Tim Pyron et al.

D0520200

SAMS
Teach Yourself
Microsoft® Project 98
in 24 Hours

SAMS

A Division of Macmillan Computer Publishing
201 West 103rd St., Indianapolis, Indiana, 46290 USA

Copyright © 1998 by Sams Publishing

FIRST EDITION
FIRST PRINTING—1998

All rights reserved. No part of this book shall be reproduced, stored in a retrieval system or transmitted by any means, electronic, mechanical, photocopying, recording, or otherwise, without permission from the publisher. No patent liability is assumed with respect to the use of the information contained herein. Although every precaution has been taken in the preparation of this book, the publisher and author assume no responsibility for errors or omissions. Neither is any liability assumed for damages resulting from the use of the information contained herein. For more information, address Sams Publishing, 201 W. 103rd St., Indianapolis, IN 46290.

International Standard Book Number: 0-672-31258-1

Library of Congress Catalog Card Number: 98-84400

01   00   99   98   4   3   2   1

Interpretation of the printing code: The rightmost double-digit number is the year of the book's printing; the rightmost single-digit, the number of the book's printing. For example, a printing code of 98-1 shows that the first printing of the book occurred in 1998.

Composed in AGaramond and MCPdigital by Macmillan Computer Publishing

Printed in the United States of America

Trademarks

All terms mentioned in this book that are known to be trademarks or service marks have been appropriately capitalized. Sams Publishing cannot attest to the accuracy of this information. Use of a term in this book should not be regarded as affecting the validity of any trademark or service mark.

EXECUTIVE EDITOR
Jim Minatel

ACQUISITIONS EDITOR
Jill Byus

DEVELOPMENT EDITOR
Rick Kughen

TECHNICAL EDITOR
Henry Staples

MANAGING EDITOR
Thomas F. Hayes

PROJECT EDITOR
Lori A. Lyons

COPY EDITORS
Lisa Lord
Alice Martina-Smith

INDEXERS
Becky Hornyak
Craig Small

PRODUCTION
Lisa England
Chris Livengood
Becky Stutzman

Overview

Contents

Dedication

To Jill Byus

Jill made the completion of this book possible. I have wanted to write it for a long time and was excited to reach an agreement with Jill, Acquisitions Editor for the book. Unfortunately, about halfway into it, I was distracted by thoughts of immortality, and the more likely alternative, as my body effectively demonstrated its seniority. Now, publishing is a business, and an unusually competitive business at that. Jill could have sent me a sympathetic email while giving the book to someone else. Instead, it was flowers she sent, and she very efficiently found other writers to help out; but she left the book in my hands. I'd like to think it's because she had faith in me, but I suspect it's because she is an uncommonly decent person. Thank you, Jill.

Acknowledgments

Even a small book owes its existence to many more people than the one whose name appears as author. I am immensely grateful to the other writers who jumped in to help complete this book and who contributed a great deal to the text: **Laura Monsen**, **Jo Ellen Shires**, **Ira Brown**, **Gus Cicala**, **Helen Feddema**, and **Joe Habracken**. **Rick Kughen** has done a masterful job of ferreting out the meaning I intended and tactfully suggesting that clarity is considered a virtue by Sam's readers. Technical errors, though unintentional, are still a sin in technical writing. **Henry Staples** expertly pointed out the sins of both commission and of omission, and he even exorcised some of the devils found in the details. Those errors that remain are entirely my responsibility.

Writing, especially against intense deadlines, takes a toll on the writer's family. The family and pets always sacrifice more than the writer is aware of (even though occasional hints may be dropped from time to time). I know I speak for the other writers when I thank my family for their patience and forbearance. My wife, Gerlinde, could write her own book on the topic. Hopefully, she will leave it in private circulation.

About the Authors

TIM PYRON is the Information Systems Manager for the South Central Region of Productivity Point International, a leading worldwide provider of computer training and support services. Tim provides consulting services and conducts training in Microsoft Project and in spreadsheet and database applications. His previous Microsoft Project books include *Using Microsoft Project 4* and *Special Edition Using Microsoft Project 98*, which have sold over 140,000 copies. He can be contacted at tpyron@tx.direct.net.

IRA BROWN is the senior vice president of Project Assistants, Inc. based in Wilmington, DE. Ira is a leading authority in integrating Microsoft Project with other products, including the Microsoft Office suite of applications. In addition, Ira has many years of experience developing and implementing automated methodologies centered around Microsoft Project. To contact Ira, call (302) 475-8322, or email him at ibrown@projectassistants.com.

Gus Cicala is the President of Project Assistants, a firm that specializes in administrating, installing, and training corporations on project management systems. His company produces "Project Assistant," an add-on product that customizes Microsoft Project to each company's specific needs. He is also a contributing author to *Special Edition Using Microsoft Project 98*.

HELEN FEDDEMA earned a B.S. in Philosophy from Columbia and M.T.S. in Theological Studies from Harvard Divinity School. Helen co-authored *Inside Microsoft Access*, and co-authored *Access How-Tos* for the Waite Group Press. She is also a regular contributor to Pinnacle's *Smart Access* and *Office Developer* journals and *Woody's Underground Office* newsletter.

JOE HABRAKEN is a freelance writer and has served as an author, editor, curriculum designer, and software instructor during his career as a computer technology professional. Joe earned his MA in Communications from American University in Washington, D.C. Most recently, he has written the *Internet 6-in-1* and the *Complete Idiot's Guide to Access 97*.

LAURA MONSEN is a professional instructor with more than seven years' experience teaching computer application classes. For the past five years she has been teaching a variety of spreadsheet, project management, database, and graphic application classes for Productivity Point International (PPI), a leader in computer software training solutions. She teaches at the PPI site in San Antonio, Texas. Laura is the author of *Using Microsoft Excel 97* and *Migrating to Office 97*, both recently published by Que. Laura has a B.A. in Economics from the University of the South, Sewanee, Tennessee.

Jo Ellen Shires is an independent consultant and trainer who has been specializing in Microsoft applications since 1984. She owns Common Sense Computing, and has been designated by Microsoft as Project Champion for the Portland, Oregon area and for small businesses regionally. Construction and information systems are her areas of project management experience. Her firm writes and delivers customized training and programmed solutions to Project users at all levels in a wide variety of industries. She holds a B.S. in Economics and an M.S. in Biometry.

Tell Us What You Think

As a reader, you are the most important critic and commentator of our books. We value your opinion and want to know what we're doing right, what we could do better, areas in which you'd like to see us publish, and any other words of wisdom you're willing to pass our way. You can help us make strong books that meet your needs and give you the computer guidance you require.

If you have access to the World Wide Web, check out our site at `http://www.mcp.com`. If you have a technical question about this book, call the technical support line at (317) 581-3833 or send email to `support@mcp.com`.

Your comments will help us to continue publishing the best books available on computer topics in today's market. You can contact us at

Publisher
Sams Publishing
201 West 103rd Street
Indianapolis, Indiana 46290
USA

Introduction

Is This the Book for You?

Absolutely…if you have to plan how to coordinate a lot of different activities and people to reach a specific goal—and if you're already planning to use Microsoft Project 98 to help you do it. If you're still undecided about using project management software, or about which software to use, then this book will show you how instrumental Microsoft Project 98 can be to the success of your project. This book is as much for those who support the manager of the project as it is for the manager.

Almost every adult has to organize a project at some time. It's common enough in the workplace: planning conferences and conventions, a move to a new office, the introduction of a new product, the construction of a skyscraper, a landing on the moon, that sort of stuff. I've even known people to use Microsoft Project to plan weddings and the remodeling of their home. (The wedding was great, thank you; the remodeling is finally just a painful memory.) And if the stars on *Touched by an Angel* don't whip out a laptop on camera, you can bet the producers do so to coordinate all the details that go into filming the travails of those poor lost souls. Why, just what do you think made it possible for Him or Her to pull off a Creation in just six days? But, I digress…

Microsoft Project is a great friend to have if you are responsible for putting together a plan of action for reaching a goal (or if you are the one who supports the person with that responsibility). It helps you block out the big picture and then fill in and organize all the details that must be completed if the goal is to be reached. Of course, you have to provide the inspiration; but Project helps you capture your thoughts in an organized way so that you can turn them into a workable plan. Working with Project, you can easily estimate completion dates for each task or phase of the project, ensuring that you complete your project on time.

If you assign people and other resources to the tasks, Project will show you who's working when, and how much the project is going to cost, and it will alert you when someone's assignment schedule is beyond reason—the stuff that only a slave-driver's dreams are made of.

When work finally gets started on your project, you can update the schedule with the actual dates as tasks are started and completed, and Project will recalculate the schedule, showing you the implications when tasks are finished late or early.

Finally, and maybe most importantly, if you use Microsoft Project you will be able to print reports throughout the planning and production stages that illustrate and explain your plan and the progress that's being made. As you know, if more than one person is involved, good communication is essential to success.

This book is designed to help you quickly gain control of the planning, implementation, and recording of your project. All the essentials for using Microsoft Project 98 effectively are included, but I've omitted as much theory as possible, giving you only as much as you need to make good choices. If you need more details, you should see my comprehensive guide *Special Edition Using Microsoft Project 98*, published by Que.

How This Book Is Organized

Part I , "Getting Started with a Basic Schedule" (Hours 1 through 3), gets you up and running quickly with Microsoft Project 98. You learn early how to manage the main screen that displays project data, how to start a new project, and how to put together the list of tasks or things to do in the project.

Part II, "Developing the Timeline" (Hours 4 and 5), shows you how to give Microsoft Project the information it needs to turn the list of tasks into a reasonable schedule of dates for working on the tasks.

Part III, "Displaying and Printing Your Schedule" (Hours 6 through 8), shows you some of the alternative ways you can view a project in Microsoft Project 98 and then shows you how to get printed reports and copies of the project that look the way you want them to look.

Part IV, "Assigning the Resources and Costs to Tasks" (Hours 9 through 13), is where you learn how to let Project know who is going to do the work, when they are available, and how much it costs to use them and the other resources they need to do the work. This section also deals with how changes in resource availability and assignments can affect your schedule.

Part V, "Finalizing and Publishing Your Plan" (Hours 14 through 16), covers the steps you should take to review and optimize your plan. You will also see how to generate reports that explain the project in varying levels of detail, including how to publish your project on Web pages.

Part VI, "Managing and Tracking the Project" (Hours 17 and 18), explains how to track progress after the work is underway and how to analyze the progress to help keep things on track.

Part VII, "Beyond One Project, One Application" (Hours 19 through 21), expands your horizons to include combining multiple project plans into a master plan, using the work-group features of Project to communicate changes and progress via email and the Internet, and exchanging data between Microsoft Project and other software applications.

Part VIII, "Customizing Microsoft Project" (Hours 22 through 24), shows you how to create your own reports and views of the project data, how to create macros to automate processes, and how to customize the toolbars and menus.

Conventions Used in This Book

This book uses the following conventions:

Text that you type and text that you see onscreen appear in <u>monospace type</u>:

`It will look like this.`

> A **Note** presents interesting information related to the discussion.

> A **Tip** offers advice or shows you an easier way to do something.

> A **Caution** alerts you to a possible problem and gives you advice on how to avoid it.

NEW TERM   New terms are introduced using the New Term icon.

PART I

Getting Started with a Basic Schedule

Hour

Hour 1

Getting Started with Microsoft Project 98

You might be reading this because you just found out that you have to organize a project of some kind or because you work for someone who has to get one organized—meaning you have to do much of the work yourself. On the other hand, if you're like most people who have come to my Microsoft Project classes, you're already into a project of some kind and realize that you need to get a grip.

In this hour, you learn how to take charge of your project with Microsoft Project 98.

The Life Cycle of a Project

Most of the hour-long lessons in this book parallel the process that you would normally go through using Microsoft Project to help you plan and manage a project. Have the big picture in mind as you start so that you can understand how one lesson leads into the next. The following sections give you a brief overview of Project's features and how they can help you track and manage your projects.

Clarifying the Goal of the Project

Start by writing down the objective or goal of your project in a short sentence or two. It's essential that you clarify what you hope to accomplish with this project before you start the planning process. If you don't know where you're going, you're likely to wind up in a strange place. You have a chance to record the goal when you start a project file so that you have it handy if you need to explain the project to anyone.

Be specific about what exactly has to happen in order for the "powers that be" to judge the project a success. The following are a few questions to answer before beginning a project:

- What must be delivered or accomplished by the project? Be specific not only about what has to be produced or what the outcome must be, but also about the quality standards that must be met to satisfy those who commissioned the project.

- Are there deadlines that must be met? When must the work start or when must it be finished?

- What are the budget constraints that you have to consider?

Planning the Schedule

Next, do some brainstorming and put together a list of the major phases of activity—the blocks of work that must be completed. After you have identified the major blocks of work, you can start filling in the details, listing the tasks that fall under each of the major phases.

After you have the list of tasks organized, Project can help you organize the task list into a schedule of work with calendar dates. Of course, you still have to do most of the work—Project just helps you get it together and puts it all into time frames so that you can see when things start and finish. The following are some ideas to consider when preparing your schedule:

- You first need to check the calendar that comes with Project and record any holidays or other nonworking time Project needs to work around in its scheduling.

- You then estimate how long you think each task takes to complete.

- You also take note of any deadlines that must be met during the project.

- You link tasks that must follow one another in a required sequence so that Project won't schedule the cart before the horse.

- If you want, you can assign tasks to people or other resources. Project can schedule tasks around vacations and other off-days that you've defined for the resources assigned to a task.

Organizing a task list into a schedule takes work, but after it's done, Project will have calculated when each task needs to start, how long it is to take, and when it is to finish so that the next task can get under way. Also, Microsoft Project will have calculated when you can expect the project to be completed, based on the information and assumptions you provided, or when it must start in order to be completed by a certain date.

If the calculated schedule is not acceptable, you need to rethink some of the assumptions you've entered about what should happen. (By the way, Project includes a number of tutorials and *wizards* to help you with the planning process. I show you how to use those later in this hour.)

Publishing the Schedule

After your plan is complete, you want to print copies of the schedule and distribute it to other people. You probably need to get the plan approved; you definitely need to show it to those you've assigned to do the work, and you may need to explain to other people in the organization (or in the community) what's going to happen and when. Indeed, the capability to print meaningful and helpful reports is the main reason some people use Microsoft Project. Project makes it relatively easy to publish reports on both paper and on Web pages for the Internet or an organizational intranet.

Tracking Progress and Adapting to Change

After the work starts on the project, you can use Microsoft Project to record the actual dates that work begins and ends on individual tasks. As you enter these dates, Microsoft Project notes any differences between the scheduled dates and the actual dates and automatically calculates new dates for the remaining tasks in the schedule. In this way, you get an early warning if deadlines are in jeopardy of not being met, and you can give resources advance notice of necessary changes in the schedule.

If you want to record costs for your project, your tracking efforts can give you a heads-up when it begins to look like costs are going over budget. This gives you time to find ways of reducing the remaining costs to stay on target.

Wrapping up the Project

At the end of the project, you probably want to submit a report glorifying its successful completion (or putting a good spin on what went wrong). Microsoft Project can help you prepare good-looking, informative descriptions and analyses of the project. After all, if you don't objectively report on your work, who's going to give you the credit you deserve?

Using Project 98's Tutorials and Help Features

The first thing to do with any new software is to get used to the user interface—the screens, menus, and toolbars that you use to run the program. Microsoft Project offers an impressive array of learning aids, starting with the opening welcome screen. When you start Microsoft Project, the Welcome! dialog box offers immediate access to tutorials on using Project to develop a project plan.

The Welcome! dialog box (see Figure 1.1) appears each time you start Project until you select the check box in its lower-left corner labeled **D**on't Display this Startup Screen Again. Use the Close button in the upper-right corner of the Welcome! dialog box if, for the time being, you just want to close it without selecting any of the learning aids. (The Welcome! screen's three tutorials are described below.)

FIGURE 1.1

The Welcome! screen offers three different kinds of help for getting started with Microsoft Project 98.

Learn While You Work

The Learn While You Work tutorial is a great learning aid that guides you through the steps of setting up a new project document. After reading the initial screen to learn how to use the tutorial, click the Next button to view the list of lessons (see Figure 1.2).

FIGURE 1.2

The Learn While You Work tutorial has 12 basic lessons.

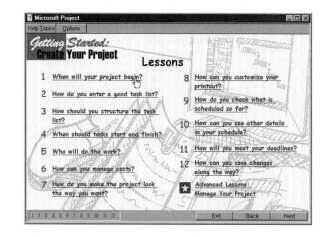

When you choose a lesson you see a description of the steps to be executed in that lesson. For example, in Lesson 1 (see Figure 1.3), click the first action step, "Set the project's start or finish date," to display a help screen dialog box (see Figure 1.4) that explains the detailed steps you need to follow to set a project's start or finish date. While the help screen is displayed, you can actually follow the instructions and work on your project document, selecting menu choices and typing text.

FIGURE 1.3

A lesson contains action steps that provide explicit instructions for each step.

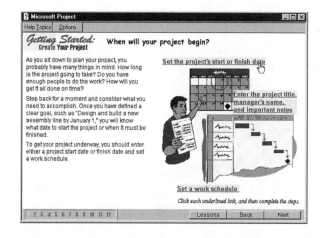

When you're finished with the action steps, choose one of the buttons at the top of the help screen to return to the lesson or to go on to the next step.

You can stop the Learn While You Work tutorial at any time. Later, you learn how to start it again.

FIGURE **1.4**

The help screen pro-
vides the exact steps
that you take to com-
plete the action.

Quick Preview

The second tutorial on the Welcome! screen is **W**atch a Quick Preview. This is just a slide show that identifies the major features of project scheduling with Microsoft Project. If you go all the way through the Preview, the last screen enables you to start the other tutorials from the Welcome! screen.

Navigate with a Map

The third tutorial on the Welcome! screen is **N**avigate with a Map (see Figure 1.5). This tutorial also enables you to continue working while using the tutorial as a guide. The Map is a graphic pathway with numbered steps along the way that display instructional help screens just like the **L**earn While You Work tutorial. Special Hints along the pathway are jump points that display animated explanations of the process.

Running the Tutorials from the Menu

Unfortunately, when you work your way through one of the tutorials on the Welcome! screen, it's difficult to find your way back if you want to try one of the other tutorials. You could exit Project (by choosing File, Exit from the menu) and start it again to display the Welcome! screen, but there's an easier way.

All three of the tutorials can be run from the Help menu, although, as you can see from the following list, the names are changed, making it somewhat confusing to run the desired tutorial. The following list helps you choose the correct tutorial:

- You can run Learn While You Work by choosing **H**elp, **G**etting Started, **C**reate Your Project.

- You can run Watch a Quick Preview by choosing **Help, Getting** Started, **Quick** Preview.

- You can run Navigate With a Map by choosing **Help, Getting** Started, Microsoft Project 101: Fundamentals. Choosing buttons located at both the top and bottom of the screen displays the map (see Figure 1.6).

  With numbered buttons, you can access six topics in this tutorial. Topics number 1 and 2 can be accessed only from this screen. The other topics correspond to the Hints on the Map.

FIGURE 1.5

The Map provides numbered steps to help guide you through a task.

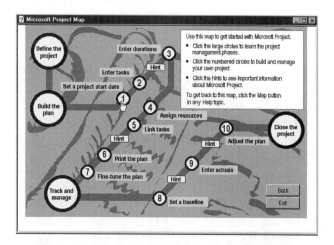

FIGURE 1.6

Microsoft Project 101: Fundamentals is a companion tutorial to the Map.

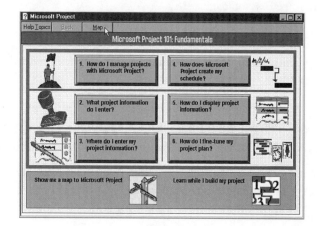

Using the Office Assistant

When you close the Welcome! dialog box, the Microsoft Office Assistant pops up (see Figure 1.7) and offers you a tip about using Microsoft Project. If you leave the Assistant on the workspace, you can click it at any time and type in a question or a word about which you want information. You can ask your questions in your own nontechnical words, and the Assistant responds with a list of Help topics that may be relevant to your question. The Assistant also displays warning messages and helpful hints about how to use Microsoft Project more effectively as you work. Personally, I find the Assistant obtrusive, so you won't see him on the screen in my figures after this. If you are new to Project, however, you might find the Office Assistant helpful until you become more comfortable with Project.

FIGURE 1.7

For experienced Project users, the Office Assistant is somewhat obtrusive, but can be helpful to new users.

If you want to hide the Office Assistant, choose the Close button in the upper-right corner of the Assistant window. You can activate the Assistant again from the main menu by choosing **H**elp, Microsoft Project **H**elp or by clicking the Office Assistant tool at the end of the first toolbar.

Using Other Sources of Help

The Help menu also offers the standard Windows **C**ontents and Index access to the help files. You can look up answers by:

- Browsing through the Contents tab, where topics are organized into books
- By searching the alphabetized index of help topics on the Index tab
- By using the Find tab to have Project search for key words in the list of topics

Choose What's **T**his? on the **H**elp menu to turn the mouse pointer into a question mark. Then, click a toolbar button, a menu choice, or any screen element and see a description of the object that you clicked. This is a great way to gain familiarity with the screen.

Choose Microsoft on the **W**eb from the **H**elp menu to open World Wide Web sites that offer everything from technical support and free software for Microsoft Project to links to Microsoft Office and other sites that may prove helpful.

Exploring the Microsoft Project Window

1

Figure 1.8 shows the Project window after closing the Welcome! screen and Office Assistant. The major components of the window are identified in the following list:

- The title bar at the top of the screen indicates the name of the project file on which you are working.
- Below the title bar, you see the menu, toolbars, and an entry bar for typing and editing data.
- Running down the left side of the screen is the View Bar, which provides a quick way to choose the display format for the project data.
- Running across the bottom of the screen is the status bar.
- You view the project data in the center of the screen.

Each element of the window is described in the following sections.

The Menu Bar

The menus listed on the Microsoft Project Menu bar are very similar to the menus in other Microsoft Office products (Word, Excel, PowerPoint, and Access). The menus and the commands they display are defined and described in detail in later sections as the functions they perform are discussed.

Toolbars

The toolbar buttons provide shortcut access to frequently used menu choices or special functions. The individual tools are described as you encounter them in the following sections. A brief description (called a *ScreenTip*) appears beneath a tool if you position the mouse pointer over the tool for a second or two.

For more complete descriptions of the tools, use the What's This? command on the Help menu. Choose **Help**, What's **T**his? (or simply press Shift+F1) and then click a tool. A mini help screen provides additional information about that tool.

Microsoft Project 98 provides 12 toolbars. The two that are displayed initially are the Standard and Formatting toolbars. You can add and remove toolbars to the Project window, or create your own custom toolbars. For a detailed description of all the Project toolbars, choose **Help**, **C**ontents and Index. On the Contents tab, select Microsoft Project Reference (it's toward the bottom of the list), select Toolbars and Buttons, and finally, select Toolbars. This help screen lists all the toolbars. Clicking one of the toolbar names displays its tool buttons with descriptions of the tools.

FIGURE 1.8

The parts of the Microsoft Project window.

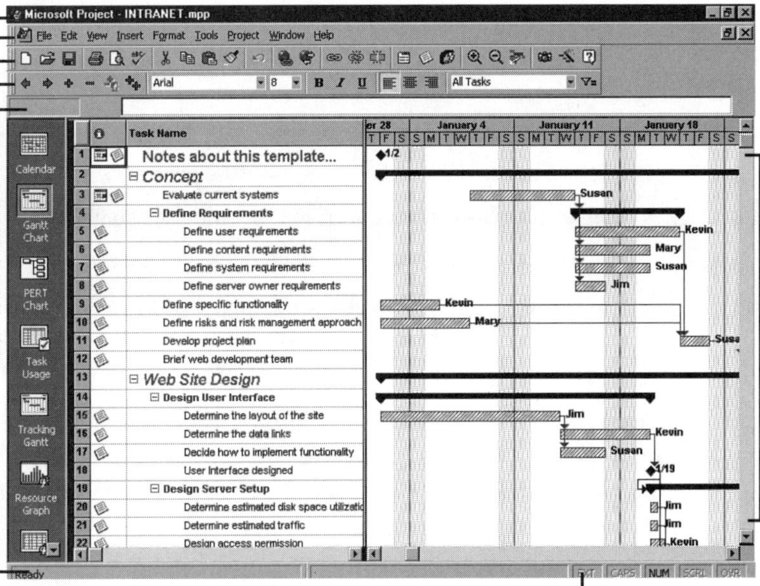
The Standard toolbar has buttons for the menu commands that you most often use.
Choose menus from the Menu bar to access commands.
The filename appears in the Title Bar. In this example, the project is a plan for installing an intranet.
The Formatting toolbar has buttons to manage a task outline, change the font of text, align text, and apply filters.
The Entry bar is where you type and edit data in the project.
The View Bar has icons to activate the most commonly used views.
The status bar is used to display messages when Project is processing a time-consuming command. It also shows the status of special keys such as Caps Lock, Num Lock, and the Insert key.
A "view" is the Microsoft Project term for the way the project information is displayed. The Gantt Chart is the name of this view of tasks in a project. Its display elements are the table on the left and the timescale on the right. Many other predefined views enable you to see your project data in different ways.
Microsoft Project - INTRANET.mpp
File Edit View Insert Format Tools Project Window Help
Calendar
Gantt Chart
PERT Chart
Task Usage
Tracking Gantt
Resource Graph
Task Name
Notes about this template...
Concept
Evaluate current systems
Define Requirements
Define user requirements
Define content requirements
Define system requirements
Define server owner requirements
Define specific functionality
Define risks and risk management approach
Develop project plan
Brief web development team
Web Site Design
Design User Interface
Determine the layout of the site
Determine the data links
Decide how to implement functionality
User interface designed
Design Server Setup
Determine estimated traffic
January 4
January 11
January 18
Ready

To show additional toolbars, or to hide one that is currently displayed, choose **V**iew, **T**oolbars from the menu. Toolbars that are checked are currently displayed (see Figure 1.9). Click a checked toolbar to hide it; click an unchecked toolbar to display it.

FIGURE 1.9

Display or hide tool-bars by clicking them in the Toolbars list.

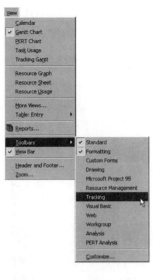

The shortcut menu is a quick way to show or hide toolbars. Position the mouse over any visible toolbar and right-click to display the shortcut menu (see Figure 1.10). Toolbars that are checked are currently displayed. Choose a checked toolbar to hide it; choose an unchecked toolbar to display it.

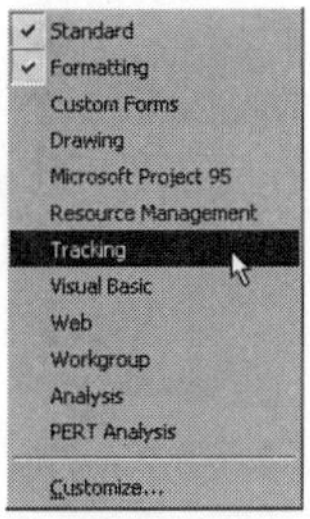

FIGURE 1.10

You can use the short-cut menu to show or hide toolbars. Simply click the toolbar name to change its display status.

The Entry Bar

The entry bar is on the line below the toolbars. The entry bar performs several functions:

- The left end of the entry bar displays progress messages that indicate when Microsoft Project is engaged in calculating, opening and saving large files, and so on.

- The center of the entry bar contains an entry area where data entry and editing takes place. During Entry and Editing modes, Cancel and Enter buttons appear.

Use the entry area to enter data in a field or to edit data previously placed in a field.

 When the entry bar is active, many features of Microsoft Project are unavailable. Most menu commands, toolbar buttons, and shortcut keys are also unavailable. Make sure that you close the entry bar by pressing Enter after entering or editing data in a field.

The Status Bar

The *status bar* is located at the bottom of the window. It shows the status of special keys and displays advisory messages (refer to Figure 1.8). At the left end of the status bar is the *mode indicator*. This indicator displays Ready when Microsoft Project is waiting for you to begin an operation. The mode indicator displays Enter when you initially enter data, and it displays Edit when you edit a field where you have already entered data. The mode indicator is also used to provide information for some actions that are in progress, including messages while displaying a dialog box, opening or saving a file, and previewing the document before printing.

The middle of the status bar displays warning messages when you need to recalculate and when you've created circular relationships while linking tasks. The far right end of the status bar indicates the status of special modes or keys: Extend (EXT), Caps Lock (CAPS), Num Lock (NUM), Scroll Lock (SCRL), and Insert (OVR). When you press one of these keys to activate it, the key name changes from gray to black on the status bar. Choose **H**elp, Contents and Index, and use the Index tab to look up more information on these keys.

The View Bar

The View Bar displays a column of icons that represent the select set of *views* that are listed on the View menu. You can display any of the views represented on the View Bar by simply clicking its icon. If a view icon appears depressed, then the active view is displayed. The scroll arrow at the bottom of the View Bar displays additional view icons.

To show or hide the View Bar, choose **V**iew, **V**iew Bar. Similar to the way views and toolbars are checked, choose the checked View Bar to hide it; choose the unchecked View Bar to display it.

Use the shortcut menu to show or hide the View Bar. Simply right-click in front of the bar to display the shortcut menu, and click next to View Bar to toggle its display status on and off.

Understanding Views

Microsoft Project provides 26 predefined formats or views for viewing project information, and this book explores all the most often used views. The only views we do not explore are those that are for advanced topics or those that have been superseded by improved views.

Help has a good review of all the views. Choose **Help, Contents** and Index and choose the Contents tab. Choose the topics Working with Views, Tables, and then choose Filters, Working with Views, View Basics, Available views.

The View menu includes eight of the most commonly used views for quick access, and provides a **M**ore Views command for selecting the rest of the views. These are the same views that are represented by icons on the View Bar.

View is the term Microsoft Project uses to describe the way in which the project data is displayed on the screen and in printing. Figure 1.8 is an example of a view: It displays part of the information in a spreadsheet-like **table** on the left side and additional information in a bar graph under a **timescale** on the right side. A view can also contain a **form,** which has the advantage of presenting a lot of information about one task in a compact way. **Combination views** are made up of two separate views that are coordinated to present even more information in one display. You can create your own views to add to the set provided by Microsoft.

A Sampling of the Major Views

If you examine the next four figures (1.11 to 1.14), you see how different the views in Microsoft Project can be. Each of these views draws on the same set of data, but presents it differently to stress particular aspects of the project or to help managers analyze the project in different ways. Learning to make good use of the different views is an important key to the successful use of Microsoft Project.

FIGURE 1.11

This view of the project presents a traditional calendar format for the scheduled activities and is most effective when focused on a subset of tasks—for example, showing the assignments for just one resource.

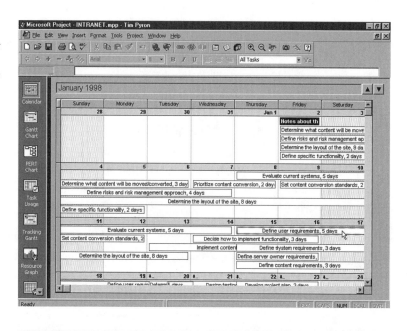

FIGURE 1.12

This view of the same project is like a flow chart, and it empha-sizes very effectively the planned sequence of tasks.

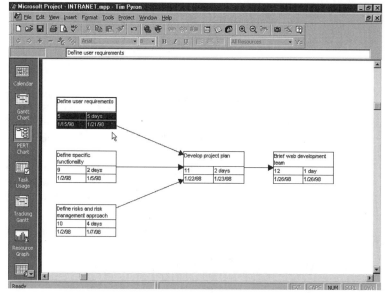

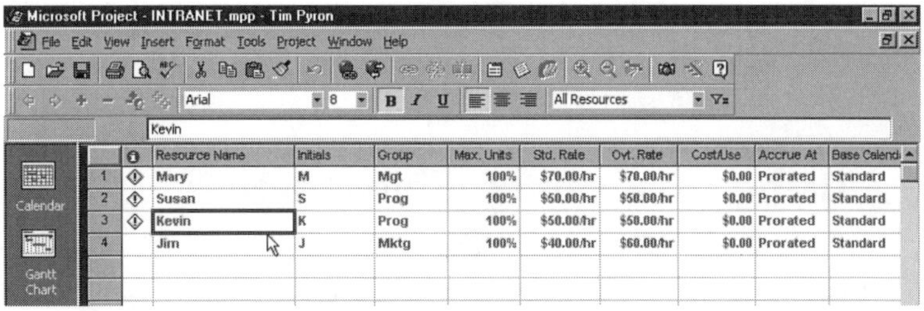

FIGURE 1.13

This view is like a spreadsheet with columns and rows and is called a Sheet or Table view. Sheet views provide lots of infor- mation in the compact table format preferred by many for data entry.

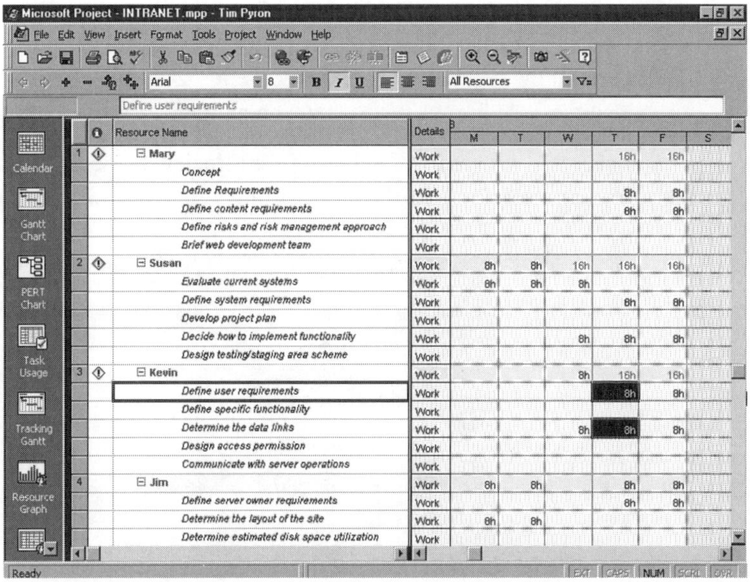

FIGURE 1.14

This view displays the task assignments for each resource along with the amount of work that is scheduled each day.

Learning to make use of the different views is a key to successful use of Microsoft Project. Each of these views draws on the same set of data, but presents it differently.

- In Figure 1.11, the Define User Requirements task begins on January 15 and extends into future dates.

- In Figure 1.12, the same task is to take place before the task Develop Project Plan starts.

- In Figure 1.13, you see information about Kevin, the resource assigned to the Define User Requirements task.

- In Figure 1.14, the Define User Requirements task is one of the five tasks assigned to Kevin. In the timescale to the right, Kevin is assigned eight hours of work on this task for Thursday.

Using Views in Combination

You can use the **W**indow, **S**plit command with any view to split the window into a top pane and bottom pane. If the view in the top pane is a task view, then after the split, the default view in the bottom pane is the Task Form. (Figure 1.15 shows the Gantt Chart in the top pane and the Task Form in the bottom pane.)

The view in the bottom pane always displays only information related to the selection in the top pane. For example, Figure 1.15 shows the Gantt Chart in the top pane and the Task Form in the bottom pane. The task Define User Requirements is selected in the top pane, and the Task Form shows details about the task in the bottom pane.

Combination views are extremely useful for reviewing details about one task in the bottom pane while seeing how the task fits in with the rest of the project in the top pane.

FIGURE 1.15

Splitting the window in the Gantt Chart produces the Task Entry view, with the Gantt Chart in the top pane and the Task Form in the bottom pane.

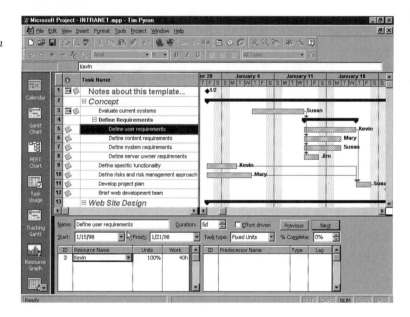

You can remove the split view by choosing **W**indow, Remove **S**plit. You learn more about managing split views in Hour 2.

Exiting Microsoft Project 98

You can exit Microsoft Project by choosing **F**ile, **E**xit, or you can click the application's Close button in the upper-right corner of the window.

> Use the Alt+F4 shortcut key combination to quickly close an application. You are prompted to save your latest changes before the application closes.

When you exit the application, all open project files close. If any changes have been made in a project file since you last saved it, a dialog box prompts you to save the changes before closing the file. Choose **Y**es to save the changes, choose **N**o to close without saving the changes, or choose Cancel if you want to return to work on the project.

> If the Planning Wizard asks you about saving a baseline when you save a file, just click OK for now; you don't need a baseline this early in the game.
>
> The *baseline* is a copy of the way the schedule looks at this moment. The baseline copy does not change as you make changes in the project schedule. It's useful for comparing later versions of the schedule with the original intentions. Always capture a baseline copy of your project before you start tracking work so that you can compare the plan with actual outcomes.
>
> You can select the Don't Tell Me About This Again check box to avoid seeing the Planning Wizard baseline warning every time you close a file.

Hour 2

Becoming an Instant Project Guru

In this hour, you learn how to read what the primary Microsoft Project display indicates about a project plan, and you learn techniques, tips, and tricks to make Project display the plan the way that you want to see it.

You may be anxious to start putting a task list together, but some of you have already been given a project file to make sense of and start using right away. Besides, after this hour you are better prepared to start building the task list because you are familiar with the workspace.

Practicing with a Sample File

You get the most benefit from this hour if you can display on the screen a project file that is already developed. I recommend that you open the file I use as the basis for my illustrations. It's one of the Project 98 templates that is copied to your hard disk when you install Microsoft Project. If you already have a project file that you are going to be working with, you can open it also and try things out with both files.

To Do: Opening the Project Template File

1. Choose **File**, **O**pen from the menu (or click the Open tool on the Standard toolbar) to display the File Open dialog box. Use the Look **I**n list box to locate the drive and directory where the file is stored. Microsoft Office is usually installed in C:\Program Files. If you installed Office elsewhere, you have to substitute that drive and directory path in the steps that follow.

2. In the Look **I**n list box, select drive C.

3. Select the directory Program Files.

4. Select the directory Microsoft Office.

5. Select the directory Templates.

6. Select the directory Microsoft Project to display the templates in that directory.

7. Select the file Intranet and click the **O**pen button (or just double-click the file name).

New Term **Intranet** An *intranet* is a computer network within an organization that works like a local version of the Internet but is available only to members of the organization. Users can publish or exchange information in the HTML (Hypertext Markup Language) format used by the Internet. For example, you can publish your project plans and progress reports for interested parties to review on your intranet.

Figure 2.1 shows the Project template files. Notice in the figure that they all have the extension MPT, which is the Microsoft Project file extension for templates, whereas MPP is the extension for regular project files.

> By default Windows Explorer hides file extensions for registered files. I've disabled that feature for working with Microsoft Project. If you also want to disable that feature, open Windows Explorer by choosing Start, Programs, Windows Explorer. On the Explorer menu choose **V**iew, **O**ptions. Clear the check box for Hide MS-DOS File Extensions For File Types That Are Registered. Then click OK and close Explorer. You now see file extensions in Windows dialog boxes.

If you also want to look at your own file during these exercises, you can open it now. To switch back and forth between your file and the Intranet example, open the **W**indow menu and select the file that you want to activate from the numbered list at the bottom of the menu.

FIGURE 2.1

Microsoft Project installation includes six templates for common projects like renovating an office, planning an event, and launching spacecraft.

File Open					
Look in: Microsoft Project					
Name	Size	Type	Modified		Open
Aerospace.mpt		224 KB Microsoft Project...	9/23/97 12:00 AM		Cancel
Event Planning.mpt		102 KB Microsoft Project...	9/23/97 12:00 AM		
Intranet.mpt		144 KB Microsoft Project...	9/23/97 12:00 AM		ODBC...
ISO 9000.mpt		122 KB Microsoft Project...	9/23/97 12:00 AM		Advanced...
Renovation.mpt		182 KB Microsoft Project...	9/23/97 12:00 AM		
Software Launch.mpt		101 KB Microsoft Project...	9/23/97 12:00 AM		Read Only

Find files that match these search criteria:
File name: Intranet.mpt   Text or property: Find Now
Files of type: Microsoft Project Files (*.mp*)   Last modified: any time   New Search
6 file(s) found.

Because we're going to be experimenting in ways that could permanently change the display of the project, save the open file with a different name to create a working copy. By doing so, you won't run the risk of accidentally saving the results of our experiments over the original.

To Do: Making a Working Copy of the Internet Template

▼To Do

1. Choose **File, Save As** from the menu. The file extension is changed automatically from MPT to MPP, the extension for regular project files. So, if you had simply issued a save command, the original template would not have been overwritten after all. You would, however, have saved the file back in the Microsoft Project Templates directory, which is not a good place for it to be.

2. Change the location for the file in the Save **In** list box or change the name of the file in the File **Name** text box—or do both. You now have a separate, working copy of the original project file.

▲

Do the same thing to create a working copy for your own file if you have opened one.

Understanding What You See

Figure 2.2 shows the Intranet project screen (with a few changes I've made for illustration purposes). The display consists of a listing of task names on the left and a timeline with horizontal taskbars on the right. Details of a project can be displayed many other ways, but this is the display, the Gantt Chart view, that is most often used in Microsoft Project.

Long ago, Henry Gantt introduced the use of graphical bars drawn on a timeline in his studies of industrial management. It's such an easily understood way to compare and contrast the timeframe for events that it's not only widely used by project managers, but also by historians and scientists who want to explain time relationships. Microsoft Project has paired Gantt's chart with a spreadsheet-like table and called it the Gantt Chart view.

Now, let's start poking around in the Gantt Chart view. Before you get too adventurous, however, let me warn you that the Gantt Chart view is a dangerous place for click-and-drag fiends. The mouse can do powerful things in Microsoft Project, and you need to be especially careful about using click-and-drag until you know what it does. I'll show you those techniques later. For now, just say no.

FIGURE 2.2

This is the Gantt Chart view of the Intranet project (with some additions for illustration purposes).

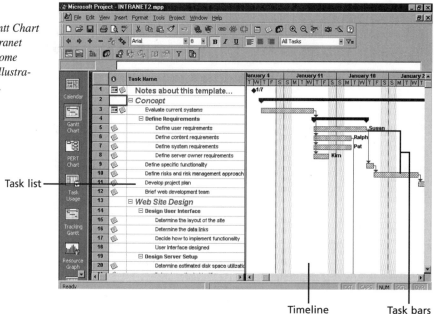

Task list

Timeline   Task bars

The Task Table

The spreadsheet on the left of the view (see Figure 2.3) contains a table that displays the list of tasks that are to be completed for the project. The table has rows, columns, and cells where data is entered and displayed, just like a spreadsheet. Each row represents a project task. Each column displays information from one of Microsoft Project's database fields.

The row numbers on the left are the ID numbers for the tasks. Graphical icons or indicators appear in the second column. The indicators provide important information about the task. If you pause your mouse pointer over an indicator cell, a ScreenTip shows you the meaning of the indicators for that task. For example, Figure 2.3 shows the ScreenTip for the indicators for task 3. The first indicates that a constraint has been placed on task 3, and it cannot start any earlier than 1/8/98. The second indicator is the Notes indicator, and you see the note for the task at the bottom of the ScreenTip.

FIGURE 2.3

You can review the meaning of an indicator by displaying its ScreenTip.

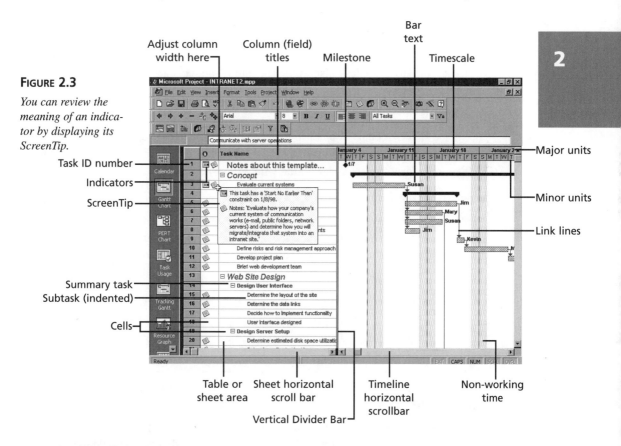

Outlined Task Lists

The Task Name column shows the name of each task. If the task list is outlined, the display uses indentation to show the outline hierarchy. If a task name is indented, it is a *subtask* belonging to the *summary* task under which it is indented. An outline symbol (a small icon with a plus or minus sign in it) appears to the left of summary task names. If the outline symbol has a plus sign, then subtasks have been hidden from view (meaning that their rows are not displayed). You can click the plus sign to display the rows for those subtasks. If the outline symbol has a minus sign, then all the subtasks are displayed, and you can click the outline symbol to hide them.

NEW TERM   **Summary task**   A *summary task* summarizes the important details for its subtasks (those that are indented under it). For instance, the start and finish dates for
the summary task span the time between the earliest start and latest finish of any of its
subtasks. The cost of the summary task is calculated as the sum of the cost of all its
subtasks.

You can do the following with the minus sign and plus sign outline symbols:

- Click a minus sign outline symbol to hide the summary task's subtasks, leaving
  only the summary task displayed. The minus sign changes to a plus sign.

- Click a plus sign outline symbol to display a summary task's hidden subtasks (and
  to restore the minus sign icon).

Hiding the subtask details in order to focus on the larger task groups is a great way to
view a summary of what happens in a project. (You learn more about outlining in Hour
3, "Starting a New Project and Working with Tasks.")

Viewing the Other Columns

The table has more columns, but the timeline area on the right hides them. Use the scroll
bar below the table, or use the right arrow key, to bring those columns into view. I
describe the data that's displayed in these columns later in this Hour in the section
"Working with the Task Table."

> You can also drag the Vertical Divider bar that separates the sheet and time-
> line areas to change how much of the window is devoted to each area (refer
> to Figure 2.3).

The Timeline

The right side of the screen in the Gantt Chart view is sometimes called a *timeline*. It
includes the *timescale* (the grid or ruler of time units located at the top) and the bars and
other symbols underneath the timescale. Microsoft Project locates the Start and Finish
dates for each task row in the timeline area and connects those end points with a line or
bar in that task row. This device enables you to see at a glance how the start and finish
dates for different tasks are related to each other. The vertical shading represents nonworking days like weekends and holidays.

The Timescale

The default timescale displays weeks divided into days. The weeks are the major time
units, and their dividing line extends all the way down the timeline. The days are minor

time units. You can easily display different time units and different ways to label those time units. By default the week starts on Sunday, and it is the Sunday date that is used to label each week (refer to Figure 2.3.)

Task Bars

By comparing a task bar to the timeline above, you see when an event begins and ends. Longer bars generally appear to identify the events with longer duration. That can be, however, a little misleading, because the bars may include nonworking days, as we saw in the description for Duration.

The task bar for a summary task is black and it spans all the task bars for its subtasks; thus, it shows the overall duration of that group of subtasks.

When a task is represented by a diamond shape in the timeline (see tasks 1 and 18 in Figure 2.3, for example), the task is a milestone, not really a task with work to be done. Milestones mark important events in the project, such as completion of a significant phase of the project.

NEW TERM   **Milestone**   *Milestones* are flags or reference points that mark significant events or accomplishments in the project. Although they are entered as tasks, they typically have no work associated with them directly and are instead markers indicating turning points in the project.

Use the scroll bar beneath the timeline to scroll to later or earlier dates and view other task bars and milestones.

Bar Text

You can display text next to the task bars. For instance, task 1 is a milestone, and by default Project displays the date next to the diamond shape for milestones. Also, the standard Gantt Chart shows resource names to the right of task bars. I've assigned some resources to tasks in this project to illustrate that feature. The template has no resources assigned.

Link Lines

The lines with arrow points that connect tasks represent *links* between tasks that define the order in which they must be executed. For example, the arrow drawn from the finish of task 3 points to the start of task 4. That means that task 3 must be finished before task 4 can start. Task 3 is said to be the *predecessor* of task 4.

NEW TERM   **Links, Predecessors, and Successors**   *Links* are used to define the sequence in which tasks must be scheduled. When two tasks are linked, one is called the *predecessor* and its schedule determines the schedule for the other task, which is called the *successor*.

Displaying the link lines is optional. If you don't want the lines cluttering up the space you can hide them. Choose Format, Layout from the menu to display the Layout dialog box (see Figure 2.4) and select the first button in the Links group. Click OK.

FIGURE 2.4

You can govern the display of task links with the Layout dialog box.

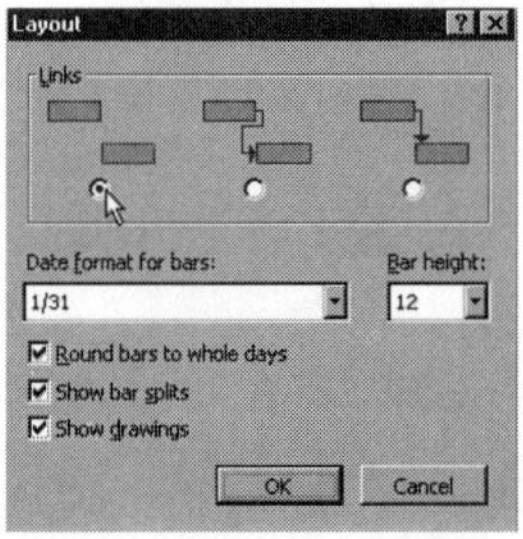

Working with the Timeline

Now that you know a little more about what the Gantt Chart view indicates, let's look at the techniques for moving around in the view to see different parts of the project and for changing the way it's displayed. We'll start with the timeline on the right side of the screen and then move back over to the table in the sheet area.

Scrolling the Timescale

Use the horizontal scroll bar below the timeline to scroll back and forth in time from the start date to the finish date of the project. If you drag the scroll button, a ScreenTip indicates what date is displayed at the left edge of the timescale when you release the button. Drag the horizontal scroll button all the way to the left to go to the beginning of the project and all the way to the right to go to the end of the project.

The following are some handy keyboard alternatives for scrolling the timeline in the Gantt Chart view:

- Alt+Home jumps to the start date for the project.
- Alt+End jumps to the finish date for the project.
- Alt+Right arrow and Alt+Left arrow scroll right and left, one day at a time.
- Alt+Page Down and Alt+Page Up scroll right and left by one screen at a time.

I suggest you place a bookmark on the Help screen for these and other special keys for working in views that have tables. To locate the Help screen, choose Help, Contents and Index from the menu. Scroll toward the bottom of the Contents tab and double-click the book labeled Microsoft Project

Reference. Double-click the volume labeled Keyboard Reference and then the page labeled Keyboard Commands for Selecting and Editing. Finally, click the jump point labeled Move, Select, and Edit in a View Using the Keyboard. You don't want to have to go through that again, so place a bookmark on this page by selecting **O**ptions, **D**efine Bookmarks. Edit the label for the reference if you want and then click OK. You can print the list of keys by choosing **O**ptions, **P**rint Topic.

If you drag the horizontal scroll button all the way to the right (or press Alt+End), you are at the finish of the project. You probably have to scroll down the task list to find the tasks whose task bars appear in this date range.

Finding a Task Bar or a Specific Date in the Timeline

If you have selected a task in the table and you want to see its task bar in the timeline, click the Go To Selected Task tool on the Standard toolbar. Project scrolls the timeline to show the beginning of the task bar.

Use the **E**dit, **G**o To command (Ctrl+G) to display the Go To dialog box (see Figure 2.5) if you want to jump to a specific date in the timeline. Enter a date in the **D**ate box or click the down arrow in the **D**ate box to display the date-picker calendar. You can scroll the months with the arrows at the top of the little calendar and then click a date to select it. Click OK to jump to that date in the timeline. You can also type in just a number to jump to that date in the current month. For example, if the current date is May 25, 1998 and you want to go to May 3, 1998, just type in the number 3.

The Date box also accepts the words "today" and "tomorrow" and jumps to those dates. This is especially helpful for those of us who don't know what day it is.

Adjusting the Units on the Timescale

The timescale has two rows. The top row is called the *major* scale and its tick lines run all the way down the screen. The bottom row subdivides the major scale and is called the *minor* scale. You can customize the amount of time encompassed by the units on each of the scales and you can change the labels that appear in the units. The following techniques provide quick adjustments to the timescale.

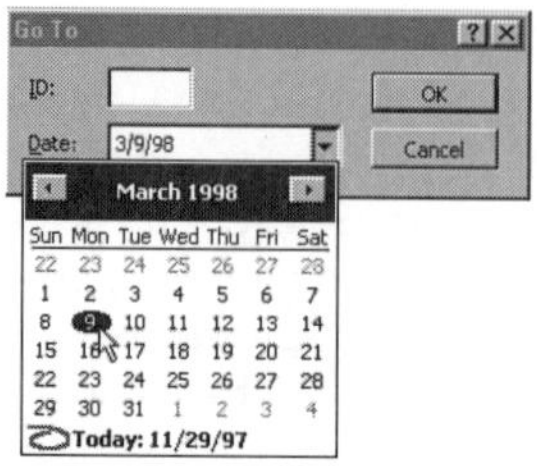

FIGURE 2.5

Use the Go To command to jump to specific dates in the timeline.

You can quickly zoom in to see smaller time units (for example days instead of weeks or hours instead of days) or zoom out to see longer time periods compressed in the display area. Clicking the Zoom In tool on the Standard toolbar (the magnifying glass with the plus sign) expands the timescale so that task bars become longer, and you see more detail in the same area of the screen. If you get carried away clicking the Zoom In tool, you can display time units as small as 15-minute intervals. You could micromanage restroom breaks with this display.

If you want to compress the timescale so that you see less detail and a longer span of time on one screen, click the Zoom Out tool (the magnifying glass with the minus sign). You can zoom out so far that you see seven or eight years at once, each divided into two half-year periods.

Project can adjust the timescale so that your entire project fits tidily in the space that is currently available on the screen. To do this, you need to choose **V**iew from the menu, and select the **Z**oom command to display the Zoom dialog box (see Figure 2.6). Select **E**ntire Project and then OK. In most cases the timescale no longer shows successive days after this adjustment. The **R**eset button in the Zoom dialog box returns you to the default timeline (weeks divided into successive days).

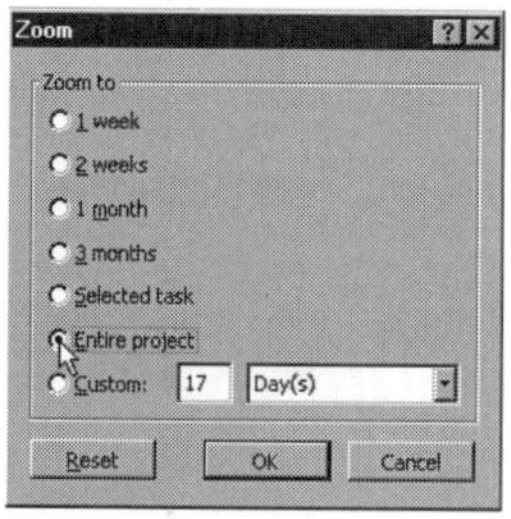

FIGURE 2.6

Use the Zoom command for special calculated adjustments in the timescale.

For ultimate control over the timescale, double-click over the timescale itself to display the Timescale dialog box. In Figure 2.7, I have changed the Major scale Label to include the year (because I always want to see that) and I've changed the Minor scale Label to display the month/day number instead of the week/day letter. You can see the results in the background in Figure 2.8.

FIGURE 2.7

The Timescale dialog box enables you to customize every part of the timescale.

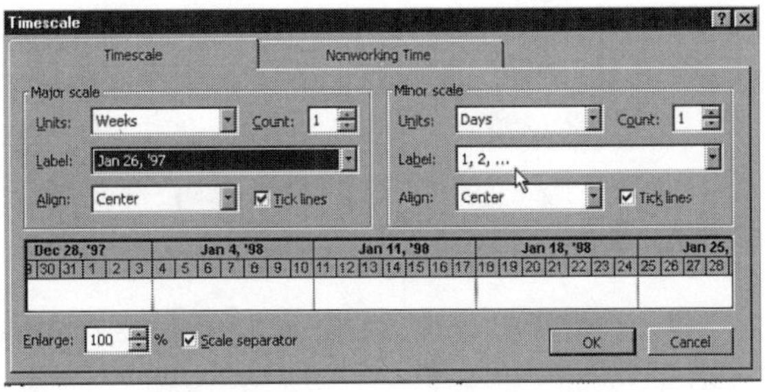

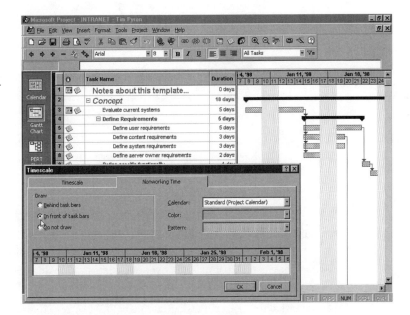

The Nonworking Time tab enables you to control how the shading is displayed for nonworking days. In Figure 2.8, I've chosen to display the shading in front of the task bars. Many people prefer this because it hides the nonworking parts of task bars, and the visible length of the bar more accurately reflects the duration. The shading also avoids agitating a work force that would otherwise see task bars stretching across Thanksgiving and Christmas holidays, creating the impression that people would have to come in to work on those days. By placing the shading in front, it's obvious that work is not scheduled for those nonworking days.

FIGURE 2.8

You can also control the display of shading for nonworking days with the Timescale dialog box.

Working with the Task Table

In this section we look at some techniques for finding information quickly in the table and for changing the way the data is displayed.

As pointed out earlier, you can drag the vertical divider bar right and left to change the amount of the table that you see. If the divider bar falls in the middle of a column, you can double-click the divider bar to make it snap to the nearest column border.

With the vertical divider bar moved out of the way in Figure 2.9, you can see all the columns in the task table.

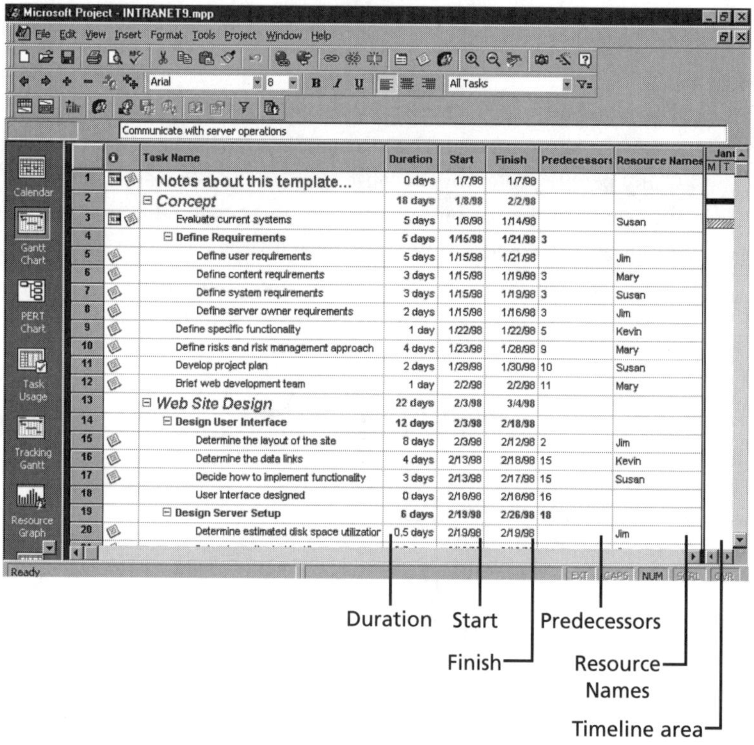

FIGURE 2.9

With the vertical divider bar moved to the far right, you can see all the columns in the task table.

Duration   Start   Finish   Predecessors   Resource Names   Timeline area

The following list provides a brief description of each additional column:

- *Duration*. Duration is the number of hours, days, or weeks during which work is going on for the task. The duration for task 3 (Evaluate Systems) is five days. Notice that its task bar extends over and seems to include the weekend days; however, those days are shaded to indicate that they are nonworking days.

  Some tasks, for example task 1 and task 18, have zero duration. Tasks with zero duration are called *milestones*, and although they are usually not actual tasks, they are important events in the project. The authors of the Intranet template assigned a zero duration to the task named "Notes about this template…" because they wanted to create a place for some general comments.

- *Start*. The Start column shows the start date for the task.

- *Finish*. The Finish column contains the finish date for the task.

- *Predecessors*. This column shows the ID number for a task's predecessors—other tasks that need to go before this task. (We look at linking tasks into predecessor sequences in Hour 5.)

- *Resource Names*. If resources have been assigned to tasks, their names appear here.

> To change the width of a column, place the mouse over the right edge of the column title (over the line dividing the column title from the column title to the right). When the mouse turns into a double-headed arrow pointing left and right, drag the dividing line left or right. If you double-click the dividing line, Project adjusts the column on the left of the dividing line to accommodate the widest cell entry in that column. In the case of the Predecessor column, the widest entry is the column title itself.

Navigating Through the Task List

The vertical scroll bar at the far right of the window adjusts the rows of the table that you see, and consequently the section of the timeline that you see also. If you drag the scroll button, a ScreenTip indicates the ID number and name of the task that appears at the top of the screen when you release the scroll button. Dragging the scroll button all the way to the bottom of the scroll bar displays the last task in the task list.

> You can also use the keyboard to move through the task list, as described in the following list. Using the keyboard, however, actually moves the cell selection, whereas using the scroll bar enables you to look at a different part of the task list without changing the cell that is selected and, consequently, losing your place.

The Up-and-Down arrow keys move through the task list a row at a time. The Page Up and Page Down keys move whole screens at a time. Alternatively, other keystroke combinations enable you to move quickly through the table.

- Ctrl+Up arrow jumps to the first task row but keeps the selection in the same column in which you start.

- Ctrl+Down arrow jumps to the last task row keeping the selection in the same column in which you start.

- Ctrl+Home jumps to the first task row and selects the first column.
- Ctrl+End jumps to the last task row, but it selects the last column. You need to press Home to see the task name for the row.
- Home jumps to the first column of the task row in which you start.
- End jumps to the last column of the task row in which you start.

Finding Tasks by Name

If your project has a long list of tasks, you may find it helpful to search for a task by name. For that matter, you can search any of the columns for a particular value, but finding task names is the most common objective.

Note that your selection doesn't have to be in the column that you want to search. The search commences, however, from the row your selection is in and proceeds down the list. After the search reaches the last task, it continues from the top of the task list until it reaches the task row in which you started. You also have the option of reversing the direction of the search, to search up from the starting row. After the search reaches the first task, it continues from the bottom of the list until it reaches the starting point.

To Do: Finding a Task

To find a task in the Intranet project that has the word "server" in its name, follow these steps:

1. Choose **Edit**, **Find** from the menu to display the Find dialog box (see Figure 2.10).
2. Type the word or series of letters for which you are searching in the **Find** What text box. I've typed in server.
3. The **Look In** Field box displays the field (column) "Name" by default. This is the actual name of the data field displayed in the Task Name column. You can change the field to be searched by selecting a different field name. For example, if you want to search task notes, you would click the **Look** in Field box and select the Notes field.
4. The entry in the **Test** box determines the type of comparison that is to be made between your search value and the values Project finds in the search field. The default test is "contains" because it is the most commonly used. This test finds any task name that contains the letters "server" anywhere in the name. Other tests are available, but you and I only have 24 hours, so we have to pass on explaining them.
5. Change the direction of the search, if you prefer, by clicking Up or Down in the **S**earch box.

▼   6. If you want to find only instances that match the exact upper- and lowercase letters
        that you typed in, fill the Match Case check box. Leave it unchecked to accept
        either case.

     7. To initiate the search, click the Find Next button. If a match is found, the cell con-
        taining the match is selected. Click Find Next again until the match for which you
        were looking is found. You can also Close the dialog box after the first match is
        found and use the Shift+F4 key combination to continue searching in the direction
        you chose. That way, the dialog box is not in the way when you look at the select-
▲   ed cells.

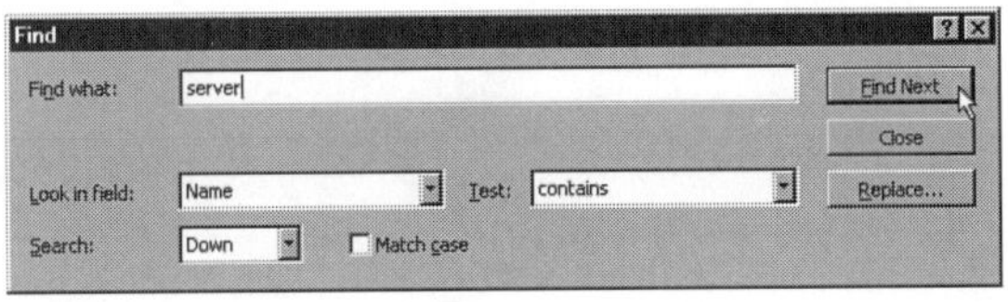

FIGURE 2.10

*Use the Find command
to locate tasks by key-
words in their names.*

Changing the Date Format

The default format for dates is the mm/dd/yy pattern, and this is the format that you see
in the Start and Finish columns of the Intranet project. You can add the time of day to the
display, or switch to any one of a number of date format options. Be aware, however, that
the display will be the same for all date fields throughout all the views in Microsoft
Project, and it applies to all the project files that you view. While looking at some projects you may want to include time of day, for example, and for others you might want to
include the day of the week.

To Do: Changing the Date Display Format

To change the date display format, follow these steps:

     1. Select Tools, Options from the menu to display the Options dialog box (see Figure
        2.11).

     2. On the View tab, select the format that you want in the Date Format box.

     3. Click the OK button to make the change effective.

     4. If any cells in the Start or Finish columns display all # signs, you need to widen
        the column to display the new format. Simply double-click the column divider line
        to the right of the title for the column you want to adjust. For example, if the Start
        column needs to be adjusted, double-click the line separating the titles Start and
▲   Finish.

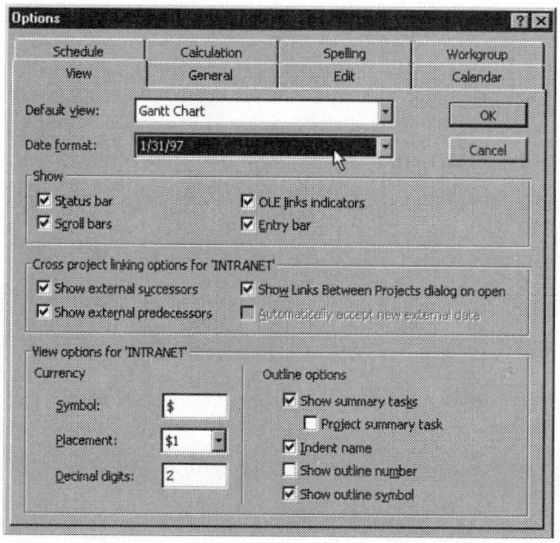

FIGURE 2.11

Select the format for dates in the Options dialog box.

For international changes in date and time formats, you must use the Regional Settings applet in the Microsoft Windows Control Panel.

Using Wordwrap to See Long Task Names

One way to see more columns in the table or sheet portion of the Gantt Chart is to reduce the width of the Task Name column, but then you usually can't see all the task name text. The solution is to increase the height of the rows; Microsoft Project automatically word-wraps the entries in each cell. Note that you can't adjust the height of just one row—when you change one row, Project changes all rows.

To Do: Displaying Task Names

To display task names on two or more rows, follow these steps:

1. Move the mouse pointer over the line dividing any two row numbers in the task ID column.

2. When the pointer's shape changes to two arrows pointing up and down, drag the dividing line up or down to the new row height that you want to use. Row heights cannot be varied in infinite gradations but must always be multiples of the original one-row height.

3. Adjust the width of the Task Name column and Microsoft Project automatically wordwraps any entry that needs more than one line to display.

Changing the Columns

Sometimes, you may want to change the column titles to match common usage within your organization, or you may even want to change the contents of a column. For example, you could change the title of the Name column to "What has to be done," or you could display the Notes field in place of the Resource Names field in the last column. To modify the column, simply double-click the column title and Project displays the Column Definition dialog box (see Figure 2.12). The following list describes the options in the Column Definition dialog box.

- If you want to change the content of the column, select a different field in the Field Name box.

- Change the entry in the Title box to modify the column title. If you don't supply an entry in the Title box, Project displays the field name as the column title.

- You can select the alignment (left, right, or center) for the title with the Align Title box and for the data with the Align Data box.

- Clicking the OK button installs the changes you have selected.

- Clicking the Best Fit button installs the changes just like the OK button does, but it also adjusts the column width to the longest cell entry.

FIGURE 2.12

Change what is displayed in a column by double-clicking the title itself.

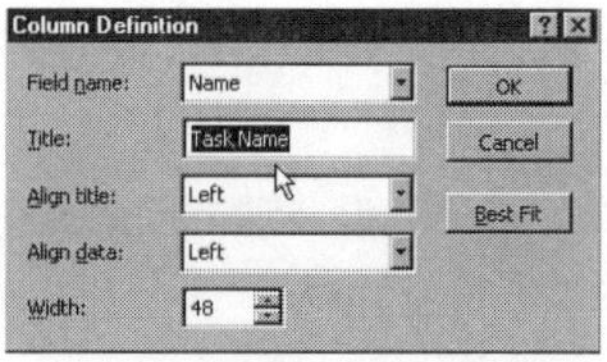

If you don't care to see a column, you can delete it from the sheet without losing the data that it displays. Simply click the column title to select the entire column and then press the Delete key.

To insert a new column in the table, select the column title that's now in the place you want the new column to be and press the Insert key. The Column Definition dialog box appears, and you can select the column options as described above.

Viewing More Task Details

The Gantt Chart view packs a lot of information. You can see even more details about individual tasks with either the Task Information dialog box or by splitting the screen and viewing the Task Form. We look at both these ways to view more information before we wrap up this hour.

Using the Task Information Dialog Box

Click the Task Information tool on the Standard toolbar to display a pop-up dialog box that displays many details about the selected task (see Figure 2.13). The five tabs in the dialog box provide access to many additional fields. If you have a summary task selected, the Summary Task dialog box is displayed. Some fields are dimmed and unavailable on the Summary Task dialog box because those fields are calculated by Project from the subtasks for the summary task.

For now, just note that in any view where you can select a task, you can see all these fields by selecting the Task Information tool—even if the fields are not normally displayed in the view with which you are working. Also note that the last tab, the Notes tab, contains the full text of the Notes field. You can go directly to this tab for the selected task by clicking the Task Notes tool on the Standard toolbar.

FIGURE 2.13

The Task Information dialog box provides a great deal of information that can't be fitted into the Gantt Chart view.

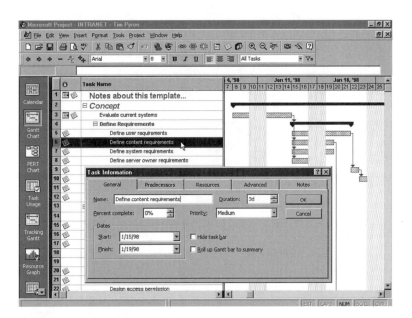

Using Combination Views

One of the most useful and powerful display techniques that Microsoft Project provides is the capability to split the screen in half and see two different views of the project simultaneously. Choose Window, Split to split the screen. You can also double-click the split box, which is located immediately below the arrow at the bottom of the vertical scroll bar (see Figure 2.14).

The window is split into two panes: the top pane shows the view with which you were working and the bottom pane shows either the Task Form (if you started with a task view) or the Resource Form (if you started with a resource view). Because the Gantt Chart is a task view, the bottom pane is the Task Form (see Figure 2.14). You can remove the split just as easily: choose **Window**, Remove **S**plit or double-click the split box, which is now at the center of the screen. Drag the Split bar up or down to change the division of the screen between the top and bottom panes.

Task number 6, "Define Content Requirements," is selected in the top pane in Figure 2.14, and that is the task whose details appear in the bottom pane. The bottom pane displays all the fields that are in the columns of the Gantt Chart. This arrangement enables you to see those field values and more of the timeline at the same time. You are also able to see additional fields—Effort Driven, Task Type, and % Complete—as well as much more detail about resources and predecessors. Altogether, this split screen is a very efficient way to view the tasks in a project. You can see how the task fits into the overall scheme of things in the top pane, and you can see many significant details in the bottom pane.

FIGURE 2.14

The combination view of the Gantt Chart and the Task Form shows the essential details for the task that is selected in the top pane.

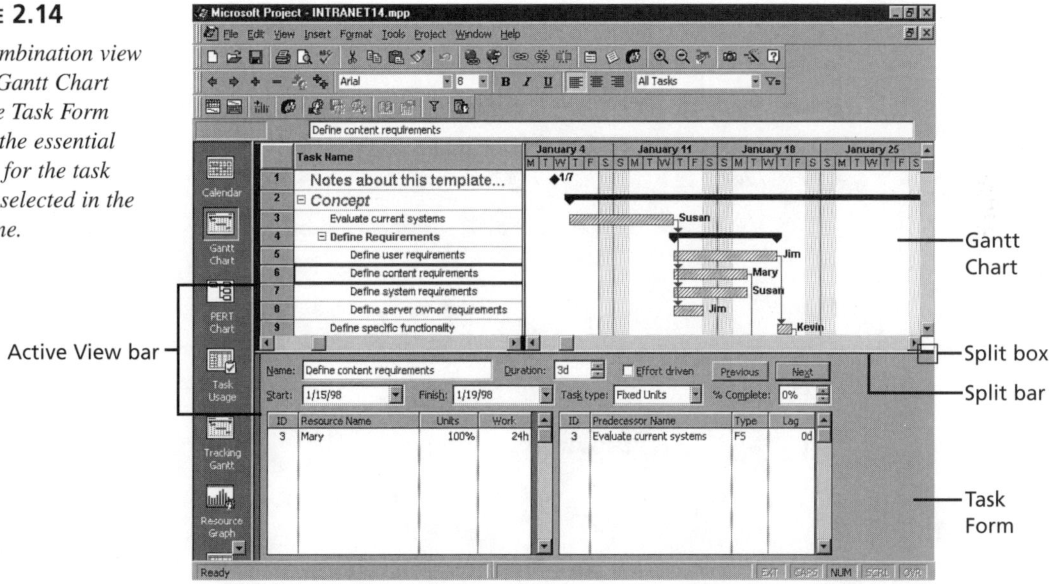

You can enter task information in either pane, but you must activate the pane before you can use it. To activate the bottom pane, simply click anywhere in the bottom pane. You can also use the F6 function key to toggle back and forth between the panes. The pane that is active at the moment displays a dark blue color in its half of the Active View bar.

The two mini-tables at the bottom of the Task Form initially display resource and prede-cessor details. You can select different details to display in this area. First, activate the bottom pane. Then choose Format, **D**etails from the menu to display the list of details you can display. (You can also right-click the bottom pane to display the list of available details). For example, if you choose **N**otes, you see the full text of the Notes field. You can then move down the task list in the top pane and read the notes attached to each task in the bottom pane. It's a good way to review all the notes.

Hour **3**

Starting a New Project and Working with Tasks

In this hour, you begin the new document for your project. If you've been given a project file to work with, you can use it to work through the features presented here. This hour covers preparing for your first project file, starting the project file, and putting together the list of things to do in the project—the task list. Hours 4 and 5 show you how to turn that list of tasks into a schedule or timeline.

Things To Do When Starting a New Project File

It's ironic that many people adopt Microsoft Project to help them get organized, but then don't want to bother with an organized approach to using Project. There are just three things I urge you to do at the beginning of any new project:

- Set the start or finish date for the project, which gives Project a peg on which to base its schedule calculations.
- Record the goal or objective of the project to guide your planning. It will prove invaluable in keeping you focused on the end result.
- Change any of the critical default options that govern how Microsoft Project calculates the schedule for your project.

You can do these things after you've already started a project file, and you can change them as often as you want, but it saves time to take care of them up front.

Starting a New Project File

When you start a new project document, you need to define for Microsoft Project the start or ending date for the project—usually the date on which work will begin or a deadline date by which the project must be completed. Project schedules your tasks based on the fixed start or finish date. You should also record the project goal when you start the new document and select any of the option settings that you want to change for that project.

Setting the Start or Finish Date for the Project

When you start a new project document, Microsoft Project displays by default the Project Information dialog box. In this dialog box you are expected to tell Project whether a fixed start date or a fixed finish date governs the schedule. Project schedules all work from the date you select.

NEW TERM **Fixed Start Date and Fixed Finish Date Projects**   If you know when you want work to start on your project, and you don't have a deadline by which it must be finished, then enter the date you want work to start and let Project calculate a schedule from that date forward. The project is said to be scheduled from a *fixed start date*.

If your project has a deadline date by which it must be finished, enter that date as the project's finish date and let Microsoft Project calculate a schedule backward from that date that guarantees all tasks will be completed by the finish date. The project is said to be scheduled from a *fixed finish date*.

Unless you have a mandated finish date for the project, you can pick a start date and let Project schedule tasks from that date. Project schedules all tasks as soon as possible after that date based on other information you enter, including the order in which tasks ought to occur, any intermediate deadlines that have to be met, and the availability of resources assigned to work on the tasks. The schedule that Project calculates will produce a finish date for the project.

If your project is required to be finished by a deadline date over which you have no control, then enter that finish date and tell Project to schedule the project to be finished by that date. Project schedules all activity to be completed by the fixed finish date. The schedule Project calculates will produce a project start date that tells you when work has to begin to finish by the deadline.

To Do: Starting a New File and Defining Start or Finish Date

To start a new file and define the start or finish date for the project, follow these steps:

1. Choose **File, New** from the menu or click the New tool on the Standard toolbar to open a new project document. Project displays the Project Information dialog box (see Figure 3.1).

2. In the Schedule From box, select Project Start Date or Project Finish Date, depending on your project's requirements.

   If you select Project Start Date, the Start **D**ate box is accessible and the Finish Date box is dimmed. If you select Project Finish Date, the Start **D**ate box is dimmed and the **F**inish Date box is accessible.

3. Enter the project start date or finish date in the appropriate box.

   Click the down arrow in the date box if you want to select the date from a pop-up calendar. Change months with the scroll arrows on either side of the calendar's title bar, and click on the date you want to be entered in the box.

> Project also stores the time of day as part of these dates, even if you are not displaying one of the date formats that include the time of day.
>
> If you enter a project start date, Project includes the default start time you entered in the Calendar tab of the Options dialog box. If you enter a project finish date, Project includes the default end time as part of the date. If this project is to begin or end at a non-default time, be sure to include the time with the date you enter.
>
> For example, if you have set the default end time to be 5:00 p.m., but you want this project to end by noon on January 4, 1999, then you would enter "1/4/99 12:00 p.m." in the Finish **D**ate box.

▲   4. Click OK to close the dialog box.

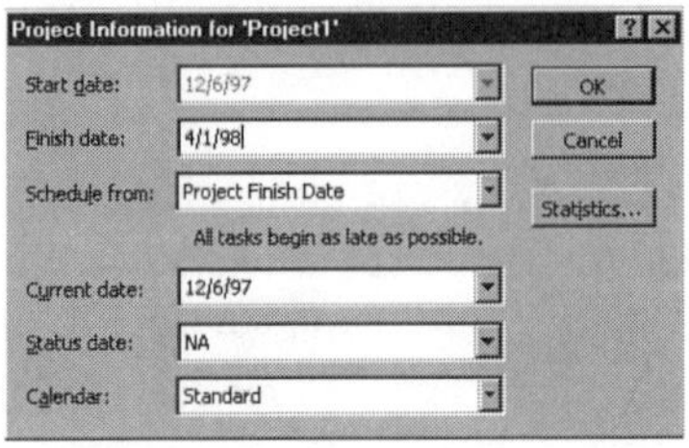

FIGURE 3.1

The Project Information dialog box determines whether the project is scheduled from a fixed start date or to meet a fixed finish date.

You can access the Project Information dialog box at any time by choosing **P**roject, **P**roject Information from the menu. You can change the start or finish date as needed, and you can change whether the project is to be scheduled from a fixed start date or a fixed finish date.

Record the Goal and Scope of the Project

When starting a new project, one of the first things you should do is to state clearly the project's objective or goal. The goal must include a well-defined deliverable or final result, something that can be measured to determine whether the project is meeting or has met its objectives. There should be a clear statement of any important assumptions or limitations, such as time and budget constraints or the quality of the final product. You should show this statement to all parties with an interest in the project outcome and protect yourself against future misunderstanding by getting an agreement from them that this statement of the objective is accurate.

The goal or objective statement for the project doesn't have to be a lofty, superbly crafted statement. It just needs to state clearly in a few sentences what the project is designed to accomplish. If you don't have this goal clearly in mind, your plans are going to lack the direction and clarity of purpose they need to succeed.

A good place to record the project goal is in the Comments box of the Properties dialog box. This dialog box is also the place to enter items such as the project's title, the company or organization's name, and the project manager. It's important to supply these entries because they will be used in headers and footers on printed reports to identify the project.

To Do: Recording Document Properties

To record the document properties, do the following:

1. Choose **F**ile, Properties from the menu to display the Properties dialog box (see Figure 3.2).

2. In the **T**itle box, enter the project title that you want to appear on printed reports. Project places the filename in this box until you type something of your own there.

▼ 3. Your user name should appear automatically in the **A**uthor box. Change it if necessary to the spelling you want to appear on reports.

4. Place the project manager's name in the **M**anager box. This information is also commonly used in reports.

5. Place the company or organization name, also for use in reports, in the **C**ompany box.

6. Place the project goal in the **C**omments box. This box can hold several thousand characters, but the typical goal statement is much shorter than that.

▲ 7. When finished, click the OK button.

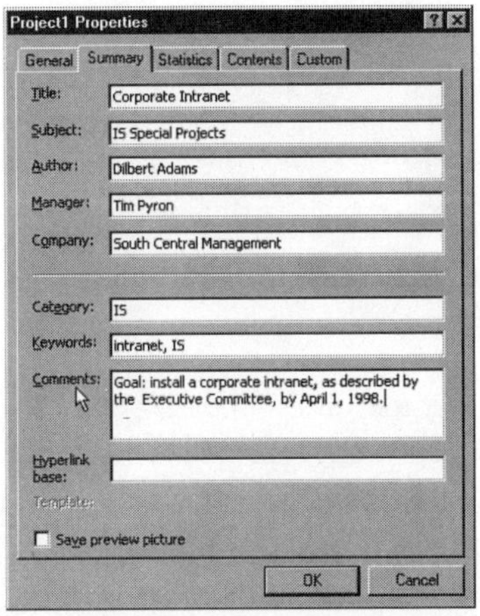

FIGURE 3.2

Supply information about the project in the Properties dialog box.

3

Choosing Microsoft Project's Operating Defaults

The first time you use Microsoft Project you should take the time to set the options that govern Project's default assumptions and behavior. A few of these options are critical because they affect the data values that Project records when you add to or edit the project document. I'm going to suggest the settings I think best in this Hour, and show you how to make them the standard settings for all your future work. However, I'll defer any thorough explanation of them until later chapters where the operations they affect will be discussed.

To Do: Setting Default Values for Critical Options

To set default values for the critical options, follow these steps:

▼ 1. Choose **T**ools, **O**ptions from the menu to display the Options dialog box (see Figure 3.3).

▼ 2. Select the General tab and clear the check box for Automatically Add New Resources And Tasks. We'll see why in Hour 9, "Defining Resources and Costs."

   Click the Set As **D**efault button to make this the default for all future projects. Otherwise, you will be changing the settings just for the current project.

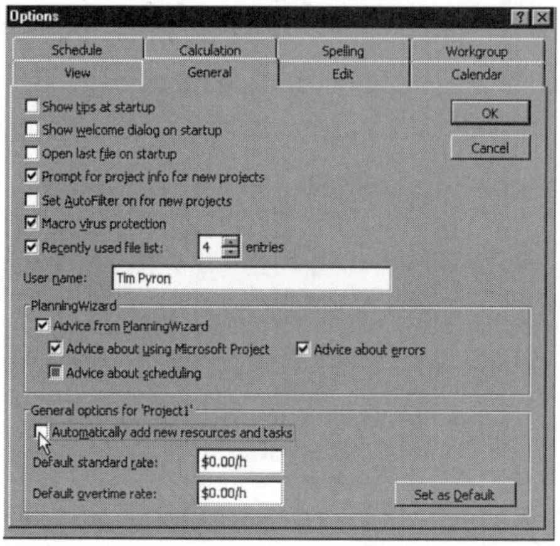

FIGURE 3.3

The Options dialog box is your control panel for determining critical features of Project's calculations.

3. Select the Calendar tab and set the values in each box described in the following list to match your organization's work schedule. These are critical options that determine how Project interprets the data you enter, so it's important that they reflect your organization's practices.

   • Set Default Start **T**ime to the time people normally begin work in your organization. The default is 8:00 a.m., but if your organization's hours are from 7:00 a.m. to 4:00 p.m., for example, change this entry to 7:00 a.m.

   • Set Default **E**nd Time to the normal end of the working day for your organization.

   • Set Hours Per Da**y** to the normal hours for employees in your organization. The default is 8 hours a day. If your organization lets people work four 10-hour days a week, with three days off, then you should enter 10 in this field. This value determines how Project interprets this information when you set the length of a task in "days."

   • Set Hours Per **W**eek to match the total hours employees work per week. The default is 40. This value determines how Project interprets this information when you set the length of a task in "weeks."

   Click the Set As **D**efault button to make these Calendar options the default for all
▼ future projects.

▼

4. Select the Schedule tab and clear the check box for the option **A**utolink Inserted Or Moved Tasks. This option will be explained in Hour 5, "Turning the Task List into a Schedule—The Rest of the Story."

   Click the Set As **D**efault button to make this setting the default for all future

▲   projects.

When you start a new project document from now on, these default values will be in place.

Now that you have entered the information that defines the project, the next step is to start defining the major tasks or groups of tasks for the project.

Starting the Task List

You can put together the list of activities or tasks for the project in several ways. The most common method is to build an outline of the work that has to be done on the project. Start by listing the large blocks of activity or major phases of the project. Then break each phase down into greater detail by listing more narrowly defined tasks, known as *subtasks*, that contribute to completing the major phase. Continue to break down the work into subtasks until you have identified all the activities you want to keep track of in the project.

NEW TERM   **Subtask**   A *subtask* is a detail item that is part of a larger task. If Relocate Wall is a task in a remodeling project, one of its subtasks might be Tear Down Existing Wall and another one could be Frame New Walls.

If you were remodeling a house, for example, the phases or major tasks might be Relocate Walls, Painting, and Carpeting. Each phase or major task can be broken down into smaller tasks. Subtasks for the Relocate Walls task might be Tear Down Existing Wall, Frame New Wall, Install New Wiring, Install New Plumbing, and so forth.

> It's an art deciding how finely detailed your task list should be. For the Relocate Walls example, subtasks such as Tear Down Existing Wall, Frame New Wall, and Install New Wiring might be reasonable. However, breaking the list down to the level of Pull Out Old Nails and Carry Debris Outside is too detailed to be useful. Monitoring that level of detail would not be useful.

Don't list every little thing that has to be done, but list everything you want to monitor to be sure it's completed. The smallest tasks—the lowest level of the outline—should be fairly short in duration (no more than a couple of weeks) and should be easily observed or monitored.

It's also possible to create the task list by importing an already prepared task list from another source. You can start with a template like those supplied by Microsoft Project during installation, or you can import into Project a task list that was created in some other application like Excel or Word. You learned how to open a template in the last Hour. In this Hour, we'll first build a list from scratch, but I'll also show you how to import an already prepared task list.

One final note: I'm going to concentrate in this Hour on building and editing the task list and defer until later the discussion of how you turn that list of tasks into a schedule with start and finish dates. After you know how to use Project, you might prefer to combine some of these techniques and enter scheduling details as you create the task list.

As you add tasks to the list, Project is going to fill in some scheduling information in its calculated fields. You will see a default Duration of "1 day" appear as soon as you enter the task name. You can change that entry if you want, but I will defer discussing duration and other scheduling issues until the next Hour. You will also see default Start and Finish dates appear, which are both initially set to the project's fixed start or finish date. Don't worry about them for now. We'll give Project better information for calculating those dates in the next Hour.

Creating the Initial List

The easiest way to build the task list is to start brainstorming and list the top-level tasks in the table on the left side of the Gantt Chart view. Click in a cell in the Task Name column and type in the name of a major phase or top-level task for the project. You can use any characters on the keyboard as part of the task name, including numbers and spaces. Names do not have to be unique, so you can have, for example, several tasks named "Stop to Assess Progress."

When you press Enter, Project automatically fills in a default Duration (1 day) and schedules the task to start and finish on the project's fixed start date (or fixed finish date).

Project then moves the selection to the cell below so you can enter the next task.

You can leave blank rows in the list where you plan to fill in details later, or you can wait and insert blank rows when you get ready to type in the details.

Keeping Notes About Tasks

It's an excellent idea to attach lots of notes to tasks to remind yourself of important ideas and also to explain why you've done particular things in the project plan that others might need explained. The notes can also be included in printed reports you prepare for the project.

 To add a note to a task, select the task and click the Task Notes tool on the Standard toolbar. The Task Information dialog box will appear with the Notes tab selected (see Figure 3.4). Type the note in the Notes box.

You can enhance the notes text with the formatting controls at the top of the Notes box:

- Use the font control to change font styles of the text you have selected. You can also use the traditional Windows shortcut keys for **bold** (Ctrl+B), *italic* (Ctrl+I), and underlining (Ctrl+U).

- Use the alignment controls to change the text's justification to left, centered, or right.

- Use the bullet control to indent a paragraph with a bullet.

- Use the graphic control to embed an image, such as a logo or drawing, into the note.

FIGURE 3.4

You can use formatting to emphasize important points in the notes that document your project.

Font control   Bullet control

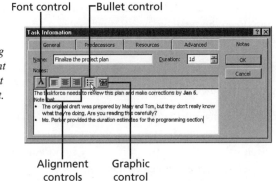

Alignment controls   Graphic control

Click OK to close the Task Information dialog box. Tasks that have Notes attached also have an indicator in the second column that resembles the icon on the Notes tool.

Entering Milestones

As you build the task list, you will probably want to include some checkpoints or *milestones*. Usually these are points in the life of the project that signal significant events or the completion of major phases. You enter a milestone just as you do any other task except that you change its *duration* to zero. Project treats any task with a zero duration as a milestone and represents it with a diamond shape instead of a bar on the Gantt Chart.

Editing the Task List

You will most likely decide at some point to change the name of a task, or to go back and insert a task, or change the order of the tasks in some way. You can easily type over old names with new ones, and you can insert, delete, move, and copy task names to your heart's content.

Undoing Changes

Before you start changing the task list, remember that you can usually reverse the last change you have made in a project with the **Edit, Undo** command or by clicking the Undo button on the Standard toolbar. The shortcut key is Ctrl+Z. Microsoft Project does not have a separate Redo command. If you use Undo to reverse a change, using Undo again reverses the reversal. Remember, it's only the most recent change that you can undo.

Inserting and Deleting Tasks

If you need to insert a task in the list, click on the row where the new task should go and press the Insert key (or choose **Insert, New Task** from the menu). Project will create a blank row by pushing down the task that was in that row and other tasks below. You can also copy a task from another location in the list.

To Do: Copying Tasks

To copy a task from another location, follow these steps:

1. Select the row for the task (or tasks) you want to copy by clicking on the row numbers (the task ID numbers). (See Hour 2, "Becoming an Instant Project Guru," for more information on task ID numbers.) It is very important that you select the entire row for the task, not just a cell in the row.

2. Click the Copy Task tool or choose the **Edit, Copy Task** command. Note that the ScreenTip for the tool and Copy command on the menu read "Copy Cell" if you haven't selected the entire task.

3. Select the row, or a cell in the row, where you want the new duplicate task or tasks to be placed. You do not have to insert a blank row ahead of time to receive the new task(s).

4. Click the Paste tool or use the **Edit, Paste** command to paste in the duplicate task.

If the selection is not the entire task row when you copy or move a task, you will be copying or moving only the cell or cells that were actually selected. Always click the task ID number to select the entire task before using the Cut or Copy command if you want to use the entire task.

If you decide to remove a task from the list, click on any cell in the task's row and press the Delete key. If you want to go the menu route, choose **Edit**, **D**elete Task.

Note that in the preceding paragraph the Delete key (or the menu choice) removes the entire row for a task. If you want to clear the contents of just the selected cell, you need to use the Ctrl+Del key combination (or choose **Edit**, **Cl**ear, **C**ontents) from the menu.

Rearranging the Task List

You can rearrange the order of the tasks by moving tasks into new positions on the list. In general, you should list the tasks in the approximate order in which you want the work to be scheduled. It isn't necessary, but it makes your task list easier to understand.

To Do: Moving a Task

To move a task to a new location in the list, do the following:

1. Select the ID number for the task that you want to move. Never select just the task name or any other single cell because you then move just that single cell instead of the whole task row.

2. Choose the **Edit**, **Cu**t Task command from the menu or click the Cut Task tool on the Standard toolbar. This action removes the task from the list and places it in Window's Clipboard memory. Don't go for coffee at this point. Finish the remaining steps, or you might forget and lose that information in the Clipboard.

3. Select the row that is to be the task's new home (click the task ID for that row). You do not have to create a blank row to receive the new task.

4. Choose the **Edit**, **P**aste command or click the Paste tool on the Standard toolbar. Project will move the existing task on that row down out of the way and insert the new task.

Arranging Tasks with an Outline

After the top-level tasks are defined, you can use the outline tools to start filling in the details under each phase of the project. You insert blank rows beneath a top-level task, list the subtasks in the blank rows, and then indent the subtasks under the top-level task. When you indent tasks, Project turns the task they are indented under into a *summary* task.

Summary tasks serve to summarize many aspects of their subtasks. A summary task's bar in the Gantt Chart spans all the task bars of its subtasks so you can see the life span of that part of the project. Later we will see that if you assign resources and costs to tasks, the cost of a summary task is the combined cost of all its subtasks.

Indenting and Outdenting Tasks

To indent one or more tasks, select the task(s) and choose the **P**roject, **O**utline, **I**ndent command, or click the Indent tool on the Formatting toolbar. Project shifts the display of the subtasks to the right and changes the task immediately above into a summary task.

You can reverse this process, also. If you decide that a task should not be a subtask under its summary task, you can shift the task leftward, or "outdent" it, with the **P**roject, **O**utline, **O**utdent command (or click on the Outdent tool on the Formatting toolbar).

When you outdent a task that has other tasks at the same outline level just below it, Project makes the outdented task a summary task for the tasks just below it. So, if you had indented five tasks under a new summary task and then decided to outdent the third task, Project would make it the summary task for the fourth and fifth tasks. If you want to avoid this, you should move the task you plan to outdent to the bottom of the list of the subtasks before you outdent.

Working with Summary Tasks

Summary tasks "contain" the subtasks beneath them. Anything you do to the definition of the summary task is also done to its subtasks.

- If you indent or outdent a summary task, its subtasks move with it and are further indented or outdented also.
- If you delete a summary task, you also delete its subtasks.
- If you move a summary task, its subtasks go right along with it, in a subordinate position, to the new location.
- If you copy a summary task, you also copy its subtasks.

If you want to delete a summary task without deleting its subtasks, you must first outdent its subtasks so that it is no longer a summary task. Then you can delete it without losing its former subtasks.

Hiding Subtasks

One advantage of outlining is the ability to collapse the outline to show only high-level tasks or to expand it to show all the details. By default, Project displays a small icon to the left of summary task names that both identifies them as summary tasks and also indicates whether their subtasks are hidden or displayed. Each summary task can be collapsed or expanded separately.

A small plus sign icon, similar to the Show Subtasks tool on the Formatting toolbar, means that there are hidden subtasks. Click the plus sign icon, or select the summary task and click the Show Subtasks tool, to display the subtasks. You can also select the summary task and then use the **P**roject, **O**utline, **S**how Subtasks command to display its subtasks.

A small minus sign icon similar to the Hide Subtasks tool means that all the subtasks immediately under the summary task are shown and that clicking the icon will hide them. You can also select the summary task and click the Hide Subtasks button or use the **P**roject, **O**utline, **H**ide Subtasks command.

If you want to collapse the entire outline to top-level tasks only, click the Task Name column title to select all tasks and then click the Hide Subtasks tool. With all tasks still selected, you can click the Show Subtasks tool repeatedly to progressively show additional levels of the outline.

If you want to instantly show all tasks in the outline, click the Show All Subtasks tool.

Selecting the Display Options for Outlining

You can choose options for how summary tasks are displayed or decide if you want them displayed at all. If you choose to hide the display of summary tasks themselves, the task list shows only non-summary tasks (tasks with no subtasks under them).

It is also handy to choose to display a summary task for the entire project. You do not have to create this task; Project can calculate it and display it as a task with ID number zero. The task bar for the project summary task stretches from the project's start to its finish, and its cost measures the total cost of the project.

To Do: Changing Display of Summary Tasks

To change the display of summary tasks, including the display of a project summary task, follow these steps:

1. Choose **T**ools, **O**ptions from the menu to display the Options dialog box (see Figure 3.5).

▼   2. Click the View tab. The options for outlining are in the lower-right corner.

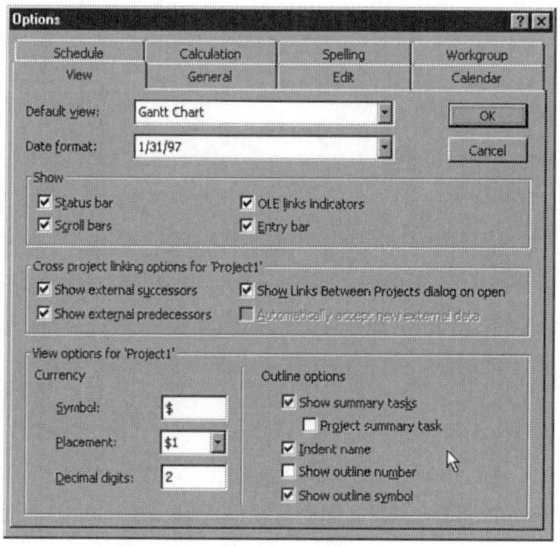

FIGURE 3.5

Adjust the display of outlines in the Options dialog box.

3. Clear the check box for Show Summary Tasks to suppress all summary tasks in the view. The default is for this option to be activated.

4. Fill the Project Summary Task check box to display an overall summary of the project as task ID zero.

5. Clearing the Indent Name check box suppresses the outline format. All task names will appear lined up against the left margin.

6. Fill the Show Outline Number check box to display numbers next to each task name. The numbering system will be the legal numbering system as illustrated in Figure 3.6. You can tell by the outline number where a task lies in the project plan. If the number is "3.2.4," it means this is the fourth subtask under the second sub-task under top-level task 3.

▲   7. If you don't want the outline icons to appear next to task names, clear the Show Outline Symbol check box.

Entering Recurring Tasks

If you have an activity such as a regularly scheduled meeting that you want to include in the task list, you can create a *recurring task*. Project asks you how often the task will occur and to indicate how long it will last each time. Project then schedules each of the occurrences and creates a summary task for the series of events. If you show the subtasks for this new summary task, you can see each event is a separate task. Instead of a contin-uous bar for the summary task, each of the individual events is *rolled up* to display on the summary task row. Figure 3.7 shows a weekly project meeting scheduled at the top of the intranet project. Note the circular icon in the indicator column for this task.

FIGURE 3.6

The outline numbering system is like the "legal" numbering system.

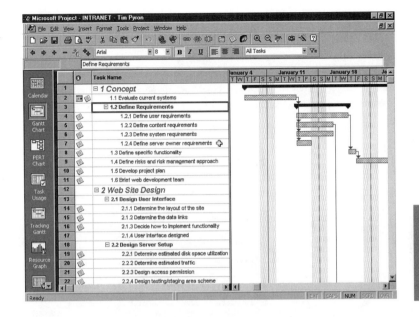

FIGURE 3.7

Enter regularly repeating events as recurring tasks.

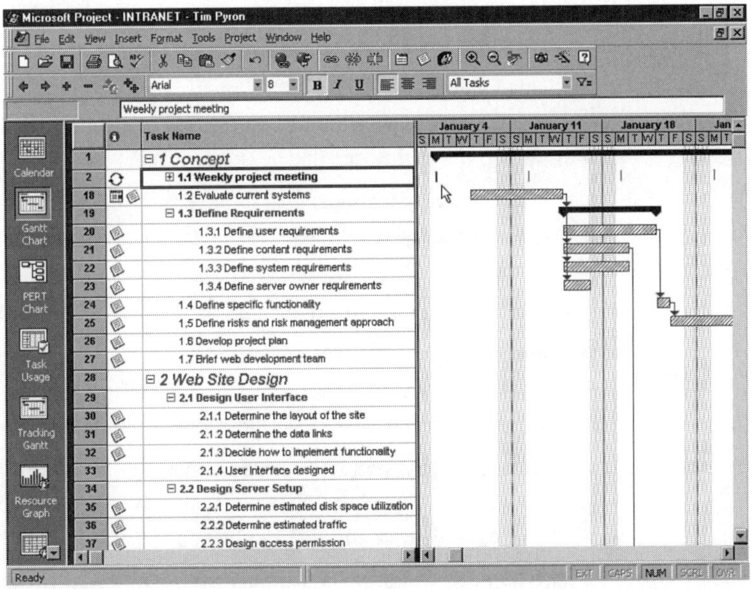

When you enter a recurring task, Project asks for the duration of each occurrence of the task and how often the task occurs. The default time unit for duration is one day (d). You can also use minutes (m), hours (h), and weeks (w) as time units.

To Do: Creating Recurring Tasks

To create a recurring task, do the following:

1. Select the task row where you want the task to go.

2. Choose Insert, Recurring Task from the menu to display the Recurring Task Information dialog box (see Figure 3.8).

3. Enter a name for the task in the Name box.

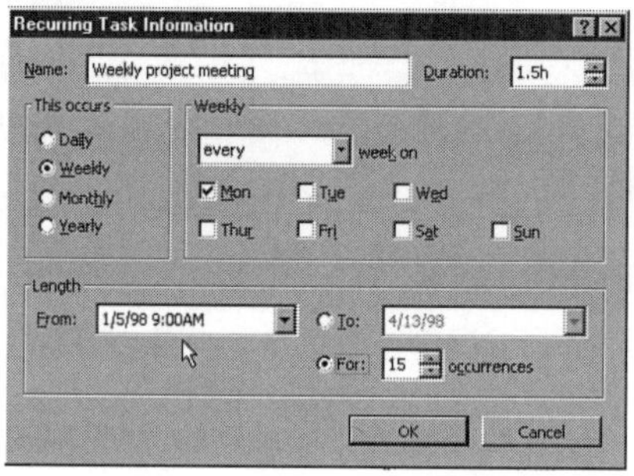

FIGURE 3.8

The Recurring Task Information box gives you great flexibility in defining recurring events.

4. Enter how long each event will be in the Duration box. For example, if the event is to be scheduled for 2 hours each time, enter 2 hrs in the Duration box.

5. In the This Occurs group, select the recurring time period (Daily, Weekly, Monthly, or Yearly). Your choice in the This Occurs group determines the options that appear to the right for your next selection.

6. If you selected Daily occurrences, choose the frequency of the event in the list box and select either Day or Workday. For example, the events might take place "every other" Workday.

   If you select Weekly occurrences, choose the frequency and the day of the week.

   If you select Monthly occurrences, you can define the frequency in terms of the day number in the month or in terms of a specific day of the week. For example, you could select Day 1 of every month or the third Thursday in every month.

   If you select a Yearly occurrence, you can define the event as a specific date in the year or as a specific weekday in a particular month. For example, you could select April 15 of each year or the last Wednesday in July.

7. Finally, you need to define how many times the event (task) will take place. You must specify the date for the first event in the From date box. If the task takes place at a particular time of day, be sure you add the time of day to the date in the From date box. In Figure 3.8, the meeting is set to start at 9:00 a.m. every Monday.

▼   You can then specify an ending date in the **To** date box or a specific number of occurrences in the For Occurrences box. Project supplies the finish date for the project as a default in the **To** box, but you can change that if needed.

8. When you have completed your choices, click OK and Project will attempt to schedule all the events. If any of the occurrences fall on a weekend or other non-working day, Project warns you with the alert dialog box shown in Figure 3.9. Choose **Yes** to let Project reschedule those occurrences that fall on nonworking days to the next working day. Choose **No** to have Project omit scheduling those occurrences, or choose Cancel to cancel the recurring task.

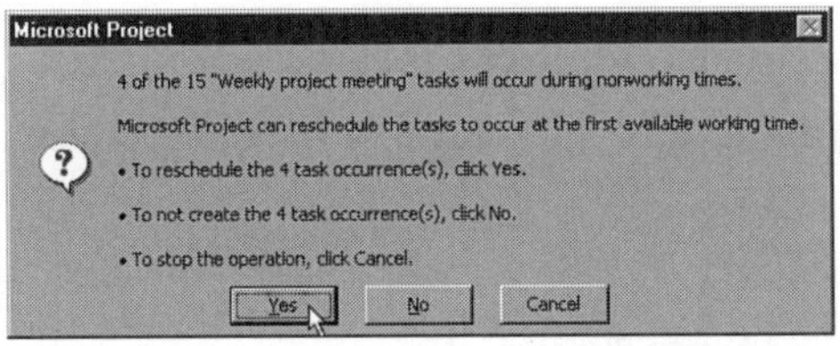

FIGURE 3.9

Project can detect any occurrences that fall on nonworking days and offer to move them to the next available working day.

If you want to modify a recurring task, select the task and choose **P**roject, Recurring Task **I**nformation (or simply double-click the recurring task) to display the dialog box again and modify any of the selections.

Using Other Techniques to Create Tasks

Typing in a task list is by far the most efficient way to create a large project. After the task list is developed, however, you might find it more convenient to add tasks with other methods. If your project is small, you might even want to begin creating the task list with one of the other methods, instead of building an outline.

Most of these other options involve scheduling tasks as you create them. For example, you can create a task on the Gantt Chart by dragging the mouse from the start date of the task to the finish date (or vice versa), or you can drag task bars from one date to another on the Calendar view. Both these methods schedule the task immediately, but they also involve other things that I want to wait until a later Hour to describe in more detail.

There is one other way of creating a task list that I want to mention because you might find it very helpful in getting started. If you already have a list of tasks in another application, such as a word processor or spreadsheet, you can copy the task list from that application and paste it into Project. However, you should be aware that you cannot import an outlined task list with this method. Even if the task list is outlined in the word processor, it will not be outlined in Project. You will have to indent tasks to create the outline after you get the tasks into Project.

In Hour 21, "Exchanging Project Data with Other Applications," you will see more elaborate ways to move data between Project and other applications.

To Do: Pasting a Task List from Another Application

▼ To Do

To paste a task list from another application into Project, follow these steps:

1. Select the task list in the other application. In a spreadsheet, the task names must each be in a separate cell in a column. In a word processor, each task name must be on a separate line in the text.

2. Copy the task list to the Windows Clipboard.

3. Select a cell in the Task Name column of the Project document. It does not have to be the first row.

▲   4. Choose Edit, Paste or click the Paste tool on the Standard toolbar to copy the list into the Project sheet.

In Hour 4, "Turning the Task List into a Schedule," I'll show you how to import not only the task names, but also the task durations and the start and finish dates if they were included in the original document.

Getting a Simple Printout of the Task List

If you're like me, you still want to see it on paper. There are several ways to print data from your project. The most common method is to get the screen to look the way you want it to look in the printed copy and then print that view. There are also some canned reports that emphasize various aspects of the project. To get a simple copy of the task list, your best bet is to simply print the Gantt Chart.

Adjust the vertical divider bar and the column widths as you did in Hour 2 to get the look you want on paper. Because we have focused on the task names and the outline this hour, the remaining columns in the table and the Gantt Chart are not very interesting. You might prefer to widen the Task Names column a bit and hide the other columns behind the chart.

If you hide subtasks on the screen, they will be hidden in the printed copy. For example, you could print just the top-level tasks or any combination of summary and subtasks.

To print the Gantt Chart view, you simply need to click the Print tool on the Standard toolbar and Project will print the current view. By default, Project prints all the tasks you see on the screen. You will learn how to customize the printout in Hour 8, "Finalizing and Printing Your Schedule."

Saving the New File

You can save Microsoft Project data in a variety of formats, but the standard format uses the file extension .mpp.

To Do: Saving a Project Document

To save a project document, follow these steps:

1. Choose **F**ile, **S**ave from the menu or click the Save tool on the Standard toolbar to display the Save dialog box (see Figure 3.10).

2. The Save **I**n box suggests the default directory. Select the directory you want to use.

   Like the other Microsoft Office products, Microsoft Project uses a default directory for saving and opening files. Unlike the other Office products, Microsoft Project does not provide a place where you can name a different default directory.

   If you know how to edit the Windows 95 Registry and are foolhardy enough to try it, you can change Project's default directory. It's a safer course for you to just use the default directory and put special folders in that directory to keep your files compartmentalized.

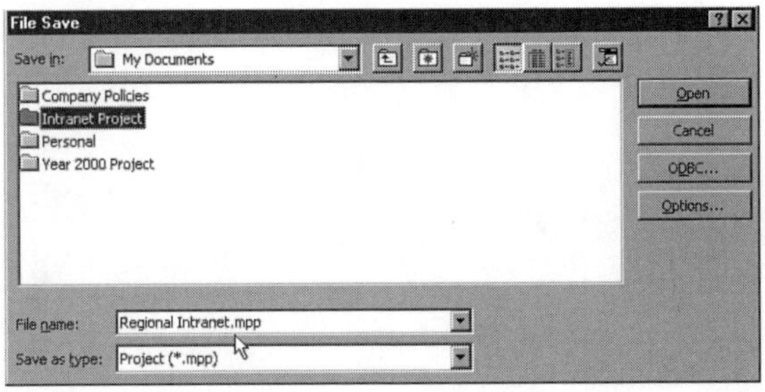

FIGURE 3.10

Save your project document as a Project file type.

3. Provide a name for the project in the File **N**ame box.

4. If you want to provide password protection for the file, click the **O**ptions button to display the Save Options dialog box (see Figure 3.11).

   Type a password in the **P**rotection Password box if you want to keep people who don't know the password from opening the file. Type a password in the **W**rite Reservation Password box if you want to prevent people who don't know the password from saving changes over the original.

   Both of these passwords can contain up to 17 characters and are case sensitive. Be sure you write down the passwords you use and store them in a safe place. You must remember the password to be able to use the file.

▼

FIGURE 3.11

You can provide password protection in the Save Options dialog box.

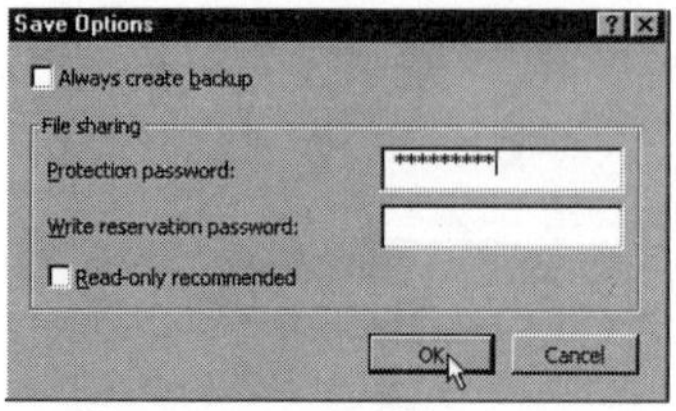

▲   5. Click the **Save** button to save the file.

PART II

Developing the Timeline

Hour

HOUR 4

Turning the Task List into a Schedule

In Hour 3, "Starting a New Project and Working with Tasks," you put together the list of tasks that need to be completed in your project, but that list is not a workable *schedule* until you attach realistic dates showing *when* work on each task is expected to start and finish. Microsoft Project automatically calculates default start and finish dates when you first enter tasks (see Figure 4.1), but that schedule calls for everything to start at once, like horses racing out of the starting gate. You have to give Microsoft Project instructions for calculating a more meaningful schedule, and that's what this Hour is all about.

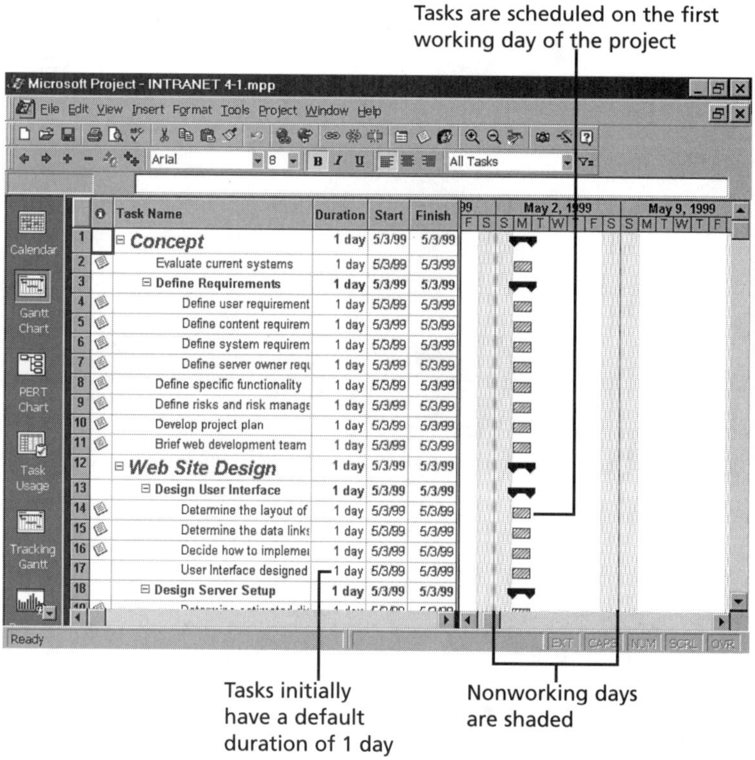

Tasks are scheduled on the first
working day of the project

FIGURE 4.1

*In the initial task list,
the tasks are lined up
at the start date and
ready to race off to the
finish line all at once.*

Tasks initially
have a default
duration of 1 day

Nonworking days
are shaded

The next section, "Understanding How Tasks Are Scheduled," gives you an overview of the factors Project considers in calculating dates for tasks. You learn in this and the next Hour how to control these factors with your instructions. However, the story will not be complete until Hour 10, "Understanding Resource Scheduling in Microsoft Project 98," where we look at how changing resource assignments affects the schedule.

Before we start discussing dates, you should be aware that almost every date field in Microsoft Project also includes the time of day. If you want to see both the time and date for scheduled events, change the display format for dates to include the time of day. However, you will usually have to widen the date columns to display this format, which takes much space onscreen (see Figure 4.2). Still, it can be a helpful temporary aid in troubleshooting problems.

If you want dates to include the time of day, you can change the default display for all dates in Microsoft Project with the Options dialog box.

FIGURE 4.2

Dates have a time component, but the format for date and time takes a lot of screen space.

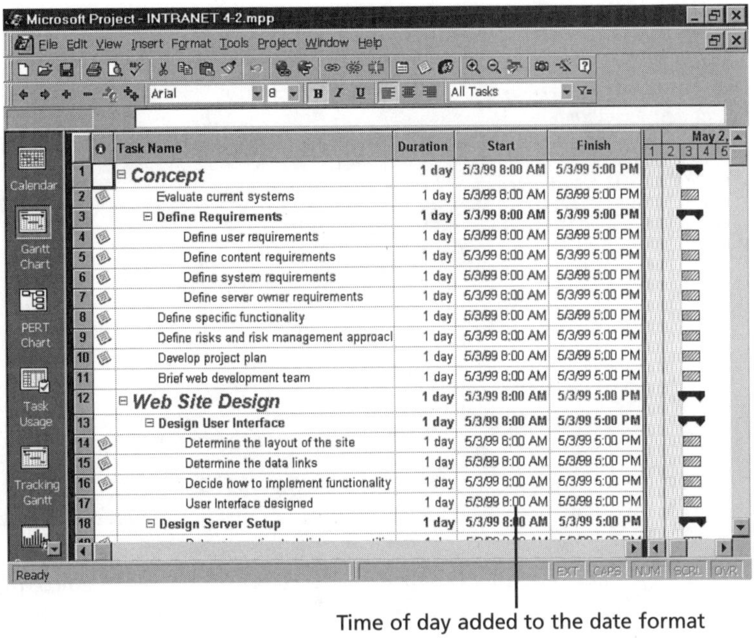

Time of day added to the date format

4

To Do: Selecting a Default Format for Dates

To select the default format for dates, follow these steps:

1. Choose **T**ools, **O**ptions from the menu to display the Options dialog box. Make sure that the View tab is displayed.

2. Click the list arrow in the Date Format list box and select the format you want to use (see Figure 4.3). The first choice in the list displays both the date and time of day.

3. Click the OK button to close the dialog box.

Understanding How Tasks are Scheduled

As soon as you enter a new task in your project, Microsoft Project immediately places it on the schedule calendar. Exactly where it gets placed depends on whether your project is scheduled from a fixed start date or from a fixed finish date. These and other factors controlling the scheduling of tasks are in the following list, which includes several new terms. They will be defined more precisely in the extended coverage for each factor—in most cases, later in this Hour.

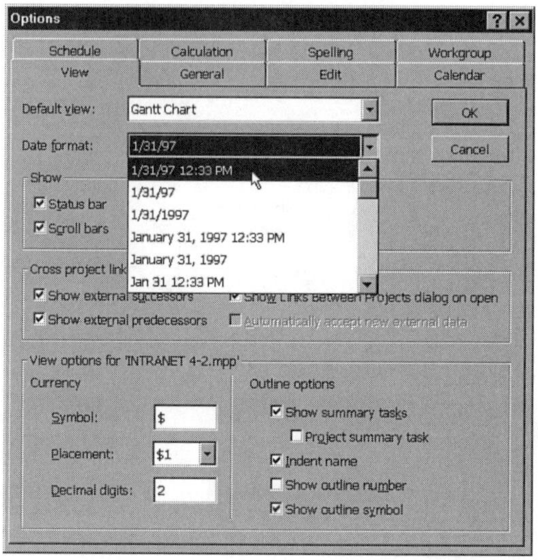

FIGURE 4.3

Sometimes displaying the time of day with dates helps you understand peculiarities in the schedule.

- Tasks are usually scheduled to start as soon as possible, which means as soon after the start of the project as the other factors listed here will allow. (You learned how to set the start date for the project in the previous Hour.) If your project is scheduled from a fixed finish date, then tasks are scheduled to finish as late as possible, which means as close to the end of the project as possible. For example, if you start a new project file and give the project a fixed start date of May 1, 1999 (as in Figure 4.1), then as you add tasks they are all initially scheduled to start as soon as possible after May 1, 1999.

- Microsoft Project includes a built-in calendar that defines working days and non-working days (such as weekends and holidays). The calendar also defines the times of day when work can be scheduled. For the most part, tasks are scheduled only during the working times defined in the calendar. The Gantt Chart shades the non-working days in the timeline area. As you can see in Figure 4.4, if you select a start date for your project that falls on a Saturday, Project schedules tasks to start on the following Monday, the first working day after the start of the project. Similarly, if you entered a time of day for the start of your project that is not a working hour on the calendar, Project would schedule tasks to begin in the first working hour thereafter. You will see much more about the calendar and working times in this Hour.

- Some tasks take longer to complete than others, and you give Project that information by your entry in the Duration field. When you first create a task, Project assigns a default duration of one day, and schedules the finish date at the end of one full working day. If you later enter a different duration estimate for the task,

Project reschedules the finish date. If, however, your project has a fixed finish date, then Project would not adjust the finish date, but would move the start date to an earlier time period.

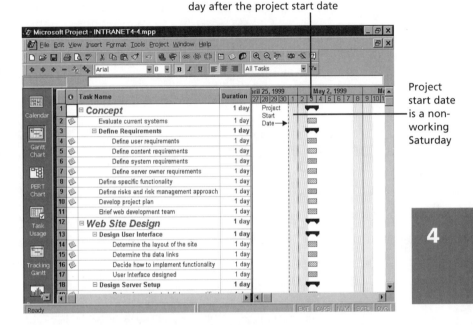

Tasks are scheduled on the first working day after the project start date

Project start date is a non-working Saturday

FIGURE 4.4

Tasks are scheduled only on working days.

In Figure 4.5, the duration estimates for the intranet project have been entered. Some task bars are longer, others are shorter, and the task finish dates reflect the duration values.

- Normally, Project assumes that once work begins on a task, it continues uninterrupted (except for nonworking days) until the task is finished. However, you can introduce arbitrary *splits* that interrupt the scheduled work on a task. In other words, you can schedule a task to start, stop, and start again at intervals of your choosing, and as often as you choose. For example, if an employee is unavailable or a piece of equipment breaks down (hopefully not vice versa), you could interrupt the task schedule until a replacement is available. In Figure 4.5, task 15 shows a split that was introduced because the person doing that task was away at a conference during that time.

Durations affect
the finish dates

Task with a
fixed date

FIGURE 4.5

*Adding duration esti-
mates to tasks causes
Project to adjust their
scheduled dates.*

Split task

- If there is a fixed date defined for the individual task, it overrides Project's attempt
  to schedule the task as soon or as late as possible. For example, in the intranet
  example in Figure 4.5, the start date for the Briefing (task 11) has been fixed at
  May 10, 1999, because the Web development team won't be hired and in place
  until that date. After you add this fixed date constraint to the task, its scheduled
  start date shifts to the fixed date. Using constraints is covered in Hour 5, "Turning
  the Task List into a Schedule—The Rest of the Story."

- Most of the time, the start or finish of a task is dependent on the start or finish of
  some other task. For example, in a residential construction project, the start of the
  Frame Walls task must wait until the finish of the Prepare Foundation task. You
  define this dependency in Project by linking tasks. In Figure 4.6, task 8 (Define
  Specific Functionality) is linked to task 4 (Define User Requirements) and should
  not be started until task 4 is finished; you shouldn't attempt to define what the Web
  site is going to do until you know what the users' requirements are. Linking tasks
  is covered in the next Hour.

FIGURE 4.6

The appropriate sequence for working on tasks is defined by linking tasks.

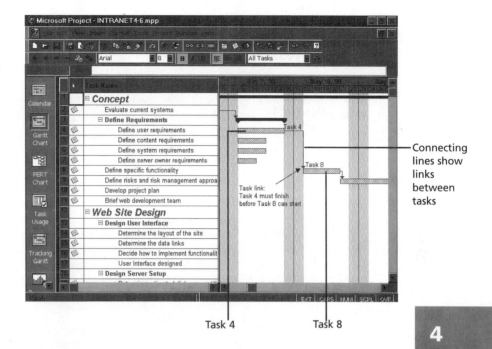

• When you assign resources to work on tasks, it can affect the schedule in a number of ways. Changing the number of people or machines assigned to a task can affect the task's duration and, therefore, the task's finish date. For example, if you double the number of people working on a task, it usually means the task is finished more quickly. The availability of the resources also affects the schedule for the task; work must be scheduled around vacations and other nonworking times for the resources, which could lengthen the schedule for the task. And, if the same resource is assigned to two overlapping tasks, you might have to delay the work on one task while the resource works on the other task. Resource assignments are covered in Hour 10, "Understanding Resource Scheduling in Microsoft Project 98," Hour 11, "Assigning Resources and Costs to Tasks," and Hour 12, "Editing Resource Assignments."

In the following sections, you learn how to control all but the last three items in the preceding list. You learn how to constrain and link tasks in Hour 5 and how to manage resource assignments starting in Hour 10.

Setting the Start or Finish Date for the Project

As you saw in Hour 3, all projects are scheduled from a fixed start date or a fixed finish date. New projects are, by default, scheduled from the beginning of the work day on the current date (your computer's internal clock date) as a fixed start date. So, if you start Microsoft Project at 3:00 p.m. on June 1, 1999, and start entering tasks in the new document (project1.mpp), the tasks are scheduled to start at 8:00 a.m. on that date—unless you change the project's fixed start date or finish date.

Even if you don't display the time of day in the date format, Project attaches the default time for the start of the work day (normally 8:00 a.m.) to the fixed start date or the default time for the end of the work day (normally 5:00 p.m.) to the fixed finish date. The section "Adjusting the Start and End of the Working Day" shows you how to change these default times.

Project assigns new tasks a default duration of 1 day (normally, that means the task will require 8 hours of work) and schedules an initial start and finish for each new task. If the project is scheduled from a fixed start date, Project schedules a new task to start as soon as possible after the start of the project and to finish at the end of one working day.

If the project is scheduled from a fixed finish date, then new tasks are scheduled to finish at the end of the project finish date. The task's start date is then calculated as one working day before the task's finish.

You must set the fixed start or finish date for the project because the rest of the project schedule is pegged to this date.

To Do: Setting the Fixed Start or Finish Date

To set the fixed start or finish date for the project, follow these steps:

1. Choose **P**roject, **P**roject Information from the menu to display the Project Information dialog box (see Figure 4.7).

2. Click the arrow in the Schedule From list box and choose either Project Start Date or Project Finish Date. If you chose Project Start Date, click the Start **D**ate field to enter the fixed start date for the project in the next step. If you chose Project Finish Date, click the **F**inish Date field to enter the fixed finish date.

3. Either type in the date or click the arrow in the cell and select the date from the calendar control.

▼ • Even if the time of day is not displayed in the current date format, Project attaches the default start time of day (normally 8:00 a.m.) to your entry in the Start **D**ate field or the default finish time of day (usually 5:00 p.m.) to your entry in the **F**inish Date field.

• If you want to specify a time of day that differs from the default time of day, type in the time of day either before or after the date. For example, to be sure that the project starts at 7:00 a.m. on December 1, 1999, you could type 12/1/99 7:00 AM into the Start **D**ate field or you could type 7am December 1, 1999. We'll discuss default times in more detail later in this chapter.

▲ 4. Click the OK button to close the Project Information dialog box.

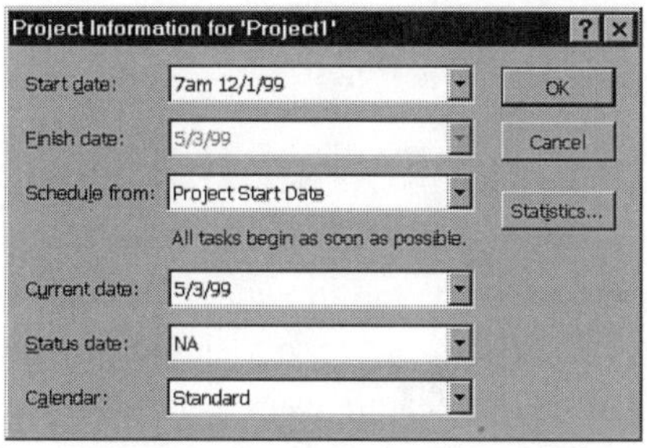

FIGURE 4.7

You should define the date from which the project starts or must finish when you start a new document.

When you want to enter today's date or a date within the next seven days, you can type in the words "today," "tomorrow," or the name of any day of the week, either spelled out or abbreviated (for example, "Friday" or "Fri"). Project will replace your text with the full date for the day you typed. For day names, Project uses the next occurrence of that name after the current date. For example, if the current date is Thursday, July 1, 1999, and you type in "9am Monday," Project will supply "7/5/99 9:00 AM."

If the date and hour you define for the project to start or finish are not a working day and hour, then tasks are scheduled on the nearest working date and hour. The next section shows you how to determine the working days and hours. In Figure 4.7, the start of the project is being set to 7:00 a.m.. If the first working hour on the calendar is 8:00 a.m., the tasks are scheduled to start at 8:00 a.m.

Defining the Standard Working Days and Times

When you install Microsoft Project, there are default settings for the start and end of the working day and a Standard calendar to define the working days and the working hours in each day:

- The default start of the working day is 8:00 a.m. and the default end of the working day is 5:00 p.m.
- The Standard calendar defines Mondays through Fridays as working days.
- The hours available for work on Mondays through Fridays are 8:00 a.m. to 12:00 p.m. and 1:00 p.m. to 5:00 p.m. This schedule provides a one-hour break in the middle of the day.
- Saturdays and Sundays are nonworking days.

Adjusting the Start and End of the Working Day

If you define the fixed start or finish date for the project, or if you type in a date for an individual task to start or finish, and you fail to include the time of day with the date, then Microsoft Project adds the default start time to any start date entry and the default end time to any finish date entry. This feature can create a nuisance for you if the default values don't match the actual start and end of the workday for your organization.

To Do: Setting the Default Start and Finish Time of Day

To set the default start and finish time of day, follow these steps:

1. Choose **T**ools, **O**ptions from the menu to display the Options dialog box, and select the Calendar tab.
2. Enter the standard start of the working day for your organization in the Default Start Time field and the standard end of the working day in the Default End Time field (see Figure 4.8).
3. Click the Set As **D**efault button if you want to make these times the defaults for all new project documents in the future.
4. Click OK to close the dialog box.

When you change the default start and finish times of day, Microsoft Project does not apply those new times to any existing task dates or calendar definitions in the project file. That's why you should make sure these times are set correctly for your organization and make them the default for all future project documents early in your career with Microsoft Project.

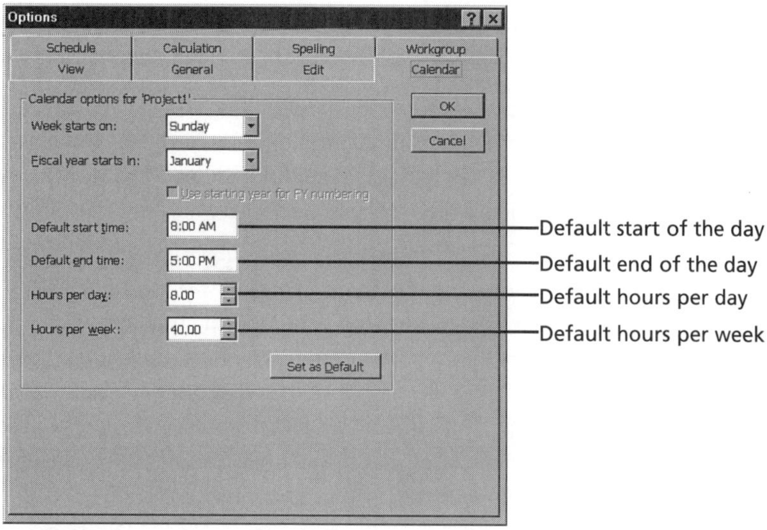

FIGURE 4.8

Change the default start and end of daily working times to match your workplace.

Default start of the day
Default end of the day
Default hours per day
Default hours per week

How Calendars Are Used in Scheduling

Microsoft Project bases its schedule for tasks on the working days and times defined in a base calendar to which the project is linked. At least, that's the case until you assign a resource to work on the task; then, the calendar for the resource determines when work can be scheduled. However, each resource calendar is also linked to a base calendar, usually the same one to which the project is linked. The resource calendar just has additional nonworking days and times (such as vacations, scheduled sick leave, or special working hours) that apply only to that resource.

NEW TERM **Base Calendar** Each project is linked to a *base calendar* that defines the normal working days and times of day in that project. Each resource you define is also linked to a base calendar—for most resources, it's the same base calendar to which the project is linked.

New project documents start out as copies of the Global project template (the file named global.mpt), and that template initially contains three base calendars supplied by Microsoft Project—one is named the Standard calendar. Initially, all new projects and all newly defined resources are linked to the Standard calendar in their project file as their base calendar.

The features of the three base calendars supplied by Microsoft Project are described in the following list. Any one of them can be used as the base calendar for your project or as the basis for the calendars governing working times for groups of employees. They can all be edited and adapted to your organization. Remember, these calendars are just copies of those in the template; these copies reside in the file for your project. If you edit them, you are not editing the originals in the template. I'll show you later how to copy your adapted calendar back to the template.

- The *Standard* calendar has Mondays through Fridays as working days, with Saturdays and Sundays as nonworking days. The working hours on Mondays through Fridays are 8:00 a.m. to 12:00 p.m., and then 1:00 p.m. to 5:00 p.m. There are no holidays defined in this or the other calendars listed here.

- The *24 Hours* calendar has 24 hours of working time every day, with no nonworking days defined. Use this calendar as the base calendar for your project if the project involves continuous, around-the-clock operations. You would also use this as the base calendar for any resources that can be scheduled around-the-clock (such as equipment and other nonhuman resources, or human resource groups that are staffed around the clock). You would not use this as the base calendar for a human resource who works only part of the day.

- The *Night Shift* calendar's working hours are from 11:00 p.m. to 8:00 a.m. the next morning. Use this calendar, or a modification of it, as the base calendar for resources who work the night shift. If the project will be worked on exclusively by the night shift workers, make this the base calendar for the project also, so that unassigned tasks are scheduled in the same working hours.

You should adapt the Standard calendar to fit your organization, and generally use it as the base calendar for your projects, but you can also create customized base calendars. This is frequently done when a group of resources has unique scheduling requirements (like the night shift workers mentioned in the preceding list). For example, if your organization hires students on work-study programs, you might create a custom base calendar to use for those resources. If a project was worked on by those resources only, you could also name that custom base calendar as the base calendar for the project.

To Do: Selecting the Base Calendar

▼ To Do

To select the base calendar for the current project, follow these steps:

1. If you are going to use a customized base calendar, create the calendar first. See the next section, "Editing the Standard Calendar," for instructions.

2. Choose **P**roject, **P**roject Information from the menu to display the Project Information dialog box.

3. In the **C**alendar field, use the list arrow to display the base calendars that are already defined. If you have defined resources already, their calendars are listed here also.

   In Figure 4.9, the base calendars provided by Project are displayed along with a special calendar that has been prepared for Work Study Students.

▼

▼ 4. Select the calendar you want to use as the base calendar for the current project.

▲ 5. Click OK to save the change and close the dialog box.

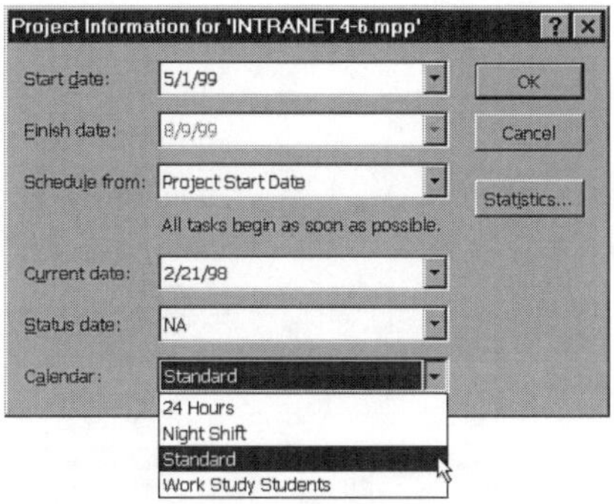

FIGURE 4.9

You can change the base calendar for your project in the Project Information dialog box.

Project Information for 'INTRANET4-6.mpp'

Start date:	5/1/99
Finish date:	8/9/99
Schedule from:	Project Start Date
	All tasks begin as soon as possible.
Current date:	2/21/98
Status date:	NA
Calendar:	Standard

OK
Cancel
Statistics...

24 Hours
Night Shift
Standard
Work Study Students

Remember: If you change the default start and end of the working day in the Options dialog box, you will also need to edit the working hours in your calendars to use these start and end times.

4

Editing the Standard Calendar

You can adjust the working days and hours for any calendar with the Change Working Time command. The original calendars have no holidays, so you must supply them yourself. For example, in Figure 4.10, December 31, 1999 is selected and has been set as a nonworking day in recognition of the inevitable.

To Do: Changing the Working Dates

To change the working dates on a calendar, follow these steps:

To Do

1. Choose the **T**ools, Change Working Time command from the menu to display the Change Working Time dialog box (see Figure 4.10).

2. Select the calendar you want to modify in the **F**or list box.

3. Use the scrollbar in the calendar to change the month and year. There's no quick way to go directly to a specific month or year.

4. Select a specific date whose working status you want to change by clicking it. You can drag to select a series of dates, and use the Ctrl key to click on multiple non-adjacent dates in the same month.

▼

▼   To change a day of the week for all weeks (for example, to change all Fridays),
         select the letter for the day of the week at the top of the day's column. Note that
         you are changing that day of the week for all months and all years in the calendar.

FIGURE 4.10

Adapt calendars to your organization's work schedule with the Change Working Time dialog box.

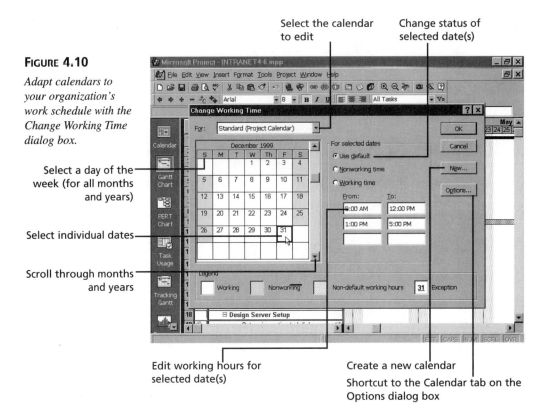

Select the calendar to edit

Change status of selected date(s)

Select a day of the week (for all months and years)

Select individual dates

Scroll through months and years

Edit working hours for selected date(s)

Create a new calendar

Shortcut to the Calendar tab on the Options dialog box

5. Use the radio buttons to the right of the calendar to change the status for the date
   or dates you have selected.

   • Select Nonworking Time to make the selected date(s) nonworking dates.

   • Select Working Time to make the selected dates into working dates with the
     default hours for that day of the week (usually 8:00 a.m. to 12:00 p.m. and
     1:00 p.m. to 5:00 p.m.).

   • Select Use Default to return the selected date(s) to the default status after
     they've been edited. Mondays through Fridays will become working days
     with the default working hours; Saturdays and Sundays will become non-
▼   working days.

▼ 6. Change the working hours for selected dates by defining up to three "shifts" or working periods per day in the **F**rom and **T**o boxes. You must fill these pairs of times from the top down. For example, you can't enter times in the second row if the first row is empty.

7. If you're finished editing calendars, click the OK button to save your changes. However, if you want to make changes in another calendar, repeat step 2. You will be asked if you want to save the changes in the first calendar. After choosing either **Y**es or **N**o, you're free to edit the next calendar.

At this point, the Cancel button in the Change Working Time dialog box changes to a Close button. Use the Close button to close the dialog box without saving any changes you've made to the second calendar. You've already saved the changes to
▲ the first calendar you edited.

The legend shows how you can tell the status of a date: Nonworking days are shaded, working days with the default times are clear, working days with customized times are striped, and any date that has been edited has an underscore under the label.

4

Creating Additional Calendars for Special Scheduling Needs

When creating special calendars, you can start with a copy of the Standard calendar so that most of your organization's holidays will already be in place, or you can start with a default calendar (working times of 8:00 a.m. to 5:00 p.m., every Monday through Friday).

To Do: Creating a New Calendar

To create a new calendar, follow these steps:

1. In the Change Working Time dialog box, click the New button to display the Create New Base Calendar dialog box (see Figure 4.11).

2. Enter a name for this calendar in the **N**ame field.

3. If you want to start from scratch, choose Create **N**ew Base Calendar.

   • If you want to start with a copy of another calendar that has holidays and other exceptions already entered, select the calendar you want to copy in the **M**ake A Copy Of field.
▼

▼   • If you have just been editing another calendar, you will be asked if you want
       to save those changes. Choose **Y**es to save the changes and **N**o to abandon
       them.

   4. You will then have a new calendar you can change as needed. After the changes are
▲   complete, click OK to save the new calendar.

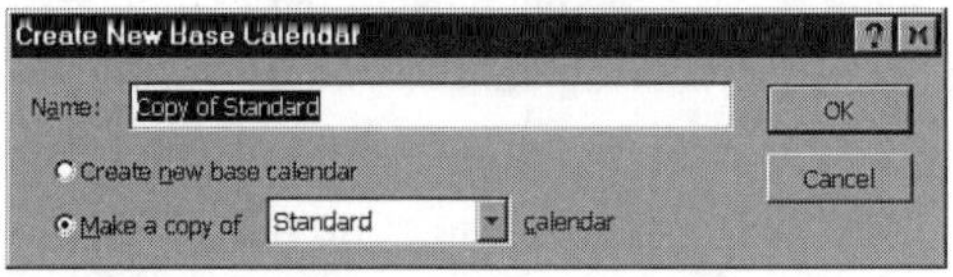

FIGURE 4.11

You can create a new
calendar by starting
with a copy of an exist-
ing calendar to keep
from having to enter
all the holidays.

Create New Base Calendar	? X
Name: Copy of Standard	OK
○ Create new base calendar	Cancel
● Make a copy of Standard ▾ calendar	

Managing Your Calendars

When you edit or create a calendar, the changes exist only in the calendars in the project
document that's currently active. If you edit the Standard calendar, for instance, you
aren't changing the Standard calendar in other project files. If you want the changes to
be included in other project documents, then you must copy the revised Standard calendar into those projects and replace their version of the Standard calendar. If you want the
changes to be included in all new projects, then you must copy the revised calendar into
the Global template file (the file named global.mpt).

I recommend that you edit the Standard calendar early in your career with
Microsoft Project and enter all holidays and other details that differ for your
organization. Do that for several years into the future, and then copy this
revised Standard calendar to the Global template so all new project files
have the Standard calendar already set up for your organization.

Use the Organizer to copy calendars from one project file to another. If you are copying
calendars to other project documents, they must be opened (using **File, O**pen) before you
start the Organizer.

To Do: Copying a Calendar

To copy a calendar to the Global template or to another project, follow these steps:

   1. Be sure that the file containing the new calendar (the source) and the file you want
      to copy it to (the target) are open in memory. The Global template is always open
      while you work in Project.

▼   2. Choose **Tools**, **Organizer** from the menu to display the Organizer dialog box (see Figure 4.12).

FIGURE 4.12

Copy calendars from one project file to another with the Organizer.

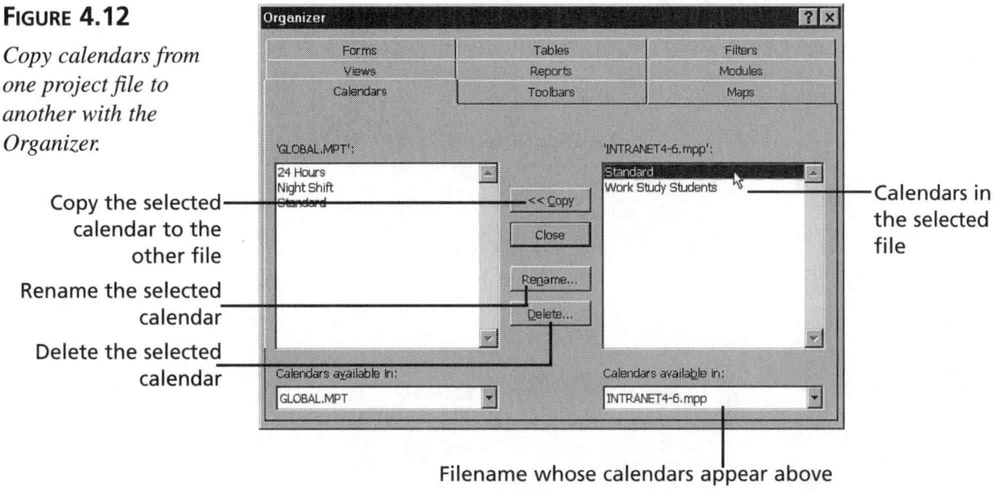

Copy the selected calendar to the other file

Rename the selected calendar

Delete the selected calendar

Calendars in the selected file

Filename whose calendars appear above

4

3. Select the Calendars tab. The GLOBAL.MPT file will be selected in the list box at the bottom of the dialog box on the left, the one labeled Calendars Available In.

   The project file that was active when you started the Organizer will be selected in the list box on the right, the one labeled Calendars Available In. A list of all the calendars contained in each file will appear above the selected filenames.

4. If you want to change the file that is selected, use the arrows in the list boxes to display the names of all files that are open (plus the GLOBAL.MPT). Be sure that both the source file (the one containing the revised calendar) and the target file (the one into which you want to copy the calendar) are displayed.

   In Figure 4.12, the GLOBAL.MPT on the left is the target, and the file on the right named INTRANET4-6.mpp is the source.

5. Select the calendar name to be copied in the source file. In the example, the Standard calendar is selected.

   The Copy button will automatically point from the source file to the target file.

6. Click the Copy button.

7. If a calendar with the same name is already listed in the target file, you will be asked if you want to replace the old version (see Figure 4.13).

▼

▼
- Click **Yes** to replace the old version with the revised calendar.

- Click **No** to cancel the copy operation.

- Click Rename to copy the revised calendar into the target file with a new
▲   name. If you click Rename, you can enter the new name in the Rename
   dialog box (see Figure 4.14).

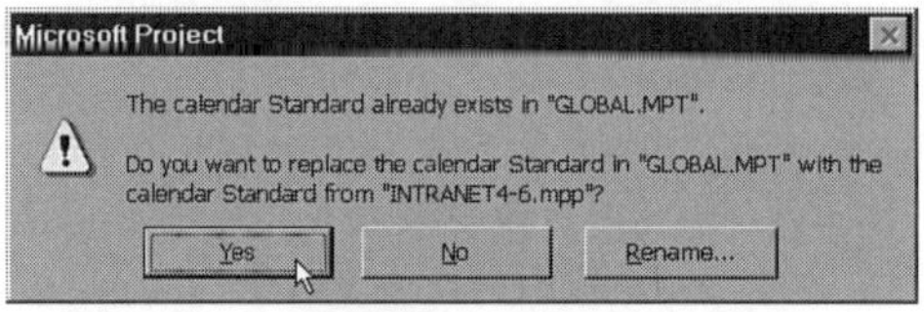

FIGURE 4.13

*You must decide what
to do when the target
file contains a calen-
dar with the same
name as the one being
copied.*

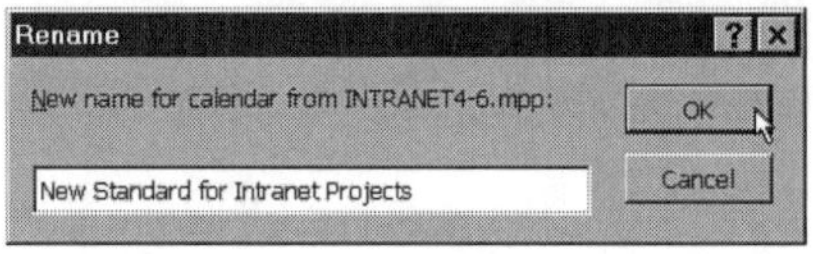

FIGURE 4.14

*Enter a new name for
the copy of the calen-
dar that will reside in
the target file.*

You must use the Organizer if you also need to rename or delete a calendar.

To Do: Renaming or Deleting a Calendar

To rename or delete a calendar, follow these steps:

1. Open the Organizer by choosing **T**ools, **Or**ganizer from the menu and select the
   Calendars tab.

2. Select the calendar to be deleted or renamed.

3. Click the Delete button to delete the selected calendar. When asked to confirm the
   deletion, click **Yes**.

4. Click the Rename button to rename the selected calendar. Supply the new name in
   the Rename dialog box (refer to Figure 4.14) and click OK.

▲   5. Click the Close button to close the Organizer.

Printing the Calendar Details

If you want to review the working and nonworking dates and times in your base calendars, print the Working Days report. It prints a separate page for each base calendar in
the current project file, showing the standard working days and hours and listing all the
exceptions, such as holidays, unusual hours, and so forth.

For instructions on printing this report, see Hour 8, "Finalizing and Printing Your Schedule," especially the section on the Working Days Report.

Estimating Task Duration

When scheduling tasks, Microsoft Project needs to know how long each task will take to complete. In other words, Project needs to know how much time should be allowed between the start and finish dates for the task. You supply an estimate of that time in the task Duration field.

The term *duration* is used to refer to the amount of working time it will take to finish a task. Duration can be measured in minutes, hours, days, or weeks, and it always means an amount of working time. Project places a default value of 1 day in the Duration field for each new task, but that means a working day, usually 8 hours, not the 24 hours defined in the dictionary.

NEW TERM **Duration**   Duration is the amount of time during which work on a task actually takes place. Duration units, such as "day" and "week," mean the amount of work done in a day or a week.

You can type a new duration over the default value Project supplies, or you can use the spin control in the Duration field to increase or decrease the number for the existing duration units.

Defining Duration Units

Duration values are entered and displayed in any one of four time units (minutes, hours, days, or weeks), and you can spell out the units, use an abbreviation, or use an initial. For example, a duration of 2 weeks could be displayed as 2 weeks, 2 wks, or 2 w. Project automatically changes the unit to plural form when appropriate. You control how duration units are displayed with settings in the Options dialog box.

To Do: Controlling the Display of Time Unit Labels

To control the display of time unit labels, follow these steps:

1. Choose **T**ools, **O**ptions to display the Options dialog box and select the Edit tab (see Figure 4.15).
2. Use the list arrow in each field (**M**inutes As, **H**ours As, **D**ays As, **W**eeks As, and **Y**ears As) to select the initial, abbreviation, or word as the default label for that unit.
3. Fill the check box next to Add **S**pace Before Label to separate the label from the number value.

4

▲

4. Click the Set As **D**efault button to apply these defaults to all new project documents in the future.

FIGURE 4.15

Control the display of time unit labels for all tasks in the Options dialog box.

Separate the number from label

Set each time label separately

Set default for future project documents

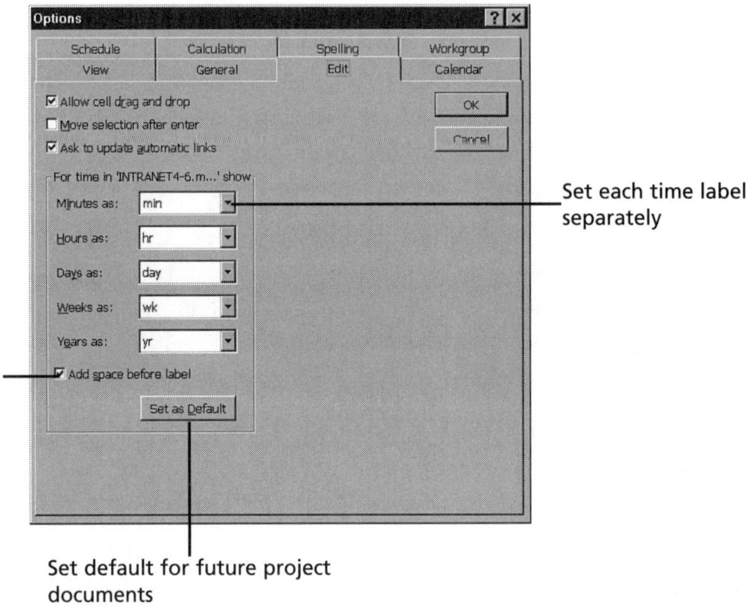

> The "year" unit is not used in the Duration field. It's used when entering an annual salary for a resource's cost rate.

If you enter a number in the Duration field without including the unit label to indicate whether the number represents minutes, hours, days, or weeks, then Project adds the default time unit, which is "days." If you would prefer a different default duration unit, change the setting in the Options dialog box.

To Do: Changing the Default Unit for Duration

To change the default unit for duration, follow these steps:

1. Choose **T**ools, **O**ptions to display the Options dialog box, and select the Schedule tab (see Figure 4.16).

2. In the **D**uration Is Entered In list box, select one of the four units: Minutes, Hours, Days, or Weeks.

▼ 3. If you want to use this default unit for all future project documents, click the Set As **D**efault button.

▲ 4. Click OK to save the new setting.

FIGURE 4.16

The default time unit for duration values is "Days," but you can change that.

Default duration unit

If a task has a duration of 40 hours, that means it will take 40 hours of time spent working on the task before the task is completed. The terms "minutes" and "hours" are unambiguous, meaning that they have a universal definition. However, if someone says "It'll take me a week to finish," we don't really know for sure what that means in terms of hours, although we can be fairly certain that it doesn't mean working continuously for 7 days and nights—168 hours.

Therefore, Project requires that you define, using the unambiguous unit "hours," what you mean by a "day" of work and a "week" of work. The default values are 8 hours in a day of work and 40 hours in a week of work (refer to Figure 4.8). These are fairly standard expectations of employees, at least in the United States. So, when you estimate the duration of a task to be a week, Project thinks you mean a working week, or 40 hours, spread over 5 days with 8 hours of work each day. If your organization has different standards for the number of hours worked in a day or a week, you need to change the definitions in Project so that you can use the terms in Project the way you use them in conversation on the job.

4

To Do: Defining the Working Hours in a Day and a Week

Follow these steps to define the working hours in a day and a week:

1. Choose **T**ools, **O**ptions to display the Options dialog box, and select the Calendar tab (refer to Figure 4.8 earlier in this chapter).

2. Enter the hours in a day in the Hours Per Day field.

3. Enter the hours in a week in the Hours Per Week field.

4. Click OK to close the dialog box.

> The working hours in your Standard calendar should be defined to match these entries in the Hours Per Day and Hours Per Week fields. The calendar is **not** automatically changed to match these definitions of days and weeks.

When you enter the duration for a task, Project schedules the duration of the task in the calendar, using the working times the calendar makes available. For example, if you estimate the duration of a task to be 2 days (16 hours) and work starts on the task at 8:00 a.m. on a Friday, Project calculates that the work will continue for the next 16 hours of available working time. At the end of the day on Friday, there will still be 8 hours of work to do (assuming you're using the default calendar). Because Saturday and Sunday are nonworking days, work will resume on Monday and continue to the end of that day. If the Monday in this example is a nonworking holiday, then the task will be scheduled to continue through the end of the day on Tuesday.

The Special Case of Continuous Working Time

The usual meaning of duration presumes that you can stop and start work on a task without difficulty. For example, if the task is to assemble a complex machine or to develop an architectural plan, you can stop when 5:00 p.m. comes along, and start back the next morning; you can even go home for the weekend if you're not finished. The time you spend on these tasks doesn't have to be continuous time.

Some tasks, however, require continuous time—once the task starts, the work must continue uninterrupted until the task is finished. For example, pouring concrete in a form in a construction project is a continuous process; once you start, you have to stay with it until you have completely filled the form and the concrete has dried and hardened successfully. Not only will the concrete go on drying out and hardening if the 5:00 whistle blows, but workers will need to stay and tend to it to be sure it doesn't dry too quickly.

This process can't be stopped once it's started. For tasks like this, you need Project to schedule the task with continuous time, right through the nonworking times in the calendar. In Microsoft Project, you enter *elapsed duration* units to signal that continuous time is required.

NEW TERM **Elapsed Duration**   Like duration, *elapsed duration* is a measure of the number of working minutes, hours, days, or weeks required to complete a task. Unlike regular duration, however, elapsed duration time units are the same as those used by people in normal conversation. An "elapsed day" is 24 hours, and an "elapsed week" is 7 elapsed days or 168 hours. Project schedules elapsed duration around the clock, in the calendar's working and nonworking hours and days alike.

To enter an elapsed duration, you simply add the letter *e* before the units label. For example, the duration for a task that should take 24 continuous hours would be entered as 24 ehrs or 1 eday.

Letting Project Calculate Duration For You

In some cases, you might not know the exact duration for a task, but you have other information that can be used to calculate it. Suppose you have been given a list of tasks to work with that includes start and finish dates for each task. You can import the list of tasks and their predetermined dates into Project, and Project can use those dates to calculate the duration. See Hour 21, "Exchanging Project Data with Other Applications," for instructions on importing data into Project.

If you know how much work a task involves and you also know how many resources you plan to assign to the task, Project can calculate how long it will take the resources to complete the work (that is, the duration). There are settings you can use at the time you assign the resources that cause Project to calculate duration for you. See Hours 10 and 11 for guidelines and the steps to take to get Project to do this for you.

Finally, if you have enough experience with the tasks to be able to give reasonable estimates of the longest possible duration, the shortest possible duration, and the most likely duration, you can use Microsoft Project's PERT analysis tools to calculate a statistically likely duration.

PERT analysis is beyond the scope of this book, but you can learn how to use it in Chapter 5 of my book *Special Edition Using Microsoft Project 98* (also published by Que).

Splitting Tasks

The last scheduling trick we will look at in this Hour is splitting tasks.

NEW TERM   **Task Split**   A *task split* is an interruption in the work on a task: Work stops at the start of the split and resumes at the end of the split. As far as Project is concerned, you can introduce as many splits in a task as you want.

Usually, a task split is introduced because we know that the resources who have to work on the task will be needed elsewhere for the duration of the split, or work has already started on a task and we need to stop it for a while before resuming later. Splits allow us to let a task get started, then be put on hold while attention is on other tasks, and then be completed later.

Until you assign resources to a task, you can create splits only in the Gantt Chart view, using the mouse. With resources assigned, you can also introduce splits in other views (see Hour 12 for more details).

To Do: Splitting a Task

Follow these steps to split a task:

1. With the task displayed in the Gantt Chart view, click the Split Task tool on the Standard toolbar, or choose **E**dit, Split Tas**k** from the menu.

2. Position the mouse pointer over the task bar you would like to split. The Split Task information box will tell you the date when the split will begin (see Figure 4.17). Position the mouse so that the date in the information box is the date you want the split to begin.

3. Click the mouse button to start the split on the date in the information box. If you just click and release the mouse button, a 1-day split will appear in the task bar and a new segment will begin after the split.

   If you drag the mouse to the right, you can position the new segment on the time period you want the task to resume. A second Split Task information box tells you the dates the segment you are dragging will start and finish (see Figure 4.18).

When you position the mouse pointer over a split task segment, the pointer turns into a four-headed arrow and you can drag the segment to the left or right to reposition it. If you drag the first segment of a split task (or if you hold down the Shift key as you drag a later segment), then all the segments move together, maintaining their splits. If you drag any but the first segment, it moves independently of other segments until it touches another segment. If you drag a segment until it touches another segment, the split between them is removed.

FIGURE 4.17

The Split Task information box tells you where the split will start if you click the mouse pointer now.

Split Task information box

Date split will start if you click now

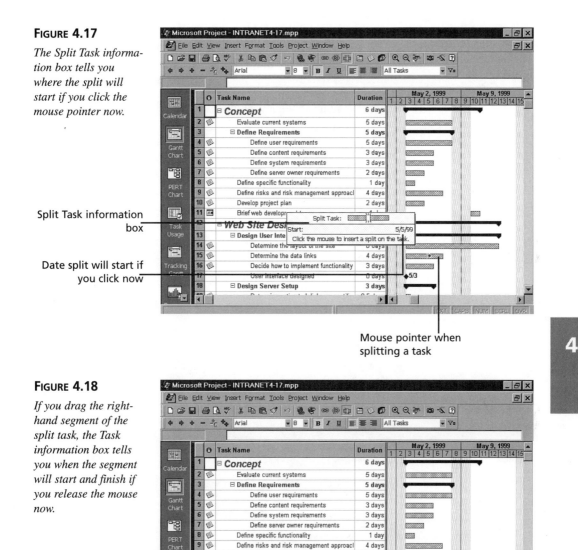

Mouse pointer when splitting a task

4

FIGURE 4.18

If you drag the right-hand segment of the split task, the Task information box tells you when the segment will start and finish if you release the mouse now.

Task information box

Start and finish dates for the segment at the current mouse position

Shadowed segment being moved by the mouse

Be very careful with the mouse in the timeline area of the Gantt Chart. If the mouse cursor is not the right shape when you start dragging, you could create unexpected results—such as linking two tasks (see Hour 5, "Turning the Task List into a Schedule—The Rest of the Story") or creating a new task (see Hour 6, "Working with the Other Task Views").

HOUR 5

Turning the Task List into a Schedule—The Rest of the Story

In Hour 4, "Turning the Task List into a Schedule," we began our coverage of the instructions you can give Project to impose terms and conditions on how it calculates the schedule for you. You saw how to define the times when tasks can be scheduled with calendars and how to enter estimates of task duration for both regular working hours and for continuous or elapsed time. You also saw how to split an individual task into multiple work sessions.

Although the calendar and duration estimates are essential, you didn't see much change in the schedule in Hour 4. This hour, however, you will see dramatic changes. In this hour, we will look at specifying the order in which tasks should be scheduled, which is called *linking* tasks, and defining fixed date requirements, which are called *constraints*.

Linking Tasks

Most of the tasks in your project should probably be done in a definite order. For example, it usually makes a significant difference whether you frame the walls of a new house before or after you lay the foundation. One way to put the tasks in order is to go through the task list and enter start dates for each task manually, making sure that tasks like "frame walls" start after "lay foundation" tasks. But that's the hard way to do it, and it's definitely not the best way. If you later found that you had left out a task toward the beginning of the sequence, or that you didn't allow enough time for one of the early tasks, you would have to enter all the subsequent dates again. Furthermore, you will see later in this hour that by entering dates for tasks, you are setting up constraints that keep Project from rescheduling tasks freely.

The best way to ensure that tasks are scheduled in the requisite order is to *link* the tasks and let Project calculate the start and finish dates for each task. Then, if you need to insert another task early in the process or revise the duration estimate for a task, Project can recalculate the dates much faster than you could.

NEW TERM   **Linking Tasks**   *Linking tasks* defines the order in which they should be scheduled. The task links are represented in the Gantt Chart with lines that connect (link) the tasks.

> Do not use linking to make one task follow another so that a resource can work on both tasks. We will look at better ways to handle that problem in the section on resources starting in Hour 9, "Defining Resources and Costs."

Understanding Task Links

The basic idea of linking tasks is easy enough to grasp—you link the tasks, like stringing beads or hooking up railroad cars, in the order in which you want them to be scheduled. Sometimes you link tasks because the laws of nature decree that one task follow the other in time; the link allows you to teach Project a physics lesson. The example of framing the walls after laying the foundation is a case in point, as is applying the final coat of paint after applying the primer coat.

Other times, you link one task to follow another because it just ought to be that way. In the intranet project example you saw back in Hour 4, which is replicated in Figure 5.1, the task "Define Specific Functionality" should take place only after you have found out what the users' needs are in the "Define User Requirements" task. Although computer system projects often seem to proceed unencumbered by concern for what the user needs, you know that's not the way it ought to be. Without the links, Microsoft Project has no way of knowing the order in which tasks ought to be scheduled.

FIGURE 5.1

Without linking, tasks loiter around the start date of the project, all ready to start up the minute the project starts.

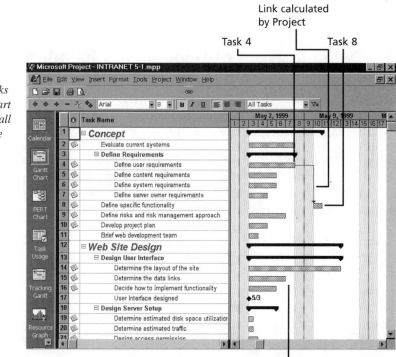

Link calculated by Project

Task 4   Task 8

Unlinked tasks start when project starts

However you arrive at the decision of which tasks to link, linking means you tell Microsoft Project to, for example, "schedule this task first, then calculate the schedule for the next task so that it starts the moment the first task finishes." A task whose schedule depends on another task is called a dependent task. Microsoft Project automatically recalculates the scheduled dates for the dependent task when anything changes the scheduled dates for the task on which it depends.

The terms *predecessor* and *successor* are usually applied to linked tasks, with predecessor designating the task whose schedule must be calculated first and *successor* designating the task whose schedule is calculated only afterward.

NEW TERM **Dependent, Predecessor, and Successor Tasks**   A task whose scheduled start or finish date is dependent on the scheduled start or finish date of some other task is called a *dependent* task. The task its schedule depends on is called its *predecessor*, which makes it seem only natural to also call the dependent task the predecessor's *successor*. The schedule for the predecessor is calculated first, and it sets limits for scheduling the successor.

Defining Types of Dependency Relationships

In most dependency relationships between tasks, the finish date for the predecessor determines the start date for the dependent (successor) task. That's the case, for example, with the foundation–frame walls sequence. This is called a *finish-to-start* relationship (see Table 5.1) because you link the finish of the predecessor to the start of the successor.

The finish-to-start link is only one of several possible links, however. For example, we can also link tasks so that they start together or finish together. Table 5.1 (and Figure 5.2) show the four possible linking relationships. In each case, the name of the relationship is made up of the predecessor's start or finish date and then the successor task's start or finish date.

Project also uses a shorthand code for each type of relationship. The first letter in the code refers to the predecessor's date (start or finish) and the second letter refers to the successor task's date (start or finish).

TABLE 5.1.   LINKING RELATIONSHIPS AVAILABLE IN MICROSOFT PROJECT

Dependency Type	Code	Description
Finish-to-Start	FS	The predecessor's finish determines when the successor can start
Start-to-Start	SS	Both tasks start when the predecessor starts
Finish-to-Finish	FF	Both tasks finish when the predecessor finishes
Start-to-Finish	SF	The start of the predecessor determines when the successor must finish

FIGURE 5.2

The types of dependency relationships are built around the schedule for the predecessor.

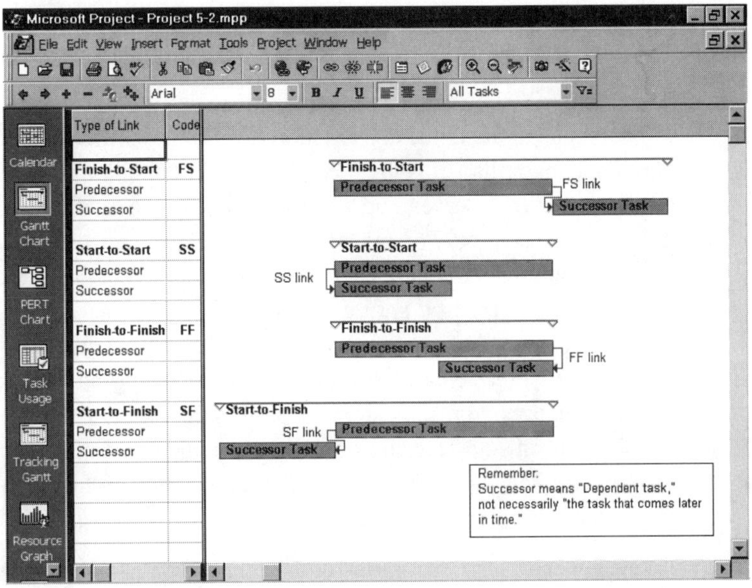

When you link summary tasks, you can use only the Finish-to-Start or Start-to-Start type links; in other words, you can link the start of a summary task to a predecessor, but you can't link the finish of a summary task to a predecessor.

If you need to use the Finish-to-Finish or Start-to-Finish link types for summary tasks, you must apply the link directly to the subtasks under the summary task.

Linking a summary task has the effect of applying the same link to all its subtasks. So, be careful when you link both the summary task and one of its subtasks to predecessors outside the summary task group—it's easy to create conflicting or redundant links.

Everyone seems to understand how two tasks can be linked Finish-to-Start, with one task not able to start until another is finished, and most people have no trouble understanding how two tasks might be linked Start-to-Start and Finish-to-Finish so that they are scheduled to start together or finish together. However, many people have a hard time understanding why we have the Start-to-Finish link, when a task is scheduled to finish when another task starts. Why not just use the Finish-to-Start link—both link types place the tasks end to end, as you can see in Figure 5.2. The difference lies in which task drives the other task. In the Finish-to-Start link, the task that comes earlier determines the schedule dates; in the Start-to-Finish link, the task that comes later calls the shots and its schedule is calculated first.

For example, in the home construction task, laying the foundation determines when you can frame the walls—it is the predecessor to framing the walls. Framing the walls requires lumber, however, and you can't start framing until you get the lumber. Therefore, a case could be made for making Get Lumber the predecessor to Frame Walls, but you need to get the lumber only because you're planning to use it in framing, and there's no need getting it until it's needed. Doesn't it make more sense to see when the framing can take place and then schedule the lumber delivery just in time for the framing? That way, for instance, if rainy weather interrupts and keeps the foundation from finishing on time, you can enter that information in Project as you're tracking the work, and Project can automatically delay the scheduled start of framing the walls and consequently also delay acquiring the lumber. Then you won't have to provide dry storage for the lumber during the bad weather.

Figure 5.3 shows both scenarios of the framing walls example. With good weather, the tasks will take 10 days to complete. (So, it's a small house, a bungalow.) In the bad weather scenario, I've introduced a split starting on Wednesday when the rains came. The split extends the completion of the foundation, which delays the start of the framing. Because getting the lumber is tied to the framing task, it's also delayed so that it's not delivered too early and left lying around in the rain.

The same principle is used to save storage costs and interest on the money used when ordering materials and parts for manufacturing processes. Parts are ordered just in time for the assembly process that will use them. "Just in time" scheduling has become an important cost-saving tool in many industries, and that's precisely what the Start-to-Finish link describes.

Allowing for Delayed and Overlapping Links

Frequently, the successor task cannot start immediately on the finish date of the predecessor. For example, when the foundation is poured in the construction task, we really should wait a day or two for the concrete to harden completely before we start framing the walls. Or, imagine the tasks in painting the exterior of a house. First, there should be a primer coat, then you apply the final coat, and finally you have to clean up (see Figure 5.4). In reality, however, we have to let the first coat dry before starting the final coat.

In both scenarios in Figure 5.4, these tasks are linked in Finish-to-Start relationships. In the second scenario, however, Painting with Greater Realism, the Final Coat does not follow immediately on the heels of the Primer Coat; there's time allowed for drying.

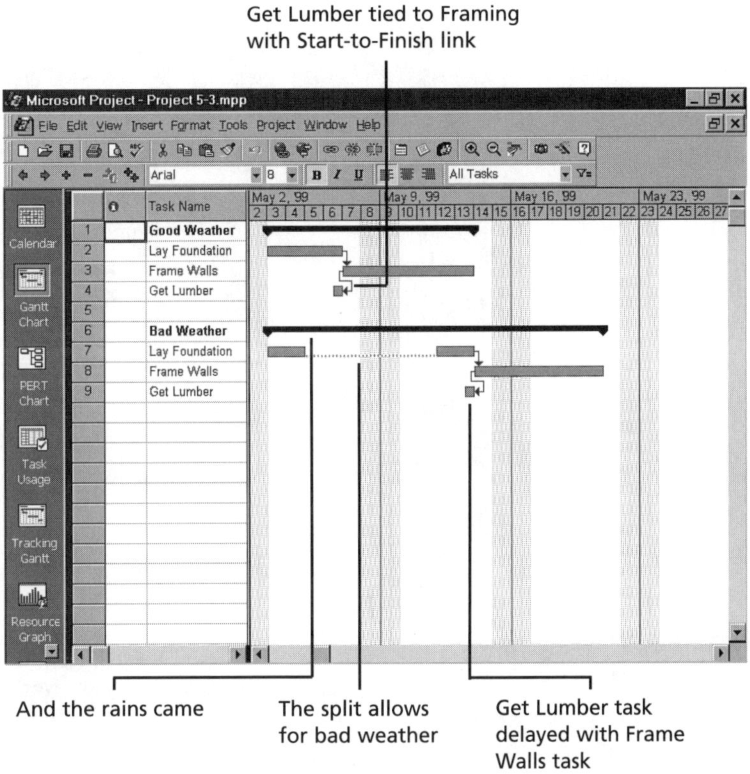

Figure 5.3

If bad weather forces a delay in framing, you want the lumber delivery delayed also.

Get Lumber tied to Framing with Start-to-Finish link

And the rains came   The split allows for bad weather   Get Lumber task delayed with Frame Walls task

Because the first coat of paint needs to dry for two days (two elapsed days, mind you), I have built a *lag* into the link between the tasks. I told Project to start the successor task two elapsed days after the predecessor task finishes.

New Term   **Lag Time**   *Lag time* is extra time allowed between the dates that link the predecessor and successor tasks. The effect is to delay the scheduled date for the successor.

This is actually Project's formula for calculating successor schedules:

```
Predecessor linked date + Lag time = Successor linked date
```

In Figure 5.4, I also decided that the Clean Up task could actually start a little before the Final Coat is completed. So, I built in some *lead time* for the Clean Up task by telling Project to start the successor task one half-day earlier than the link would otherwise dictate.

5

FIGURE 5.4

Lags and Leads give added realism and flexibility to the schedule.

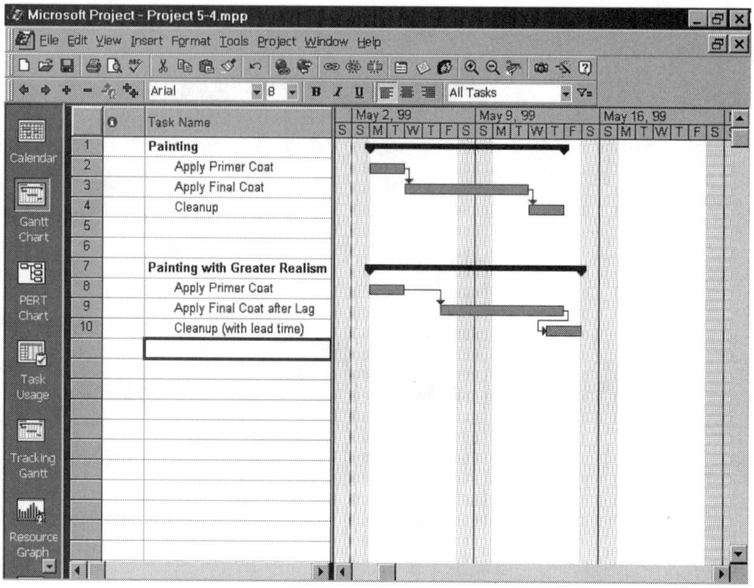

NEW TERM   **Lead Time**   *Lead time* is used to move the scheduled date for the successor task to a little earlier time. The effect is usually to overlap the linked tasks. Lead time is entered as negative lag time in Microsoft Project (see the formula in the preceding definition of Lag).

> Lags and Leads are usually entered as time units (for example, two days), but you can also enter them as a percentage of the predecessor task's duration. A 10% Lag means lag by 10% of the predecessor's duration value. A 10% Lead (entered as -10%) means start the successor earlier by an amount of time equal to 10% of the predecessor's duration value.
>
> Therefore, a Start-to-Start link with a 10% Lag would mean "start the successor only after the predecessor has started and 10% of the work is done." And a Finish-to-Start link with a 10% Lead would mean "start the successor when the predecessor is within 10% of being finished."
>
> There are a number of ways you can create task links. In this book, we'll look only at those most commonly used with the Gantt Chart—using the Link Tasks tool, the mouse, or the Task Form in the lower pane of a split window. For these methods, you create the link first, being careful to correctly identify the predecessor and the successor; then you can edit the link to change the type or to add Leads or Lags.

Linking and Unlinking Tasks with the Toolbar

 The simplest and easiest way to link tasks is to select the tasks in the task list and then click the Link Tasks tool on the Standard toolbar, or choose Edit, Link Tasks from the menu. If the task bars are visible in the timeline, you will see the linking lines appear immediately.

There's no limit to the number of tasks you can select for linking before you click the Link Tasks tool. You can link just one predecessor and one successor at a time, or you can link all the tasks in the project in the same operation.

If you select the tasks for linking by dragging to select adjacent tasks, tasks higher up on the task list (with lower ID numbers) are always the predecessor to tasks lower in the selection (with higher ID numbers), no matter which direction you drag the mouse in the selection. If you use the Ctrl key to select tasks that aren't adjacent, the task you click first is the predecessor to the next task you click. For example, if you hold down the Ctrl key and click tasks 5, 2, and 12 in that order and then click the Link Tasks tool, task 5 will be the predecessor to task 2, and task 2 will be the predecessor to task 12.

If you find a link between tasks is no longer necessary, you need to remove the current link. There are several ways to remove links.

 You can unlink tasks by using the menu or toolbar. Select the tasks you want to unlink in the task list in the top pane, and click the Unlink Tasks tool on the Standard toolbar or choose Edit, Unlink Tasks from the menu.

If you select multiple tasks and then choose Edit, Unlink Tasks or click the Unlink Tasks button, Project removes all links between any pair of the selected tasks. To remove all links from the project, select all tasks by clicking a field name, such as Task Name, and choose Edit, Unlink Tasks or click the Unlink Tasks button.

5

> If you select a single task and then click the Unlink Tasks tool or choose Edit, Unlink Tasks, Project removes all predecessors for that task.

Editing Links with the Task Form

If you have split the window to display the Task Form beneath the Gantt Chart, you can view details of the linking relationships in the bottom pane (see Figure 5.5).

To Do: Displaying Predecessor and Successor Details

Follow these steps to display predecessor and successor details:

1. Display the Gantt Chart and split the window with the **W**indow, **S**plit command. The Task Form will be displayed in the lower pane.

2. Activate the lower pane by clicking anywhere in it.

3. Choose **F**ormat, **D**etails, **P**redecessors & Successors from the menu.

   Predecessors for the task that's selected in the top pane are described on the left, and successors for that task are described on the right.

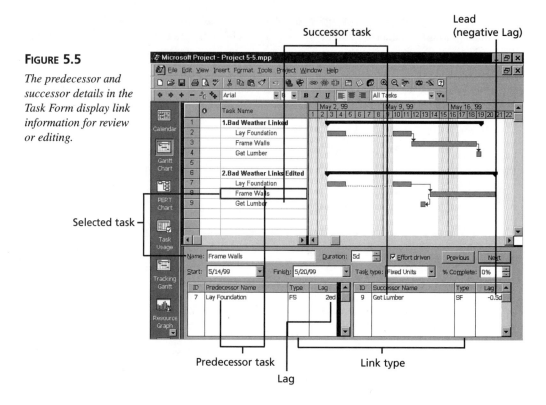

FIGURE 5.5

The predecessor and successor details in the Task Form display link information for review or editing.

The first set of tasks in Figure 5.5 are the bad weather tasks from the earlier example, after being linked with the Link Tasks tool. The link types are the default Finish-to-Start and there are no Lags or Leads.

The second set of tasks (2. Bad Weather Links Edited) show the results of editing the links. The Frame Walls task is selected in the top pane, and the details of its links are displayed in the bottom pane.

A Lag of two elapsed days has been added to the predecessor link with Lay Foundation. Remember that you insert an *e* before the time unit for elapsed duration entries. The type of link to Get Lumber has been Start-to-Finish. A list arrow appears when the Type field is selected, and the list displays the four possible link types. A Lead of one-half day has been entered for the link by typing -0.5d into the Lag field. Remember, Leads are entered as negative Lags.

You can delete a link in the Task Form by clicking anywhere in the row for the link and pressing the Delete key. Then click OK to complete the change in the task.

  You can edit task links in the Task Information dialog box. However, you must apply the dialog box to the successor task because the dialog box displays only predecessor links.

Creating Links Using the Mouse

You can use the mouse to link task bars on the timescale side of the Gantt Chart or in the PERT Chart or the Calendar view (see Hour 6, "Working with the Other Task Views"). You can also use the mouse to edit the linking relationship.

 Be careful! Clicking the mouse pointer in these views can produce strange and wondrous results. It's easy to accidentally reschedule the task, change its duration, or mark the task as being partially complete if you're not careful. Watch the shape of the mouse pointer carefully after you start dragging because each action has its own pointer shape.

For linking, the mouse pointer must change to the shape of chain links when you hover over another task. You must drag from the center of the predecessor task to the center of the successor task, or the mouse will not change into the chain-links shape, and you won't be linking the tasks.

5

> If you start dragging the mouse from a task bar to link it to another task and the mouse does *not* change into the chain-links shape, you can abort the operation (with or without colorful epithets) by dragging the pointer outside the Gantt Chart.

Dragging the mouse pointer from the middle of one task bar to another task bar establishes a Finish-to-Start link between the tasks. The task you start on is the predecessor, and the task you drag to is the successor task.

To Do: Linking Tasks with the Mouse

To link tasks with the mouse, follow these steps:

1. Scroll the task list so that the predecessor task is visible onscreen.

2. Position the mouse pointer over the middle of the predecessor task. It's not necessary to select the row for the task in the Gantt Chart table. In Figure 5.6, the mouse was over task 4, "Define User Requirements," when the button was pressed to drag.

3. Click and drag toward the middle of the successor task ("Define Specific Functionality" in the figure). The mouse pointer should change to the chain-links shape by the time you are positioned over the successor. If it doesn't, you weren't in the middle of the task bar when you started dragging, and you should abort by dragging the pointer off the Gantt Chart.

   A Finish-to-Start Link information box will identify the predecessor task you started on and the dependent task bar you have positioned the mouse over (see Figure 5.6). If the dependent task you're seeking is off the screen, move to the edge of the screen, and Project will scroll the task list or the timescale to bring the task bar into view.

4. When in position over the successor task, release the mouse button.

Editing and Removing Links Using the Mouse

The dependency type created by dragging the mouse is always a Finish-to-Start relationship. You can change the link type, add a Lag or Lead, or even delete the link in the timescale with the mouse.

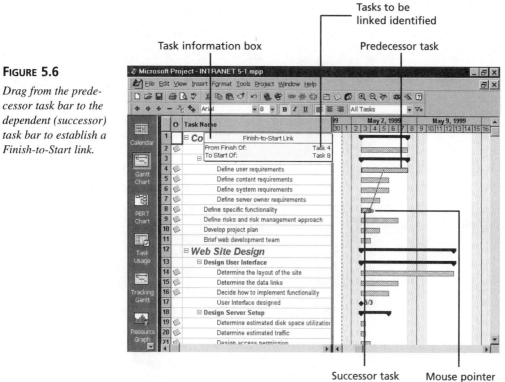

FIGURE 5.6

Drag from the predecessor task bar to the dependent (successor) task bar to establish a Finish-to-Start link.

Task information box

Tasks to be linked identified

Predecessor task

Successor task

Mouse pointer (chain links)

To Do: Modifying a Link with the Mouse

To remove or modify a link with the mouse, follow these steps:

1. Position the tip of the mouse pointer on the line connecting the tasks whose link you want to delete or change.

2. Double-click the linking line. The Task Dependency dialog box appears (see Figure 5.7).

3. Change the type of link in the **T**ype list box.

4. Edit the Lag or Lead in the **L**ag box.

5. To remove the link, click the **D**elete button.

6. Click the OK button to complete the deletion or change in the link definition.

5

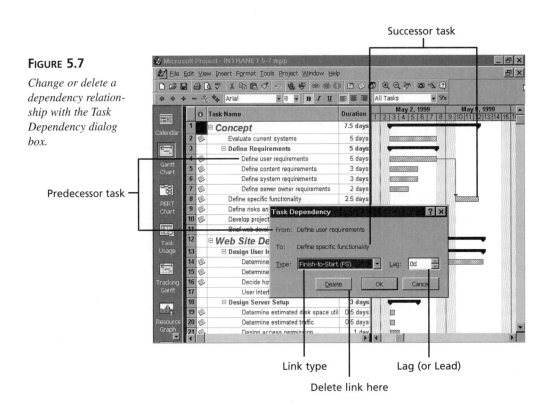

FIGURE 5.7

Change or delete a dependency relationship with the Task Dependency dialog box.

Working with the Automatic Linking Option

Microsoft Project's Autolink feature will keep chains of linked tasks intact when you break the chain by deleting or inserting tasks within the chain—but only if tasks in the chain are linked Finish-to-Start. Autolink is enabled by default, but you can disable it in the Options dialog box.

To Do: Disabling or Enabling Autolink

To disable or enable Autolink, follow these steps:

1. Choose **T**ools, **O**ptions to display the Options dialog box and select the Schedule tab.

2. Deselect the **A**utolink Inserted or Moved Tasks check box. This disables Autolink. To turn it back on, select the check box again.

3. To set the option status as a global default for all new projects, click the Set as **D**efault button. Otherwise, the change you make will affect only the active project document.

4. Click the OK button to close the dialog box.

Reviewing Your Task Links

The project schedule is heavily influenced by the linking relationships you establish among tasks. It's very easy to accidentally link tasks or break task links, so you should review the link relationships carefully before committing to the project schedule. Accidental links could easily skew the project's finish date.

You should also review the links with an eye toward shortening your project schedule. Identifying task relationships where overlap between tasks is possible is one of the best ways to shorten the overall time it takes to finish a project. So look for opportunities to use Start-to-Start and Finish-to-Finish links or to use Leads and Lags to overlap tasks.

When you link tasks, you create task sequences or chains of events. The longest chain in a project, the chain with the latest finish date, determines the finish of the project. The way to shorten the project is to shorten that chain of tasks by decreasing the duration of individual tasks or by overlapping tasks. Because shortening projects is often one of the big chores of project management, Project identifies those tasks that are on the longest chain by labeling them as *critical* tasks, and the chain itself is cryptically called the *critical path*. (You can call it "the longest chain of events.")

You will see more about critical tasks, critical paths, and shortening the project in Hour 14, "Optimizing the Project Plan."

The Gantt Chart shows the task links as arrows connecting the task bars, with the arrow always connecting the linked dates and pointing to the dependent (successor) task. Other views are useful, too, when reviewing the links defined in a project.

You saw in Figure 5.5 that the Task Form can be used to review the links for each task. Use the Previous and Next buttons in the bottom pane to step through all the tasks in the project, examining the links for accuracy.

You can also review your task links in the PERT Chart view. The PERT Chart view concentrates on linking relationships by representing each task as a box with arrows from predecessor to successor tasks (see Hour 6, "Working with the Other Task Views").

Working with Constraints

Another category of special scheduling instructions you provide to Microsoft Project are those that tell Project about deadlines and fixed dates for individual tasks or groups of tasks.

5

NEW TERM   **Constraint**   A constraint is a limitation on the range of dates when a task can be scheduled.

When you add a new task to a project that's scheduled from a fixed start date, Microsoft Project automatically assigns the default constraint that the task is to be scheduled as soon as possible after the start of the project. When you add a task to a fixed finish date project, Project assigns the constraint that the task is to be scheduled as late as possible before the end of the project. These are two relatively mild constraints, if they can be considered constraints at all. There are other cases, however, when you need to be more restrictive, as shown in the following examples:

- You might have contractual agreements that bind the start or finish of a task to a specific date. If the project involves work for a customer, there could be specific intermediate deadlines defined in the contract. Or, your agreement with a contractor or vendor might stipulate the earliest date you can expect completion of the parts of the project they're responsible for.

- Government regulations could impose date constraints. For instance, income and payroll taxes must be filed no later than designated dates, and environment laws also have compliance dates.

- Your own internal management might impose arbitrary deadlines for individual tasks in the project.

All these special scheduling instructions, including as soon or as late as possible, are entered into Project by defining a constraint type for the task and, when appropriate, a constraint date.

Understanding the Types of Constraints

The eight constraint types are described in Table 5.2. The order of the listing in the table is not alphabetical (as it will be when you pick a constraint type on the screen), but is arranged to help you understand the constraint types. The abbreviations are occasionally found in Project's Help texts and are included here just for reference.

TABLE 5.2.   THE CONSTRAINT TYPES IN MICROSOFT PROJECT

Constraint Type	Description
As Soon As Possible (ASAP)	Marks a task as essentially unconstrained. There's no constraint date for the task.
As Late As Possible (ALAP)	Delays the task as long as possible, without holding up the finish of the project. There's no constraint date for the task.

Constraint Type	Description
Start No Earlier Than (SNET)	The task can't start before the defined constraint date. It must be scheduled to start on or after that date.
Finish No Earlier Than (FNET)	The task can't finish before the defined constraint date. It can be scheduled to finish on or after that date.
Start No Later Than (SNLT)	The task must be scheduled to start on or before the defined constraint date.
Finish No Later Than (FNLT)	The task can't finish any later than the defined constraint date. It can be scheduled to finish on or before that date.
Must Start On (MSO)	The task must start on the defined constraint date, not earlier or later.
Must Finish On (MFO)	The task must finish exactly on the defined constraint date, not earlier or later.

 Summary tasks can only be assigned constraints that relate to the start of the summary group: As Soon As Possible, Start No Earlier Than, and Start No Later Than.

Flexible and Inflexible Constraints

When a task has a constraint type other than As Soon As Possible or As Late As Possible, you will see an icon in the Indicators field (see Figure 5.8). These icons resemble little calendars with either a red or a blue "dot" in the icon. The red dots indicate an *inflexible constraint* and the blue dots indicate a *flexible constraint*.

NEW TERM   **Flexible and Inflexible Constraints**   *Inflexible constraints* are those that can potentially create scheduling conflicts—they can present barriers to Project's capability to schedule all your tasks while honoring the constraints. *Flexible constraints* are those that are unlikely to create problems with the schedule.

FIGURE 5.8

All constraints except As Soon As Possible and As Late As Possible display special indicators.

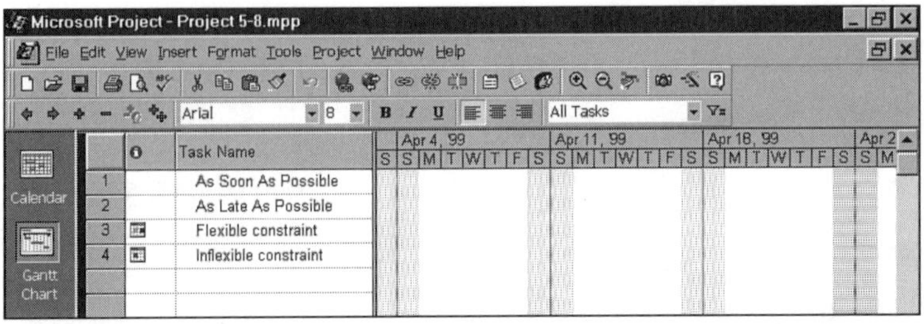

NEW TERM **Scheduling Conflict** Predecessors other than Start-to-Finish tend to push successor tasks to later and later dates in projects with a fixed start date. If a successor task has an inflexible constraint, a *scheduling conflict* exists when the predecessors try to push the task past the constraint date.

In projects with fixed finish dates, the predecessors tend to push successor tasks to earlier dates, and a *scheduling conflict* arises if the predecessors try to push the successor task to a date earlier than the inflexible constraint date.

All constraints restrict Project's freedom to schedule tasks to some degree, but inflexible constraints are called that because they can potentially keep Project from scheduling tasks as your linking instructions require. Whether a constraint is inflexible depends on the constraint type and whether the project is scheduled from a fixed start date or a fixed finish date.

- When projects are scheduled from a fixed start date, Project generally has to push the schedule toward later and later dates to accommodate all the linked tasks. The inflexible constraint types are those that might keep Project from rescheduling tasks to later dates—they are the Must Start On, Must Finish On, Start No Later Than, and Finish No Later Than types.

- If the project is scheduled from a fixed finish date, Project has to push the linked tasks to earlier dates to get everything done by the finish date. For a fixed finish date project, the inflexible constraints are those that might prevent Project from rescheduling tasks to earlier dates—they are Must Start On, Must Finish On, Start No Earlier Than, and Finish No Earlier Than.

Creating Task Constraints

You can enter task constraints in the Task Information dialog box. In Figure 5.9, the task "Brief Web Development Team" is to be constrained to start no earlier than 5/10/99 because the members of the team won't be in place until that date.

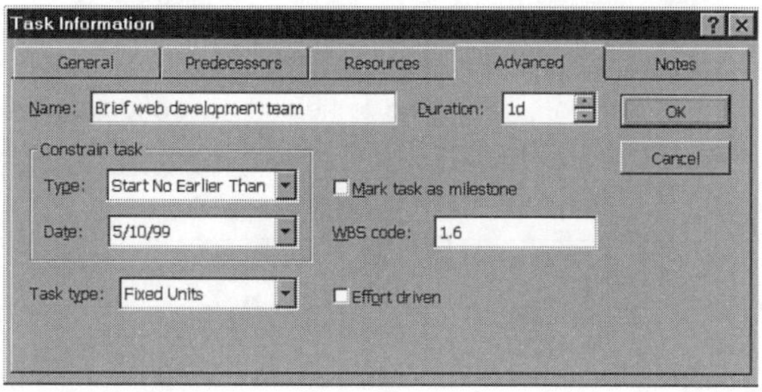

FIGURE 5.9

Choose the type of constraint from the Type entry list on the Advanced tab of the Task Information dialog box.

Task Information

| General | Predecessors | Resources | Advanced | Notes |

Name: Brief web development team   Duration: 1d   OK

Constrain task

Type: Start No Earlier Than   ☐ Mark task as milestone   Cancel

Date: 5/10/99   WBS code: 1.6

Task type: Fixed Units   ☐ Effort driven

To Do: Entering Task Constraints

To enter task constraints, follow these steps:

1. Select the task you want to constrain.

    2. Choose **P**roject, Task **I**nformation, or click the Information button on the Standard toolbar to display the Task Information dialog box.

3. Select the Advanced tab.

4. From the drop-down list in the Constrain Task Ty**p**e field, select the constraint type you want (see Figure 5.9).

5. In the Constrain Task Da**t**e text box, enter the constraint date, if necessary. The As Soon As Possible and As Late As Possible constraints do not require a constraint date, but all others require a date entry.

6. Click OK to close the dialog box.

> While you have the Task Information dialog box open, it's a good idea to add a note to the task indicating why the constraint was set. This gives you a reminder, and if you are sharing the project file with colleagues, gives them important information, too. To add a note to the task, simply click the Notes tab and type the note in the Notes field.

To remove a constraint, change the constraint type to As Soon As Possible for fixed start date projects or to As Late As Possible for fixed finish date projects.

5

You should avoid placing constraints unless absolutely necessary. Otherwise, you'll find yourself having to help Project find ways to work around them, or you'll find them getting in your way as you try to shorten the duration of the overall project.

If you enter a date in the Start or Finish field for a task, of if you drag a task bar to a later date, Project makes that date a constraint, albeit a flexible constraint. For example, if you enter a date in the Start field, Project makes that a constraint date and assigns the Start No Earlier Than constraint type.

You should generally avoid entering specific dates for tasks unless they really are required. Let Project calculate the dates for you. Project is generally not free to reschedule constrained tasks to optimize your schedule.

When you attempt to apply an inflexible constraint to a task that has predecessor tasks, Project's Planning Wizard warns you that the constraint could potentially cause a scheduling conflict and asks you to decide whether to continue (see Figure 5.10). The Wizard's dialog box offers you three choices:

- Cancel and don't set a constraint. This is the default selection, and it's the same as clicking the Cancel button. So if you don't change the selection, you will fail to set a constraint whether you click OK or Cancel.

- Continue, but set a flexible constraint instead of the inflexible constraint you requested.

- Continue setting the inflexible constraint, despite any possible scheduling conflicts.

You can also suppress the future display of this warning for inflexible constraints by selecting the Don't Tell Me About This Again check box.

If you go ahead and apply the constraint and it does in fact create a scheduling conflict either immediately or later, because of changes in the schedules for predecessor tasks, you will see another Planning Wizard warning that a conflict is about to occur (see Figure 5.11). Your choices now are simply to cancel the action and avoid the conflict, which is the default selection, or to continue and allow the scheduling conflict. You must select the Continue option and then click OK to go ahead with the change you requested.

Cancel without
setting a
constraint

FIGURE 5.10

If an inflexible con-
straint is entered for a
task with predecessors,
Project warns you and
gives you a chance to
change your mind.

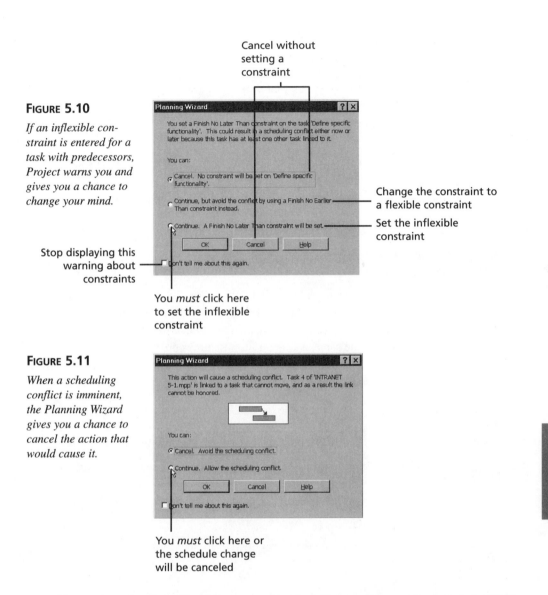

Change the constraint to
a flexible constraint

Set the inflexible
constraint

Stop displaying this
warning about
constraints

You *must* click here
to set the inflexible
constraint

FIGURE 5.11

When a scheduling
conflict is imminent,
the Planning Wizard
gives you a chance to
cancel the action that
would cause it.

5

You *must* click here or
the schedule change
will be canceled

If you proceed with a change that creates a scheduling conflict, you have to deal with the conflict somehow (see the next section) because it's an indication that your project is not workable as defined.

You get only one Planning Wizard warning about each scheduling conflict you create. If you create a conflict and don't deal with it right away, you will have to find a solution on your own at some later point. The next section shows you how to find unresolved scheduling conflicts.

Resolving Conflicts Caused by Constraints

If you decide to go ahead with a change that creates a scheduling conflict, then you must deal with the conflict resulting from the constraint. When a scheduling conflict occurs, Project has to honor the link to the predecessor (and schedule the constrained task past its constraint date), or it has to honor the constraint and not observe the link to the predecessor. By default, Project honors constraint barriers at all times and ignores the link instructions because constraints are normally what we call "hard" constraints.

With hard constraints, the screen really doesn't tell you for certain that a scheduling conflict exists. The link arrow doubles back on itself in a tortured S-shape (see Figure 5.12). However, this could just as well be the link arrow for a Finish-to-Start link with lead time. The indicator is just the same as it is for all inflexible constraints, so you can't tell that there's a scheduling conflict just from looking at the screen. Furthermore, you have seen the last warning from the Planning Wizard. You're on your own if you want to find the conflict and fix it.

If you would like Project to honor the predecessor link, it must ignore the constraint. You can choose that option by instructing Project to make all constraints *soft constraints*.

NEW TERM **Hard and Soft Constraints**   Microsoft Project must honor tasks' constraint dates (and ignore their predecessor links) if constraints are *hard constraints* in that project; it honors the predecessor links, and not the constraint dates, if the project uses *soft constraints*.

You can change the way a project uses constraints, from hard to soft, with the Options dialog box.

FIGURE 5.12

A scheduling conflict is not really evident on the screen when the constraint is honored.

Could *you* tell there's a scheduling conflict here?

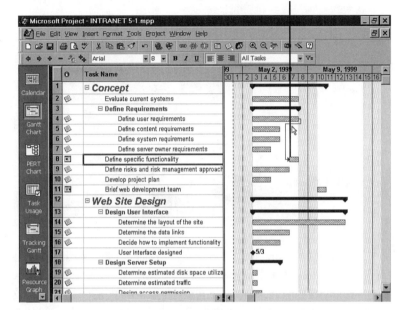

To Do: Making Constraints Hard or Soft

Follow these steps to make constraints in the project hard or soft:

1. Choose **T**ools, **O**ptions to display the Options dialog box and select the Schedule tab (see Figure 5.13).

2. Clear the check box next to **T**asks Will Always Honor Their Constraint Dates to make constraints soft constraints. Fill the check box to make them hard constraints.

3. Click OK to close the dialog box.

> Note that the choice of hard or soft constraints is not made task by task: The choice affects the way all constraints are used in the project.

5

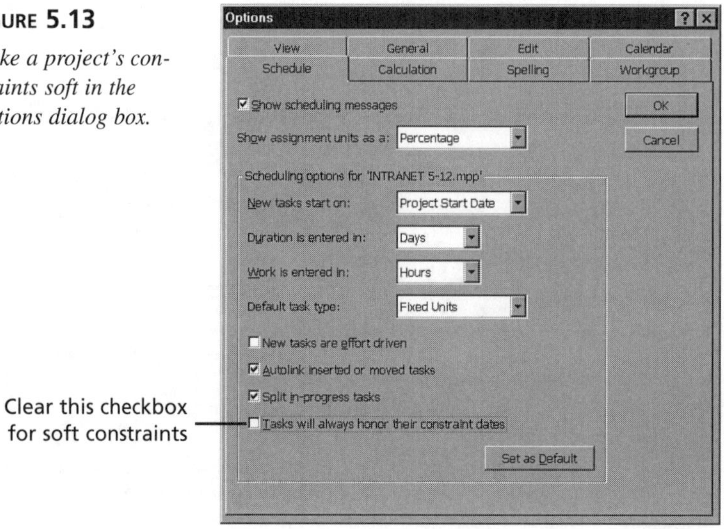

FIGURE 5.13

Make a project's constraints soft in the Options dialog box.

Options	? X
View	General	Edit	Calendar
Schedule	Calculation	Spelling	Workgroup

☑ S̲how scheduling messages

OK

Cancel

Sho̲w assignment units as a: Percentage ▾

Scheduling options for 'INTRANET 5-12.mpp'

N̲ew tasks start on: Project Start Date ▾

Du̲ration is entered in: Days ▾

Wo̲rk is entered in: Hours ▾

Default task type: Fixed Units ▾

☐ New tasks are e̲ffort driven

☑ A̲utolink inserted or moved tasks

☑ Split i̲n-progress tasks

Clear this checkbox
for soft constraints ☐ Tasks will always honor their constraint dates

Set as D̲efault

If any task constraint is not honored, Project displays a special indicator next to that task (see Figure 5.14). This indicator is the only easy way to identify scheduling conflicts after the Planning Wizard warnings have ceased being displayed. You can make constraints soft to display the indicator where conflicts exist, find those tasks with conflicts, and figure out what to do about the conflict.

If soft constraints are in effect, you can still see the Planning Wizard warning when you set inflexible constraints, but you won't see a warning when a scheduling conflict actually occurs.

You can apply the filter named Tasks With Fixed Dates to the task list to filter out all but the tasks with fixed dates. The list includes all tasks with constraints, but it also includes tasks that have already had dates recorded for the beginning of actual work (because dates for actual work are fixed, too, as far as Project is concerned). Nevertheless, the filter can significantly reduce the number of tasks you need to look over to see if the scheduling indicator is showing. And, if you apply the filter before you start tracking actual work, only tasks with constraints are displayed.

FIGURE 5.14

The scheduling conflict indicator appears only when you select soft constraints for the project.

Indicator for missed constraint date

Task link honored instead of constraint

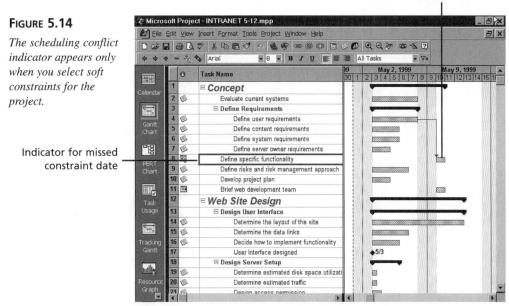

To Do: Applying the Tasks with Fixed Dates Filter

Follow these steps to apply the Tasks with Fixed Dates filter:

1. In the Gantt Chart, choose **P**roject, **F**iltered For, **M**ore Filters to display the More Filters dialog box.

2. Scroll down to select the Tasks With Fixed Dates filter.

3. Click the App**l**y button to close the dialog box and apply the filter.

   The filter restricts the display to only those tasks with constraints or tasks with actual start dates already entered.

4. When finished, you can remove the filter by pressing the F3 function key or by choosing **P**roject, **F**iltered For, **A**ll Tasks from the menu.

You can correct a scheduling conflict in three ways:

- Change the constraint by changing its type or date or by eliminating it altogether.

- Change the predecessor link or eliminate it altogether.

- Reduce the duration of the predecessor task, or the duration of its predecessors, so that the immediate predecessor to the constrained task finishes in time to allow the constraint to be honored.

PART III

Displaying and Printing Your Schedule

Hour

HOUR 6

Working with the Other Task Views

Besides the Gantt Chart view, several other views in Microsoft Project can be used to work with your task list. The Calendar view displays the task list in a typical monthly calendar format. Some of your project team members might find it easier to monitor their specific tasks using printouts based on the Calendar view. Another useful view is the PERT Chart. The PERT Chart view is often used as a flowchart of the tasks in the entire project. It provides an overview of the project tasks and the sequence of events.

Working with the Calendar View

The Calendar view displays project tasks in a familiar monthly calendar format. Each task is represented by a bar or line that includes the task name and duration. The Calendar view is most useful for viewing all the tasks being performed during a specific set of weeks. You can insert, delete, and link tasks from the Calendar view. You can filter the task list to display only specific tasks, such as milestone tasks or tasks performed by a particular resource.

Exploring the Calendar View

You can display the Calendar view by clicking the Calendar button on the View Bar or by choosing **View, Calendar**. The standard Calendar view appears (see Figure 6.1).

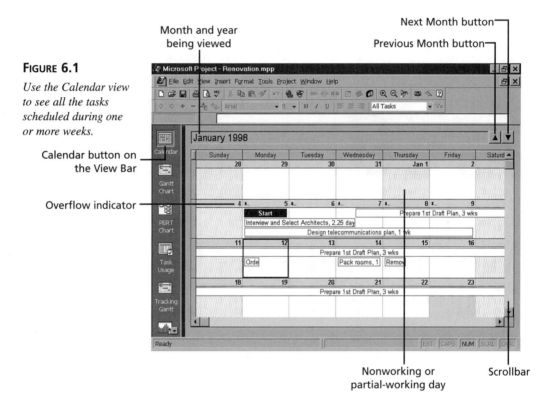

Figure 6.1

Use the Calendar view to see all the tasks scheduled during one or more weeks.

Month and year being viewed

Next Month button

Previous Month button

Calendar button on the View Bar

Overflow indicator

Nonworking or partial-working day

Scrollbar

The default display shows the four weeks at a time. Bars or lines for tasks include the task name and duration. Any nonworking or partial-working days you have identified in the project base calendar appear with a gray background.

The Previous Month and Next Month buttons, along with the scrollbars, are used to display other weeks or months onscreen.

Normal tasks are displayed with task bars outlined in blue. Milestone tasks are represented by black task bars with white text. In Figure 6.1, the Start milestone task is displayed. Summary tasks, except the Project Summary Task, are not displayed by default. You can include the summary tasks by customizing the Calendar view.

To Do: Displaying Summary Tasks in Calendar View

To display summary tasks in Calendar view, follow these steps:

▼ To Do

1. Choose Format, Bar Styles to open the Bar Styles dialog box, shown in Figure 6.2.

2. Choose Summary from the list of Task Types.

3. Change the Bar Type from None to either Bar or Line.

4. Click OK.

▲   5. To update the Calendar view display, choose Format, Layout Now.

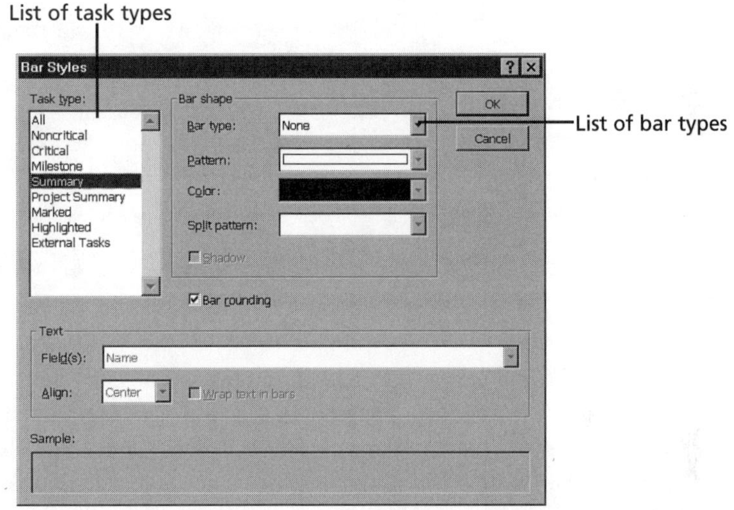

List of task types

FIGURE 6.2

*Use the Bar Styles dia-
log box to customize
the appearance of the
task bars in the
Calendar view.*

List of bar types

In some cases, there isn't enough room in the calendar to display all the tasks whose
schedules fall on a particular date. When this happens, you see an overflow indicator in
the left corner of the date box (refer to Figure 6.1). The overflow indicator is a black
arrow with an ellipsis that indicates additional tasks, which are not being displayed, are
scheduled for this date.

You can see all the tasks scheduled for a given date by displaying the Tasks Occurring
On dialog box for that date (see Figure 6.3). Simply double-click the gray band at the top
of the date box.

The Tasks Occurring On dialog box lists all tasks whose schedule dates encompass the
date you selected. Tasks visible in Calendar view have a check mark to the left of the listing. Tasks that are not being displayed in the Calendar view do not have a check mark.

6

FIGURE 6.3

*All tasks that occur on
a specific date are
shown in a list.
Double-click any of the
tasks to see details for
that task.*

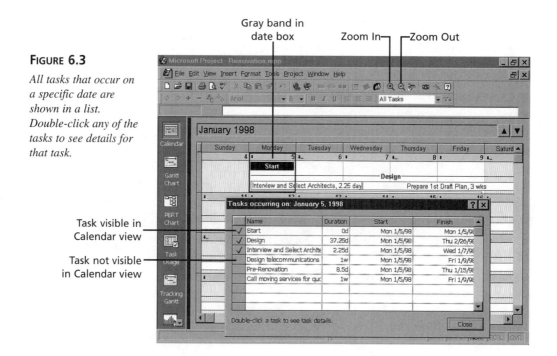

To increase the number of tasks that appear in the Calendar view, use the Zoom In button
on the Standard toolbar (see Figure 6.3). This action changes the number of weeks visible in the Calendar view. You can display 1, 2, 4, or 6 weeks by clicking the Zoom In
and Zoom Out buttons. Changing the zoom in the Calendar view has no effect on the
printed Calendar view; it affects only the screen display.

Moving Around in the Calendar View

There are several ways to effectively move around the Calendar view and find the information you want to focus on:

- Use the Previous Month and Next Month arrow buttons to display the week in
  which the first day of the previous or next month occurs. The beginning of each
  successive month appears in the first row of the calendar, no matter how many
  weeks you displayed in the view.

- The scrollbars move forward and backward in time on the calendar. When you drag
  the scroll box on the vertical scrollbar, a date indicator pop-up box helps you locate
  a specific date (see Figure 6.4).

FIGURE 6.4

Drag the scroll box to move quickly to a spe-cific date.

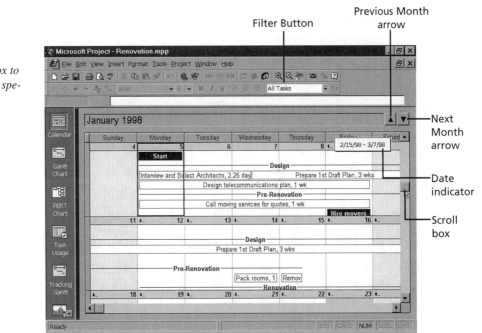

Filter Button

Previous Month arrow

Next Month arrow

Date indicator

Scroll box

- Press Alt+Home and Alt+End to jump to the beginning and ending dates of the project, respectively. You also can use the Page Up and Page Down keys to scroll through the display, showing successive weeks in the life of the project.

- Use the Go To command to move directly to a specific task ID or date. Choose **E**dit, **G**o To. The Go To dialog box appears (see Figure 6.5). Type in the desired task ID or date and click OK. If the bar for the task is not visible, try using the Zoom In button to display more task bars for each day.

FIGURE 6.5

Use the Go To dialog box to quickly locate a specific date or task ID.

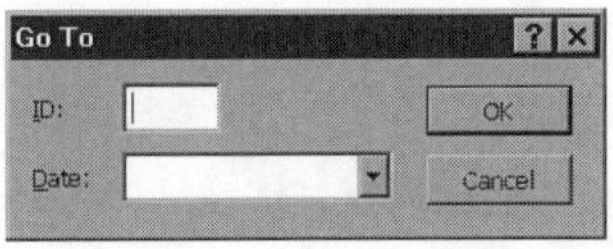

6

The Go To command does not select tasks that don't display task bars in the Calendar view. Therefore, because the default display doesn't display sum-mary tasks, you can't go to a summary task unless you change the task bar styles.

Using Filters to Clarify the Calendar View

When a project has many overlapping tasks, the Calendar view can quickly become very cluttered. As previously discussed, you can zoom in to see more detail, but you can also use filters to reduce the list of tasks that display at one time.

A *filter* limits the display of tasks to just those that match the defined criteria. For example, you can have Project display only the critical tasks in the project by applying the Critical filter. You might display tasks that a specific resource is working on by applying the Using Resource filter. When the project is underway and you want a record of what has been accomplished so far, use the Completed Tasks filter.

To apply a filter to a Calendar View, click the Filter button on the Formatting toolbar and select the list of built-in filters available on the drop-down list.

Editing a Project in the Calendar View

The Calendar view is not designed for creating complex projects. This view is more useful for reviewing and printing tasks and the time frames in which they occur. As you work in the Calendar view, you might need to look up and modify task information. Instead of switching back to the Gantt Chart view, you need to know how to display and edit tasks in this view.

> Although the Calendar view is not a good view for creating the details of large projects, it's a great device for sketching out the major components of projects in initial planning sessions, when a group is trying to block out time on a calendar to see how long it will probably take to get it all done.
>
> You can quickly use the mouse to create the tasks by dragging from the estimated start to the estimated finish, access the Task Information dialog box to name the task, and link the tasks. Then you can just as quickly adjust task durations as the group debates possible scenarios.

Viewing Task Details in Calendar View

To display individual task information, you must select the task and open the Task Information dialog box, or you can split the screen displaying the Calendar view in the top part of a dual-pane view, with the task details in the lower pane.

To display the Task Information dialog box (shown in Figure 6.6) while you're in Calendar view, double-click the task bar, or select the task bar and click the Task Information button on the Standard toolbar. If the task bar is not displayed, you must first select the task by using the Go To command.

FIGURE 6.6

The Task Information dialog box offers easy access to most of the data fields for a task.

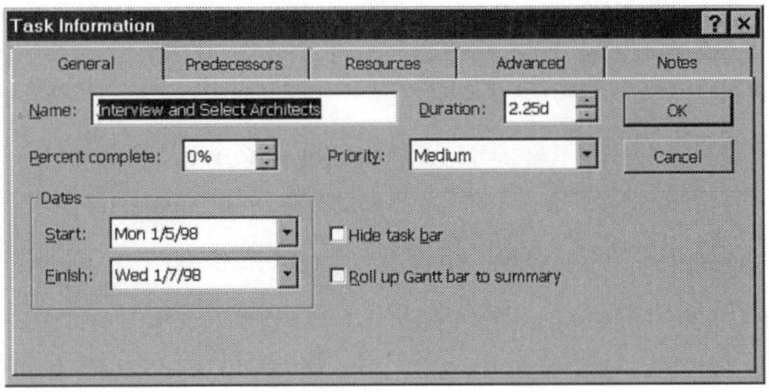

> Another way to view task details is to split the screen by choosing **W**indow, **S**plit. The Calendar view appears in the top pane and the Task Form view in the bottom pane.

Inserting Tasks in Calendar View

You can create tasks in Calendar view by choosing **I**nsert, **N**ew Task or by dragging the mouse to create a new task bar in the calendar. Although it's easy to create tasks in the Calendar view, there are several reasons why you might not want to:

- Unlike the Gantt Chart view where you can insert a new task ID in the middle of the project near other tasks to which the new task is related, when you create a task in Calendar view it is always given the highest ID number in the project. If you view the new task in Gantt Chart view, the task is at the bottom of the list—even if its dates fall in the middle of the project or you link it to tasks in the middle of the task list.

- The task you create in Calendar view is often automatically given a flexible date constraint to hold it on the date you set the task on. If you want to remove the constraint, set the constraint type to As Soon as Possible in the Advanced Tab of the Task Information dialog box.

6

> Recall from the previous Hour that flexible constraints do not generally hinder scheduling. They can, however, make it difficult to reduce the project's overall length.

To Do: Inserting a New Task from Calendar view

To insert a new task from the Calendar view, follow these steps:

1. Select the date for the start of the task if you want the start date constrained to that date, or select any task if you do not want the task to be constrained.

2. Choose **I**nsert, **N**ew Task or press the Insert key on the keyboard.

3. Choose **P**roject, Task **I**nformation (or click the Information button on the Standard toolbar) to open the Task Information dialog box.

4. Supply a name and duration for the task.

5. Because most tasks created in Calendar view are automatically given a date constraint, select the Advanced tab and change the entry in the Constrain Task **Ty**pe field to As Soon As Possible, if necessary.

6. Click OK to close the dialog box.

Deleting Tasks in Calendar View

To delete a task, simply select it and choose **E**dit, **D**elete Task or press the Delete key on the keyboard. If the task bar is not visible onscreen, use the Go To command to select the task. If you accidentally delete a task, choose **E**dit, **U**ndo or click the Undo button to get it back.

Creating Links Between Tasks in Calendar View

Creating task dependency links in Calendar view is similar to creating links in the Gantt Chart view. Select the tasks you want to link and click the Link button on the Standard toolbar.

To change to a different kind of relationship or to add lag or lead time, you must select the dependent (successor) task and display the Task Information dialog box. Use the Predecessors tab to change the dependency link, and add lag or lead time.

Working with the PERT Chart

The PERT Chart is a graphical display of tasks in a project; each task is represented by a small box or *node*, and lines connect the nodes to show task dependencies. The PERT Chart is most useful for an overall view of how the process or flow of task details fit together.

> While in the PERT Chart view, you can't filter the task list or copy a task.

Exploring the PERT Chart View

The PERT Chart is named for the Program Evaluation and Review Technique, a project management methodology introduced by the U.S. Navy in 1958. The PERT Chart has evolved into several species of network diagrams. The popular version used in Microsoft Project reveals information about the individual task, as well as information about the task's place in the flow of activity.

To display the PERT Chart, click the PERT Chart button in the View Bar or choose View, PERT Chart. Figure 6.7 shows the PERT Chart view of the Renovation project. Interview and Select Architects is the selected task; its name appears in the Entry Bar. The default format for nodes displays five fields for the task: the name, ID, duration, start, and finish.

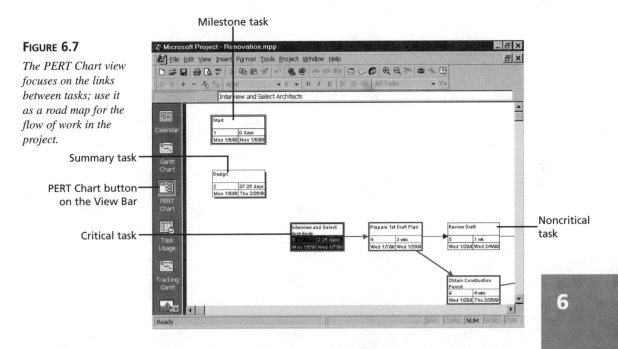

FIGURE 6.7

The PERT Chart view focuses on the links between tasks; use it as a road map for the flow of work in the project.

Each node represents a task, which is connected to predecessors and successors by lines. In the diagram, dependent (successor) tasks are always placed to the right of, or beneath, predecessors. Different border styles or colors distinguish summary tasks, critical tasks, and milestones. Summary tasks are above and to the left of subordinate tasks.

Table 6.1 describes a few of the node borders displayed in Figure 6.7.

TABLE 6.1. EACH TYPE OF TASK HAS A UNIQUE NODE BORDER

Tasks	Node Borders
Summary task	Thin border with shadow box
Milestone	Double border
Critical task	Red heavy border
Noncritical task	Black thin border

Zooming the PERT Chart View

The PERT Chart in Figure 6.7 displays each node enlarged enough to read the field data easily. If you want to get an overview of the links among more tasks, you can zoom the view to show more tasks. Figure 6.8 shows the same task selected, Interview and Select Architects, as in Figure 6.7. When you zoom out, you get a better feel for how that task fits into the overall project.

FIGURE 6.8

The PERT Chart displays dashed lines to show where page breaks occur when you print the view.

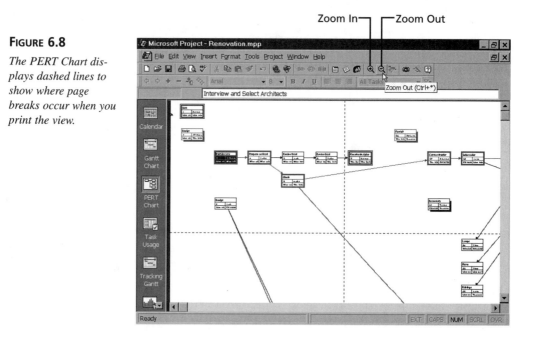

You can zoom to view more tasks by using the Zoom Out button on the Standard toolbar; use the Zoom In button to see the task details. The Zoom In and Zoom Out buttons change the zoom to specific increments each time you click the button, ranging from 25 to 400 percent. Choose View, Zoom to enter a custom zoom percent.

Using the Zoom command affects only the screen view in the PERT Chart. It does not affect how much of the chart is printed.

Scrolling and Selecting in the PERT Chart

You can use the horizontal and vertical scrollbars or the movement keys (the arrow keys, Page Up, Page Down, Home, and End) to scan through the PERT chart.

Scrolling does not change the currently selected node. After you scroll, you probably can't see the selected node, although the name remains in the Entry Bar. To select one of the visible nodes after scrolling, click anywhere on the node, except the ID field. To return to the selected node, press the Edit key (F2) as though you plan to edit the selected node, and then press the Esc key (to cancel the editing).

You can also use the movement keys to move around the PERT Chart. When you use one of the movement keys, the selected node changes. The rules that the movement keys follow in selecting the next node are not apparent. The following list defines these rules:

- *Right-arrow key.* Selects nodes to the right that are closest to it, including nodes that are above or below the active node.
- *Down-arrow key.* Selects nodes directly below that are closest to it, whether the node is to the left or right.
- *Left-arrow key.* Selects nodes to the left that are closest to it, including nodes that are above or below the active node.
- *Up-arrow key.* Selects nodes directly above that are closest to it, whether the node is to the left or right.

The rest of the movement keys simulate repeated use of the arrow keys. The newly selected task name appears in the Entry Bar. If the selected task is not visible after the move, press the Edit key (F2) and then press Esc to place the selected task in the center of the screen. Here's what the other movement keys do:

- *Page Down.* Simulates repeated down arrow for one screen.
- *End.* Simulates repeated down arrow until it reaches the bottom row of the PERT Chart.
- *Page Up.* Simulates repeated up arrow for one screen.
- *Home.* Simulates repeated up arrow until it reaches the top row of the PERT Chart.
- *Ctrl+Page Down.* Simulates repeated right arrow for one screen.
- *Ctrl+Page Up.* Simulates repeated left arrow for one screen.

6

- *Ctrl+End.* Simulates repeated right arrow until it reaches the last column of the PERT Chart.

- *Ctrl+Home.* Simulates repeated left arrow until it reaches the first column of the PERT Chart.

> To move to the beginning of the PERT Chart, press Ctrl+Home and then press Home.

Editing a Project in the PERT Chart

Although the PERT Chart view can be used to create a project, it's more useful for reviewing the sequence of events and the overall flow of the project tasks. As you work in the PERT Chart view, you can change task data, add and delete tasks, and create and modify task links.

To Do: Changing Task Data in the PERT Chart

To change the field data displayed in a node, follow these steps:

1. Select the task to edit by clicking the mouse pointer on the node or by using the selection keys.

2. Select the field to edit by pressing the Tab and Shift+Tab keys or by clicking the field.

3. In the Entry Bar, type the new data or edit the existing data.

4. Complete the change by pressing Enter, by selecting the Enter box in the Entry Bar, or by selecting a different field or node.

If you want to change data in fields that don't appear in the node (such as constraints, fixed duration, and so on), you must use the Task Information dialog box. To display the Task Information dialog box, select the node you want to edit and choose **P**roject, Task Information.

> You can also double-click the center of the node to display the Task Information dialog box, or click the Task Information button on the Standard toolbar. (Double-clicking the border of a node takes you to a formatting dialog box.)

Inserting Tasks in PERT Chart View

You can add tasks directly to the project in the PERT Chart view. You must select the insertion position carefully, however, if you want to control the ID number of the new task. Project inserts a task you add in PERT Chart view just after the currently selected task.

To Do: Adding a New Task via the PERT Chart

To add a new task through the PERT Chart, follow these steps:

1. Select the task you want the new task to follow. This step makes sure the new task node will be placed to the right of the selected task and has an ID number that follows that of the selected task.

2. Choose **Insert**, **N**ew Task (or press the Insert key) to insert a blank node to the right of the selected task.

   The ID number for the new task is one greater than the selected task, and all existing tasks with ID numbers higher than the selected task increase by one, just as they do when you insert a task in the Gantt Chart view. The new task appears directly to the right of the selected task. If there is already a task in that position, the new task hides it

3. Type the name for the new task. Tab to the Duration field and estimate the duration. Do not enter the start or finish date unless you want the task constrained to one of those dates.

   You will have to create the links required for the newly inserted task. Automatic linking of tasks is not enabled while you add, delete, or move tasks in PERT Chart view.

Deleting Tasks in PERT Chart View

You can delete normal tasks and milestone tasks while in PERT Chart view. However, summary tasks can't be deleted in the PERT Chart view. The Autolink option is not active in PERT Chart view. If you delete a task in the middle of a linked chain of tasks, you must manually rejoin its predecessor and successor to preserve the chain.

To delete a task, select the task and choose **E**dit, **D**elete Task or press Delete.

Linking Tasks in PERT Chart View

You can create task links in PERT Chart view by dragging the mouse from the middle of the predecessor task to the middle of the successor task (see Figure 6.9). Be careful to start in the middle of a task node; dragging the border of a task node merely repositions the node. The task relationship of Finish-to-Start is created with no lead or lag time.

6

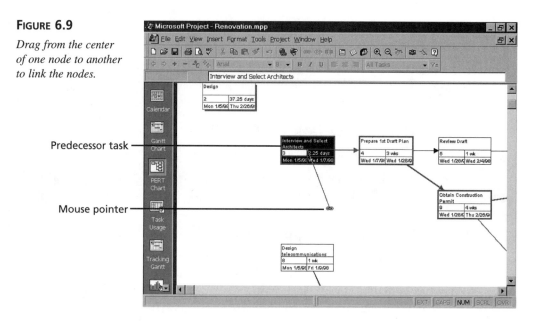

FIGURE 6.9

Drag from the center of one node to another to link the nodes.

Predecessor task

Mouse pointer

If you want to change the relationship, enter lead or lag time, or delete the task link, you must activate the Task Dependency dialog box. Double-click the line that links two tasks to display the Task Dependency dialog box. Make sure the very tip of the mouse pointer is on the line that links the tasks when you double-click.

Moving Task Nodes in PERT Chart View

You can change the layout of the PERT Chart by moving individual task nodes or groups of nodes to new positions in the PERT Chart view. If you move a group of nodes simultaneously, the nodes retain positions in relation to one another as you move them. The linking lines also follow task nodes to the new locations.

To Do: Moving the Task Node

To move the task node, follow these steps:

1. If necessary, zoom out so you can see an overview of the task layout of the PERT Chart.

2. Click on the border of the task node you want to move. If you are moving several nodes, click on the borders of each task to be moved; the border changes color to indicate it is selected.

3. Hold down the mouse button on the border of a selected node and drag the node(s) to the new location (see Figure 6.10).

4. After it's moved to the proper place, click away from the node to turn off the selection.

▲

FIGURE 6.10

You can reposition nodes with the mouse.

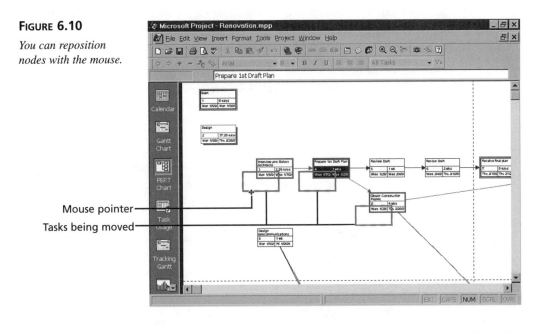

Mouse pointer

Tasks being moved

> If you press the Shift key as you select the border of a task, Project selects that task plus all its dependent (successor) tasks. You can quickly select all of a summary task's subtasks by holding down the Shift key as you click the border of the summary task. Drag the border of any task in the selected group to move the entire selected group.

When you rearrange the PERT Chart, you want to see the page break lines, so you don't place a task node on a page break. If you place a node on a page break line, part of the node prints on one page and the remainder prints on another page. The following section explains how to display and use page break lines.

Customizing the PERT Chart with the Layout Dialog Box

You can customize the layout of the PERT view through the Layout dialog box (see Figure 6.11). To display it, choose Format, Layout. The following choices are available in the dialog box:

6

- With the **L**inks option, the dependency lines can be drawn diagonally or at right angles from predecessor to successor tasks.
- The Show **A**rrows option displays (or removes) an arrow on the linking line from the predecessor to successor task.
- The Show **P**age Breaks option displays (or removes) the dotted page break lines.
- Select the **Ad**just for Page Breaks option if you want Project to automatically adjust task nodes to avoid page break lines when you execute the Layout Now command (see the following section). This way, no task node can be split by a page break. If a node must be adjusted to avoid a page break, Project moves the node to the right or down until it fits entirely on the next page.

The **L**inks, Show **P**age Breaks, and Show **A**rrows options are carried out immediately. The **Ad**just for Page Breaks option doesn't take effect until the next time you choose **F**ormat, Layout **N**ow.

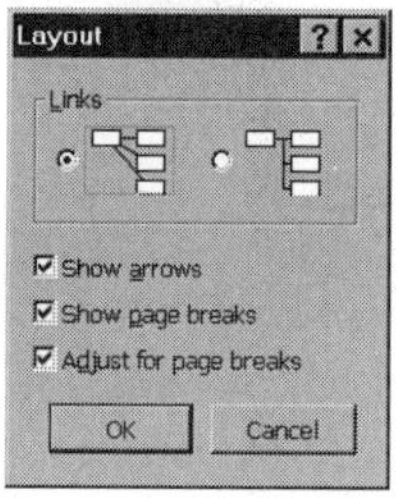

FIGURE 6.11

The PERT Chart Layout dialog box controls PERT Chart display features.

Hour 7

Formatting Views

As you've already learned in earlier hours, Project offers several different ways to view the various aspects of your projects. These major Project views include the Gantt Chart, which displays information in both a sheet and chart format; the Calendar view, which emphasizes how your various tasks are scheduled; and the PERT Chart, which emphasizes the tasks in your project and their relationships.

Project gives you a great deal of flexibility to enhance and change these available views. You can format selected text in a view. You can format timescales. You can zoom in and out on a particular view, to change the level of detail shown. You can add graphics and text to a view. There is even a Gantt Chart Wizard that you can use to format your Gantt Charts.

In this hour, you learn how to format the various Project views. You will customize the standard views, using format options for everything from text to graphics to timescales to Gantt Charts.

Using the General Format Options

Using formatting options to change your Project views can help you emphasize certain information (by changing the font of selected text), change your perspective of the information displayed (by using the Zoom feature), and customize how that information is displayed (by changing the graph type or an object's color).

You will find that the different views you work with in Project fall into three categories: sheets, forms, and graphical views. All the sheet views (such as the left side of the Gantt Chart) share certain characteristics, such as gridlines. Most graphical views, such as the Gantt Chart, contain timescales.

NEW TERM **Timescales**   A *timescale* is the time-period indicator that appears at the top of the various Gantt views, the Resource Graph view, the Task Usage view, and the Resource Usage view. The indicator consists of a major timescale and, below it, a minor timescale. Both the major and minor timescales can display units of minutes, hours, days, weeks, thirds of months, months, quarters, half years, and years.

This sharing of characteristics means that after you learn to modify the gridlines for one sheet view, such as the left side of the Gantt view, you will be able to modify them in other sheet views. The same goes for the timescale display for Project's graphical view types, such as the Gantt Chart; after you learn how to modify the timescale for one graphical view, you will know how to do it for the other graphical views.

> The Project views that fall into the form category are pretty inflexible when it comes to formatting. This makes sense, however, because the various forms you work with are designed more for data entry than for providing a particular view of the information in the project.

Formatting Selected Text

You can easily format the text for a particular resource or task in a particular view. For instance, in the Gantt Chart sheet view, you might want to use text formatting to emphasize a particular task.

You can format selected text in three ways. You can use the Format menu, use the Formatting toolbar, or copy formatting from one text entry to another by using the Format Painter button on the Standard toolbar.

To Do: Formatting Text Using the Format Menu

▼ To Do

To format text using the Format menu, follow these steps:

1. Use the mouse to select the text you want to format.

2. Choose Format, Font to open the Font dialog box, shown in Figure 7.1.

3. Select a new font type in the Font box. To change the style of the text to bold or italic (or both), use the Font Style box. To change the size of the font, make a new selection in the Size box. This dialog box also allows you to underline selected text and change the color of the text.

FIGURE 7.1

The Font dialog box and Formatting tool-bar allow you to select the font attributes you use in your projects.

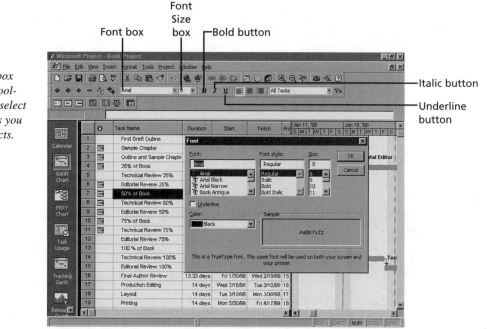

4. After you make your selections in the Font dialog box, click OK to assign the new attributes to the selected text and close the Font dialog box.

You can also use the Formatting toolbar to change the format of selected text. Buttons are available for the font, font size, bold, italic, and underline. Simply select the text and click the appropriate button or buttons on the toolbar (refer to Figure 7.1).

If you've already assigned formatting to a particular text entry, it is very easy to copy the format to another text entry by using the Format Painter on the Standard toolbar. Select the text with the formatting. Click the Format Painter button; the mouse

7

pointer changes to a Format Painter pointer. Click the text you want to copy the formatting to. The text is then displayed in the new format.

When you use the Format Painter to copy text attributes from one text entry to another, you will find that the Undo feature is not available. To remove the copied format, you must change each of the font attributes back to the default, or copy the set of normal attributes to the text from an entry that still appears in the default.

Formatting Text by Category

Another way to change text formatting in your projects is to change the format of entire categories of tasks or resources. This allows you to differentiate certain groups of tasks or resources by their font, type size, style, or color. For example, you might want to format your summary tasks in a certain color to make them stand out on the Gantt Chart sheet, or you might want to change the format for the Monthly and Daily titles on the Calendar view.

Changing the text format for an entire category of items in a particular view is done by selecting a new text style in the Text Styles dialog box.

To Do: Selecting a New Text Style

To select a new text style for a particular category, follow these steps:

1. Choose the view in which you want to change the formatting from the View bar.

2. Choose **F**ormat, **T**ext Styles. The Text Styles dialog box appears (see Figure 7.2).

3. To select a category of items to format, click the **I**tem to Change drop-down box. Select a particular category.

4. Select the font formats from the appropriate drop-down boxes (**F**ont, Font Style, Size, and Color).

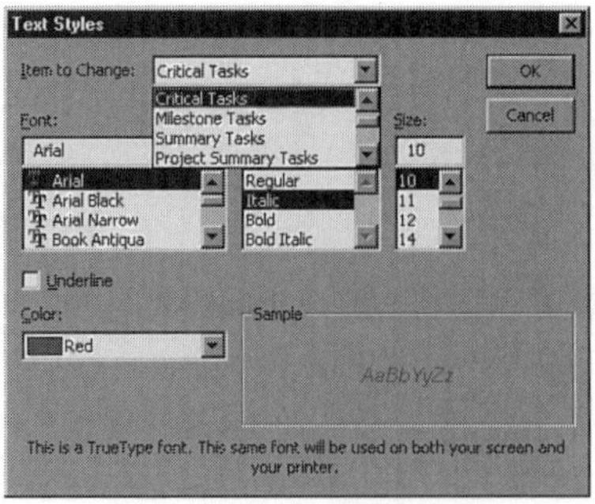

FIGURE 7.2

The Text Styles dialog box allows you to select formatting attributes for an entire category of items.

▼

▲

5. Click OK after you have made your selections. The category of items (or categories of items) that you selected in the Text Styles dialog box will appear in the new format in the current view.

> You can format several categories by opening the Text Styles box once. Select a category, change the format, and then select another category and do the same. You can format all the categories by selecting All in the Item to Change box.

Formatting Timescales

You can change the format of the timescales that appear in views such as the Gantt Chart (formatting the Calendar timescales will be covered later in this hour). You can choose the time units and the date formats for the timescale. Normally, a timescale displays two levels of time units: the major units scale and the minor units scale. For example, the major units scale might use weeks as its unit, but the minor units scale displays days.

To Do: Changing the Timescale

To change the timescale, follow these steps:

1. Choose **F**ormat, **Ti**mescale. The Timescale dialog box appears (see Figure 7.3).

2. In the Units drop-down boxes in the Major Scale and Minor Scale sections, select the units of time you want to use. All the changes that you make to the timescale format for the current view will appear in the preview box at the bottom of the Timescale dialog box. This feature allows you to preview different format attributes.

> The Timescale dialog box can also be opened by double-clicking on the timescale in the Gantt Chart view or by double-clicking on nonworking days.

> If you don't want to display two levels of time units on the timescale, you can select None in the Minor Scale's Units drop-down box.

▼

7

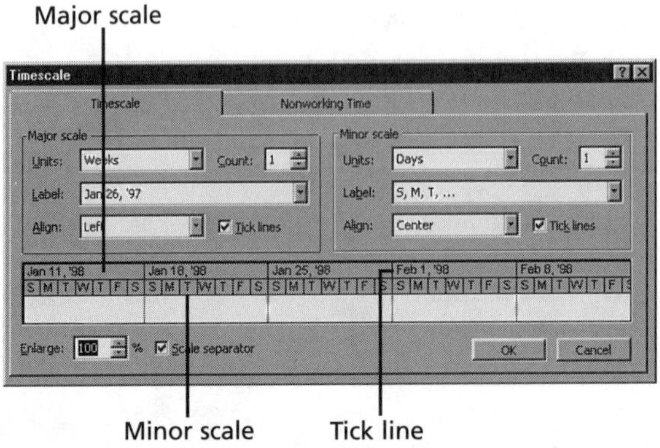

▼

FIGURE 7.3

The Timescale dialog box allows you to format the timescale in a particular view.

Major scale

Minor scale   Tick line

3. Each set of units (Major and Minor) also has a Label drop-down box. Select the labels you want to use for the scale in these boxes.

4. Each of the units also has an Align box. Select the alignment you want to use for each of the Major and Minor Scale units.

Three other format attributes that can be changed in the Timescale dialog box are the tick lines, the size of the timescale, and the scale separator.

The *tick lines* are the vertical lines that separate the labels for a scale. Use the Tick Lines check boxes to toggle these lines on and off (a check mark is "on"). The Scale Separator check box controls the horizontal line that separates the Major and Minor scale (a check mark is "on").

The Enlarge box allows you to increase or decrease the timescale by a particular percentage. Click the increase or decrease arrows to change the percentage. Enlarging the timescale allows you to see less time in the same space; decreasing the size allows you to see more time.

▲   5. After you have finished your selections, click OK.

Formatting Gridlines

Some of the views that you use in Project contain gridlines. You can find them on sheets (in tables), timescales (the lines separating the Major and Minor units), and even on Gantt Charts (lines between the bars in the bar chart).

To Do: Formatting the Gridlines for a View

To format the gridlines for a particular view, follow these steps:

1. Choose Format, Gridlines from the menu. The Gridlines dialog box appears, as shown in Figure 7.4.

FIGURE 7.4

The Gridlines dialog box allows you to format the lines in your various views.

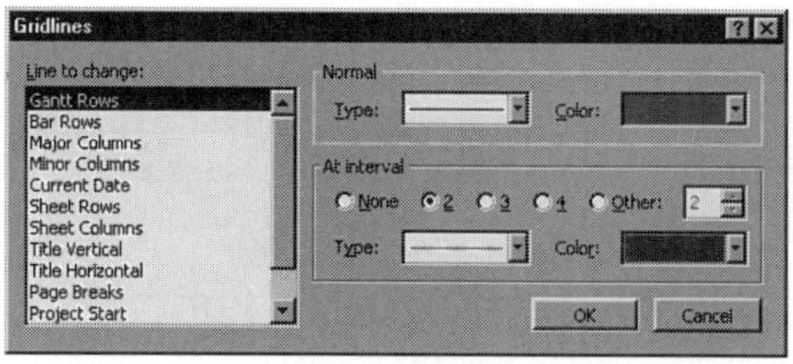

2. In the Line to Change list, choose the line type you want to format. The new settings will apply to all the lines in the group you select (such as Major Columns), unless the radio buttons in the At Interval section are active (as is the case for the Gantt Rows group). Choose a particular interval, and the lines will be formatted only at that interval (every second occurrence of the line if the 2 radio button is selected, for example).

3. In the Normal section, use the Type drop-down box to select a new type for the line and the Color drop-down box to select a new color. If the At Interval section is active, you can select different line types and colors (using the Type and Color drop-down boxes) for a particular interval that you select.

4. After you have made your gridline format selections, click OK. The new gridline formats will appear in the current view.

Special Formatting for the Gantt Chart

The Gantt Chart makes it easy to see the schedule for the tasks that make up your project. It gives you both a text view in columns and a bar graph. Because the Gantt Chart is commonly used as the view to initially build a plan, a number of formatting options are available. Also keep in mind that the Gantt Chart view is the best view to use when periodically reviewing your plan, so it must provide viewing flexibility for both building and reporting information in your project.

Using the Gantt Chart Wizard

The quickest way to format the Gantt Chart is to use the Gantt Chart Wizard. It guides you through several formatting options.

7

To Do: Formatting the Gantt Chart Using the Wizard

To Do

To format the Gantt Chart using the Wizard, follow these steps:

1. Choose Format, GanttChartWizard from the menu. The first screen welcomes you to the Wizard. Click Next to continue.

2. The next screen asks you to determine how your project's tasks should be displayed in the Gantt Chart. Several possibilities are offered:

   - *Standard.* Displays the taskbars in the default format.

   - *Critical path.* The critical path is a series of tasks that must be completed on schedule for a project to finish on schedule. This view helps identify the critical tasks in the critical path.

   - *Baseline.* Displays Gantt bars that show the baseline for each task. This display is useful when comparing the baseline with the actual schedule as the tasks are completed.

   - *Other.* Offers variations of the standard, critical path, and baseline formats.

   - *Custom Gantt Chart.* Select this option if you want to select each format option for the Gantt Chart. You are walked through a number of formatting steps, including choice of colors, patterns, and shapes for Critical, Normal, Summary, and Milestone tasks. You get additional options for adding a baseline bar and adding text to the bars. This selection gives you the greatest control over the various formatting options.

3. Select the radio button for the format you want to use and then click Next.

4. If you chose an option on the previous screen other than Custom Gantt Chart, the next screen asks you what information you would like displayed with the Gantt bars (see Figure 7.5). You can elect to display resources and dates, resources, dates, or none. A Custom Task Information radio button is also available that allows you to select additional text to display with your Gantt bars. Make a selection and click the Next button.

5. The next screen displays the Format It button. Click the button and the Gantt Chart will be formatted according to the choices you've made. When the final screen of the Wizard appears, click the Exit Wizard button to finish the process.

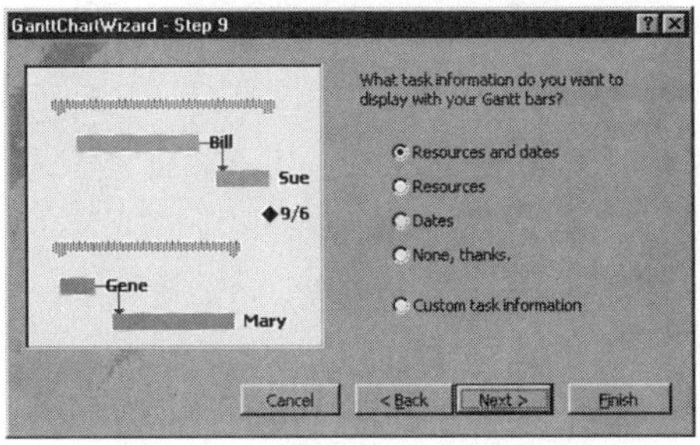

FIGURE 7.5

The Gantt Chart Wizard walks you through the formatting steps of your Gantt Chart, including the text you want to display with the Gantt bars.

GanttChartWizard - Step 9

What task information do you want to display with your Gantt bars?

- ○ Resources and dates
- ○ Resources
- ○ Dates
- ○ None, thanks.
- ○ Custom task information

Bill
Sue
♦ 9/6
Gene
Mary

Cancel   < Back   Next >   Finish

Your Gantt Chart will display the formatting attributes you chose using the Wizard. If you don't like the way the chart is formatted, you can rerun the Wizard or make changes to the formatting by using the techniques described in the following sections.

Using the Bar Styles Options

You can also change the way the bars are displayed in your Gantt Charts. You can change the bars for all the tasks, or just format the bars for a category of tasks, such as milestones or critical tasks.

> You can also format a bar for a specific task in the Gantt Chart. Select the task name in the Task Name field, click Format, and then click Bar. Select the Bars tab. You can choose shapes, patterns, or colors for the bar in the Start Shape, Middle Bar, and End Shape drop-down boxes.

To Do: Formatting Gantt Chart Bar Styles

To format Gantt Chart bar styles, follow these steps:

▼ To Do

1. Make sure you are in the Gantt Chart view, and choose Format, Bar Styles. The Bar Styles dialog box appears.

2. In the table at the top of the dialog box, select the category row (such as Summary) you want to change, as shown in Figure 7.6.

3. Under the Start Shape, Middle Bar, and End Shape sections, select shapes, patterns or types, and colors for the bar.

   Some of the task categories, such as Milestone and Task, have only a start shape for their bar. Others, like Summary Task, have a start shape, middle bar, and end shape.

▼

7

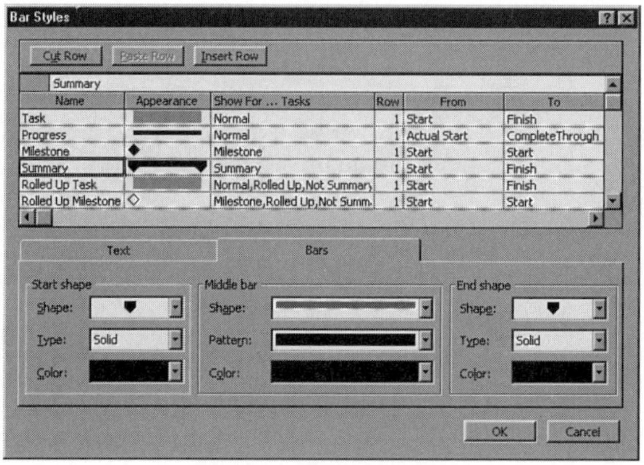

▼

FIGURE 7.6

The Bar Styles dialog box allows you to change the look of the task bars (by category) that appear on the Gantt Chart.

4. After you have completed your changes, click the OK button to close the dialog
▲   box. The bar changes you have made will appear on the Gantt Chart.

The Rollup Views

Using rollup views gives you another strategy for emphasizing and de-emphasizing items in the Gantt Chart and the tasks sheet that accompanies it. You can apply rollup views to the tasks sheet items and the different bars on the Gantt Chart.

If you have divided your project into summary tasks, you can expand and contract the subtasks they consist of. Select a summary task in the Task Name field.

To show the subtasks, click the Show Subtasks button on the Project Formatting toolbar. To hide the subtasks, click the Hide Subtasks button. Showing and hiding subtasks affect your view of their name in the task sheet and their bars on the Gantt Chart.

You can also expand and contract the subtasks for a summary task by using the outline symbol that appears to the left of the summary task name in the Task Name field. When this button displays a plus sign (+), click it to show the subtasks.

Adding Graphics and Text to Gantt Charts

Microsoft Project has several drawing tools you can use to enhance your Gantt Charts. You can add graphics, such as arrows and rectangles, to highlight tasks on the chart. You can also add free text to the Gantt Chart that provides additional information or notes for a particular task or group of tasks.

Introducing the Drawing Toolbar

To add the Drawing toolbar to the toolbars currently displayed, right-click on any toolbar and select Drawing from the shortcut menu that appears.

To use the buttons on the Drawing toolbar, you select a particular button and then click and drag on the Gantt Chart to create the object. The Drawing toolbar buttons and their uses are described in the following table:

Icon	Button Name	Objects
	Line	Lines without arrows
	Arrow	Lines with arrowheads
	Rectangle	Rectangles
	Oval	Circles and other elliptical graphics
	Arc	Arcs
	Polygon	Many-sided figures
	Text Box	A box containing text
	Cycle Fill Color	Allows you to change the fill color of the selected object
	Task	Opens the Format Drawing dialog box so you can change how an object is anchored to a bar on the Gantt Chart

You can use the Shift+click technique to enhance the drawing of a rectangle, oval, arc, or text box. Holding down the Shift key as you drag draws a perfect object, such as a perfect square or perfect circle.

The extraneous first button on the Drawing toolbar is a drop-down list. It contains tools you can use to arrange and edit the objects that you draw with the other buttons. You must select an object before these options are available.

7

- *Bring to Front.* Brings the selected object to the forefront if other objects currently overlay it

- *Send to Back.* Sends an object to the very back of the currently overlaying objects

- *Bring Forward.* Moves the object forward one object at a time in a group of overlaying items

- *Send Backward.* Moves an object behind overlaying items, one object at a time

- *Edit Points.* Allows you to edit the shape of a polygon

Working with Drawing Objects in the Gantt Chart View

To draw a particular item on the Gantt Chart, click the appropriate button and drag to create the object. The item will be attached to the date on the timescale where you draw it. When you move an item, it will attach to the date on the timescale at the new position.

To attach an item to a task, open the Format Drawing dialog box by double-clicking on the object or by selecting the object and clicking the Attach to Task button.

In the Format Drawing dialog box, you must place the ID number for the task (in the **ID:** box) that you want to attach the object to (the ID numbers are in the ID column on the Gantt sheet). You can also select where the object is connected to the Gantt bar for the task (either the beginning or end of the taskbar). Figure 7.7 shows the Format Drawing dialog box. The Line & Fill tab of this dialog box also allows you to control the line style and color, and the fill pattern and color for the object.

FIGURE 7.7

The Format Drawing dialog box allows you to attach an object to a taskbar and to change the look of the object.

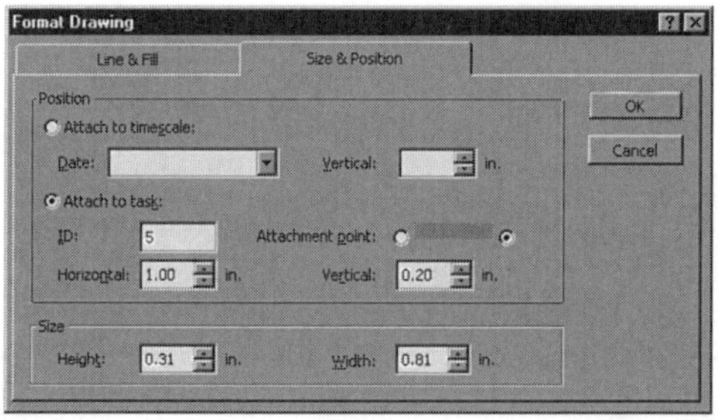

You can also easily remove or hide the objects that you place on the Gantt Chart. Select an object and then press the Delete key to remove it. You can hide the objects on the Gantt Chart by choosing Format, Layout. In the Layout dialog box, clear the Show Drawing check box. Click OK to close the dialog box.

Placing Free Text on the Gantt Chart

Place free text on the Gantt Chart by using the Text box button. When you create the text box, a insertion point appears in the box. Type the text you want to appear in the text box.

Double-click on the text box to edit the settings in the Format Drawing dialog box. You can attach the text box to a particular date on the timeline or to a task bar on the chart. If you want to edit the text in a box, select the text box and then drag to select the text. Type in new text or edit the current entry.

If you want to change the text font, select the text in the box and then click the various formatting options on the Formatting toolbar, or choose Format, Font to open the Font dialog box. You can change any font attribute for the text box in the Font dialog box.

Special Formatting for the Calendar

Project offers several methods for changing the view of the calendar and for formatting the timescale and bars that appear on the calendar. These formatting options either use the mouse to drag a vertical or horizontal line on the calendar to a new position, or use dialog boxes opened through the Format menu. Make sure you are in the Calendar view so that you can see the results of your formatting changes.

Formatting the Timescale for the Calendar

To format the timescale for the calendar, choose Format, Timescale. The Timescale dialog box appears. This dialog box contains three tabs: Week Headings, Date Boxes, and Date Shading (see Figure 7.8).

The Week Headings tab allows you to change the calendar display by changing the Monthly, Daily, and Weekly titles for the calendar (each has its own drop-down box). You can also select to show the week with 7 or 5 days. A sample box at the bottom of the dialog box shows you the results of the changes you make.

The Date Boxes tab allows you to include additional elements in the top or bottom row of each of the individual date boxes. You can include Overflow indicators that appear when all the tasks for a given day cannot be displayed in the Calendars date box. Other options include drop-down boxes for the pattern and color of these additional elements.

7

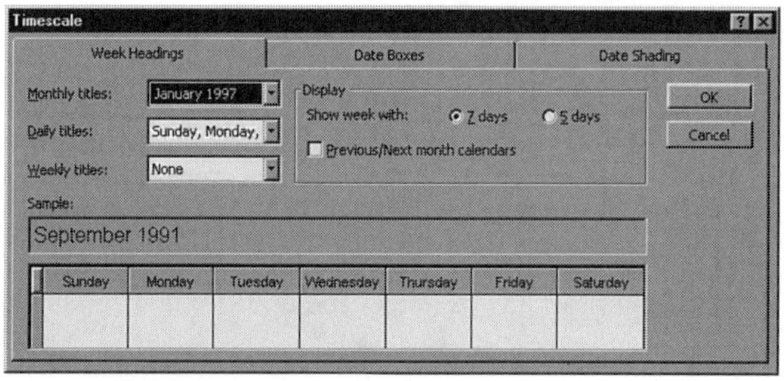

FIGURE 7.8

The Timescale dialog box allows you to change the display settings for the Calendar timescale, include special timescale elements, and use shading to indicate working and nonworking days in the schedule.

Selecting Calendar Bar Styles Options

You can also control the formatting of the bars on the Calendar. In the Calendar view, choose Format, Bar Styles to open the Bar Styles dialog box.

A Task Type box allows you to select the category of bars that you will change the formatting for. Drop-down boxes for Bar Type, Pattern, Color, and Split Pattern give you access to the different formatting options for the bars. Check boxes are also included for Shadow and Bar Rounding.

A Text Box area in the dialog box allows you to choose fields that will be displayed inside the bars. For instance, you might want to include the Actual Cost field in the Milestone task bars to see the dollar amount cost for a particular task on the Calendar.

> You cannot add fields to Summary bars. However, you can add fields, such as Actual Cost, to the various subtask bars making up a Summary task.

After you have made your bar style formatting selection, click the OK button in the Bar Styles dialog box. The changes you have made to the various bar categories will appear on the Calendar.

Setting the Layout Options for the Calendar View

You can also set certain layout options for the Calendar. Choose Format, Layout to open the Layout dialog box, which gives you the following options:

- *Use Current Sort Order radio button.* This button allows you to toggle the current sort order for the Calendar view. The default sort view for the Calendar is ascending by the ID field.

- *Attempt To Fit As Many Tasks As Possible radio button.* The Calendar shows as many tasks as it can in the week rows without overlapping the task bars.
- *Show Bar Splits check box.* Selecting this check box will show split task bars in the Calendar. This setting is on by default.
- *Automatic Layout check box.* The Calendar adjusts the available space to show new tasks that you add to the task list. The check box toggles this feature.

Special Formatting for the PERT Chart

Some special formatting options are available for the PERT Chart view of your project, too. You can rearrange the PERT task boxes, change the borders of the boxes, and zoom in and out to change your perspective in relation to the entire project.

NEW TERM **PERT Chart**   The *PERT Chart* view displays tasks and task dependencies as a flowchart. A box (sometimes called a "node") represents each task, and a line connecting two boxes represents the dependency between the two tasks.

Reviewing the Format Options for the PERT Chart

The PERT Chart Format menu options consist of Text Styles, Box Styles, Layout, and Layout Now. You have already worked with the Text Styles dialog box earlier in this Hour.

The Box Styles dialog box (choose Format, Box Styles) allows you to change the box style and color by using drop-down boxes. It consists of two tabs: Borders and Boxes.

On the Borders tab, to change the box border style or color for a particular category of tasks (Critical, Noncritical, Critical Summary, Noncritical Summary, and so forth), choose the task category in the Item To Change list. After you choose the task category, use the Style and Color boxes as desired. To put your format changes into effect, click OK.

NEW TERM **Critical Task**   A *critical task* must be completed before the next task can be started. A noncritical task does not have to be completed before the next task in the timeline is begun.

NEW TERM **Critical Summary**   A summary task is made up of a set of subtasks. A *critical summary* task is a set of subtasks that must be completed before the next critical task on the timeline can be started. A noncritical summary task contains subtasks that do not affect the start time of the next task in the project.

The Boxes tab allows you to control the size of a particular node and what is displayed in it by using a number of drop-down boxes.

7

Five drop-down boxes are allocated for the field information that appears in the task boxes. The default selections show the Name, ID, Duration, and the task's Start and End dates (see Figure 7.9). You can change any of the default selections. For instance, you can replace the Name field with a Linked Fields or Notes field. The Duration field can be replaced with the % Work Complete or the Actual Cost field. You can even choose to show fewer than five fields in the node, if you like.

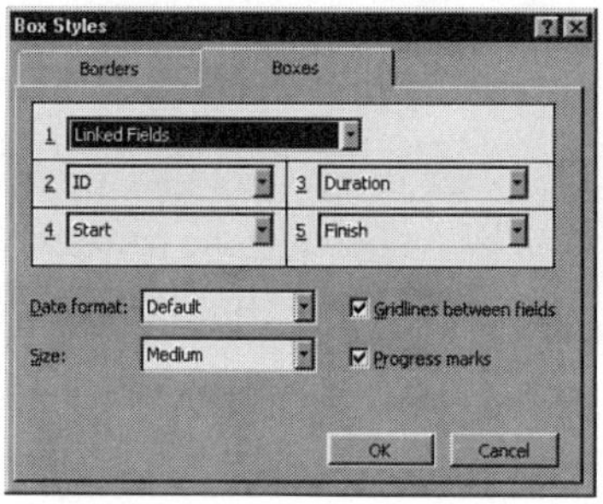

FIGURE 7.9

The Box Styles dialog box allows you to format the look of the node boxes as well as the fields displayed in them.

A **D**ate Format drop-down box and a **S**ize drop-down box are also available that allow you to change the format of the date and to size the node box (smallest, small, medium, or large). Check boxes for **G**ridlines Between Fields and **P**rogress Marks allow you to toggle these features.

Selecting Layout Options

You can also control the layout of the links between the task boxes and whether the arrows show on the links. Choose F**o**rmat, **L**ayout to open the Layout dialog box. You are given two layouts for the links between the tasks: straight lines or right-angled lines. Check boxes for Show Arrows, Show Page Breaks, and Adjust For Page Breaks are also available in the Layout dialog box. After you make your selections, click OK to close the dialog box.

When you are ready to redraw the PERT Chart using your new layout, choose Format, Layout Now. Your changes will be put into effect on the PERT Chart. You can remove the changes, if you want, by clicking the Undo button on the Standard toolbar.

Using the Zoom Command

You can also use the Zoom command to change your view of the information shown in the PERT Chart. When you use the Zoom command, you are increasing (Zoom out) or decreasing (Zoom in) the timescale in which your information is displayed.

To change the zoom percentage for your view of the PERT Chart, choose View, Zoom to open the Zoom dialog box. Radio buttons are available that allow you to zoom from 200% to the entire project. A Custom radio button and a percentage indicator allow you to select custom zoom percentages. After you've selected the zoom percentage, click OK. To return to the previous zoom percentage, open the Zoom dialog box and make the appropriate selection.

7

HOUR 8

Finalizing and Printing Your Schedule

Now that you have created the task list, established the dependency links between tasks, and explored the most popular task views, it's a good time to print your schedule. There are several choices when printing the project data. You can print the data as it appears in a view—such as the Gantt Chart, PERT Chart, or Calendar views. On the other hand, you can print one of the 22 predesigned reports in Microsoft Project. These reports often consolidate the data or include calculations, which can help you analyze your schedule.

This hour concentrates on printing views and reports that focus on the project tasks. You will learn how to check your task list for spelling errors, set layout and print options for views, and explore the built-in reports. Hour 15, "Printing Views and Reports with Resources," explains how to print views and reports that focus on your project resources.

Checking for Spelling Errors

Before you print a schedule or report, you should spell check the project file. Nothing is more embarrassing than handing a report or printout to a boss or client with misspelled words! The spell checker verifies the spelling of your list of task names and any notes you have added to a task.

Using the Spelling Command

If you have used the spelling feature in other Windows programs, you will be right at home using it in Project 98. To access the spell check feature, click the Spelling button on the Standard toolbar or choose **T**ools, **S**pelling from the menu. The Spelling dialog box (shown in Figure 8.1) appears when Project can't find a word in its internal dictionary.

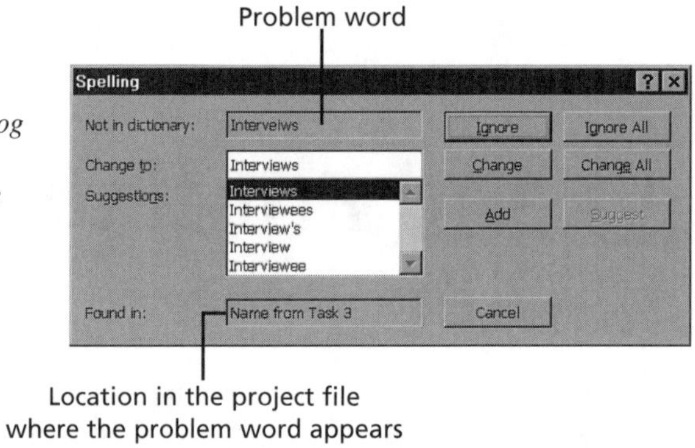

FIGURE 8.1

Use the Spelling dialog box to decide how to treat words not in the internal dictionary.

Problem word

Location in the project file
where the problem word appears

The first word not found in the dictionary is listed in the box at the top of the Spelling dialog box. In Figure 8.1, the problem word is *Interveiws*. The Change **T**o box proposes the most likely correction to the problem word. A list of possible variations on the problem word is displayed in the Suggestions box. You can accept the proposed correction, select one of the alternative words, or type in a correction in the Change **T**o box.

Table 8.1 describes the uses of the buttons on the right side of the Spelling dialog box.

TABLE 8.1. THE SPELLING DIALOG BOX OPTION BUTTONS

Button	Description
Ignore	Ignores this occurrence of the word.
Ignore All	Ignores all occurrences of the word found in this file.
Change	Replaces only this occurrence of the problem word with the word you select or type in.

Button	Description
Change All	Replaces all occurrences of the problem word found in this file.
Add	Adds the word listed in the Not In Dictionary box to the custom user dictionary. The spell checker will ignore this word if found again in this or any other file.
Suggest	By default, the spell checker is set to always offer spelling suggestions. You can change this setting so that you see a list of suggestions only when you click the **S**uggest button. To change the default setting, choose **T**ools, **O**ptions from the menu.

Setting the Spelling Options

There are several options you can set for spell checking in Microsoft Project. To access these settings, choose **T**ools, **O**ptions and select the Spelling tab. The Spelling tab, shown in Figure 8.2, lists the fields that are checked when you activate the spell checker.

FIGURE 8.2

You can modify the field and spelling settings from the Spelling tab in the Options dialog box.

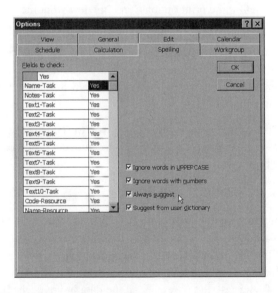

In addition to selecting the fields that should be checked for misspelled words, there are four settings you can turn off or on to control the way Project checks the spelling, listed in Table 8.2.

TABLE 8.2. THE SPELLING SETTINGS IN THE OPTIONS DIALOG BOX

Setting	Description
Ignore Words In UPPERCASE	Ignores acronyms in all capital letters, such as IBM, AFB, or NYSE. Turn this setting off if you enter all text in capital letters.
Ignore Words With Numbers	Ignores words that contain both letters and numbers.
Always Suggest	Displays spelling suggestions in the Spelling dialog box.
Suggest From User Dictionary	Checks problem words against words added to the custom user dictionary, as well as the main dictionary.

Printing Views

One way to share your project task list with others is to print a task view, such as the Gantt Chart, PERT, or Calendar. Before you print a view, however, it's important that you prepare the view, set up the print options, and preview what the printout will look like.

As in all Windows applications, the print commands are located on the File menu. The Page Setup command defines page orientation, headers, footers, and so on, for printed views. The Print Preview and Print commands are used to print views. In addition to using the File menu, you can access the Print Preview and Print commands through buttons on the Standard toolbar.

Clicking the Print Preview button allows you to see what the printed copy will look like and also gives you access to the page setup and print commands. You should always preview before you print.

Preparing the View for Printing

The first step in preparing the project view for printing is to select the view you want to print. Choosing which view to print largely depends on which view you think others can easily follow. After the desired view is displayed onscreen, you can modify the project data so that it looks just as you want it to when printed. Although you might be seeing only a portion of your task list onscreen, all the data in your schedule will be printed. In Hour 7, "Formatting Views," you learned how to alter the appearance of the task list by using the buttons on the Formatting toolbar and through commands on the Format menu.

Options in the Format menu vary, depending on which view is displayed. In most task views, you can format the task names and other text to accentuate one or more tasks. In the Gantt Chart and Calendar views, there are a wide range of formatting options for the task bars. In the Timescale dialog box in the Calendar view, you can change the number of days per week displayed and control shading options. The PERT Chart view allows you to select the box and linking line styles for the task nodes. In the Task Usage view, you can choose the level of details displayed in the timescale side of the view.

 The timescale increments in the Gantt Chart and Task Usage views can be in minutes, hours, days, weeks, months, quarters, or years. To quickly adjust the timescale increments, use the Zoom In or Zoom Out buttons on the Standard toolbar.

 Using the Zoom In or Zoom Out buttons in the Calendar view has no impact on what is printed. Each month is printed on a separate page.

If you want the printed view to display only a subset of tasks in the project, you might want to apply a filter to the task list. Refer to Hour 14, "Optimizing the Project Plan," for descriptions and examples of filters available in Microsoft Project.

Page breaks are automatically determined when a view is printed. In the Gantt Chart and Task Usage views, you can set the page breaks manually instead of using the default page breaks. In the PERT Chart view, you can move the task node boxes to place tasks on specific pages. Sections later in this hour describe exactly how to insert your own page breaks.

Changing the Page Setup

In addition to making changes to how the view is displayed onscreen, you need to select options for how the data will appear on the printed page. Page margins, orientation, headers, footers, and the legend can all be modified. Separate print options can be set for each view or report. For example, adding or changing a header for Gantt Charts does not change the header for PERT Charts. The next time you print the Gantt Chart view, the print options previously set for it are automatically included. However, the print settings are saved only with the active project file. When you print the Gantt Chart view using another project file, you need to select the print options for the view in the other file. This allows you to establish unique print options in each file.

To change the print settings for the active view, choose File, Page Setup to display the Page Setup dialog box for the active view. Figure 8.3 shows the Page tab of the Page Setup dialog box for the Gantt Chart view.

 There are some views that you cannot print. If the File, Page Setup command is not available, the active view can't be printed.

8

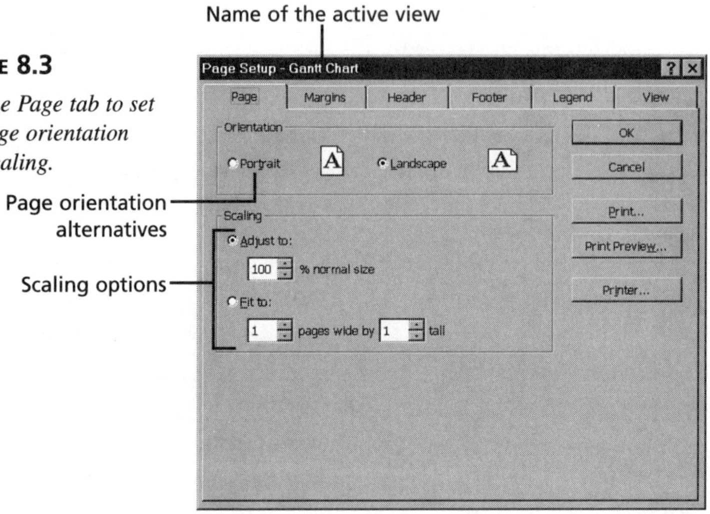

FIGURE 8.3

Use the Page tab to set the page orientation and scaling.

Name of the active view

Page orientation alternatives

Scaling options

As with other dialog boxes, the Page Setup dialog box has multiple tabs, each one representing a different collection of settings. Table 8.3 describes the print settings on each tab.

TABLE 8.3. THE PAGE SETUP DIALOG BOX PRINT OPTIONS

Tab	Options
Page	Choose a Portrait or Landscape page orientation. Enlarge or reduce the scale of view by a specified percentage or by a given number of pages.
Margins	Select the top, bottom, left, and right margins. Microsoft Project prints with a quarter (.25) inch margin, even if you reduce the margin to zero (0). Borders can surround the page and separate the printed view from the header, footer, and legend. By default, borders are printed with every page. The Outer Pages option is available only with the PERT Chart view.
Header/Footer	Headers or footers that you want to appear on every printed page can be aligned on the left, center, or right side of the page. Buttons and a drop-down list are used to insert system codes in the header and footer areas.
Legend	If a printed view can have a legend, you can place text in the lower-left corner of the legend area. You can have up to three lines of text inside this area. Some views contain a default legend text consisting of the project title and the current date. The Width option controls the horizontal size of the legend text area, with the maximum width being 5 inches (or half the legend area in landscape

Tab	Options
	orientation). The buttons and drop-down list are used to insert system codes into the legend text area. The legend can appear at the bottom of every printed page or on its own separate page, or you can choose not to print a legend.
View	This tab displays options specific to the active view being printed. Some options on the View tab might be unavailable (dimmed), depending on the view being printed. Descriptions of the options on the View tab are described later in this Hour in sections devoted to printing each view.

Understanding Headers and Footers

On the Header and Footer tabs of the Page Setup dialog box are seven buttons and a drop-down list that can be used to format text, insert system codes, or insert graphic images into the header or footer. A sample of the header or footer as currently defined is displayed in the top portion of the dialog box. There are no default headers. You can have up to five lines of header text. Most views have a default footer for the printed page number located on the center alignment tab. You can have three lines of footer text. Figure 8.4 shows an example of a header with the Project Title, Company, and Project Manager displayed in the upper-left corner of each printed page. The text has been formatted by using the Font button.

FIGURE 8.4

The Header tab of the Page Setup dialog box.

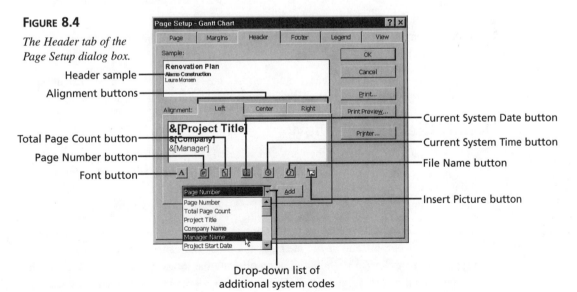

Header sample

Alignment buttons

Total Page Count button

Page Number button

Font button

Current System Date button

Current System Time button

File Name button

Insert Picture button

Drop-down list of
additional system codes

Headers and footers can be placed on one or more of the Alignment tabs. You can type in text or insert system codes using one of the buttons or the drop-down menu. Many of the system codes insert data that appears in the Properties dialog box (**File**, **Properties**).

> When printing draft copies, it's extremely useful if you put the filename and view name on your printouts. This will help to remind you exactly what was printed. Additionally, you should place the system date and system time on printouts to record the day and time the draft was printed. This will ensure you're working with the very latest copy.

To Do: Entering a Header or Footer

To enter a header or footer, follow these steps:

1. Select either the Header or Footer tab.
2. Choose the desired Alignment tab.
3. Use the box below the Alignment tabs to type the appropriate text you want to appear on the header or footer.

   Or, choose one of the buttons or items from the drop-down list to insert a system code. If you use one of the items in the drop-down list, click the **Add** button to insert the information into the header or footer.
4. To format any of the text or codes in the header or footer, highlight the text or code and use the Font button.

After you have established the page setup options, the settings become a permanent part of the view in that project file. However, you may change the settings at any time.

Using the Print Preview

After you have formatted the view and selected the page setup options you want, it's a good idea to preview what the printout will look like before you actually print the view. You can choose **File**, **Print Preview** or click the Print Preview button on the Standard toolbar. Figure 8.5 shows the Print Preview screen.

If multiple pages exist, you can use the buttons at the top left of the Print Preview screen to display left, right, up, and down one page at a time. You can zoom in on the details of a page by clicking the Zoom In button or by clicking the mouse pointer on the part of the page you want to see in greater detail. Click again to zoom out. Additionally, you can view multiple pages in the Print Preview screen. Figure 8.6 shows the multi-page view of a Gantt Chart.

8

Move down one page
Move up one page
Move right one page
Move left one page

Zoom in
View one full page
View multiple pages

Display the Page Setup dialog box

Display the Print dialog box

Close the Print Preview screen

Display help on using the Print Preview screen

FIGURE 8.5

The initial Print Preview screen shows the entire first page of the view to be printed.

Mouse pointer for zooming in

Legend text

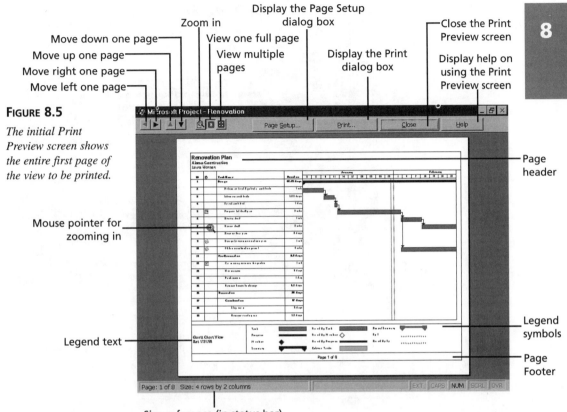

Page header

Legend symbols

Page Footer

Size reference (in status bar)

In this example, the size of the printout is 4 rows by 2 columns. Pages are numbered down the columns, starting from the left. Page 4 of the report is the bottom page in the left column in this example of the Print Preview screen.

From the Print Preview screen, click the Page Setup button to open the Page Setup dialog box. The Help button displays information about using the Print Preview screen. When you are ready to print, click the Print button to display the Print dialog box. To make changes to the view, or if you decide not to print at this time, click the Close button to display the project view.

Using the Print Command

When you have formatted the view onscreen and the page setup and printer options are selected, the final step is to print the view. Choose File, Print and the Print dialog box shows you choices for printing the current screen view (see Figure 8.7). You can also click the Print button from the Print Preview screen to open the Print dialog box.

FIGURE 8.6

The multi-page view of a Gantt Chart in the Print Preview screen helps you see how your pages will fit together.

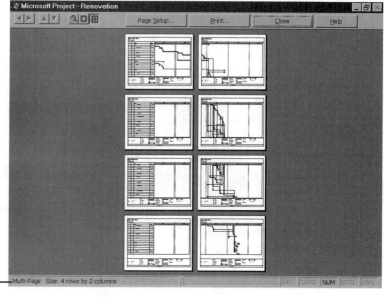

Status line indicates the number of pages that will print

 The Print button on the Standard toolbar causes data to be sent to the printer immediately; you don't get a chance to make selections in the Print dialog box.

FIGURE 8.7

Some options in the Print dialog box do not apply to all views and may be dimmed (meaning inactive).

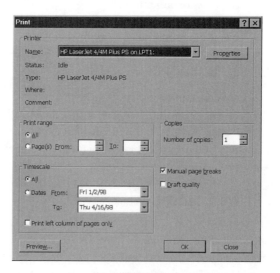

The default printer appears in the Name drop-down list. You can select an alternative printer if necessary. The printer Properties include selecting legal or letter size paper, selecting a paper feeder source, and changing the resolution of graphics objects.

Unless you specify otherwise, all pages shown in the Print Preview screen will print. To print only a few pages, select the Page(s) From and To options in the Print Range area, and type the page numbers you want to print.

By default, the view prints all the information from the start date of the project through the finish date. You can limit the printed output to a specific time span. Another option is to print only the pages on the far left side of the multi-page Print Preview screen. Use the Preview button to verify which pages are included in the left column.

After you have selected the print settings, click OK to start printing the view.

Printing Gantt Charts

When printing the Gantt Chart view, check the following items before you print:

- Make sure the columns you want printed are visible onscreen. The rightmost column that's completely visible in the table side of the Gantt Chart is the last column of the table that will be printed, unless you select Print All Sheet Columns on the View tab of the Page Setup dialog box.

- The increment displayed in the timescale will be the increment printed. Use the Zoom In and Zoom Out buttons or the Format, Timescale command to change the timescale increment.

- You can force a page break when printing a task list so that a new page starts at a specific task, even if the automatic page break doesn't occur until farther down the list.

To Do: Setting a Page Break

To set a page break, follow these steps:

1. Select any cell in the row just below the intended page break. This row becomes the first row on a new page.

2. Choose Insert, Page Break. A dashed line appears above the selected row to indicate the presence of a manually inserted page break.

   To remove a page break, select any cell in the row just below the page break dotted line and choose Insert, Remove Page Break.

The page break settings are tied to the view that is active when you set the page break. Even if part of the task list has been collapsed to hide detail tasks, a new page starts at the task where the page break was set.

Gantt Chart Page Setup Options

The Page Setup dialog box includes a set of options specific to the view you're printing. Figure 8.8 shows the View tab in the Page Setup dialog box. To display the Page Setup dialog box choose **F**ile, Page Set**u**p, or click the Page Setup button in the Print Preview screen.

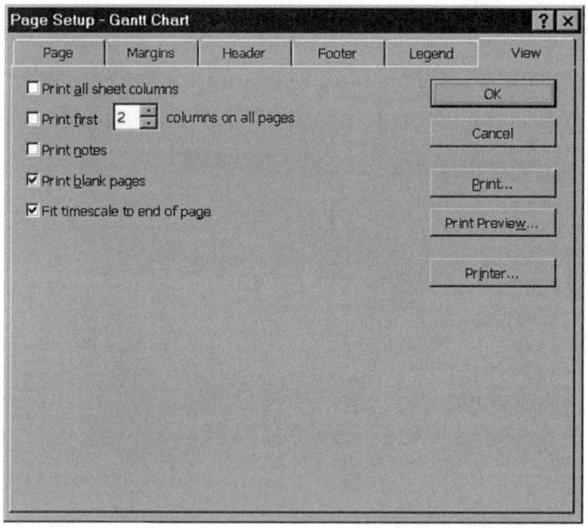

FIGURE 8.8

The View tab in the Page Setup dialog box.

These are the View options in the Page Setup dialog box for the Gantt Chart view:

- Print **A**ll Sheet Columns. Prints all columns of the Gantt Chart table, regardless of whether they are completely visible on the screen.
- Print **F**irst # Columns On All Pages. Prints the specified number of columns on all pages. Figure 8.9 shows a preview of the Gantt Chart view with the default setting, which prints only the visible sheet columns. Printing several columns on all pages makes it easier to determine the task that corresponds to each bar. Remember that the ID number and Indicator columns count as two of the columns.
- Print **N**otes. Prints the task notes on a separate page.
- Print **B**lank Pages. Uncheck to suppress the printing of blank pages. The default is for all pages to print. In Figure 8.9, the last page in the middle column does not contain any sheet columns or task bars; it's a blank page. When this setting is unchecked, blank pages appear grayed out in the preview screen.
- Fit Timescale to Pa**g**e. Leave the box checked to ensure that the timescale extends all the way to the right page margin.

FIGURE 8.9

Preview of a project in the Gantt Chart view.

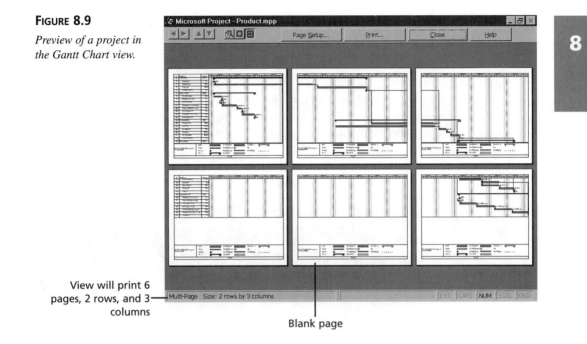

8

View will print 6 pages, 2 rows, and 3 columns

Blank page

Printing PERT Charts

When printing the PERT Chart view, check the following items before you print:

- You have a choice on the Margins tab of the Page Setup dialog box as to what type of borders you want to be printed. The default is to print borders only around the **O**uter Pages. To enclose each page in a lined border, choose **E**very Page. To suppress all borders, choose **N**one. Previewing the PERT Chart and clicking the Multiple Pages button is the best way to see the effect of changing the border options. Figure 8.10 shows the preview of the PERT Chart view.

- When you print the PERT Chart view, you have the option of printing or suppressing the blank pages. Figure 8.10 shows several blank pages that will be printed. Uncheck the Print Blank Pages option on the View tab of the Page Setup dialog box (see Figure 8.11) to suppress the printing of blank pages.

- The way in which the PERT Chart diagrams the linking lines between tasks can be adjusted through the F**o**rmat, **L**ayout command. The lines can be drawn using just straight horizontal and vertical lines at right angles, or with diagonal lines.

- In PERT Charts, page breaks are automatically displayed, but you might have to zoom out to see them. You can't change the page breaks on the PERT Chart, but you can move the task nodes to either side of the automatic page breaks or use scaling (located on the Page tab of the Page Setup dialog box) to shrink the number of printed pages. When you scale the display, the Adjust For Page Breaks option under the Layout command on the Format menu automatically moves nodes to the right and down if the nodes land on a page break. Use the Format, Layout Now command to see the result.

If you move a group of nodes simultaneously, the nodes retain positions in relation to each other as you move them. The linking lines also follow task nodes to the new locations. See Hour 6, "Working with the Other Task Views," for more information on moving task nodes.

Multiple Pages button

FIGURE 8.10

A preview of the PERT Chart view.

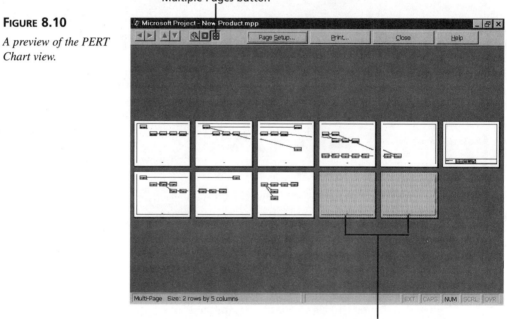

Blank pages

Printing Calendars

When printing the Calendar view, each month prints on a separate page by default. The View tab in the Page Setup dialog box includes a set of options that control what's printed (see Figure 8.12). You can change the default settings to print 2 months per page or set the number of weeks to print per page. To open the Page Setup dialog box, choose File, Page Setup or click the Page Setup button in the Print Preview screen.

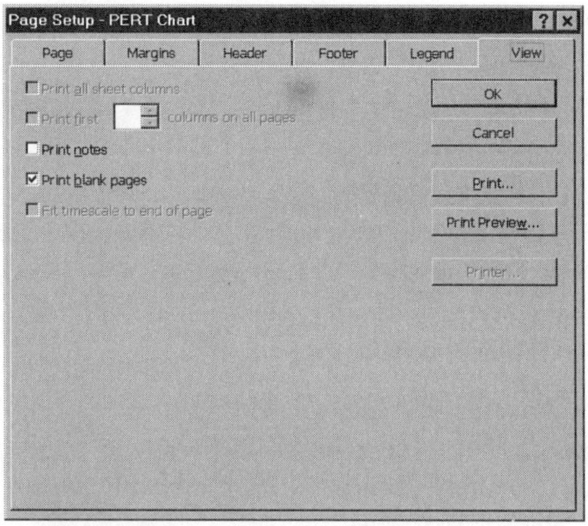

FIGURE 8.11

*PERT Chart options
on the View tab in the
Page Setup dialog box.*

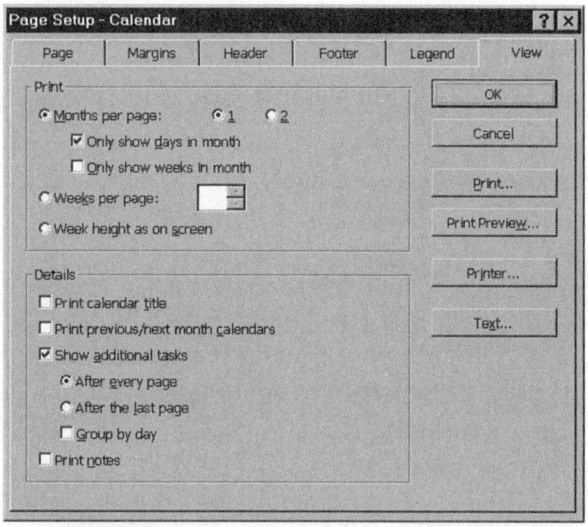

FIGURE 8.12

*The View tab of the
Page Setup dialog box,
for the Calendar view.*

The View options in the Page Setup dialog box for the Calendar view are

- **Months Per Page.** Choose to print 1 or 2 months on each page. The Only Show Days in Month option doesn't display the dates or tasks in other months on the printed calendar. If the Only Show Weeks in Month option is unchecked, 6 weeks will print, starting from the first of each month.

- **Weeks Per Page.** Type the number of weeks to print in the entry box. This option is very useful if you have many tasks and want to print one or two weeks on a page.

- **Week Height As On Screen.** Use this option if you want the printed calendar to match the week height on the screen display of the Calendar view.

- Print Calendar Title. At the top of each page, the name of the month or the span of weeks is printed.

- Print Previous/Next Month Calendars. Miniature calendars of the previous and next month appear at the top of the page.

- Show Additional Tasks. Use this option when more tasks exist than can be displayed on the calendar. You have the choice of printing these overflow tasks with the After Every Page or After The Last Page options. The Group By Day check box displays the overflow page by date with the tasks listed underneath every date the task is being worked on. The default grouping is by task.

- Print Notes. Prints the task notes on a separate page.

- The Text button. Allows you to format the font type; font style, size, and color for all printed text; monthly titles; previous/next month miniature calendars; or overflow tasks.

Printing the Overview Reports

Of the 22 predesigned reports in Microsoft Project, the Overview category contains the best set of purely task-oriented reports. To access these reports, choose View, Reports and double-click on Overview to open the Overview Reports dialog box, shown in Figure 8.13.

When you double-click a report, it's displayed in the Print Preview screen. From there, you can access the Page Setup and Print dialog boxes. The Print Preview screen, Page Setup dialog box, and Print dialog box options are used the same way for reports as for views, discussed in earlier sections of this Hour. Because of the nature of the reports, some of the Page Setup and Print options might not be available.

FIGURE 8.13

The built-in reports in the Overview category.

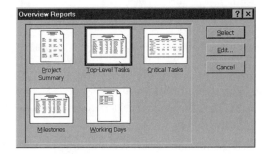

The Top-Level Tasks Report

The Top-Level Tasks report shows the highest level summary tasks in a task list. Use this report to focus on the major phases of your project. For each summary task, the ID,

Indicators, Task Name, Duration, Start, Finish, Percent Complete, Cost, and Work are printed. Figure 8.14 shows a sample of this report.

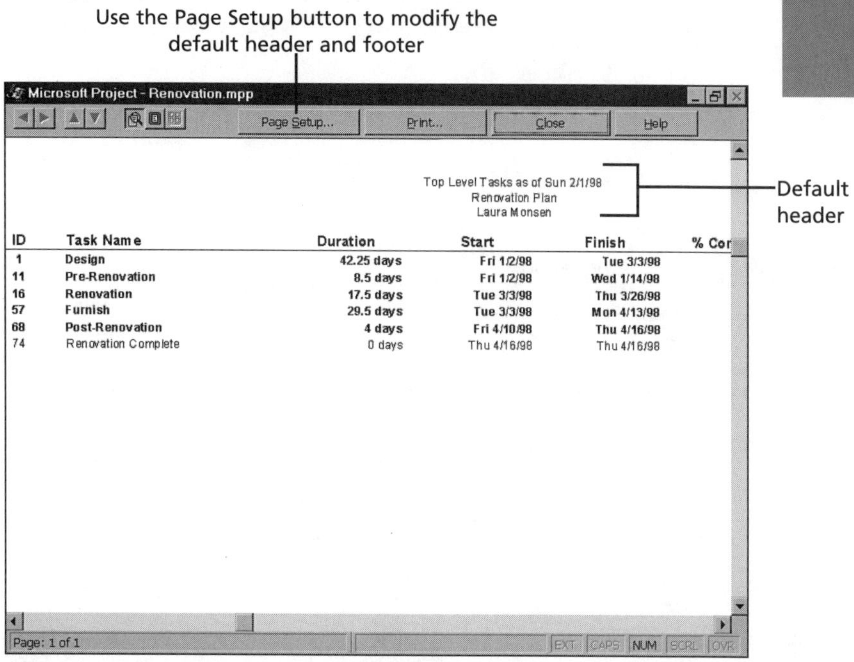

Use the Page Setup button to modify the
default header and footer

FIGURE 8.14

The Top-Level Tasks report.

Default header

The Critical Tasks Report

The Critical Tasks report (see Figure 8.15) displays all the critical tasks, categorized under their summary task. For each task, the ID, Task Name, Duration, Start, Finish, Predecessors, and Resource Names are listed.

The Milestones Report

Figure 8.16 shows the Milestones report, which offers another way to focus on the major phases or turning points in a project. This report shows the ID, Task Name, Duration, Start, Finish, Predecessors, and Resource Names for all project milestones.

The Working Days Report

The Working Days report, shown in Figure 8.17, displays a list of the working and nonworking times for each base calendar used in your project. This report provides a good way to verify that the appropriate work hours have been established and that the holidays, and other nonworking times, are incorporated into your project. The information for each base calendar is printed on a separate page.

Use these buttons to see the other
pages in this report

FIGURE 8.15

*The Critical Tasks
report.*

Summary task —

Critical task —

Successor (Dependent)
task information

Constraint indicator —

Note indicator —

Note —

Status bar indicates
the number of printed pages

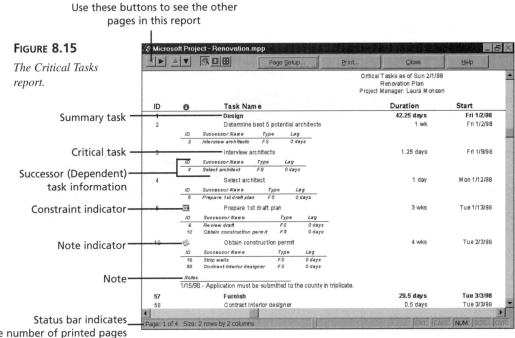

FIGURE 8.16

The Milestones report.

Note indicator —

Note —

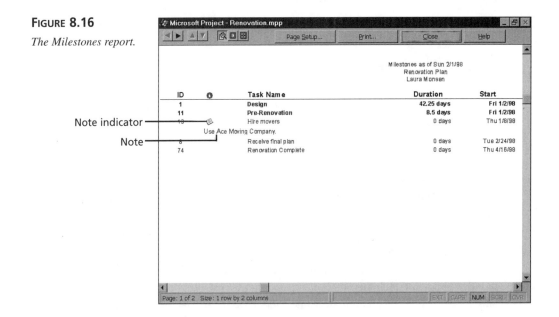

FIGURE 8.17

*The Working Days
report.*

Name of the base
calendar

Typical work days
and work hours

Nonworking or
partial working days

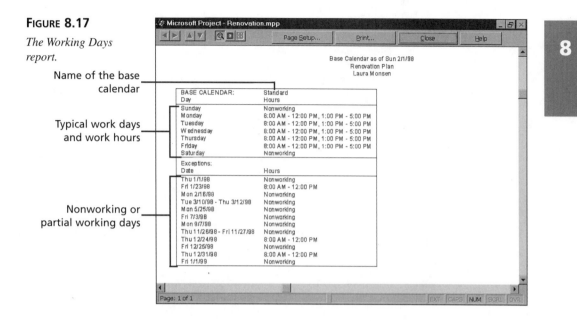

Part IV

Assigning Resources and Costs to Tasks

Hour

Hour 9

Defining Resources and Costs

In the previous hours of this book, you created your task list and organized it into a schedule of dates that shows when the project and the individual tasks will start and finish. However, you haven't yet taken into consideration these questions:

- Who is going to do the actual work, and what equipment, facilities, or materials will they need to do it? In other words, what *resources* will be needed to complete the project?

- When are they available for work on this project, and is it feasible for them to do all that your project calls for in the time you have allowed?

- What's it going to cost, and is that amount acceptable?

New Term **Resources** The *resources* for your project include the people who manage and do the work, as well as the facilities, equipment, materials, and supplies they use to complete the tasks. The people may be employees, contractors, vendors, or temporary employees. The set of resources available for working on your project is called the *resource pool*.

For the next four hours, Hours 10, "Understanding Resource Scheduling in Microsoft Project 98," through 13, "Resolving Resource Allocation Problems," you will learn how to incorporate resources and costs into the project plan to get answers to questions such as these. You rarely get to work with unlimited resources or funds, and much of project management is concerned with juggling limited resources to produce the project's output at an acceptable cost. Although adding resources and costs to the project plan requires you to devote more time to the care and feeding of the project document, it will return substantial benefits.

Improving the Accuracy of the Schedule

One of the benefits will be a far more realistic schedule of dates. If you *assign*, or allocate, individual resources to work on specific tasks and have told Project when those resources are available for work, then Project will recalculate the schedule to accommodate the working times of the assigned resources. It will schedule work on tasks around the vacations and other nonworking times you have identified for the resources. In Figure 9.1, you can be sure that the scheduled start and finish dates for each task take into account any nonworking days for the resources named next to its task bar.

New Term   **Resource Assignment**   A *resource assignment* is the result of allocating a resource's time to work on a task. You can assign resources full-time, part-time, and overtime (beyond their normal working hours). Project calculates the hours of work an assignment involves and the cost of using the resource for that many hours.

Project can help you detect when you have allocated the resource to more tasks than it can complete in the time allowed—in other words, when the resource is *overallocated*. In the resource list shown in Figure 9.2, all the overallocated resources are highlighted, but the seriously overallocated resources have an indicator as a warning. Project can help you reschedule the tasks so that resources are able to complete all the work you have assigned them.

New Term   **Resource Overallocation**   A resource is *overallocated* when it's assigned to do more work than it can complete in that time period. Most often, overallocations result from assigning resources to multiple tasks scheduled during the same time period. Hour 13 addresses the overallocation issue in more detail.

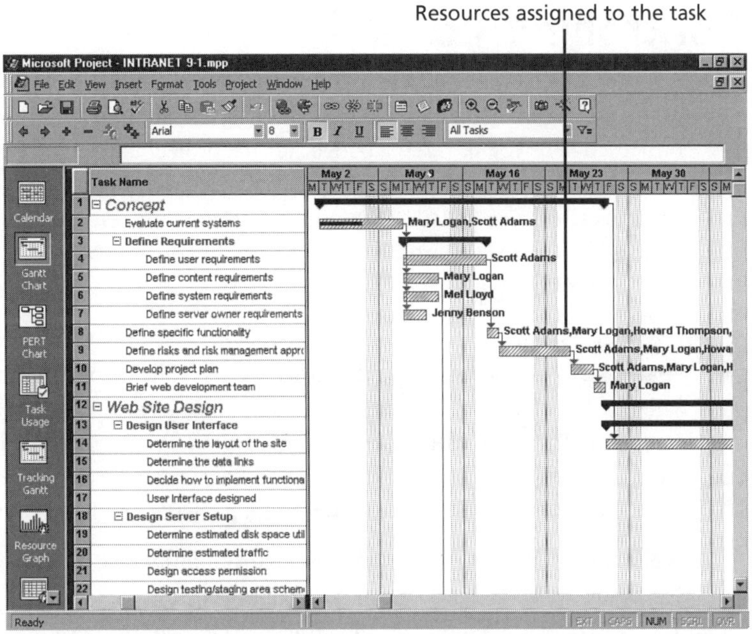

Resources assigned to the task

FIGURE 9.1

The default format for the Gantt Chart displays assigned resource names next to each task bar.

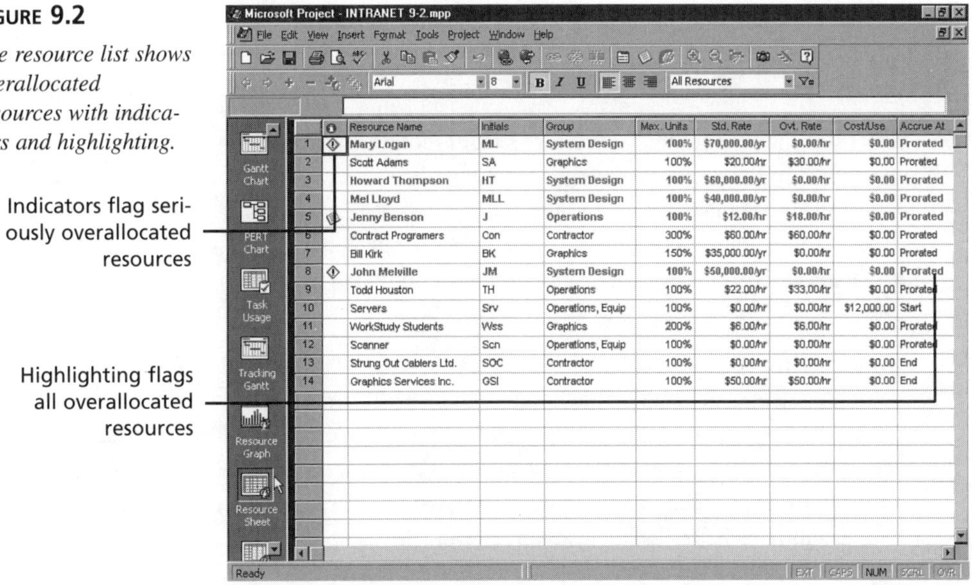

9

FIGURE 9.2

The resource list shows overallocated resources with indicators and highlighting.

Indicators flag seriously overallocated resources

Highlighting flags all overallocated resources

Controlling Costs

Another major benefit of adding resources to the project is the added help in cost control it provides. Adding resources and their costs to the project plan will allow Microsoft Project to help you develop a budget for the project and to compare the budget with the actual costs as the work on the project proceeds (see Figure 9.3). You can detect cost overruns while there's still time to take measures to correct them. And, by the time the project is complete, Microsoft Project will have accumulated the data you need to prepare your final reports.

NEW TERM   **Costs**   The *costs* of a project usually stem more from the amount of money paid for the resources that work on tasks than from anything else. These are called *resource costs*, but there can also be costs that aren't identified with specific resources. These are called *fixed costs*. Examples of fixed costs might be taxes, licensing fees, legal fees, or gifts of appreciation to the Godfather (or his governmental counterpart). *Total cost* for a task is the sum of its resource and fixed costs.

When you're planning the project, of course, the *scheduled costs* and dates for each task are entirely speculative—they're just your best estimates. The scheduled costs can be used as a planning *budget* for the project, which you can use in getting the project approved. Just before you start work on the project, save the details of the entire project plan as a *baseline*, or planned, schedule and budget for comparison later with what actually happens. (See "Setting the Baseline or Plan" in Hour 17, "Tracking Work on the Project.")

After work starts on the project, you should monitor what actually happens and enter the results in the project document—noting when tasks actually start and finish and letting Project calculate how long they actually took to complete and what the actual costs were. As you enter the *actual* dates and costs, Project automatically updates the schedule, replacing the speculative dates and costs for completed tasks with the real dates and costs.

If things haven't gone as planned (and they rarely do), Project calculates new schedule dates and estimated costs for the remaining tasks. If the completed tasks are predecessors for tasks not yet started, the dates for the unstarted tasks are recalculated based on the actual dates for their predecessors. Thus, the current schedule now shows the actual dates and cost for completed tasks; although the schedule for tasks not finished is still speculative, it will have better estimates than before.

Sometimes, you revise your estimates for unstarted tasks based on your experience thus far in the project. Microsoft Project can incorporate them into the schedule as soon as you enter them, which also improves the accuracy of the current schedule.

FIGURE 9.3

Project your budget by calculating task costs: fixed, total, baseline, actual.

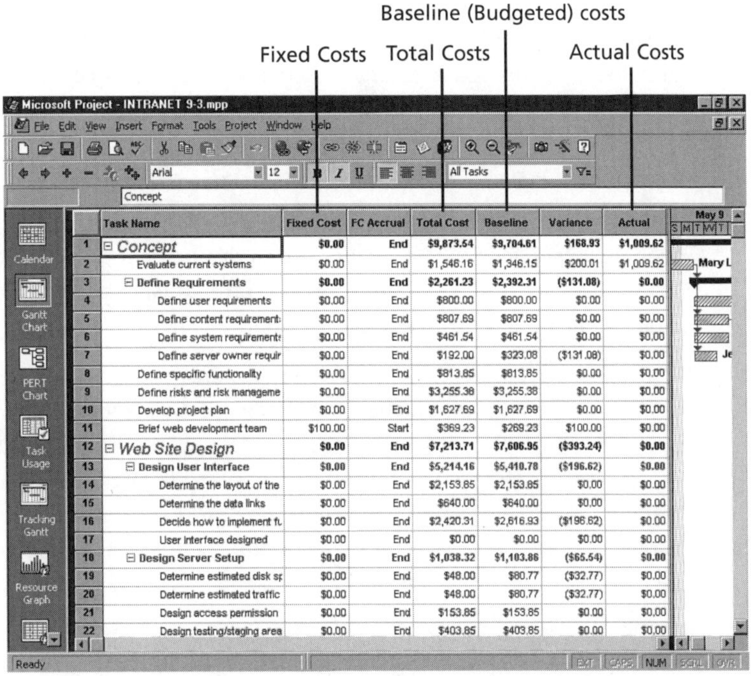

Therefore, the project schedule changes from the baseline values as you track actual performance, and you can compare the new estimates with the baseline to gauge how well you are doing. You can detect cost overruns or the possibility of not finishing on time while there's time to take corrective action. When the project is finished, you will have replaced all the estimated dates and costs with actual dates and cost. The baseline values can be compared to the final actual values to see how you did overall and what lessons can be learned for future projects.

NEW TERM **Scheduled, Budgeted, and Actual Costs** Project managers generally have to keep costs in line with a budget for the project. *Budgeted* costs are shown as *baseline* costs, and comparing the baseline and *actual* costs as the project progresses is important to cost containment.

In this hour, you learn how to create the pool of resources you will use for the project, how to define when those resources are available for work, and how much the resources cost. In the following hours, you learn how to assign individual resources to work on specific tasks and how Project then schedules the work around the availability of the assigned resources and calculates the cost of each task based on the cost of the resources that do the work.

Defining Your Resources and Costs

This section gives you a general understanding of resource and cost terms. The next section is more specific and uses the terms to define your resource pool.

Defining Resources and Their Availability

You can create a list of resources to work on your project, or you can use the resource pool already created in another project. In this hour, you learn how to create a resource pool in the current project. (You can also refer to the section "Sharing Resources Among Projects" in Hour 19, "Working with Multiple Projects.")

Many, if not most, of the names in your resource pool may be those of individual people, machines, and so forth; you have one "unit" of the resource to work with. A resource name can also represent a group of resources, as long as all members of the group have similar skills or job descriptions. For example, you might define a group of nurses in a hospital project as the Nurses resource, or a group of fork-lift trucks as the Fork-lifts resource. These are sometimes called *group resources*, but in Microsoft Project 98, they are called *resource sets*.

NEW TERM **Resource Sets**   A *resource set* is a resource name that represents a group of people or assets. You can assign several people or units from the set to the same task, but you can't specify which individuals from the group are being assigned. The members of the set all have the same pay rates and work schedules.

Resource sets represent more than one physical resource unit, and you need to let Project know how many of the units are available for assignments. A resource that represents an individual person or piece of equipment is a single unit.

NEW TERM **Resource Units**   In defining the resource pool, you enter *resource units* to define the maximum number of units of a resource that are available for assignment. This value sets a limit to the number of units of the resource that can realistically be assigned to various tasks at any one moment. When you assign resources, you specify the units assigned to that task. If you assign more units than the maximum available, Project shows an indicator next to the resource name (refer to Figure 9.2).

> The default format for resource units is the percentage format, which is covered later in this hour.

In addition to the maximum units of a resource available for assignment, you also need to indicate on the *resource calendar* the normal working days and hours for the resource and any special nonworking days (such as vacations, leaves of absence, and so forth). When you assign a resource to a task, Project uses the resource calendar to schedule the task, not the project's base calendar. We looked at base calendars in Hour 4, "Turning the Task List into a Schedule."

New Term **Resource Calendar**   A separate calendar for each resource is linked to a base calendar, so it has the same normal work days, hours, and holidays found in the base calendar. The *resource calendar* contains exceptions to the base calendar that apply only to the resource—vacation time, leave of absence, special hours, and so forth.

Defining Costs

The most common resource cost is the cost of the time the resource spends during normal working hours on a task. Project multiplies the hours of work by the hourly cost rate (the *standard rate*) you have defined for the resource to get the cost of that resource for that task. If you assign multiple resource names to a task, the sum of all the individual resource costs totals the task's resource cost. You can also define an *overtime rate* for work performed outside the normal working hours, and Project will use that rate when you assign the resource to overtime work.

New Term **Standard Rate and Overtime Rate**   The *standard rate* is the rate charged per hour of work during normal working hours for a resource. The *overtime rate* is the rate charged per hour of work outside the normal working hours.

The cost calculations described previously are designed for resources such as labor, equipment, or facilities, in which the resource cost is based on the hours of work the resource does on the task. However, for resources like material parts or supplies, you want the cost to reflect the number of resource units used, not how many hours of work are used to complete the task. These resource costs should reflect the cost per unit used (called *Per Use Cost* or *Cost/Use* in Project), not the duration of the task.

New Term **Cost/Use (Per Use Cost)**   The *Cost/Use* (or *Per Use Cost*) is a cost charged per unit of the resource used on a task. It does not change as the hours of work change. If you define a Per Use Cost for a resource, it's charged for each unit of the resource assigned to the task.

For example, when pouring a foundation in construction, there are labor costs as well as the cost of the truckloads of mixed concrete. The labor costs are determined by the wage rate (the standard rate in Project) and the hours the task takes to be completed. The concrete cost depends only on the number of loads delivered and the cost of each load (the Cost/Use in Project). For this example, the cost of a truckload of delivered concrete is entered in the Per Use field, and the number of truckloads needed is entered in the Units field. The duration of the task has no direct correlation with the materials cost.

Project can let you view the day-by-day details of resource costs for each resource and each task, or these costs can be summarized by task, by resource, or by project. When summing costs by task, Project adds the fixed costs to the resource costs and calls it *total cost* (or just *cost*).

Controlling How Costs Are Accrued

Suppose that you want to print a report to show how far along the project will be as of a certain date and how much it will have cost up to that date. The estimated cost for the project as of that date includes all the costs of tasks that should have been finished by that date and none of the costs for tasks that haven't started by that date. But what about tasks that should be started but not completed by the report date? The way the resource costs are *accrued* determines how the costs are handled in interim reports.

- Normally, Project will *prorate* the estimated costs for tasks that are only partially completed as of a given report date. If the task is 60% completed, Project reports 60% of the expected cost of the task as the estimated actual cost up to that date.

- If you have to pay a resource in full before it starts work, you tell Project to count the entire cost of that resource in any report printed on or after the *start* date of the task.

- If the resource is paid nothing until the job is finished, tell Project not to count any of the cost of that resource in reports printed before the *end* of the task.

These methods of calculating cost are called *accrual methods*, and you can select *pro rated*, *start*, or *end* as the accrual method for each resource. The accrual method doesn't affect the final cost of the project. It's important only for interim reports, when tasks might be partially complete.

Creating the Resource Pool

As you can guess from this overview, several fields in Microsoft Project define resources and costs. How many of them you use depends on what you want Project to do for you when you assign resources to tasks.

- If you just want to associate people's names with tasks to assign responsibility, you have to at least enter the resource names in the resource pool and assign them to individual tasks.

- If you want Project to schedule work around the availability of the resources, you have to also define the maximum units available and the working times for the resources.

- If you want Project to assign the cost of the resources to the tasks they work on, and thereby calculate the cost of each task and the cost of the project, then you have to define cost rates for the resources.

If you just want to use resource names without all the other information, you can enter those in the Assign Resources dialog box as you assign them to tasks, or you can prepare the list ahead of time with the Assign Resources dialog box or with the Resource Sheet. Then you can pick the names from a list as you assign them.

9

Using the Assign Resources Dialog Box to List Resources

You will use the Assign Resources dialog box (see Figure 9.4) a great deal in subsequent hours, but for now, let's see how you can use it to create the list of names in the resource pool. You can open this dialog box in any task view and leave it on the workspace as you work with the other views.

To Do: Entering Resources in the Assign Resources Dialog Box

To enter resources in the Assign Resources dialog box, follow these steps:

 1. Click the Assign Resources button on the Standard toolbar or choose Tools, Resources, Assign Resources from the menu.

2. Select a cell in the Name column.

3. Type a resource name and press Enter. Project then moves the selection to the cell below and you can type the next name.

4. Repeat step 3 until you're finished entering the names.

5. Click the Close button to put the dialog box away.

If you want to enter more information about each resource, you can double-click a resource name in the Assign Resources dialog box to display the Resource Information dialog box for that resource (see the following section), where you have access to almost all fields that define resources.

Resource names can be very long if you choose, but they cannot contain the slash(/) , brackets ([ ]), or the list separator character—usually the comma(,).

FIGURE 9.4

You can create a quick list of resources in the Assign Resources dialog box.

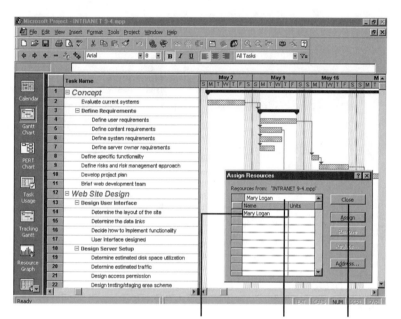

Name of resource   Edit selected   Close button
                    names here

Using the Resource Sheet

If you plan to define your resources more fully, you might want to start with the Resource Sheet view (see Figure 9.5). This view displays an entry table with columns for many of the major resource fields.

To Do: Entering Resources in the Resource Sheet

To enter resources in the Resource Sheet, follow these steps:

1. Display the Resource Sheet by choosing **V**iew, Resource **S**heet or by clicking the Resource Sheet icon on the View Bar.

2. Enter the resource information in the columns provided. You need to use the scroll-bar to view additional columns off to the right.

FIGURE 9.5

You can access the major resource definition fields in the Resource Sheet view.

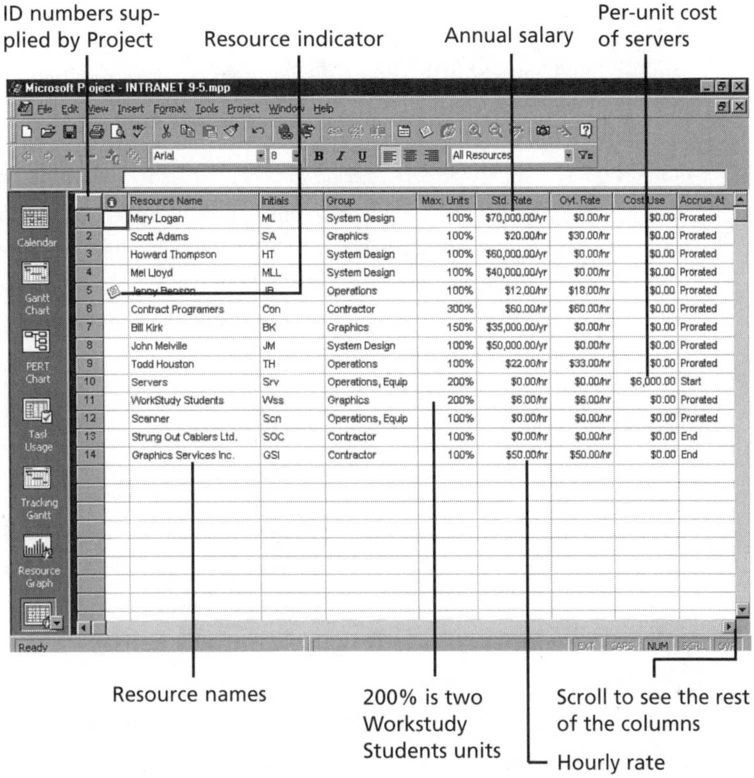

Each column in the Resource Sheet is described in the following sections.

ID Value

This is a display-only field that Project calculates for you. You can't enter an ID value, although you can change the order of the resources in the list by sorting the list and applying new ID numbers to the new sort order.

Indicators

Indicators alert you to additional information about a resource. In Figure 9.5, there is a Notes indicator next to Jenny Benson. Resource indicators are covered in greater detail in later Hours.

Name

Always identify the resource with a unique name. The name can contain any characters except the comma and the square brackets ([]). Resource names can be much longer than the space you see on the screen, but short names are easier to deal with in reports and onscreen.

Initials

Supply initials to use as a shorter display than the full resource name. For example, you can use the initials instead of the full name next to the task bars in the Gantt Chart.

Group

You can identify the resource as a member of a group (such as a department or type of cost). You can use the group label for sorting or filtering the list. You can also calculate cost subtotals for all members of the group. If the resource belongs to several groups, separate them with spaces or commas. See Hour 14, "Optimizing the Project Plan," for more information on sorting and filters.

Max Units

Use this field to tell Microsoft Project the maximum number of units of the resource that are available for assignment to tasks. Project uses the Max Units field to determine when a resource has been overallocated. Because you can assign resources to multiple tasks, it's possible to assign the same resource to tasks that wind up being scheduled at the same or overlapping times. If the sum of a resource's assignments to all tasks at a given moment exceeds the entry in the Max Units field, Project alerts you that the resource is overallocated.

You will see in the next hour that when assigning resources to tasks, the default format for the units assigned is the percentage format. Consequently, the default format for the Max Units field is also a percentage. For example, when you assign an individual person to a task, the default assignment units are 100%, which means the person will put 100% of his or her working hours into that task for the duration of the task. If that person were assigned to work only half-time on the task, the assignment units would be 50%. The maximum percentage that could be allocated for a single person would be 100%, so the entry in the Max Units field for that resource would be 100%.

If the same resource is assigned full-time (100%) to one task and half-time (50%) to another task during the same time period, then the combined assignments call for 150% of the person's time. Because the maximum available is only 100%, the resource would be overallocated.

Although using the percentage format for a resource that represents an individual person or piece of equipment is easy enough to understand, when the percentage format is applied to resource sets, it's a bit strained. For example, if a resource set represents five nurses or five machines, the maximum units available in percentage format is 500%, instead of the simple decimal value "5."

You can change the default format for resource units to decimal, if you prefer, but this change will affect all resources; it can't be limited just to resource sets. I'll continue to use the percentage format because it's the default and will have its advantages in the hours that follow.

To Do: Setting the Default Format for Resource Units

To set the default format for resource units, follow these steps:

1. Choose **T**ools, **O**ptions from the menu to display the Options dialog box and select the Schedule tab (see Figure 9.6).

2. Select the field labeled Sh**o**w Assignment Units As A, and choose either Percentage or Decimal.

3. Click OK to close the dialog box.

   Note that this choice will remain the display format for all projects until you change it again.

FIGURE 9.6

The default format for displaying resource units applies immediately to all projects, not just the one you are currently working on.

The default value for Max Units is 100% in the percentage form; in the decimal format, the default value is simply "1." The largest value you can enter in the Max Units field is 10,000 units (in decimal format) or 1,000,000% (in percentage format).

Even if you are using the percentage format, including a decimal point with your entry in the Max Units field causes Project to treat your typing as a decimal format entry. You can enter "1." as a shortcut for entering "100%" because 100% is the equivalent of the decimal value "1." So, if there are five nurses in the Nurses resource, you can enter either "5." or "500%"; in both cases, Project will display "500%."

Standard Rate

The standard rate is the cost rate to be charged for the resource's work during normal working hours. Type the standard rate as a number, followed by a *forward* slash, and one of the following time unit abbreviations: m (minute), h (hour), d (day), w (week), or y (year). For example, if a worker is paid $12.50 per hour, you would enter 12.5/h. You can use the year as a time unit if the resource is paid an annual salary. If you type just a number (without a time unit), Project assumes it's an hourly rate. For example, type 600/w for $600 per week, 35000/y for $35,000 per year, and 15.5 for $15.50 per hour.

> You can change the default currency unit, the placement of the currency symbol, and the number of decimal points to display in the Options dialog box on the View tab (see Figure 9.7). However, you must use the Regional Settings application in the Windows 95 Control Panel to change the default settings for all projects.

To Do: Changing the Default Currency Format for the Current Project

▼ To Do

To change the default currency format for the current project, follow these steps:

1. Choose **T**ools, **O**ptions to display the Options dialog box and choose the View tab (see Figure 9.7).

2. Type the currency symbol to use in the **S**ymbol field.

3. Select the **P**lacement: before or after the value, with or without a separating space.

4. Enter the number of **D**ecimal Digits to display.

5. Choose OK to close the dialog box. Note that these settings affect only the current project.

▲

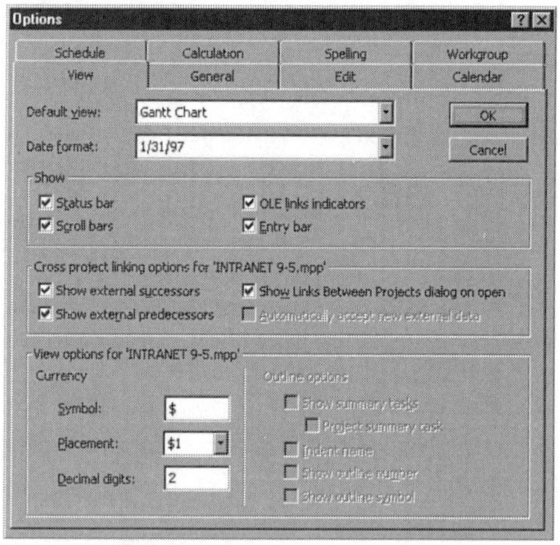

FIGURE 9.7

Set the default format for currency for this project only in the Options dialog box.

To Do: Changing the Default Currency Format for Windows 95

▼ To Do

To change the default currency format for Windows 95, follow these steps:

1. Choose Settings, Control Panel from the Windows 95 Start menu to display the Control Panel dialog box.

2. Choose the Regional Settings application and select the Currency tab.

3. Enter the currency symbol in the Currency Symbol field.

4. Select the placement in the Position of Currency Symbol field.

5. Use the Decimal Symbol field to change the decimal character to a comma or other character.

6. Change the number of decimal digits to display in the No. of Digits After Decimal field.

7. Use the Digit Grouping Symbol field to change the grouping character to a period or other character.

▲ 8. Use the Number of Digits In Group to enter a value from 0 to 9.

Overtime Rate

The overtime rate is charged for work outside the normal working hours. If the rate for overtime work is the same as the regular rate, you must enter this amount again in the Overtime Rate text box, or overtime hours will be charged at the zero default rate. For salaried employees, you can leave the overtime rate zero, or you can repeat the standard rate if overtime is compensated with comp-time (compensatory time-off during regular working hours).

Cost/Use

Use this field for costs that are charged once for each unit assigned, such as for parts or material resources, but that are not applied for each hour of work.

Accrue At

The default accrual method is prorated. If you must pay a resource in full before work starts, change the entry to Start. If you will not pay the resource until the work is complete, change it to End.

Base Calendar

Select the base calendar to which the calendar for this resource will be linked. The in-cell drop-down list displays all base calendars already defined for the project. You will edit the calendar for the resource in the following section on using the Resource Information dialog box.

Code

Use this field for any accounting or other codes that you want to associate with the cost of using the resource. You also can use this field as another Group field.

Using the Resource Information Dialog Box

All the resource definition fields displayed on the Resource Sheet are also displayed in the Resource Information dialog box (see Figure 9.8). Plus, there are additional fields that are important to the full definition of a resource that aren't accessible on the Resource Sheet. You can display the Resource Information dialog box from any resource view. You can also display it if you have the Assign Resources dialog box displayed in a task view.

To Do: Displaying the Resource Information Dialog Box

Follow these steps to display the Resource Information dialog box:

1. Display a resource view, such as the Resource Sheet or Resource Form.

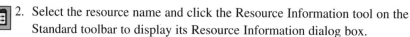

2. Select the resource name and click the Resource Information tool on the Standard toolbar to display its Resource Information dialog box.

   With some resource views (such as the Resource Sheet), you can also just double-click the resource name to display the Resource Information dialog box.

Or, from a task view, you can use these steps:

1. Display the Assign Resources dialog box in any task view with the Assign Resources tool (or by choosing **T**ools, **R**esources, **A**ssign Resources from the menu.

▲   2. Double-click a resource name to display its Resource Information dialog box.

The Resource Information dialog box contains four tabs: General, Working Time, Costs, and Notes. The following sections describe those fields on the tabs that have not already been covered.

Costs tab: Cost Rate tables

Working Time tab: Notes tab:
The resource calendar   Resource notes

FIGURE 9.8

The General Tab of the Resource Information dialog box contains additional resource availability and work-group fields.

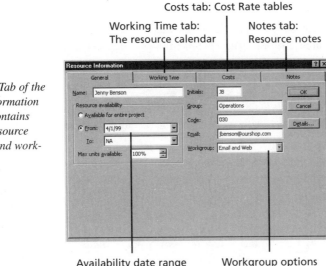

Availability date range   Workgroup options

9

The General Tab

The General tab contains the following information:

- *Resource Availability.* Normally, you leave the radio button Available For Entire Project selected. However, if the resource will come on board after the project starts, or leave before it's finished, you can enter the start date in the From field or the last working day in the To field.

- *Email.* Use this field to supply the resource's email address for use in the project's workgroup (see the next paragraph).

- *Workgroup.* If the members of the project team have communication links via email or a Web site on the Internet or the organization's intranet, you can define one or both of those links on the Workgroup tab of the Options dialog box. This field is used to specify to which link this resource has access. See Hour 18, "Analyzing Progress and Revising the Schedule," for a complete explanation of workgroup features.

- *Details.* The Details button is used to identify additional details about the work-group connection. See Hour 18 for more information.

Setting the availability dates doesn't keep Project from scheduling the resource's assigned tasks outside that range of dates, but if it does happen, Project shows you that the resource is overallocated so that *you* can deal with it. (See Hour 13, "Resolving Resource Allocation Problems," for a full explanation).

The Working Time Tab

The Working Time tab lets you edit the calendar for the resource. You can change the base calendar the resource calendar is linked to in the **B**ase Calendar field. Initially, the working days and times will be identical to those on the base calendar, but you can use this dialog box to enter exceptions to the base calendar that apply to this resource:

- If the resource is scheduled for vacation days, sick leave, or a leave of absence, make those days nonworking days on the resource calendar, even though they are working days on the base calendar.

- If the resource has special assignments, answering the phone on a day that's a non-working day for the rest of the organization, make that day a working day on the resource calendar, even though it's been made a nonworking day on the base calendar.

- If the resource has unique hours on any days, enter those in the resource calendar.

Suppose that Jenny Benson has asked to get off work at midday on the Tuesday before Thanksgiving in November, 1999, because she has asked her family and her new husband's family to come to her house for Thanksgiving dinner; she's never cooked a turkey before. She has offered to work a day and a half on the weekend before Thanksgiving to make up the hours. Every date in her calendar that differs from the base calendar has the date underlined in Figure 9.9.

- November 20 is a nonworking day on the base calendar but it's a work day with the normal working hours for Jenny. The date is underlined to show that it's an exception to the base calendar, and clear to show that it's regular hours.

- November 21 is a nonworking day on the base calendar, but Jenny will work half a day (not the normal working hours). The date is clear with diagonal stripes to indicate a working day, but one with different hours.

- November 23 is Jenny's half-day off. The diagonal stripes show that she has special hours that differ from the base calendar.

- November 24 is Mary's special full day off work, as indicated by the shading and the date underline.

- November 25 and 26 are company holidays on the base calendar, so they are shaded but have no underline.

If you create several base calendars for use by resources, remember to make company-wide changes in working days and hours on all base calendars. If your company decides to make December 24 a holiday, for example, you need to edit each base calendar used by resources to apply the holiday to all resources.

Special working day
for the resource

FIGURE 9.9

*Enter the resource's
special working and
nonworking days and
times on the resource
calendar.*

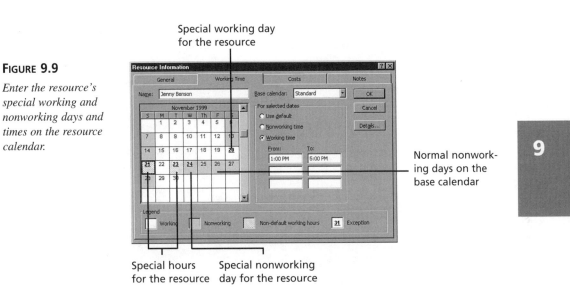

9

Normal nonwork-
ing days on the
base calendar

Special hours   Special nonworking
for the resource   day for the resource

Use the same techniques we used in "Defining Your Calendar" in Hour 4, "Turning the Task List into a Schedule," to edit the resource calendar.

You can also access the resource calendar from the Change Working Time dialog box. If you want to work on several calendars at once—base calendars and resource calendars—it's easier to work from this dialog box.

To Do: Editing All Calendars

To edit all calendars, follow these steps:

1. Select the top pane. You can't access the calendars from the bottom pane.

2. Choose Tools, Change Working Time to display the Change Working Time dialog box.

The Costs Tab

The Costs tab of the Resource Information dialog box lets you expand the cost-rate data for the resource in two significant ways: You can create different cost rates for different types of tasks, and you can define when and how cost rates will change in the future because of raises, labor contracts, or other influences.

This tab has five Cost Rate tables, labeled A–E, that you can use to define cost rates for different types of assignments (see Figure 9.10). For example, an electrician might have higher rates for tasks involving high-voltage lines. A software engineer might have one set of rates for in-house development projects, several other rates for development or consulting for clients, and another set of rates for the hated chore of writing documentation.

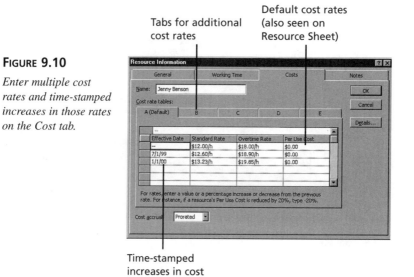

Tabs for additional cost rates

Default cost rates
(also seen on
Resource Sheet)

FIGURE 9.10

*Enter multiple cost
rates and time-stamped
increases in those rates
on the Cost tab.*

Time-stamped
increases in cost
rates for tab A

The first row on rate table A contains the rates you define on the Resource Sheet. The rates on rate table A are the default rates Microsoft Project uses for all task assignments. You can select a different rate table for specific assignments. (See "Modifying Assignments with the Assignment Information Dialog Box" in Hour 12, "Editing Resource Assignments.")

The first row on each rate table has dashes in the Effective Date column to show that those rates are effective from whenever the beginning date of the project might be. You can record future increases (or decreases) in the rates by entering the effect date for the change on the rows below, along with the rates that will go into effect on that date. For example, in Figure 9.10, you see that Jenny Benson's standard rate will go up to $12.60 an hour on 7/1/99. You can enter up to 24 rate changes beneath the initial rates. If a task assignment extends past one of these dates, the new rates will be used for the cost of work done after that date.

When entering the rate changes, you can either enter the new amount or indicate a percentage increase or decrease and Project will calculate the new rate for you. For example, the increase from $12.00/h to $12.60/h for Jenny Benson in Figure 9.10 was created by entering +5% for the new rate; Project calculated the $12.60/h and replaced the percent increase with the new rate.

The Notes Tab

The Notes tab of the Resource Information dialog box lets you record notes about the resource (see Figure 9.11). The Notes indicator will appear next to the resource name on the Resource Sheet so that you know there's a note to be read.

FIGURE 9.11

Record reminders and other information about a resource in the Notes field.

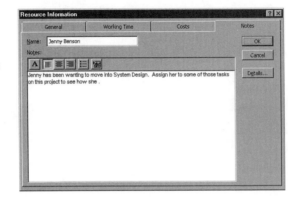

Printing the Resource Pool

As you just learned in Hour 8, "Finalizing and Printing Your Schedule," you can display a view such as the Resource Sheet and then use the **File, Print** command to get a paper copy. Printing the Resource Sheet view gives you a listing of the project's resources with the basic resource fields.

Hour **10**

Understanding Resource Scheduling in Microsoft Project 98

In this hour, you learn how Microsoft Project handles resource assignments and how it then schedules work for the resources. Although it takes more time to add resource assignments to your project, there are many benefits to be gained. Resource assignments allow you to do the following:

- Plan work around the vacations and other downtime periods for individual resources
- Examine the workload your project will impose on individual resources
- Identify those resources whose workloads in the project are unrealistically high
- Identify resources that are not fully utilized and might, therefore, substitute for overworked resources on some tasks

- Calculate the effect that changing resource assignments can have on the duration of a task
- Calculate costs for tasks based on the amount of work and the value of the individual resource's time

These benefits have a price tag attached, however. When you introduce resource scheduling into your project, you add a considerable amount of complexity to the project document. A number of settings and rules govern how Project calculates the schedule for a resource assignment. Don't worry, though—you will understand what's going on in those calculations after this hour.

Microsoft Project offers you the flexibility of assigning resources in a fairly simplistic way or of getting really sophisticated. If all you want to do is get Microsoft Project to print resource names next to the tasks on the reports you want to hand out, then you can use a fairly simple process that will not require you to master all the information in this hour. You can use this hour to catch up on your email or whatever.

SIMPLY ASSOCIATING PEOPLE WITH TASKS

If all you want to do with resource names is have them associated with tasks so that they can appear on reports, then you do not need to fill in all the details about a resource (such as a calendar of nonworking days and various cost rates). You also do not need to be concerned with most of the details covered in this hour. You can achieve your purpose by making all your tasks Fixed Duration tasks that are not Effort Driven. You should at least review the sections on those two topics later in this hour. See Hour 11, "Assigning Resources and Costs to Tasks," for the actual steps you need to take for the minimalist approach to resource assignments. Of course, you are invited to read on in this hour so you will understand *why*...as you're undoubtedly blessed with an inquiring mind.

We're not going to look at the step-by-step process of assigning resources until the next hour. There, you'll learn how to use the views and dialog boxes that give you access to the features I explain in this hour. Understanding the process is more than half the battle in this endeavor, and understanding needs to come first.

Defining the Resource Assignment Fields

When you assign a resource to a task in the project, Microsoft Project keeps track of the assignment by filling in values for several fields. The essential fields that define an assignment are the following:

- The name or ID number of the task to be completed

- The duration of the task

- The name or ID number of the resource being assigned to the task

- The number of units of the resource to be assigned to the task

- The hours of work that the resource is expected to complete on the task

Project can help you calculate values for these fields if you don't fill them in yourself. These calculations are controlled by still other fields that characterize the task. Two of the most important of these other fields are the Task Type and whether the task is Effort Driven. We'll learn how those two fields govern calculations later in this hour.

The split-window view in Figure 10.1 shows three linked tasks that I'll use this hour to illustrate resource assignment concepts. The view in the bottom pane is the Task Form, and it shows details about the task selected in the top pane. We'll use this combination view in Hour 11 to assign resources. The bottom pane shows all the fields mentioned previously.

10

FIGURE 10.1

Resource assignments in the Task Form show the essential fields.

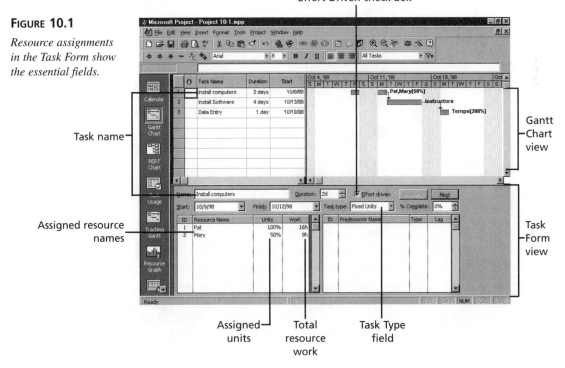

In Figure 10.1, the Install Computers task is selected in the top pane. Both Pat and Mary are assigned to that task, and their Units and Work appear in the Resource Details at the bottom of the screen.

In Figure 10.2, the Task Form is replaced by the Task Usage view in the bottom pane, which presents the same task assignments with additional detail. In the Task Usage view, the grid in the timeline area shows the hours of work scheduled as a result of the assignment. I'll use this view in the explanations that follow to help illustrate resource assignment calculations.

FIGURE 10.2

The Task Usage view shows the actual hours of work assigned during specific time periods.

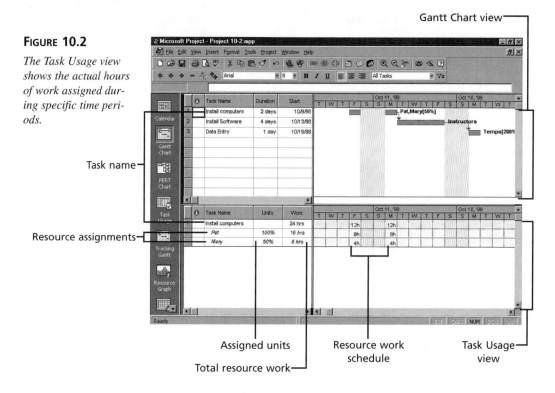

When you make an assignment, you must supply at least the name of the task and the name of the resource. If you don't specify anything more, Project calculates default values for the number of units of the resource assigned to the task and for the amount of work the resource will do. Let's examine the units assigned and the hours of work because they require additional explanation.

Defining the Resource Units

When you add a resource name to the resource pool, you define the maximum number of units of the resource that will be available for use in the project. Then, when you assign the resource to a task, you specify the number of units that will work on the task.

It is appealing to think of the value in the Units field as the physical count of resources with a specific name: for example, 1 Programmer, 5 Nurses, 2 Fork-lifts, 3 Meeting Rooms, 150 Bags of Concrete, and so on.

Recall from Hour 9, "Defining Resources and Costs," that if the resource represents multiple people or assets, the resource is known as a *group resource*. However, Microsoft Project uses a percentage format in the Units field. Let me explain why.

The reason we use resources in a project is because of the effort or work they contribute to tasks. Sometimes, especially with human resources, the resource might be assigned to work on a task only part-time. Suppose that Pat works full-time on a task and that Mary works half-time on the same task. During a day, Pat devotes 100% of his time and effort to the task, but Mary devotes only 50% of her time and effort to that task (and probably 50% to some other task). In one sense, you could say that we have assigned 1 unit of Pat and .5 units of Mary to this task. It is more accurate (and sounds better, anyway) to say we have assigned 100% of Pat's time and 50% of Mary's time to the task. Then we know that if the task lasts for 2 days, Pat will contribute work equal to 100% of 2 days (16 hours) and Mary will contribute work equal to 50% of 2 days (8 hours). If the 2 Fork-lifts mentioned previously were also assigned to the same 2-day task, we could say we assigned 200% of Fork-lift time and that Fork-lifts contribute work equal to 200% of 2 days (or 32 hours).

From this point of view, the Units field is really the multiplier that Project uses to calculate how much work can be done by a resource during each hour or day of the task's scheduled duration. Recall that Duration is the number of hours or days of working time it takes to complete the task. Multiply Duration by the Units, and you have the calculation for hours of Work, as shown here:

```
Duration × Units = Work
```

For example, if 5 Nurses work on a 4-hour task, then the total work will be 20 hours: 5 units × 4 hours, or 500% of 4 hours. If you express resource Units in percentage format (which is the default format in Project), you are recognizing the multiplier aspect of the Units value: the work for the resource will be some percentage multiple of the hours in the task's duration.

10

New Term **Resource Units** *Resource units* are a measure of resource effort or working time per unit of task Duration. Units are normally expressed as a percentage—that is, 100% means the resource can deliver one day of effort or work for every day of working time on the calendar, and 500% means the resource can deliver 5 days of work for every day of working time on the calendar.

In addition to calculating the work a resource will deliver for a given task duration, the Units field also tells Project how much of the available working hours on the calendar can be used for a task. If Pat is assigned 100%, then Project schedules him for 100% of the available hours on his calendar during the days the task is being worked on. If he has 8 available hours on a given day, Project schedules 8 hours of work for the task on that day. If Pat's calendar shows that he works only half a day, Project schedules 100% of his 4 hours for the task on that day.

If you prefer, you can format Units as decimal numbers instead of percentages. Decimal numbers are more intuitive for group resources, like 5 Nurses or 2 Fork-lifts, but they can be misleading because the physical units might not be engaged 100% on the task. If all 5 Nurses work on a task, but only half-time, then the decimal Units would need to be 2.5—even though five people are working. I think the percentage format is better because it forces you to think of Units as the work multiplier: 5 Nurses working half-time contribute work equal to 250% of the duration of the task.

To Do: Viewing Units in Decimals Instead of Percents

To view Units in decimals instead of percents, follow these steps:

1. Choose **T**ools, **O**ptions from the menu to display the Options dialog box.
2. Select the Schedule tab.
3. In the field labeled Sh**o**w Assignment Units As A, select the Decimal setting. A 100% full-time assignment would be the simple digit one (1) in decimal format.
4. Click OK to close the dialog box.

If you use the percentage display for the assignment Units field and type a units value that includes a decimal point, be sure to include a percent sign after the number, or Project will interpret your entry in decimal format instead of percentage format.

For example, if you type 12, Project treats that entry as 12%, and if you type 12.5%, Project treats that as 12.5%; but if you type 12.5, Project treats it as 12.5 units and displays 1,250% (which is 12.5 in percentage format). If you include a decimal, you must also include the percent sign for the entry to be treated as a percent.

> You can enter fractions of a percent in the Units assignment, but they will
> display as rounded whole percent numbers. So if you want to specify that a
> worker spends 1 hour per 8-hour day on a task (one-eighth or 12.5% of a
> day), you will see 13% displayed after you enter 12.5%. Project will actually
> use fractional percents in its calculations (down to tenths of a percent)—it
> just doesn't display them.

Defining the Work

Work, which is also called "effort," measures the time or effort expended by the
resources during the assignment. Work is always measured in hours in Microsoft Project.
It can be entered by the user or, if not, is automatically calculated by Project.

NEW TERM   **Work**   *Work* defines the amount of time that a resource is actually engaged on
a task. Project always measures work in hours.

If a resource works full-time on a task that lasts 2 days (16 hours), the resource will do
16 hours of work. If the resource is assigned half-time to the task, then it will do only 8
hours of work on the task (see Mary in Figure 10.2).

The amount of work scheduled depends on the duration of the task and the number of
units assigned to the task. The next section defines this relationship more precisely.

Understanding the Formula for Work

The work formula ties together the quantitative fields of an assignment: task duration,
resource units, and resource work.

This is the formula for calculating work:

Duration × Units = Work

In symbols, the formula looks like this:

D × U = W

In words, work is calculated by multiplying the task duration by the assigned units (what
you saw previously is really the work multiplier per hour of duration). For a given
Duration, the more Units, the more Work on the task. For a given number of Units, the
longer the Duration, the more Work.

Simple algebra can be used to reformulate this equation to calculate Duration when Work
and Units are given, or Units when Work and Duration are given:

Duration = Work/Units   Units = Work/Duration

In symbols, the formula looks like this:

```
D = W/U      U = W/D
```

The Duration variant of the formula shows that if you increase the Units and keep the Work the same, Duration will be reduced. The Units variant of the formula shows that if you increase the Duration and keep Work unchanged, then you can get by with fewer Units of the resource.

Although duration can be displayed in minutes, hours, days, or weeks, Project converts duration to hours when calculating work. Therefore, if a 1-day (8-hour) task has 200% units assigned to it (two full-time units of the resource), the work would be calculated this way:

```
D × U = W
8hrs × 200% = 16hrs
```

According to the work equation, when you change one of the three variables, then one of the other two variables must also change, but how do you know which of the remaining variables Project will change and which it will leave fixed? The answer to that question is important because if Project changes Duration, for example, it affects the length of time it will take to complete your project.

Project was originally conceived as a date calculator, to evaluate Work and Units and calculate Duration and the schedule of dates for the project. It was assumed that the user would enter an estimated task duration and the number of units of the resource he or she wanted to work on the task. Project was designed to calculate the Work from these two values supplied by the user. Then it was assumed that users might adjust the Units assigned to change the duration of the task (and the project), but would want the Work amount to remain unchanged.

Because of this heritage, Project tends to recalculate Duration when it has to choose between changing Duration or Work or Units. In addition, Project is generally programmed to respect the number of Units you enter for an assignment as holy writ. So, when Project has to choose which variable to change in a calculation, its bias is to recalculate Duration before Work and Work before Units. The following are other considerations:

- Given the choice between Duration and either of the other two variables, Project will choose to change Duration.
- If Duration is fixed (or you have just entered a new Duration), Project will choose to change Work before it changes Units.
- Project changes Units only when it can't change Duration or Work.

You can assert greater control over Project's calculations by defining the Task Type, as you will see in the next section.

Using the Task Type to Control Calculations

To give you more control over calculations, Project defines every task as one of three task "types," and the type determines which variable Project must keep fixed when you force it to recalculate the work formula. The three types are

- Fixed Units (the default for all new tasks)
- Fixed Duration
- Fixed Work

Fixed Units Tasks

The Fixed Units task type is appropriate when you want to control the number of resource Units assigned to the task, and there is no particular reason why you need to keep the Duration or the Work constant. As you can see in the following recap of the work formula (the brackets indicate that the Units variable is "fixed"), if you reduce Duration, then Project must reduce total Work (because Units is fixed):

```
Duration × [Units] = Work
```

If you change Work, Project must leave Units fixed and change Duration (with more Work requiring a longer Duration and less Work allowing a shorter Duration). Of course, *you* can change the Units, in which case Project's bias will dictate that it change the Duration and leave Work unchanged. Note that with Work unchanged, increasing the Units results in a decrease in Duration, and reducing the Units leads to an increase in Duration.

Fixed Duration Tasks

For some tasks, it makes sense to lock in the Duration and keep Project from changing it. For example, if you schedule meetings as part of a project, you should generally make them Fixed Duration. Otherwise, the duration of the meeting would get shorter and shorter as you assign more and more people to attend! That flies in the face of common sense: If anything, meetings get longer as more people attend.

If Duration is fixed and you change the Units assigned, Project must change Work. The more Units, the greater the amount of Work, and vice versa. If you change Work with a Fixed Duration task, Project will *have* to change the Units (with more Work requiring more Units). As you can see, when you define a task as Fixed Duration, you can force Project to overcome its bias against changing the assigned units:

10

```
[Duration] × Units = Work
```

If you change Duration yourself for a Fixed Duration task, then Project's bias causes it to recalculate Work, not Units. The longer the Duration, the more Work included in the assignment.

Fixed Work Tasks

If your project includes tasks that have a fixed or contracted number of hours of work to be delivered, then you should make those tasks Fixed Work. Then Project will leave the Work undisturbed and adjust Units or Duration in its calculations.

If the task is the Fixed Work type, then increasing Units allows Project to decrease Duration because Work is fixed and can't be changed. If you decrease the Duration, Project is forced to increase the Units because of the fixed Work:

```
Duration × Units  = [Work]
```

If you change the Work yourself for a Fixed Work task, Project recalculates Duration and keeps its hands off the Units.

Changing the Task Type

You need to change the Task Type field for those tasks with an inappropriate default type. You can also temporarily change the Task Type to control how Project adjusts to a change you want to enter, and then return the task to the original type.

You can change the task type for the currently selected task in the Task Form (refer to Figure 10.1) or in the Task Information dialog box (see Figure 10.3). As you saw in earlier hours, you can display the Task Information dialog box by selecting any field in a task view (such as the Gantt Chart, for instance) and then clicking the Task Information tool.

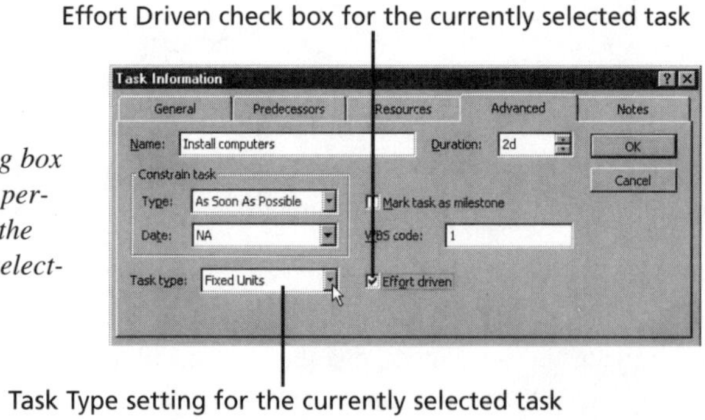

Effort Driven check box for the currently selected task

FIGURE 10.3

Use the Task Information dialog box to temporarily or permanently change the task type for the selected task.

Task Type setting for the currently selected task

As stated previously, the default task type for new tasks is Fixed Units, so all new tasks are Fixed Units type until you change them. If you think that most of your tasks in this project will be Fixed Duration or Fixed Work, you can change the default task type so that new tasks are automatically the right type. If you think that most of your projects will consist of Fixed Duration or Fixed Work tasks, you can also change the default task type for all new project documents.

To Do: Changing the Default Task Type

To change the default task type, follow these steps:

1. Choose **T**ools, **O**ptions from the menu to display the Options dialog box.

2. Select the Schedule tab.

3. Select the type you want to be the default in the Default Task **Ty**pe field (see Figure 10.4). This change affects only the current document unless you use the Set as **D**efault button.

4. If you want this task type to be the default for all future project documents, click the Set as **D**efault button.

5. Click the OK button to close the Options dialog box.

FIGURE 10.4

You can change the default task type for new project documents in the Options dialog box.

Default Task Type setting (this project only)

Default Effort Driven setting (this project only)

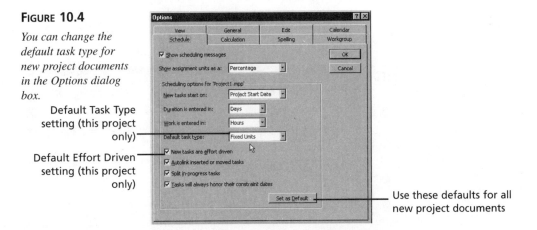

Use these defaults for all new project documents

Applying the Work Formula in an Assignment

When you assign a resource, you must define at least the task and the resource, but you can also define one or both of the units to be assigned and the work to be completed. In this section, I'll show you what happens in each of these cases. The task duration will already be defined in all cases because Project sets it to a default value (1 day) even if you don't define it yourself, so the Duration part of the work formula will already be filled in.

You Enter the Resource Name Only

If you enter just the resource name, but don't enter the units or the work, Project assigns a default value of 100% to Units and calculates the Work from the default Units and the Duration. For example, if you assign Pat to a 2-day task without entering the Units, Project first assigns 100% in the Units field and then calculates the work as 100% of the duration (16 hours). This case is illustrated by Pat's assignment to the Install Computers task in Figure 10.5.

In this figure, and in those that follow, I will show the task twice—once before the assignment I want to illustrate and then again after the assignment has been added to the task. The two versions of the task are labeled "Before" and "After." In later examples, these two versions will be useful for illustrating the impact of assignments on the schedule and on other assignments.

When Pat is assigned to the task Install Computers (After) without specifying the units or the work, Project supplies 100% as the default units and calculates the work of 16 hours.

FIGURE 10.5

You can assign a resource without specifying the Units or the Work, and Project will supply default values.

Task Duration already set to 2 days

Work calculated by Project

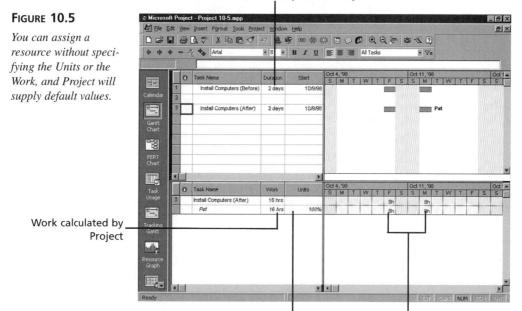

Default Units (100%) filled in by Project   Work scheduled by Project at 100% of Duration

You Enter the Name and the Units

If you enter the Units in an assignment, but not the Work, Project uses the Units and the Duration to calculate the Work. For example, if you assign a resource to a 2-day task and enter 50% in the Units field, Project calculates the Work as 50% of 16 hours, or 8 hours. Project then goes to the calendar and schedules 50% of each available working time period during the duration of the task. Figure 10.6 illustrates this case with Mary's 50% assignment to the Install Computers task.

FIGURE 10.6

If you define the Units, Project calculates and schedules the Work based on your Units and the Duration.

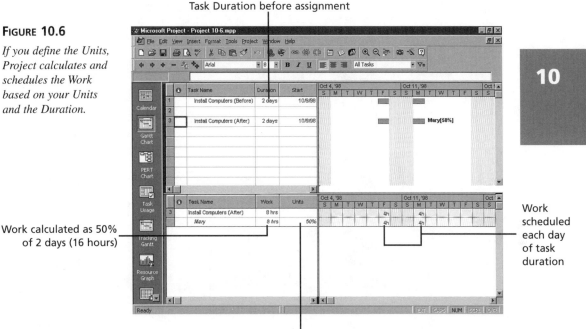

Task Duration before assignment

10

Work calculated as 50% of 2 days (16 hours)

Work scheduled each day of task duration

Units entered as 50%

Notice that Project scheduled Mary for work during each day of the task duration, but has scheduled only 4 hours (50% of her available hours) each day. When Project calculates the assignment schedule, it always schedules the resource for the same percentage of available hours during every period of the task duration.

You Enter the Name and the Work

If you enter the Work value, but do not supply the Units, then Project assumes you want the Units to be set at the default (100%) and calculates a new value for the Duration based on the specified Work and the assumed value of 100% for Units. For example, in Figure 10.7 the resource Instructors is assigned to Install Software (After), which is a

2-day task (16 hours). As part of the assignment, 32 hours was entered for the Work value but nothing was entered for the Units. Project has filled the Units field with the default 100% and calculated a new Duration (32 hours or 4 days) using this variation of the Work formula:

```
Duration = Work/Units
Duration = 32 hours/100% = 32 hours (4 days)
```

Task Duration before assignment

FIGURE 10.7

If you enter the Name and the Work, Project assigns the default Units of 100% and recalculates Duration for the Work you entered.

Task Duration recalculated to 4 days

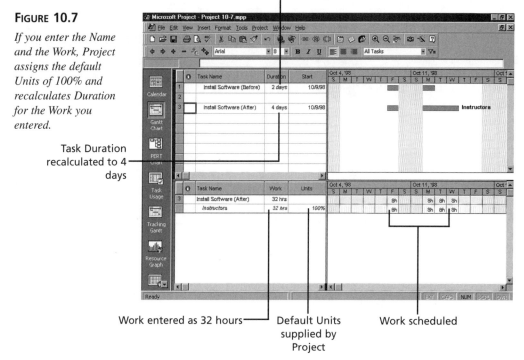

Work entered as 32 hours — Default Units supplied by Project — Work scheduled

By the way, what do you think would have happened in Figure 10.7 if the task had been a Fixed Duration task? The Work amount was entered by the user; the Duration is fixed and can't be changed (note the brackets around Duration in the following formula), so the Units is the only variable left for Project to adjust to keep the formula valid. In fact, Project would have abandoned the default Units of 100% and calculated 200% for the Units field.

```
[Duration] = Work/Units
16 hours = 32 hours/Units
Units = 200%
```

This example shows how you can get Project to calculate how many Units you need to assign if you know the Work that has to be done and how long you want the task to take. A number of organizations have tables that define the standard hours of work associated with specific tasks. Auto mechanics, for example, consult manuals published by the auto manufacturers for the standard amount of labor needed to replace a part.

> If you have a task with a known amount of work that you want completed in a specific amount of time, you can make the task a Fixed Duration task and assign the resource and the known amount of work without entering the Units. Project will calculate the Units for you.

You Enter the Name, Units, and Work

If you enter both the Units and the Work, then Project recalculates the task Duration using the values you entered. For example, Figure 10.8 illustrates an assignment to a 2-day task named Data Entry; the required work is assumed to be 16 hours. I assigned two Temps to the task, entering 200% in the Units field and 16 hours in the Work field. Project calculated a new task Duration, using this variation of the Work formula:

```
Duration = Work/Units
Duration = 16 hours/200% = 8 hours (or 1 day)
```

FIGURE 10.8

If you enter the Units and the Work, Project recalculates the Duration.

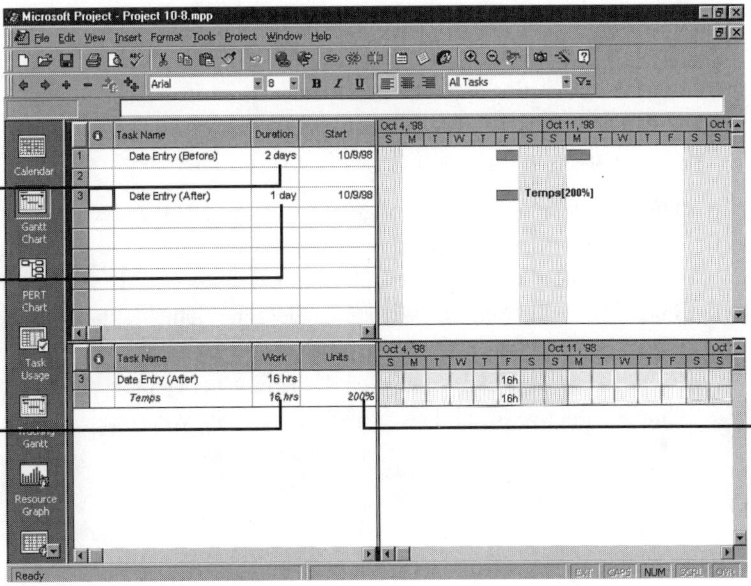

Task Duration before the assignment

New Task Duration calculated by Project

Work entered as 16 hours

Units entered as 200%

Assigning Multiple Resources to a Task

Assigning multiple resources to a task means listing multiple resource names in the task assignment. It is similar to, but a little different from, merely increasing the assigned units for a resource. In the previous examples, when we increased the Units assigned for one resource, we saw that unless it's a fixed duration task, Project adjusts the task Duration and keeps the Work the same: Increasing the Units allows Project to shorten the Duration. That's also the default behavior when you increase the units by adding another resource name and its associated Units to the assignment: Project keeps the work or "effort" for the task constant and adjusts the task duration. In essence, some of the work is shouldered by the new resource, allowing the previously assigned resource(s) to do less work. We say that the calculation is driven by (determined by) the constant work or effort, and we call such tasks Effort Driven.

NEW TERM   **Effort Driven Task**   An *Effort Driven task* is assumed to have a fixed amount of work to be done, and changing the number of resources assigned to the task causes the scheduled work for all resources to be reapportioned—usually with an impact on task duration.

For example, if one person is assigned to an Effort Driven task with a duration of 1 week, the work will be 40 hours. If we want the task to be finished sooner, we can assign additional people to work on the task. They will each do fewer than 40 hours of work, but together they can finish all the work in less than 1 week.

The Effort Driven task field is used to define a task as Effort Driven or not Effort Driven (Yes or No). This field appears on the Task Form (refer to Figure 10.1) and in the Task Information dialog box (refer to Figure 10.3). It is simply a check box; if the check box is filled, the task is Effort Driven, and if it's not, the task is not Effort Driven. By default, all new tasks in Microsoft Project are Effort Driven.

The default status for new tasks in Project is Effort Driven, but if you think that most of your tasks will not be Effort Driven, you can change the default in the Options dialog box, right next to where you change the default Task Type (refer to Figure 10.4). Choose Tools, Options from the menu and select the Schedule tab on the Options dialog box. Clear the New Tasks Are Effort Driven check box to change the default setting. Remember that you must also click the Save as Default button if you want to make this change effective for all new project documents you start.

The Effort Driven setting has no effect on the task if you list several resource names in the Task Form when you make the initial resource assignment to the task. Each resource assignment will be calculated separately. The Effort Driven setting comes into play only when you change the number of resource names on an existing list.

Understanding How Project Calculates Effort Driven Tasks

To illustrate the effect of the Effort Driven setting, I'm going to use the "Install Computers" task from the earlier examples. In Figure 10.9, Task 1, labeled "Install Computers (Before)," has both Mary and Pat assigned to the task. The column to the right of Duration in the top pane has been redefined to display the Effort Driven status of the task, and in this figure the task is Effort Driven. Todd is added to the task in Task 3, Install Computers (After), with assigned units of 50%. As a result, the task duration is reduced from 2 days to 1.5 days.

10

FIGURE 10.9

Adding resources to a task will change the existing resource assignments if the task is Effort Driven.

Effort Driven field

Task duration reduced

Total work the same after adding Todd

Work for Pat and Mary reduced

Work apportioned to resources based on share of total Units

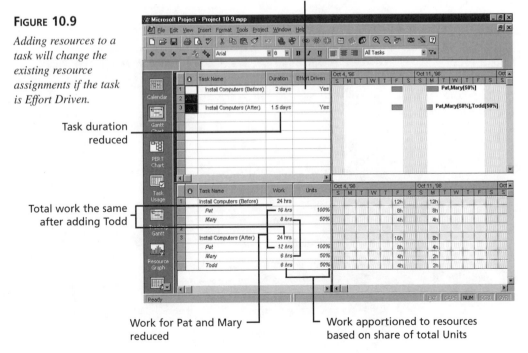

Notice in Figure 10.9 in the bottom pane that the work was redistributed when Todd was added to the task. Pat's work falls from 16 to 12, and Mary's falls from 8 to 6. Also notice that if you add up the total units assigned (100%+50%+50%) the total is 200%, with Pat contributing half of that total and Mary and Todd each contributing one-fourth of the total. That's exactly how the work is divided among the resources: Half is assigned to Pat now and one-fourth is assigned to both Mary and Todd. When you change the number of resources assigned to an Effort Driven task, Project assigns the work among the resources in direct proportion to their share of total resource units after the change.

Sometimes you might need to change the Effort Driven field for a task temporarily. For example, suppose that when initially creating the Install Computers task we had assumed that 2 days was enough if Pat, Mary, and Todd all worked on the task (with Mary and Todd only part-time), but when the initial resource assignment was made, we forgot to include Todd's assignment. If the task is Effort Driven and we later try to add Todd (refer to Figure 10.9), then the task duration will be changed to 1.5 days (which was not what we intended). To add Todd to the task without changing the duration, clear the Effort Driven check box first, add Todd (see Figure 10.10), and then change the task back to Effort Driven. As you can see in this figure, adding Todd does not change the task duration or the work loads for the other resources if the entry in the Effort Driven field is "No." The total work for the task increases by the amount of work in Todd's new assignment.

FIGURE 10.10

Make a task not Effort Driven temporarily if you forgot to include a needed resource in the initial assignment.

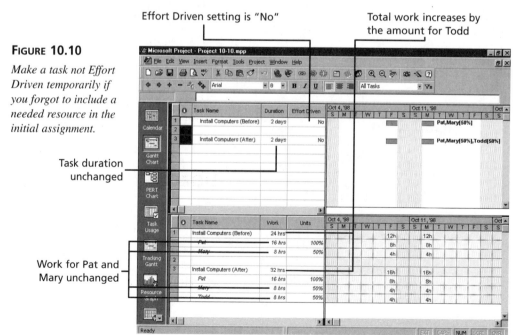

Hour **11**

Assigning Resources and Costs to Tasks

This hour shows you how to use Microsoft Project's views and tools to assign and edit resource assignments and costs. In the next hour, you see more about editing and fine-tuning resource assignments. To benefit the most from this chapter, you should understand the contents of Hour 9, "Defining Resources and Costs," and Hour 10, "Understanding Resource Scheduling in Microsoft Project 98." There are intricate relationships among task and resource fields covered in those hours.

When first assigning resources to tasks, there are a number of data fields you can use to give Microsoft Project the information it needs to calculate schedules and costs as you intend:

- You can choose the settings for Task Type and Effort Driven that control how Project will calculate changes in the schedule when you change assignments to the task.

- You can, and must, provide the resource name when you assign it to a task.

- You can define the units assigned or let Project assign the default number of units.
- You can define the amount of work the resource will perform or let Project calculate that from the task duration and number of units.
- You can choose the cost rates for the resource that will be charged to the task for the resource's time.

This hour shows you how to enter all the preceding information listed. You will also see how to use pop-up tools to record just the minimum amount of information needed to get the job done. There are a number of different views and tools you can use to assign resources, and you will see how to use the best of them. Each offers its own advantages.

You can also modify Project's calculations by assigning overtime, by introducing delays and splits in an assignment, by applying one of the predefined assignment contours, or by editing the day-to-day work assignments. These refinements will be covered in the next hour.

As you can see, Project gives you the opportunity to fine-tune resource assignments so that schedule and cost calculations can be precise. You can also get by with just the minimum amount of definition if you don't need all that sophistication.

Choosing the Task Settings for Assignments

The first thing you should do when planning to assign a resource to a task is check the task's settings for Task Type and Effort Driven. These settings govern how Project calculates the task schedule after you assign a resource. You might recall from the previous Hour that the Task Type comes into play when you change one of the variables (task duration, units assigned, or work assigned) in the work formula. The type determines which of the two remaining variables in the formula will be kept fixed.

The Effort Driven setting comes into play only if you assign more than one resource to a task. If Effort Driven is on, then all resources assigned to a task are treated as dividing up a constant amount of work; changing the number of resources changes the work load assigned to the remaining resources and usually affects task duration.

To Do: Verifying or Changing the Task Type and Effort Driven Settings

To verify or change the Task Type and Effort Driven settings, follow these steps:

1. Select the task.

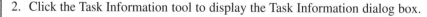 2. Click the Task Information tool to display the Task Information dialog box.

3. Select the Advanced tab.

▼ 4. Check the Task Type setting and change it, if necessary, by clicking the list arrow and selecting Fixed Duration, Fixed Units, or Fixed Work (see Figure 11.1).

5. Check the Effort Driven setting and, if necessary, turn it off by clearing the check box.

▲ 6. Click OK.

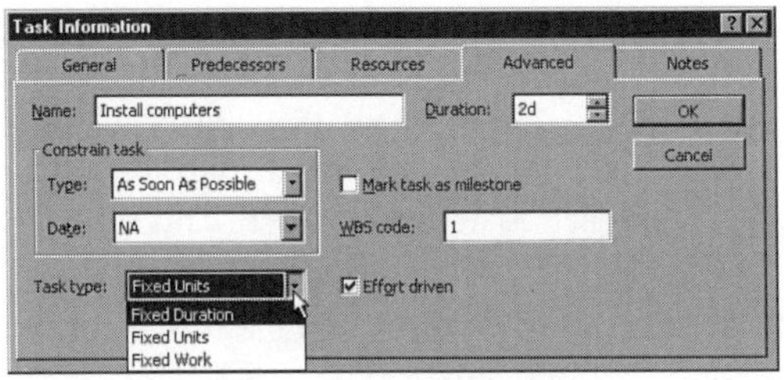

FIGURE 11.1

Check the Task Type and Effort Driven settings for a task before assigning resources to it.

Assigning Resources to Tasks

You can use a variety of views and dialog boxes, with different methods and techniques, to assign resources to tasks. They include the following:

- The Assign Resources dialog box, where drag and drop is available.
- The Task Entry view, which displays the Gantt Chart in the top pane and Task Form in the bottom pane.
- The Task Information dialog box, where a pick list of resource names is available.
- The Task Usage view, which replaces the Gantt Chart task bars in the timescale with a grid of cells that show work details for the assignment during each period in the timescale. You can edit the cells to change the work assignments in individual time periods.

The Assign Resources dialog box and the Task Information dialog box offer pop-up accessibility from any task view, but they accept and display a limited amount of assignment data. The Task Entry and Task Usage views are not pop-up objects, but they display a great deal of information at a glance, especially when used in combination with other views.

> After an assignment has been made, the Assignment Information dialog box offers still more details about the assignment. There are no regular views that show you many of the assignment fields found in the Assignment Information dialog box, so it must be used if you want to know those assignment details.

Even though pop-up forms are easy to use, and you will find yourself using them a lot once you get to know Project, I'm going to use the Task Entry view initially to create assignments. This view combines the Gantt Chart and the Task Form, and you will learn more about the process because it shows you what's going on much better than any other view.

Assigning Resources with the Task Form

The Task Form (see Figure 11.2) can display resource assignment details in a minitable at the bottom of the form. The most commonly displayed details are the resource ID, Name, Units, and Work for each assigned resource. This table is a convenient place for assigning resources because it allows you to enter either resource Units or Work, or both, for each resource assignment, and it shows you the values for those variables for each assignment. With a combination view like this, you can see how a task relates to other tasks in the top pane, along with a lot of detail about the task in the bottom pane.

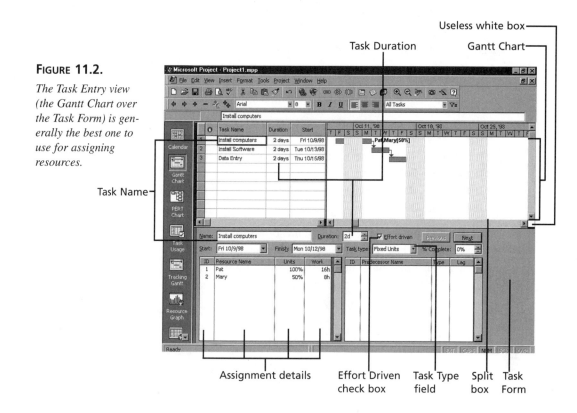

FIGURE 11.2.

The Task Entry view (the Gantt Chart over the Task Form) is generally the best one to use for assigning resources.

To Do: Displaying the Task Form with the Gantt Chart

To display the Task Form with the Gantt Chart, follow these steps:

1. Use the **V**iew menu or the View Bar to select the view you want in the top pane—in this case, the Gantt Chart.

2. Split the view by choosing **W**indow, **S**plit. You can also double-click the split box control below the vertical scrollbar.

   When you split a task view, the Task Form is automatically displayed in the lower pane.

3. Activate the bottom pane with the F6 key (or click anywhere in the bottom pane) so that you can choose the details displayed at the bottom of the form.

4. Choose F**o**rmat, **D**etails to display the Details menu. You can also display the Details shortcut menu by right-clicking anywhere in the Task Form.

5. From the Details menu, choose **R**esources & Predecessors, Resources & S**u**ccessors, or Resource **W**ork (see Figure 11.3).

   The assignment details in these three choices include the Units field along with Name and Work. The Resource **S**chedule details do not include Units, so you can't manage assignment units in that display.

FIGURE 11.3.

The Details menu for the Task Form shows the current display with a check mark and lets you select a new display.

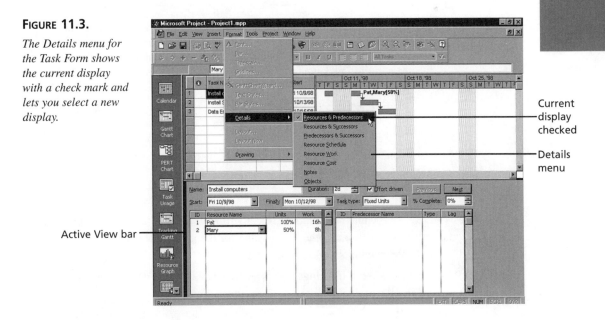

Current display checked

Details menu

Active View bar

To Do: Assigning Resources in the Task Form

To assign resources in the Task Form, follow these steps:

1. Select the task in the top pane. At this point, the task duration is already defined, even if it's only the default value of one day. This duration value will be used in the work formula when you assign a resource.

> If the bottom pane is active, you can change the task selection in the top pane with the Previous and Next buttons in the lower pane. If the task you want to select is near the currently selected task, this method will be faster than activating the top pane, selecting the task, and then activating the bottom pane again.

2. Select the Resource Name field.

3. Identify the resource by typing the resource name, typing the resource initials, or by selecting the resource name from the drop-down list available in the Resource Name field.

> If the resource name you want is not on the pull-down list, you can type in the name of a new resource and Project will add the name to the resource pool. After you complete the assignment, you can double-click the resource name in the Task Form to display the Resource Information dialog box and fill in the resource definition details.

> If you mistype the resource name, it will be treated as a new resource and added to the resource pool.

4. If you leave the Units field blank, Project will assign the default value (100%). If you want to specify some other units value for the assignment, select the Units field and enter the units you want to assign.

5. If you leave the Work field blank, Project will calculate the work based on the task duration and the assigned units.

   If you want to specify the amount of work for the assignment, select the Work field and type in the work amount. Work must be entered with a number plus the unit of

▼ measure (h, hr, hour, d, dy, day, w, wk, or week). Project's default display for work, however, is hours, and your entry will be converted to hours.

6. If you are assigning multiple resources, you can enter them in the next rows of the Resource Name column.

▲ 7. After all resource assignments are made for the task, click the OK button.

When you click OK, Project will calculate the values for those fields you did not fill in, in accordance with the principles discussed in the previous hour. If you assigned several resources at once, Project will calculate the assignment for each independently. The assignment that takes the longest time to complete will determine the task duration.

You can also remove a resource assignment easily with the Task Form.

To Do: Removing an Assignment from a Task

To remove an assignment from a task, follow these steps:

1. Select the task in the top pane.

2. Select the resource name you want to remove in the Task Form.

▲ 3. Press the Delete key and click OK.

Using the Assign Resources Dialog Box

The Assign Resources dialog box is a handy, versatile tool for basic assignment management. In addition, you can use this dialog box to add resources to the resource pool.

 Display the Resource Assignment dialog box by choosing Tools, Resources, Assign Resources or by clicking the Assign Resources tool. Figure 11.4 shows the Assign Resources dialog box over the Task Entry view in the background so you can see how the same field values are displayed differently.

In Figure 11.4, the selected task is Install Computers. If you didn't have the Task Form on the screen, you could still tell which resources are assigned to the task by the check marks next to their names in the Assign Resources dialog box. You can see more detail about the assignments (the work) in the Task Form in the bottom pane.

Adding Resources

You can add resources to the resource pool with the Assign Resources dialog box.

FIGURE 11.4.

Use the Assign Resources dialog box to create task assignments on-the-fly.

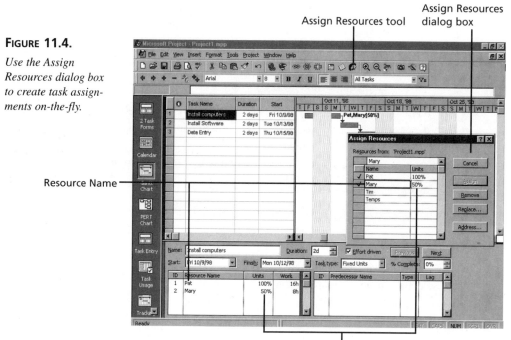

Resource Name

Assign Resources tool

Assign Resources dialog box

Assigned Units

To Do: Adding a Resource with the Assign Resources Dialog Box

To add a resource to the resource pool with the Assign Resources dialog box, follow these steps:

1. Select a blank cell in the Name column of the Assign Resources dialog box.

2. Type in the resource and press Enter.

3. Double-click the new resource name to view the Resource Information dialog box.

4. Use the tabs of the Resource Information dialog box to define the values for the resource.

5. Click OK to close the Resource Information dialog box.

> You can add resources directly from your email address book. Click the **A**ddress button on the Assign Resources dialog box to open your mail address list and select a name. When you close the address list, Project will add the name to the resource pool.

To Do: Adding a Resource Assignment to a Task

To add a resource assignment to a task or group of tasks, follow these steps:

1. Select the task or tasks to which you want the resource assigned. You can use the Ctrl or Shift keys to add additional tasks to the selection. The task Data Entry is selected in Figure 11.5.

2. If it's not already displayed, display the Assign Resources dialog box by choosing **T**ools, **R**esources, **A**ssign Resources or by clicking the Assign Resources tool on the Standard toolbar.

3. Select the row for the resource name you want to assign, or select a blank row and type in the name for a new resource. The row for Temps is selected in the figure.

4. Select the Units field and enter the units if you don't want Project to supply the default 100%. In the figure, the units will be 200% (two temporary employees).

5. Click the **A**ssign button or press Enter to assign the resource and unit information to the selected tasks.

6. If you are adding more resources to the same tasks, select the next resource name to be assigned, type the number of units in the Units field, and select **A**ssign to assign this resource to the selected tasks.

7. After the resource list is completed, click the Close button to close the Assign Resources dialog box.

11

FIGURE 11.5.

When you point to the gray button beside a selected resource, the mouse pointer appears as a selection arrow carrying a resource.

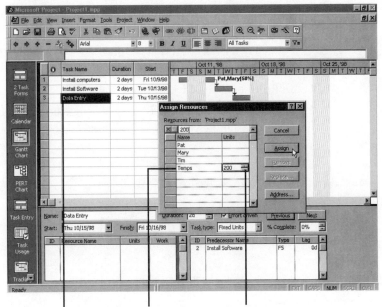

Task selected   Resource row selected   Enter Units

When you click the **As**sign button on the Assign Resources dialog box, a check mark appears to the left of the resource assigned, as shown previously in Figure 11.4. This check mark will appear only when the task is selected in the view.

Assigning Resources Using Drag and Drop

With the Assign Resources dialog box, you can also use drag and drop to assign resources to tasks. You don't have to preselect the task to which the resource will be assigned. This option gives you a quick, efficient way of assigning different resources to one task at a time. However, Project gives you no choice but to use a unit value of 100% for the resource assignment you create with this technique. Of course, you can change the units assignment later, but that will lead to other automatic calculations that might not be intended.

Do not use drag-and-drop assignments unless you want the unit assignment to be 100%.

To Do: Assigning Resources to a Task by Using Drag and Drop

To assign resources to a task by using the drag-and-drop feature, perform the following steps:

1. Display the Assign Resources dialog box by clicking the Assign Resources tool.

2. Select the resource by clicking in the Name field.

3. Position the mouse pointer in the gray rectangle just to the left of the resource name. The Assign Resources graphic appears below the mouse pointer (see Figure 11.6).

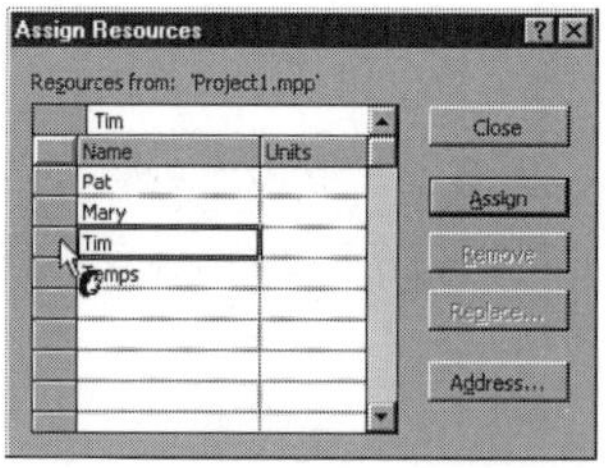

FIGURE 11.6.

When you point to the gray button beside a selected resource, the pointer appears as a selection arrow with the Assign Resources icon.

▼

▼ 4. Hold down the mouse button. A plus sign will appear next to the pointer graphic.

5. Now drag the mouse pointer over the task to which the resource should be assigned (see Figure 11.7).

FIGURE 11.7.

Drag the icon over the task to be assigned.

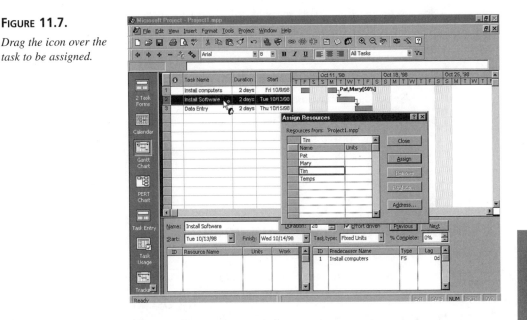

▲ 6. When the task is highlighted, release the mouse button to assign the resource.

> To assign multiple resources to a task by using the drag-and-drop feature, select multiple resource names in the Assign Resources dialog box. When you drag the mouse pointer to the task, all the selected resources are assigned at once.

Scheduling Resources for a Specific Amount of Work

If the task is not Effort Driven, then you can use the Assign Resources dialog box to calculate the number of resource units needed to complete a specified amount of work (given the task's defined duration). Normally, you enter a simple percentage in the Units column of the Assign Resources dialog box. If you enter a work amount in the Units column (a number followed by a time unit instead of a number and a percentage), then Project calculates the Units value for the resource that is needed to do the work you entered within the current duration for the task. But remember, this method will not work if the task is Effort Driven. In that case, you have to enter the work in the resource details area of the Task Form.

To Do: Assigning Resources Using a Work Amount

To assign resources using a work amount, follow these steps:

1. Select the task or tasks to which you want the resource assigned. Check to be sure the task is not Effort Driven.

 2. Display the Assign Resources dialog box.

3. Select the resource name from the Name list.

4. Select the Units field and type the work amount, followed by the unit it's measured in (h, hr, d, dy, w, wk, and so on).

5. Click the Assign button or press Enter to assign the resource and unit information to the selected tasks. Project automatically converts the work value to a percentage.

▲ 6. After the resource list is completed, click the Close button.

Removing Resource Assignments from One or More Tasks

You can use the Assign Resources dialog box to remove assignments as well as add them.

To Do: Removing a Resource Assignment from a Task

To remove a resource assignment from one or more selected tasks, follow these steps:

1. Select the task or tasks in the view that have resource assignments you want to remove.

 2. Display the Assign Resources dialog box by clicking the Assign Resources tool.

3. Select the resource or resources you want to remove from assignments by clicking the check mark or the resource name.

> Resources assigned to the selected task are identified by check marks to the left of the resource name. If a check mark is gray instead of black, then your task selection in the view includes some tasks that have that resource assigned to them and some that do not.

▼

▼
▲   4. Choose the **R**emove button. The resource (or resources) selected in the Assign
        Resources dialog box are removed from any assignments they might have with the
        task or tasks selected in the view.

> You can remove a group of resources in one step if you select all of them
> before clicking the **R**emove button.

Changing Resource Names and Unit Assignments

Use the Assign Resources dialog box to change the resource name or unit assignment for
tasks. Each resource name and unit assignment must be replaced individually.

To change units assigned for a resource, select the task and then edit the unit assignment
in the Assign Resources dialog box. When the new unit assignment is entered, click the
Re**p**lace button.

To substitute one resource for another resource in an assignment, select the currently
assigned resource and then choose Re**p**lace. In the Replace Resource dialog box, select
the new resource name.

11

To Do: Replacing an Assigned Resource with Another

To replace an assigned resource with another resource, follow these steps:

1. Select the task or tasks for which you want to substitute resources.

2. Display the Assign Resources dialog box by clicking the Assign Resources
   tool.

3. Select the resource name to be replaced. (It will have a check mark next to it.)

4. Click the Re**p**lace button. Project will display the Replace Resource dialog box
   over the Assign Resources dialog box (see Figure 11.8).

5. Select the new resource name.

6. Select the Units field for the selected resource and enter the value, if you want it
   to be something other than 100%.

▲   7. Click the OK button.

> The Replace Resource dialog box lists all resources on the project. Microsoft
> Project does not filter the list for availability during the dates for the task or
> for suitability to the task. Therefore, many of the names in the list might not
> be available or appropriate to the task assignment.

Selected task   Currently assigned resource

FIGURE 11.8.

*A second dialog box,
Replace Resource, lists
replacement resources
to choose from.*

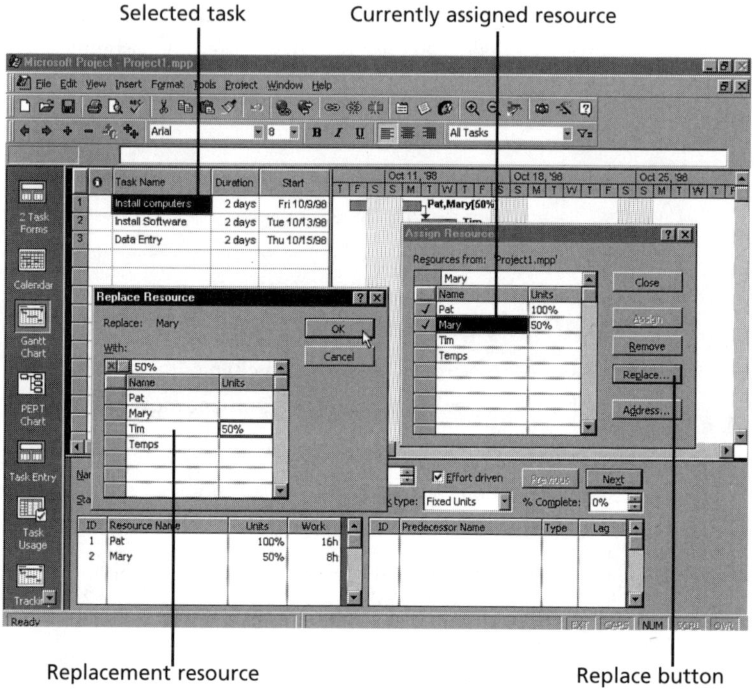

Replacement resource   Replace button

To Do: Replacing the Number of Units in a Resource Assignment

To replace the number of units in a resource assignment, follow these steps:

1. Select the task in the view. You can select multiple tasks if you plan to make an identical assignment change in all of them.

2. Display the Assign Resources dialog box by clicking the Assign Resources tool.

3. Select the Units field for the resource whose assignment is to be changed.

4. Type the new unit assignment for the resource.

5. Click Close or press Enter.

Changing the number of resource units assigned to a task causes Microsoft Project to recalculate the task duration (unless the task is a Fixed Duration task).

Using the Task Usage View

After an assignment is created in a task view, you can examine and modify details of the assignment in the Assignment Information dialog box. However, you must be in either the Task Usage view or the Resource Usage view to access the Assignment Information dialog box. So, let me first introduce you to the Task Usage view. We'll work with this view more in the next hour.

The Task Usage view displays a list of the project's tasks in a table on the left side of the screen (see Figure 11.9) with each task's assignments indented under the task listing. The table's columns are task fields or assignment fields. If the column is an assignment field, the cell in a task row will be blank (and vice versa). For example, the Units field is blank on all task rows in Figure 11.9. The Work values on task rows summarize the Work values for the assignments indented under that task.

> You can use the Assign Resources dialog box with the Task Usage view to create assignments, just as you did with the Gantt Chart.

11

The grid on the right provides work details for each assignment on a period-by-period basis. You can edit the entries in this grid, but that's a topic for the next hour.

The Resource Usage view is similar, except that the table displays a list of the resources in the resource pool with assigned tasks indented under each resource.

> For both the Task and Resource Usage views, use the Go To Selected Task tool to scroll the timeline to the grid data for the selected row in the table.
>
> To jump to the start or end of the project timeline, first click anywhere in the grid, and then press the Home or End key.

In Figure 11.9, Pat's assignment to Install Computers is selected in the table. The usage grid shows his scheduled work on Friday and Monday. The usage grid also shows that the sum of the work for all assignments (Pat and Mary) on Friday is 12 hours.

The Assignment Information dialog box provides another way you can modify an assignment—and it's the only way to modify some assignment fields.

FIGURE 11.9.

Resource assignments are indented under the task name in the Task Usage view, and work details are displayed in the grid on the right.

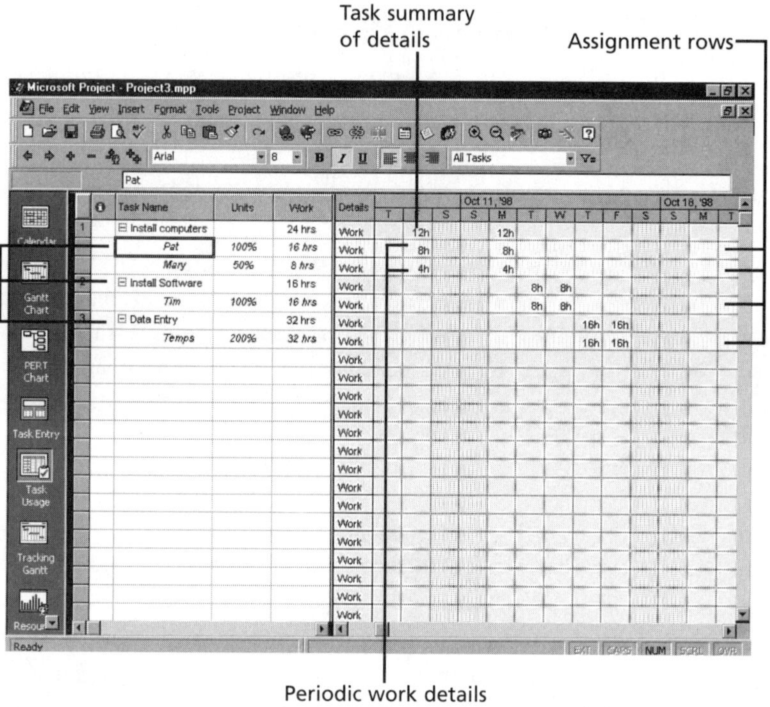

Task summary of details

Assignment rows

Task rows

Periodic work details

To Do: Displaying the Assignment Information Dialog Box

To display the Assignment Information dialog box, follow these steps:

1. Display either the Task Usage view or the Resource Usage view.

2. Select the row for the assignment you are interested in.

3. Click the Assignment Information tool on the Standard toolbar or double-click the assignment. You can also choose the Project, Assignment Information command from the menu.

Figure 11.10 shows the Assignment Information dialog box for Pat's assignment to Install Computers. As you can see, the dialog box has several familiar fields we have already worked with, including the assigned Work, the assigned Units, and the Start and Finish dates for the assignment. You can also change the name of the assigned Resource here, but there's no list to select from, and you must spell the name correctly.

New assignment fields on the Assignment Information dialog box include:

- The Work Contour field lets you choose from a set of predefined work contours. We will work with contours in the next hour.

- The Start and Finish fields will be covered in the next hour. They let you frame the time period during which the resource will do its work.

- The Cost Rate Table field lets you apply one of the five different Cost Rate tables for the resource to this assignment. The default assignment is table A. The Cost Rate Table field can also be displayed as a column in the Usage table. (The Usage table is the table displayed on the Task Usage and Resource Usage views.)

- The Cost field is a display-only field that shows you the total calculated cost of this resource for this assignment.

- On the Notes tab, the Notes field lets you record notes about an assignment. Use the Notes field liberally to explain any unique features of an assignment. You can even include the notes on printouts you distribute to the resource to explain your expectations.

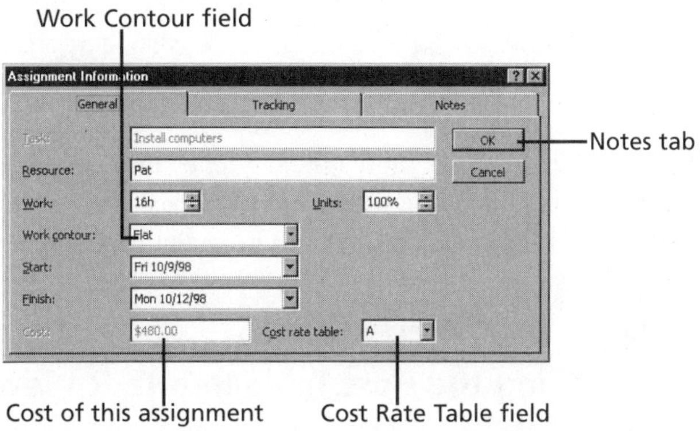

FIGURE 11.10.

The Assignment Information dialog box is the most accessible method of changing the new assignment fields in Microsoft Project 98.

Work Contour field

Assignment Information

| General | Tracking | Notes |

Task: Install computers   OK ──── Notes tab

Resource: Pat   Cancel

Work: 16h   Units: 100%

Work contour: Flat

Start: Fri 10/9/98

Finish: Mon 10/12/98

Cost: $480.00   Cost rate table: A

Cost of this assignment   Cost Rate Table field

11

To Do: Applying a Different Cost Rate Table

To apply a different Cost Rate table to a resource assignment, follow these steps:

1. Display the Task Usage or Resource Usage view.

2. Select the row for the assignment.

 3. Either double-click the assignment or click the Assignment Information tool on the Standard toolbar to display the Assignment Information dialog box.

4. Choose one of the lettered tables in the Cost Rate Table field to assign the standard rate and overtime rate from that table to the work for this assignment.

5. Click OK to complete the transaction.

You can edit the Cost Rate tables only in the Resource Information dialog box. Display the Resource Information dialog box or a view with fields for resources and double-click a resource name to display the Resource Information dialog box. Click the Costs tab to display the five Cost Rate tables, A through E.

Assigning Fixed Costs and Fixed Contract Fees

For some tasks, you need to assign costs that aren't linked to the task duration or the resource assignment. These costs, known as *fixed costs*, are entered in a task view that displays the Cost table.

You also use fixed costs when the work on a task is done by a contractor or vendor for a fixed fee. In this case, you would not want Project to track the hours of work for the task because the hours are important to the contractor or vendor, but not to you. Your cost isn't affected if the work takes more time or money than estimated. For these tasks, make the task a Fixed Duration task and assign the contractor or vendor as a resource to the task. Enter a zero in the Units field. The work amount is calculated as zero. Therefore, resource cost values from this resource are also zero. Then enter the contract cost in the Fixed Cost field of the task Cost table.

To Do: Displaying the Cost Table in a Task View

To display the Cost table in a task view, follow these steps:

1. Display the task view—for example, the Gantt Chart—that you want to work with.
2. With the task view active, choose View, Table and select the Cost table from the submenu.

The Cost table displays columns for Fixed Cost, Fixed Cost Accrual, and Total Cost (among other columns). The Total Cost column adds resource costs and fixed costs. The Fixed Cost Accrual column lets you control when the fixed cost will be included in cost figures on reports.

For example, suppose that a computer service company will install the computers for $500 (which is less than the cost of Pat and Mary's time on this task), and it promises to finish in the same time period already scheduled. The following steps would record the changed assignment.

To Do: Entering the Cost of a Fixed Contract Fee for a Task

▲ To Do

To enter the cost of a fixed contract fee for a task, follow these steps:

1. Choose a task-oriented view (like the Gantt Chart).

2. Select the task to assign to a contractor or vendor.

3. Apply the Cost table by choosing **V**iew, **T**able, **C**ost.

4. Display a combination view by choosing **W**indow, **S**plit.

5. Select Fixed Duration as the Tas**k** Type on the Task Form and deselect Effort Driven. Click OK to set these changes before continuing (see Figure 11.11).

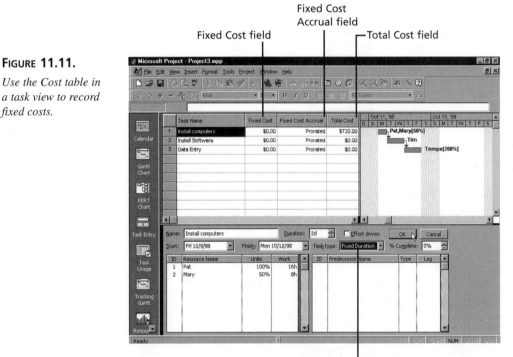

FIGURE 11.11.

Use the Cost table in a task view to record fixed costs.

6. Assign the contractor as a resource in the Resource Name field in the bottom pane.

7. Enter the resource units as zero (**0**).

8. To complete the resource assignment, click OK.

9. Activate the top pane by pressing F6 or by clicking anywhere in the top pane.

▼ 10. Select the Fixed Cost field for the task.

▲ 11. Enter the Fixed Cost amount and press Enter. Project will add the fixed cost to the Total Cost column (see Figure 11.12).

The contractor's fee

FIGURE 11.12.

Enter fixed fees or contract amounts in the Fixed Cost field for the task.

Contractor assigned with zero units

You can enter the fixed cost without assigning the contractor or vendor as a resource. Assigning the resource name just gives you a reference for determining who is responsible for doing the work.

Also note that if no resources are associated with this task, you can enter the fixed cost amount in the Total Cost field and Project will copy the amount to the Fixed Cost field.

HOUR 12

Editing Resource Assignments

In this Hour, we look at techniques you can use to fine-tune the schedule Project calculates for resource assignments and review the effects that changes in the assignments could have on the overall task schedule. We will save dealing with the problem of overallocated resources and how to adjust the schedule to resolve the overallocation problem until Hour 13, "Resolving Resource Allocation Problems."

The scheduling adjustments we will examine in this Hour are:

- Arranging for one resource to start later (or finish earlier) than other resources assigned to the same task.
- Interrupting or splitting assignments that are in progress to allow for work on other tasks.
- Applying a predefined work *contour* to an assignment.
- Manually changing or contouring daily work levels for a task.
- Assigning overtime work.

But first, it will be a good investment of your time to get a little better acquainted with the views that allow you to edit the assignment values.

You will get the most out of this Hour if you are comfortable with the material presented in Hour 10, "Understanding Resource Scheduling in Microsoft Project 98," and Hour 11, "Assigning Resources and Costs to Tasks."

Editing with the Task Usage and Resource Usage Views

You were introduced to the Task and Resource Usage views in Hour 11. We will use the Task Usage view in this Hour to view and edit several aspects of assignments, and use the Resource Usage view more in the next Hour. Let's start by getting used to the techniques you use to view and edit assignments with the Task Usage view. These techniques also apply to the Resource Usage view.

To Do: Displaying the Task Usage view

To display the Task Usage view, click its icon on the View Bar. Or, you can do the following:

1. Choose **View, More** Views from the menu to display the More Views dialog box.

2. From the **Views** list in the More Views dialog box, select Task Usage.

▲ 3. Click the Appl**y** button to display the view.

Figure 12.1 shows the Task Usage view after using the **Windows, S**plit command to display the Task Form in the bottom pane. The tasks are the same computer installation tasks used in Hour 11.

The right side of the view is a timeline with a grid of cells that show assignment details by time period. In Figure 12.1, the grid displays the default work details, but you can display other details when needed.

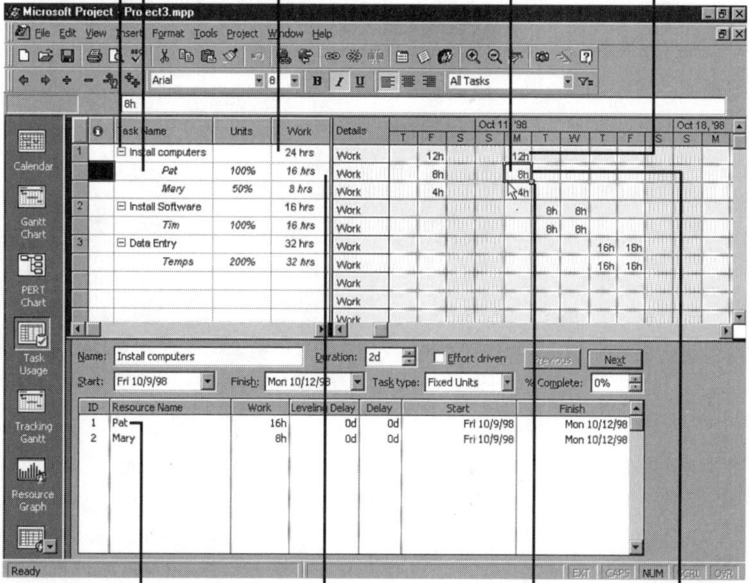

Assignment name: Double-click here
to display the Assignment Information
dialog box

Task name: Double-click here to display the Task Information dialog box

Work total for this task
for all assignments

Selected
cell with
work detail

Work total
for this task
for this time
period

FIGURE 12.1

*You can examine a
wealth of detail about a
task, its assignments,
and the resources
involved in the assign-
ments in this combina-
tion view.*

Resource name: Double-
click here to display the
Resource Information
dialog box

Work total for
this assignment

Selection copy
handle

Selection frame

12

To Do: Changing Details Displayed in the Grid

▲ To Do ▼

To change the details displayed in the grid of a Usage view, follow these steps:

1. Choose Format, Detail Styles (or double-click in any work-day cell in the grid) to open the Detail Styles dialog box (see Figure 12.2).

2. Select a detail item from the Available Fields list box on the left. These are the details that are not currently displayed.

3. Click the Show button to move the item to the Show These Fields list box. This action displays the item for the time being, but doesn't permanently add the item to the shortcut menu for easy access. If you think you will frequently want to work with this detail, then you should execute the next step.

▲
4. Select the Show in **M**enu check box to add this item to the shortcut menu (see Figure 12.3).

FIGURE 12.2

The Details Styles dialog box gives you the option to display additional assignment values.

Available details not currently displayed

Show detail selected in list on the left

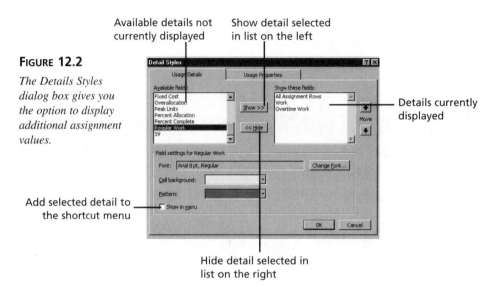

Details currently displayed

Add selected detail to the shortcut menu

Hide detail selected in list on the right

Figure 12.3 shows the Overtime Work details added to the display. It also shows the shortcut menu you can access by clicking the right mouse button over the grid or by choosing Format, Details from the menu. Currently displayed details are checked on the shortcut menu. Click a checked item to hide it; click an unchecked item to display it.

Editing Work Schedules with the Task Usage View

To change the amount of work scheduled for any given time period, simply select the cell, type in a new value, and either press Enter or select another cell. When you type in a value, Project assumes the unit is hours unless you supply a different measurement unit.

As soon as you finish a cell entry, Project immediately recalculates the following:

- The total work for the task for that period (in the task row above the selection)
- The Work field entry for the resource in the table on the left
- The Total work for the task in the table on the left
- The Duration for the task

FIGURE 12.3

The Details shortcut menu lets you change the displayed details quickly.

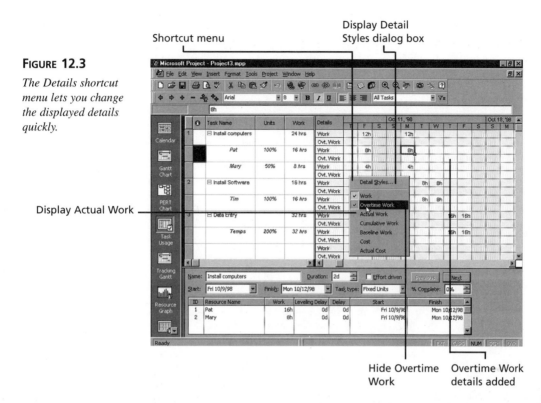

The Contoured indicator will appear in the Indicator column to signal that the work on this assignment has been edited.

Inserting and Deleting Assigned Work

You can shift assigned work to later periods by inserting zero-work cells in place of work that's currently scheduled. It's a little like inserting spaces in text to push text to the right. To insert zero-work cells in the grid, select the first of the cells to be moved to the right and choose Insert, Cells to shift that cell to the right. Or better yet, you can simply press the Insert key to shift cells to the right. If you select a string of cells before you choose Insert, the Insert, Cells command will insert as many zero-work cells as there are work days in your selection.

Unfortunately, inserting and deleting cells works better for projects that are scheduled from a fixed start date than for those scheduled from a fixed finish date. See the cautions in the "Fixed Finish Date Projects" section later in this Hour.

12

You can also delete cells; this action shifts all cells to the right of the deleted cell left-ward. To delete a cell or a block of cells, select the cell or cells and then choose **E**dit, **D**elete Cells; you can also simply press the Delete key to delete the selected cells.

By manually editing cells and inserting or deleting cells, you can fine-tune the work schedule for a resource.

> You can move work from one period to another with traditional Windows 95 cut-and-paste techniques or by dragging selected work cells to new dates with the mouse. To drag the selection, position the mouse over the frame surrounding the selection so that the pointer turns into an arrow. Then click and drag the frame selection to a new time period. Project replaces each original cell with zero-work and replaces any prior value that might have been in the target cell(s) you paste the frame over.

> You can copy a work cell to other cells by using Windows 95 copy and paste techniques. You also can use the "copy handle" that appears in the lower-right corner of the frame surrounding a selection. Position the mouse over the copy handle and it turns into a plus sign. Then drag the selection to adjacent cells to copy the work value.

Introducing Delay in an Assignment

Now, let's get back to actually working on the work assignments. You may remember from Hour 9, "Defining Resources and Costs," that when a project is scheduled from a fixed start date, Microsoft Project schedules all assignments to begin as soon as the task begins. However, you can delay the start of one or more assignments so that they start later than the other assignments for that task.

On the other hand, if the project is scheduled from a fixed finish date, then Project automatically schedules all assignments to finish just as the task finishes. You can override the default assignments by allowing one or more assignments to finish before the task and the other assignments finish.

In this discussion, it will be easier if we begin by examining projects with fixed start dates and then show how the principles apply to projects with fixed finish dates. You learned how to set the fixed start or finish date in Hour 3, "Starting a New Project File and Working with Tasks."

Fixed Start Date Projects

Many of the tasks you create for your projects actually encompass more than one action. You don't want to create separate tasks for every little step that has to be taken, that leads to projects that are too finely detailed to be practical. Consequently, some of your tasks might require work from different resources at different times.

For example, in the Install Computers task, one of the last steps in the installation process is configuring Windows to recognize the printers available on the network. Suppose Todd is assigned to the Install Computers taskforce to configure the network printers. His work needs to come toward the end of the task, but Project schedules all assignments at the beginning of the task by default. We need to be able to tell Project to *delay* the start of Todd's assignment.

This simple equation explains what we want to achieve:

```
Task start date + Assignment delay = Assignment start date
```

Assignment delays are created by entering an amount of time in the Delay field, inserting zero-work days at the start of the assignment, or specifying a new start date for the assignment. We will use the Task Form to create the delay.

To work with delays, display the Task Form in the bottom pane below a task view and apply the Resource Schedule details. Figure 12.4 shows the Task Usage view in the top pane and the Task Form with Resource Schedule details in the bottom pane.

> There are two delay fields on the Task Form—Delay and Leveling Delay. Leveling Delay is covered in the next Hour.

12

To Do: Viewing or Editing Assignment Delays

To view or edit assignment delays with the Task Form, follow these steps:

1. Display a task view, such as the Gantt Chart or the Task Usage view.
2. Split the window with the **W**indow, **S**plit command (or by double-clicking the split box).
3. Activate the Task Form by pressing F6 or by clicking anywhere in the bottom pane.
4. Use the **F**ormat, **D**etails command to display the Resource **S**chedule details.

▼   5. Enter an amount of time in the Delay column, using a number and a time unit (for
        example, "h" for hours, "d" for days, and so forth). Or, you can enter a later start
        date and time for the assignment in the Start field.

▲   6. Click OK to finish the entry. Your screen should look similar to Figure 12.4.

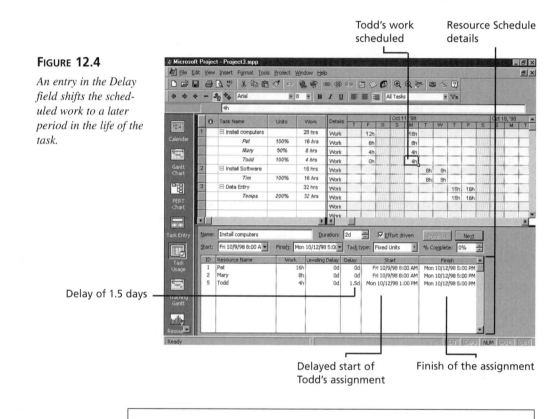

FIGURE 12.4

An entry in the Delay field shifts the scheduled work to a later period in the life of the task.

Todd's work scheduled

Resource Schedule details

Delay of 1.5 days

Delayed start of Todd's assignment

Finish of the assignment

Although changing the assignment start date is an alternative way of creating a delay, changing the assignment finish date has a different effect—it is interpreted to mean you are changing the length of the assignment and, therefore, the amount of work to be done.

Figure 12.4 shows Todd assigned to the Install Computers task. The original schedule had Todd starting at the same time Pat and Mary start—on Friday at 8:00 a.m. In this case, however, a delay has been added to shift his assignment to a day and a half later. The bottom pane shows the 1.5d entry in the Delay field. After that entry, Project changed the start date for his assignment. The delay is apparent from the zero-work entry for Todd on Monday in the top pane and from the entry in the Start field in the bottom pane. Instead of entering the delay amount, we could have entered "10/12/98 1:00 PM" in the Start field and Project would have calculated the delay value. We could also have simply inserted a zero-work day in the grid in the top pane.

The Delay field is never blank. To remove a delay, you must enter zero in the Delay field; you cannot delete the value in the field and try to leave the field blank.

Fixed Finish Date Projects

The preceding discussion is based on a project with a fixed start date, in which the delay field is used to schedule one assignment to start later than other assignments. If your project has a fixed finish date, then by default Project schedules assignments to finish when the task finishes, not to start when the task starts. The Delay field is used to cause one assignment to finish earlier than other assignments.

In the example used in the previous figures, Todd's assignment to configure the printers would automatically be scheduled at the end of the task if the project had been a fixed finish date project. There would have been no need for a delay. However, suppose Todd's assignment was to help unpack all the computer boxes at the beginning of the task. In that case his work should come at the beginning of the task. If the project is a fixed finish date project, Microsoft Project would schedule his 4 hours to finish when the task finishes, and we would need to be able to force Project to schedule his assignment to finish earlier.

"Delays" in fixed finish date projects must be entered as negative numbers in the Delay field because they move the finish date to an earlier date.

NEW TERM   **Assignment Delay**   For a fixed start date project, an *assignment delay* is the amount of time between the start of a task and the start of the resource's work on the task. The start date of the task, plus the amount of delay, yields the start date for the assignment.

For projects with a fixed finish date, an assignment delay is the amount of time between the finish of the task and the finish of the resource's work on the task. It measures how much earlier the resource's work on the task is finished compared to the rest of the work. The finish of the task, minus the delay, yields the finish of the assignment.

12

Substituting "finish date" for "start date" in the formula used earlier, we have this formula:

```
Task finish date + Assignment delay = Assignment finish date
```

In the case of fixed finish date projects, the delay value must be a negative number because the assignment finish must come before the task finish in projects with fixed finish dates.

In Figure 12.5, the Install Computers task is scheduled in a fixed finish date project, and Todd's assignment is naturally scheduled at the end of the task. To schedule his hours at the beginning, we would need to introduce a negative delay in his assignment. I have already entered the delay (-1.5d) in the bottom pane, but have not yet clicked the OK button to add it to the calculations.

> Although you can simply insert zero-work into an assignment to create a delay in a fixed start date project, that technique doesn't work with fixed finish date projects. Use extreme care when inserting and deleting cells in the Usage view grids with these projects.

FIGURE 12.5

In a fixed finish date project, schedules are calculated backward from the defined finish date for the project.

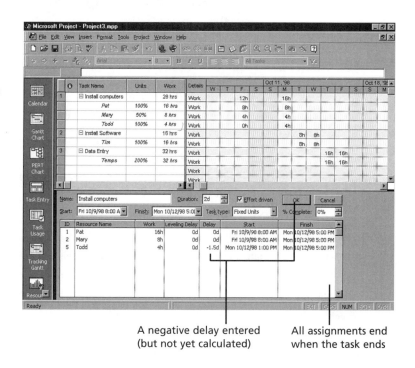

A negative delay entered
(but not yet calculated)

All assignments end
when the task ends

Figure 12.6 shows the result after the OK button is clicked. Notice that Todd's work now starts at the beginning of the task on Friday.

FIGURE 12.6

After the delay is added, Todd's assignment is scheduled to finish (and start) earlier.

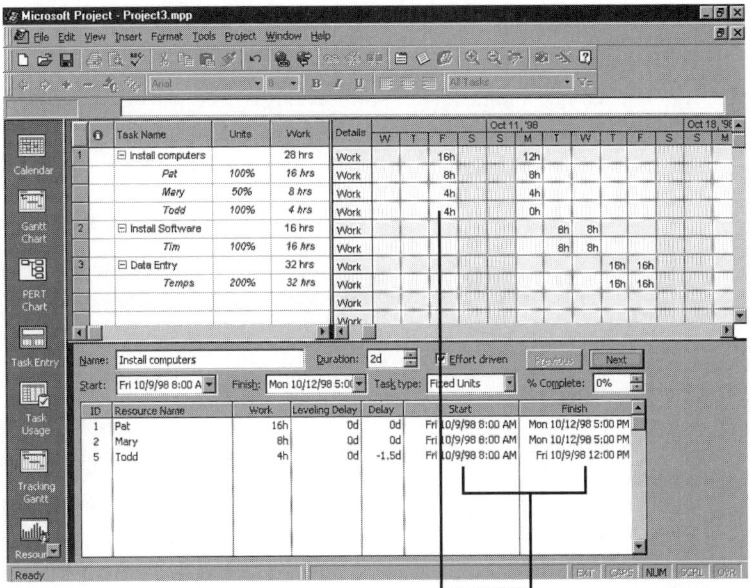

Early finish for this assignment means rescheduled start

The assignment Start field has no effect on the delay in a fixed finish date project. Instead, its changes are interpreted by Project to signal a change in the assignment work.

12

Splitting Tasks and Task Assignments

You might have noticed that you hardly ever get to work on a task from start to finish without having to stop and work on something else; you're putting out fires or you're diverted temporarily to another task with a higher priority. If you know in advance that you will have to interrupt your work on a task, you can build in a *split* in the task assignment. Project can show that the work stops at the point of the split and then resumes at a later time.

NEW TERM **Split** A *split* in a task or in a task assignment is an interruption in the schedule, so that work stops at the point of the split and then resumes later at the end of the split.

If you split a task schedule, Project also splits all the assignments to that task. In this case, the task's duration is not affected (the number of working time periods has not changed), although the time span between the start and finish of the task is now longer because of the nonworking time introduced by the split.

If you split just one assignment on a task, however, the other assignments continue unchanged and the task isn't split. The resource whose assignment was split might have to work beyond the original dates for the task to make up the time lost to the split. If that happens, then the task duration increases because of the split.

> In a fixed start date project, the resource whose assignment is split would finish later than the originally scheduled finish. In a fixed finish date project, the resource would have to start earlier than the originally scheduled start to get all the work done.

You saw back in Hour 4, "Turning the Task List into a Schedule," how to split a task with the Split Task tool on the Standard toolbar. Assignment splits have to be created in either the Task Usage view or the Resource Usage view. In both cases, you activate the grid on the right side of the view, select the time period where the split should occur, and press the Insert key. Project will insert cells with zero work in the cell(s) you selected, pushing the scheduled work cells out of the way to make room.

> For a fixed start date project, inserting cells in a Usage view pushes selected cell(s) to the right—shifting that work to later dates. For a fixed finish date project, inserting cells in a Usage view pushes the selected cell(s) to the left—rescheduling that work to start earlier.

To Do: Splitting a task assignment

To split a task assignment, follow these steps:

1. Display either the Task Usage view or the Resource Usage view. This view needs to be either full-screen or the top pane of a combination view.
2. If necessary, adjust the timescale for the grid to show the time units you plan to use for the split. For example, if you are going to split a task for a number of days, the minor units in the timescale should be days.

▼   Use the Zoom In and Zoom Out tools on the Standard toolbar to quickly change the time units displayed. See "Formatting Timescales" in Hour 7, "Formatting Views," for more details.

3. On the row for the task to be split, select the period or periods the split will occupy in the timescale grid. (See the following Warning for an exception.) You can drag with the mouse or use the Shift key with the left or right arrow keys to select multiple time periods.

4. Choose Insert, Cells or press the Insert key. Project pushes the selected cells out of the way to the right or left (depending on the type of project) and replaces them with cells having zero work (0h) assigned. For projects with fixed start dates, Project pushes the selected cells to the right to later dates, thus pushing the assignment finish to a later date. For projects with a fixed finish date, Project pushes the selected cells to the left to earlier dates, thus pushing the assignment start to an earlier date.

▲

> Project behaves differently when performing this operation in projects scheduled from a fixed finish date. Instead of starting the split in the cell you select, Project starts the split in the cell *to the left* of your selected cell. You need to select the cell to the right of the point where you want the split to start.

To illustrate, I'll introduce a new task for Pat: He needs to attend a project meeting at one of the company's other sites on Monday, but that's during the second day of the Install Computers task. We can split Pat's assignment for the Install Computers task, rescheduling his work from Monday to Tuesday. In Figure 12.7, task 4, Project planning meeting, is also assigned to Pat and scheduled for Monday. Pat's Monday assignment to the Install Computers task is selected. Pressing the Insert key inserts a zero-work cell in place of the selection and shifts the selection to the right.

Figure 12.8 shows the split in place. Pat has zero hours (0h) scheduled on the Install Computers task on Monday and 8 hours scheduled on Tuesday. Notice that because the Install Computers task now finishes later, the tasks that follow it have been pushed out to the right also, and the finish of the Data Entry task is now delayed until the following Monday.

You can also reschedule work in the Task and Resource Usage views by dragging a work assignment from one time period to another. When the mouse pointer touches the selection border around cells in the grid, it turns into an arrow, which indicates that you can click and drag the selection to a new date.

12

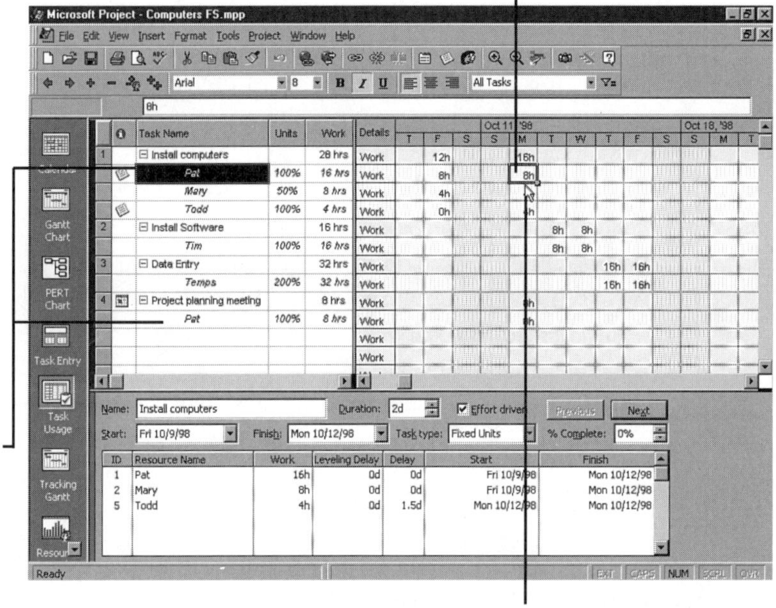

FIGURE 12.7

Pat and Mary are scheduled to finish installing the computers on Monday, but Pat needs to attend a meeting on that day. We can split the installation task so he can attend the meeting.

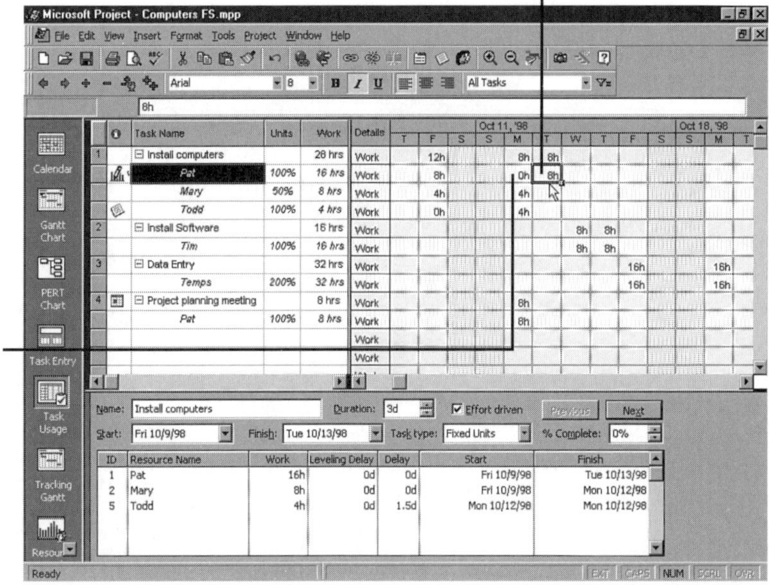

Cell where the split is to start

Pat's conflicting assignments

Pointer shape shows the mouse can drag this cell to a new period

FIGURE 12.8

Pat's assignment is split, with his last 8 hours of work on the Install Computers task now scheduled for Tuesday.

Work shifted to this period

No work scheduled for this task now in this period

Contouring Resource Assignments

When Project creates an assignment, it schedules the same amount of assigned units during each time period until the task is completed, thus producing an even, or "flat," level of activity each period. This is called a *flat* assignment profile, neither rising nor falling over time. In reality, many tasks require varying amounts of work throughout their duration; for some, most of the work comes up front and then tapers off (sometimes called a *front loaded* profile), and others start out with light work loads that build as the task nears completion (also called a *back loaded* profile).

If the actual work profile needs to vary from period to period, with peaks and valleys of activity, or a rising (or falling) trend of activity, you can use one of Project's predefined assignment profiles, called *contours*—or you can create your own contour by manipulating the scheduled work for each period.

NEW TERM **Contour** An assignment *contour* is a work profile or pattern that describes how scheduled work is distributed over time.

If the work assignment has been changed from the default Flat schedule, an icon appears next to that assignment in the Indicator column on the Task (or Resource) Usage view (see the indicators in Figure 12.9). In either of those views, you can also manually adjust the assigned hours over the course of the task duration. If you make manual changes, the icon in the Indicator column shows a pencil imposed on the Scheduling Pattern icon (see Figure 12.9).

Identifying the Predefined Contours

Microsoft Project 98 provides eight predefined work contour profiles that you can apply to a resource assignment. One of them is the default assignment profile, called *flat*, used by Project when it initially calculates an assignment. The contour profiles are indicated in Figure 12.9.

Figure 12.9 compares the schedules that Project calculates for each contour. The original task had a duration of 5 days and the resource was assigned 40 hours at 100%. The first row, labeled "Flat," shows how the default assignment looked initially. Each of the contours reduces the unit assignment during selected days in the assignment; the choice of which days are reduced is what distinguishes the different profiles and gives rise to the contour names. Because less work is scheduled on some days, the total assignment takes longer to complete; for some contours, it's doubled to 10 days in the figure.

The Resource Graph view in the bottom pane of Figure 12.9 has been formatted to show the units assigned in each period for the contour selected in the top pane (Double Peak in this instance). Notice how the graph profile is the inspiration for the contour type's indicator image.

12

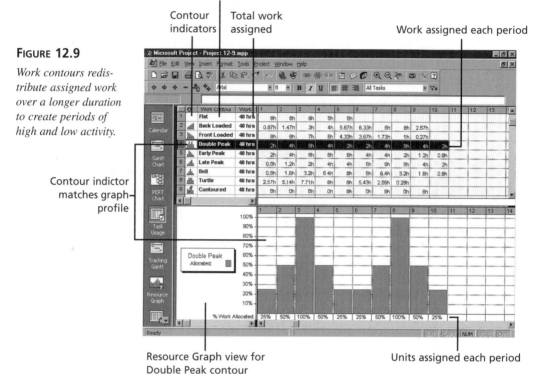

FIGURE 12.9

Work contours redistribute assigned work over a longer duration to create periods of high and low activity.

Contour names

Contour indicators

Total work assigned

Work assigned each period

Contour indictor matches graph profile

Resource Graph view for Double Peak contour

Units assigned each period

I've also represented the units assigned to each period beneath the graph bars (labeled "% Work Allocated") to illustrate that this is the real mechanism at work in contours. Project assigns different units each time period when you apply a contour, and that's what leads to different amounts of work each period.

Row 9 in Figure 12.9 is labeled "Contoured," and it represents the user manually editing the schedule to create a unique "contour," in this case by scheduling the work every other day for 9 days instead of every day for 5 days.

Applying a Predefined Contour

To Do: Selecting a Contour for an Assignment

To select a contour for an assignment, follow these steps:

▼   1. Select the assignment in the Task Usage view or the Resource Usage view.

▼   2. Display the Assignment Information dialog box by choosing **P**roject,
Assignment **I**nformation, by clicking the Assignment Information tool, or by
double-clicking the assignment row.

3. On the General tab, use the list arrow in the Work **C**ontour field to select one of
the predefined contours.

▲   4. Click OK to have Project calculate the new assignment pattern.

When you assign a contour, Project keeps the total work of the assignment constant (see
the following Caution for an exception). However, the duration of the assignment is usually longer because work in some periods is reduced. Therefore, the total work must be
spread out over a longer time period.

> If you assign a contour to a Fixed Duration task, the task duration cannot
> change. Therefore, wheile applying the contour reduces work in some peri-
> ods, the total work for the task is reduced, instead of the duration being
> extended.

> If you want to restore the assignment contour to the default pattern, or if
> you have edited the assignment and want to restore the original assign-
> ment, choose the predefined contour named "Flat."

12

Assigning Overtime Work

You can reduce the duration for a task by allowing some of a resource's work to be
scheduled as overtime work. The total work to be done on the assignment remains the
same, but the amount of work scheduled during regular working hours is reduced. Project
calculates cost for overtime work by applying the resource's overtime rate.

NEW TERM   **Overtime Work**   Work scheduled to take place outside the working hours of
the resource calendar is called *overtime work*.

Understanding How Overtime Affects the Schedule

When you assign a resource to a task for the duration of the task, Project schedules work
for the resource only during the regular working times (those times defined in the resource
calendar). If you assign overtime work, you are telling Project that part of the task will be
completed outside the regular working times (for example, in evenings or on weekends)
and that Project doesn't have to use regular hours to schedule that part of the work.

NEW TERM   **Regular Work**   Work scheduled during the working times defined on the
resource calendar is called *regular work*; it's counted when calculating the task
duration.

To Project, if part of the work on a task is to be done in overtime, that reduces the
amount of work that needs to be scheduled during the regular working times. To handle
the calculations, Project divides Work (which is total work) into Regular Work and
Overtime Work. When you assign overtime to a resource, Project subtracts Overtime
Work from Work to get Regular Work and schedules that amount of work in regular
hours. Because it's work during regular time that Project counts in calculating duration,
reducing Regular Work effectively reduces the task duration.

When you assign overtime work, this is how Project recalculates the schedule:

- Your entry in the Overtime Work field is subtracted from the assignment's total
  work, and the difference is called *Regular Work*.

- The new, reduced Regular Work is scheduled during the hours available on the
  resource calendar. If you have selected a work contour for the assignment, the new
  work Regular schedule is apportioned over time in the same pattern as the contour.

- The Overtime Work is then scheduled over the same period of time as the Regular
  Work, and with the same contour.

> If you assign all the work to be done in overtime, Project reduces the
> Regular Work, and consequently the duration of the task, to zero and auto-
> matically flags the task as a milestone. You can remove the milestone flag by
> opening the Task Information dialog box and clearing the Mark Task as
> Milestone check box on the Advanced tab. The milestone symbol will no
> longer appear in the Gantt Chart for the task, although its duration will still
> be zero.

Entering Overtime Work

You can view the assigned overtime work in the Task and Resource Usage views, but
you can't enter or edit overtime in those views. You can display the Overtime field on
several forms for editing. In each form, you must use the Format, **D**etails command to
apply the work details at the bottom of the form. You can enter overtime in these ways:

- On the Task Form, with the Resource Work details displayed at the bottom of the
  form

- On the Resource Form, with the Work details displayed at the bottom of the form

You can see the total overtime worked by a resource for all tasks by viewing the Resource Usage view or the Resource Sheet and applying the Work table to either one.

Using the Task Form to Enter Overtime

You can use any of the task-oriented views (Calendar, Gantt Chart, PERT Chart, Task Usage, Tracking Gantt, and Task Sheet) in the top pane to display and select the task for which you want to record overtime. The Task Form in the bottom pane can then be used to enter the amount of overtime.

To Do: Entering overtime in the Task Form

To enter overtime in the Task Form, follow these steps:

1. Choose a task-oriented view from the **V**iew menu for the top pane.

2. Select the task for which you want to schedule overtime.

3. Display a combination view by choosing **W**indow, **S**plit.

4. Press F6 to activate the Task Form in the bottom pane.

5. In the bottom pane, choose Format, **D**etails and select Resource **W**ork, or right-click the form and select Resource Work from the shortcut menu to display the Resource Work fields in the entry table (see Figure 12.10).

FIGURE 12.10

You can enter overtime hours, and reduce task duration, in a combination view.

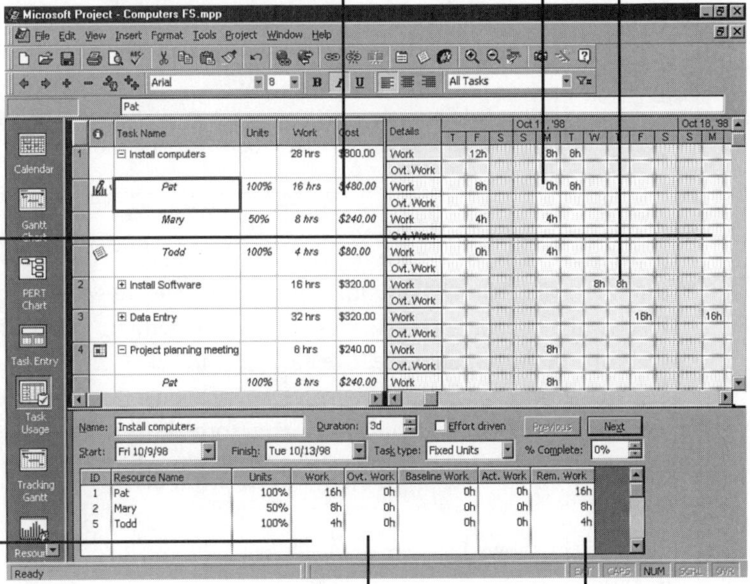

Task and assignment costs

Assignment split

Finish of subsequent tasks

Overtime work details

Overtime Work

Resource Work details

Total Work (including overtime)

12

▼   6. Select the Ovt. Work field and enter the amount of work you are scheduling in overtime. Enter a number followed by a time unit abbreviation (h, hr, or hour for hours, and so on), and then press Enter or click the Enter box on the Edit bar. Do not reduce the entry in the Work field. That field's entry must show the *total* amount of work to be done, including both the regular work and the overtime work.

▲   7. Click OK to complete the overtime assignment.

> If you want to clear an overtime entry, you must enter a *0*. You can't leave the field empty; it must have a value.

For example, in the computer installation example earlier in this lesson, Pat was scheduled for 16 hours of work on the Install Computers task. Remember that this schedule caused a conflict with a meeting on Monday, which was resolved by splitting his assignment and letting him complete the installation task after the meeting. However, another option would be to let Pat do the 8 hours originally scheduled for Monday over the weekend or after hours on Friday (assuming he's a good-natured fellow and is willing). This time would be overtime hours, and Pat's assignment would be finished by the time of the meeting.

> Although you can't edit scheduled overtime hours in Project to put them in the hours and days when you really plan for them to take place, you can record when they took place when you're tracking actual progress on the project. See Hour 17, "Tracking Work on the Project."

Figure 12.10 shows the same information that was in Figure 12.8 (where Pat's assignment was split), but with a slightly different display to get ready for adding overtime. I've added a column for Cost, and I've added Overtime Work to the details in the timescale. In the bottom pane, I've changed the details from Resource Schedule to Resource Work because that's where I will schedule the Overtime. In the Cost column, you can see that Pat's assignment costs the project $480 (because Pat's standard rate is $30 per hour). The total cost for the task is $800, which includes the costs for all three assigned resources.

Figure 12.11 shows Pat's assignment changed to include 8 hours of overtime. The overtime was entered in the bottom pane in the Ovt. Work field. Notice that the total Work for the assignment is still shown as 16 hours. Total Work includes regular work and over-time work.

Project displays the overtime hours in the timescale on Friday, although Pat can do the work whenever he wants—evenings or on the weekend. Had this assignment spanned several days, Project would have distributed the overtime hours over all the days in the duration.

> If you have applied a work contour pattern to an assignment, Microsoft Project automatically allocates overtime work for that assignment in a similar pattern, so a front-loaded resource will also have its overtime work scheduled more heavily at the beginning of the task.

FIGURE 12.11

By scheduling part of an assignment in overtime, the duration of the task is usually reduced.

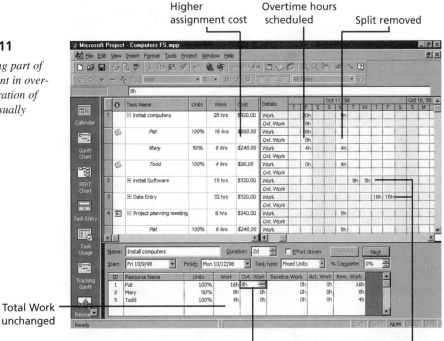

12

Notice these changes in the schedule as a result of the overtime assignment:

- The cost for Pat's assignment has risen from $480 to $600 because Pat gets more for overtime work than for regular work (see Figure 12.12).
- The overtime hours enable Pat to complete his assignment before Monday. The split that started on Monday is no longer needed (there's no more work for Pat to do), so Project has removed the split.
- The subsequent tasks are now scheduled earlier, and this little project finishes a day earlier.

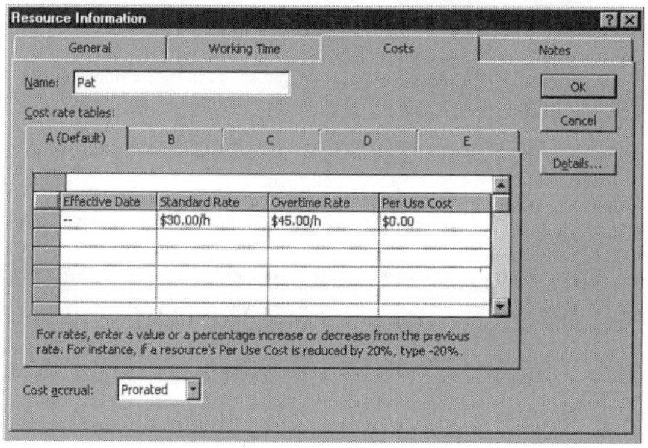

FIGURE 12.12

The Overtime rate for resources is entered on the Resource Information form.

An Alternative to Overtime: Changing the Calendar

Another way of scheduling extra time is to change the resource calendar and increase the hours when a resource is available. You edit the resource calendar and make these days and hours working times rather than nonworking times. Be aware, however, that Microsoft Project charges no overtime rate for work done during the regular calendar hours. If you don't pay premium overtime rates, then editing the calendar is satisfactory. Indeed, by editing the calendar, you can state explicitly when the extra work time takes place. If you pay premium overtime rates, however, you should enter overtime hours in the Overtime field so that costing is done at the overtime rate.

Understanding the Effects of Changing Task Duration

Recall from Hour 10 that the duration of a task is determined by how long it takes the *driver resources* to complete their assignments. Therefore, the task's finish is tied to the finish of the driver resource assignments. When you increase the duration for a task,

Project increases the assigned work for the driver resources, but leaves unchanged the assignments for resources who aren't working when the task finishes. When you reduce task duration, Project reduces the assigned work for the driver resources and reduces the work only for non-driver resources.

For projects scheduled from a fixed finish date, changes in duration affect only the assignments for resources who are working when the task starts.

12

Hour 13

Resolving Resource Allocation Problems

You undoubtedly know what it means to be assigned more work than you can possibly get done in the time allowed. You have several assignments that fall in the same time period, as though your boss assumed you could clone yourself—and would be more than willing to do so.

When you're overbooked like that, you can sometimes spread the workload out a little, getting some of it done ahead of time and finishing some of the tasks a little late, without causing any harm. However, if there are absolutely intractable deadlines, you have to get other people to take some of the assignments for you. Otherwise, you can't get the work done on time, or you have to cut corners and not do a good job.

When you schedule resources to work on tasks in your project, you almost inevitably create some of these "impossible" resource workloads. Microsoft Project calls it an *overallocation* when a resource is assigned to more work than can be realistically completed.

NEW TERM **Resource Overallocations**   A resource is *overallocated* if at any moment the sum of the units assigned to all tasks is more than the maximum number of units available (as defined in the Max Units available field on the Resource Information dialog box for that resource).

How do overallocations occur? Actually, they can happen very easily.

- You can create multiple assignments scheduled during the same time period; if the combined assignments require more work than the resource can possibly do in that time period, the resource is then overallocated. This is by far the most common source of overallocations.

- You can accidentally (or intentionally) assign more than the maximum available units of a resource to a task. Project will let you do that, but it immediately highlights that resource as overallocated.

- You can assign a resource to a task scheduled outside the dates when the resource is available. Again, Project will let you do that, but it highlights the resource as overallocated.

You need to identify these overallocations and modify the project plan to eliminate them (in a process called *leveling*). The following sections show you how to identify resource overallocation problems and how to correct them.

NEW TERM **Leveling Resources**   *Leveling* refers to adjusting the assignments for a resource to "level out" the demands for that resource's time. Leveling is necessary when assignments are bunched up and too much work falls in too short a time period, thus creating a "peak" of work that needs to be spread out more evenly (leveled) over a longer period.

Identifying Overallocated Resources

Project uses highlighting to help you identify not only which resources are overallocated, but also to pinpoint the time periods during which overallocations occur. Furthermore, Project displays a special leveling indicator to distinguish serious overallocations that need rescheduling from those that are less serious and that can be resolved by the people doing the work without having to change the project schedule.

A resource is technically overallocated if for even one minute anywhere in the project there are more units assigned than are available for assignment. Some overallocations, however, do not put the project at risk, so it's not worth taking the time to adjust the "official" schedule. In those cases, you can let the people assigned to the task make minor adjustments to the schedule.

For example, suppose Pat is assigned to only two tasks on a particular day, and each task should take about an hour to complete. If, however, both tasks were scheduled for the same time period, say 8:00 a.m., Microsoft Project would highlight Pat's name because Pat is technically overallocated. The only way Pat can finish both tasks is to delay one until the other is finished. Whether you consider this delay a serious problem is a judgment call, based largely on the nature of the project and how sensitive you think the success of the project is to delays like this.

If the project is very sensitive to delays and needs to be on schedule hour by hour, then you would take Pat's conflicting assignments seriously and make changes in the schedule to resolve the conflict so that both tasks can be completed on time. On the other hand, if you feel secure so long as the project is on schedule on a day-by-day basis, you could save the effort of tinkering with the project schedule and leave it to Pat to figure out how to get both tasks finished by the end of the day.

You can define how sensitive your project is to overallocations, whether it must be on schedule minute by minute, hour by hour, day by day, week by week, or month by month. This is called the *leveling sensitivity setting* (although Project refers to it onscreen as the "basis" for leveling calculations).

To Do: Changing the Leveling Sensitivity Setting

To Do

1. Choose **T**ools, Resource **L**eveling from the menu to display the Resource Leveling dialog box (see Figure 13.1). We'll spend more time with this dialog box shortly.

2. Click the list arrow in the box to the right of the label "Look For Overallocations On A" and select the time period sensitivity.

▲ 3. Click the OK button.

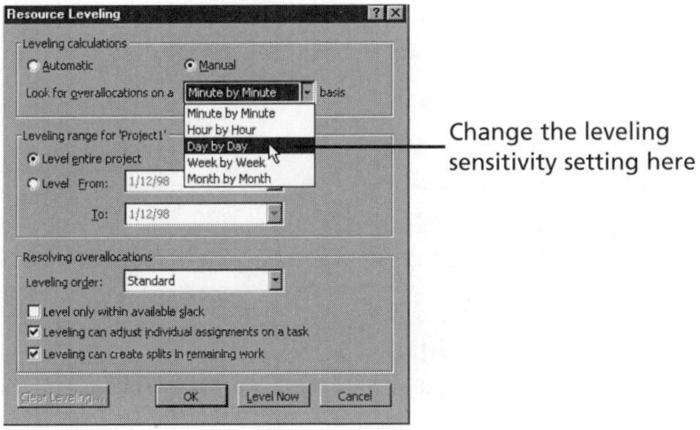

FIGURE 13.1

Select the setting for how sensitive your project is to minor delays in the Resource Leveling dialog box.

Change the leveling sensitivity setting here

13

If you select the setting Day by Day, then Project displays the leveling indicator next to any resource name that has more work assigned during any one day than can be completed in that amount of time (see Figure 13.2). If you select Hour by Hour, the indicator appears next to any resource that has any hour overbooked (like Pat in the previous example).

> All overallocated resources are highlighted; however, only those that exceed the sensitivity setting have the leveling indicator displayed.

Viewing Overallocated Resources

The Resource Usage view, shown in Figure 13.2, is the best view for finding and dealing with resource overallocations. This view displays all the resource names, with each resource's assignments indented under its name. A grid of numbers under the timescale on the right shows the amount of work scheduled during each time period. In Figure 13.2, the timescale is divided into weeks, and the numbers in the grid represent the total assigned work for each week.

To Do: Displaying the Resource Usage View

1. Choose **V**iew, **M**ore Views from the menu to open the More Views dialog box.
2. In the **V**iews list of the More Views dialog box, select Resource Allocation.
3. Click the Apply button to display the selected view.

You can easily identify the overallocated resources because they are highlighted in red text. The number in a grid cell on the resource row also appears in red if the resource is overallocated at any point during that cell's time period. Although you can't tell in the black-and-white figure, the names for both Pat and Mary in Figure 13.2 are highlighted in red.

The numbers for the work amounts annotated as "Overallocated Assignments" in Figure 13.2 are also highlighted in red. Mary is scheduled for 56 hours in the week of January 1. Because she is available for only 40 hours a week, she's overallocated. Pat is scheduled for only 16 hours in the week of February 15, yet that value is also in red. Although Pat can easily do 16 hours of work in a week, it turns out that all 16 hours are scheduled in just one day (see Figure 13.3), and that is too much work to be scheduled in one day. Because he is overallocated at some point during the week, the value for the week is displayed in red in Figure 13.2.

FIGURE 13.2

The Resource Usage view is an excellent view for analyzing and adjusting resource schedules.

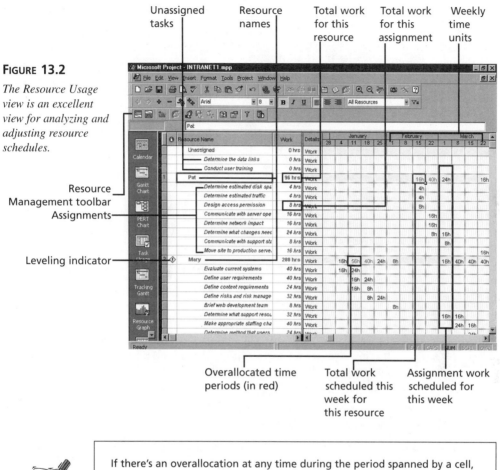

If there's an overallocation at any time during the period spanned by a cell, Project 98 highlights that period's values in red, no matter how far you zoom out to compress the timescale.

13

In Figure 13.2, you see the leveling indicator next to Mary's name but not next to Pat's. That's because the leveling sensitivity setting for this project is week by week. Mary has 56 hours scheduled the week of January 11, which is excessive for the leveling sensitivity setting. Pat has no more than 40 hours scheduled in any week, so even though Pat is overallocated on a single day, it's not too much for a week. In that case, the indicator is not applied.

FIGURE 13.3

Pat's daily detail for the week of February 15 shows that all the work falls on one day.

All work for the week of February 15 is scheduled on one day, February 19.

			Resource Name	Work	Details	Feb 15									Feb 22								
						15	16	17	18	19	20	21	22	23	24	25	26	27	28	1	2
			Unassigned	0 hrs	Work																
			Determine the data links	0 hrs	Work																
			Conduct user training	0 hrs	Work																
		1	Pat	96 hrs	Work					16h						16h	16h	8h			8h
			Determine estimated disk spa	4 hrs	Work					4h											
			Determine estimated traffic	4 hrs	Work					4h											
			Design access permission	8 hrs	Work					8h											
			Communicate with server ope	16 hrs	Work											8h	8h				
			Determine network impact	16 hrs	Work											8h	8h				
			Determine what changes nee	24 hrs	Work													8h			8h
			Communicate with support sta	8 hrs	Work																
			Move site to production serve	16 hrs	Work																
		2	Mary	288 hrs	Work																
			Evaluate current systems	40 hrs	Work																
			Define user requirements	40 hrs	Work																
			Define content requirements	24 hrs	Work																
			Define risks and risk manage	32 hrs	Work																
			Brief web development team	8 hrs	Work																
			Determine what support resou	32 hrs	Work																
			Make appropriate staffing cha	40 hrs	Work																
			Determine method that users	24 hrs	Work																

You can pause the mouse pointer over a leveling indicator to see a ScreenTip that identifies the leveling sensitivity setting. This is quicker than opening the Leveling dialog box to see how the leveling sensitivity setting is defined.

Finding Overallocations

Use the Go To Next Overallocation tool on the Resource Management toolbar to search through the project for the next date when an overallocation occurs. When an overallocation is found, Project selects the resource name or task name, depending on the type of view you are using. If you're in the Resource Usage view or Task Usage view, then after Project selects the row for the resource or the task, it also selects the cell in the timeline grid on that row for the date when the overallocation occurs (see Figure 13.4). This helps you identify the conflicting assignments that must be examined if you are to resolve the overallocation.

In Figure 13.4, the Resource Usage view shows that Pat's total assigned work for the day of February 19 is 16 hours. The grid entries below identify the conflicting assignments contributing to the workload on that date that must be adjusted to resolve the overallocation.

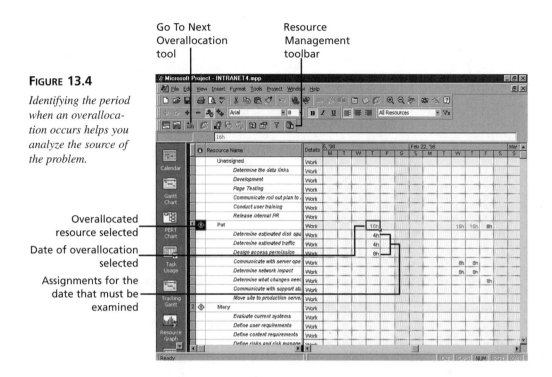

FIGURE 13.4

Identifying the period when an overalloca-tion occurs helps you analyze the source of the problem.

When you use the Go To Next Overallocation tool, again Project selects the next overal-located resource or associated task on the currently selected date before moving on to find the next date with an overallocation and selecting each of its overallocated resources or associated tasks. You must scroll the timescale to the start of the project if you want to find all overallocations. I suggest you drag the horizontal timescale scrollbar button all the way to the left to move to the start of the project.

Eliminating Resource Overallocations

Now that you know how to find overallocations in your project, let's look at ways to cor-rect them. If you want to eliminate an overallocation, you have to edit the project sched-ule to do either of the following:

- Increase the amount of the resource that's available in the time period when the overallocation occurs.

- Reduce the demands for the resource during the time period when the overalloca-tion occurs.

13

You have to identify when the overallocations occur and then either increase the availability of the resource or reduce the assignments for the resource during the period of the overallocation. The next sections offer suggestions for strategies to resolve the overallocations.

Increasing the Resource Availability

If you decide to increase the availability of the resource, you have to negotiate the change with the resource supplier and then enter the changes in the Resource Information dialog box, as you did in Hour 9, "Defining Resources and Costs." I won't repeat those steps here, but let me give you some pointers for gaining access to the Resource Information dialog box while finding overallocations.

To display the Resource Information dialog box, you must be in a view that allows you to display resource data. Of course, any of the resource views (such as the Resource Usage view and the Resource Sheet) offers this access. After selecting a resource name, you can use the Resource Information tool to display the Resource Information dialog box.

If you're in a task view (such as the Gantt Chart or the Task Usage view), you can use the Assign Resources tool to display the Assign Resources dialog box. The resources assigned to the selected task have check marks next to them. You can double-click a resource name to display the Resource Information dialog box for that resource.

> Although resource names seem to be indented in the Task Usage view, the records are really *assignment* records, not *resource* records, and the Information tool on the toolbar displays the Assignment Information dialog box, instead of the Resource Information dialog box.

Consider the suggestions in the following list for increasing the resource availability:

- The overallocation could be caused by an assignment outside the dates when the resource is available. Check the General tab of the Resource Information dialog box and, if possible, select the option Available for the Entire Project for that resource, or change the From and To dates to encompass the overallocation period.

- If a group resource is overallocated, you can increase the number of Units available by increasing the entry in the Max Units Available field.

- You can increase the hours of work the resource can deliver during the period of the overallocation by changing the working hours on the resource calendar—assuming the resource is willing to work longer hours.

You can also schedule overtime hours if the resource is willing to work more hours during the period of overallocation. However, you can't handle overtime on the Resource Information dialog box. You must display the Task Form with the Work details, as you did in Hour 12, "Editing Resource Assignments," to enter overtime.

Reducing the Workload of the Overallocated Resource

You can reduce the workload for a resource in an overallocated period in a number of ways. This list summarizes the possibilities:

- You can reduce the total work defined for one or more task assignments during the overallocated period. There could be nonessential work or "frills" included in the task definition that can be removed, or you might have to reluctantly downgrade the quality of the finished task to resolve the overallocation. However, you must consider the effect this "downscaling" will have on the ability to meet the deliverables expected for the project.

- You can reduce the number of tasks assigned to the resource during the period by canceling unnecessary tasks or by reassigning tasks to other resources. Sometimes it helps to break a large task into several smaller tasks that can be reassigned more easily than the original conglomerate task.

- You can shift the workload for one or more assignments to other periods by delaying the start of one or more tasks or by changing the assignment's contour to shift work to later time periods for those tasks. Of course, delaying any of the assigned work in the project schedule naturally extends the duration for the task and could compromise finishing the project on time.

Reducing Workload with the Resource Allocation View

The Resource Allocation view was specially designed for reassigning and delaying tasks. You can display the Resource Allocation view from the menu by choosing View, More Views, selecting Resource Allocation from the Views list, and clicking the Apply button to display the view. You can also display the view by clicking the Resource Allocation tool on the Resource Management toolbar.

This composite view shows the names and task assignments of all resources in the top pane (see Figure 13.5), highlights overallocated resources in red, and displays the leveling indicator for those resources that need your attention. When you select a resource in

13

the top pane, all the tasks assigned to that resource appear in the Leveling Gantt in the bottom pane. The Leveling Gantt has a specially formatted Gantt Chart that will be particularly helpful when we discuss delaying resource assignments.

FIGURE 13.5

The Resource Allocation view is designed specifically for dealing with resource allocation problems.

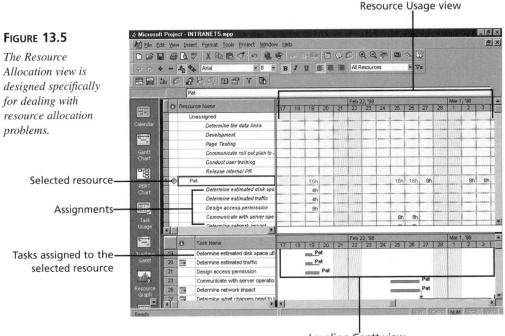

You can use the Go To Next Overallocation tool in either pane to pinpoint overallocated resource assignments. In the top pane, the Go To Next Overallocation tool identifies *resources* that are overallocated. In the lower pane, the Go To Next Overallocation tool is limited to finding overallocations for the resource you have selected in the top pane, and it selects the *tasks* associated with an overallocation.

If you want to remove an assignment from a resource without assigning another resource in its place, you can simply select the assignment and choose **Edit, Delete** Assignment (or press the Delete key). The assignment will disappear from under the resource and reappear in the Unassigned category at the top of the Resource Usage view. You can also select the row for the assignment and drag the assignment to the Unassigned group. You can assign the task to another resource later.

If you want to redefine the duration for a task, select the overallocated resource in the top pane, and then select the task in the bottom pane. Either double-click the task or use the Task Information tool to display the Task Information dialog box, where you can adjust the task duration.

Reassigning Tasks

One of the most successful methods for dealing with the problem of overallocated resources is to reassign tasks to other, underutilized resources. In Figure 13.6, Pat is the overallocated resource selected in the top pane of the Resource Allocation view. I used the Hide Assignments tool on each of the other resources so I could quickly see (without having to scroll through the top pane) the time periods in which all of them are available for additional assignments.

FIGURE 13.6

Select the resource whose overallocations you want to resolve.

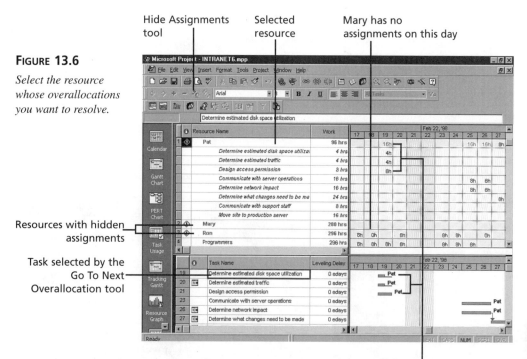

Hide Assignments tool   Selected resource   Mary has no assignments on this day

Resources with hidden assignments

Task selected by the Go To Next Overallocation tool

Conflicting assignments

To Do: Reassigning Tasks

Follow these steps to reassign tasks for overallocated resources:

1. Display the Resource Allocation view and select the overallocated resource in the top pane.

2. Activate the bottom pane by clicking anywhere in the pane.

3. Go to the start of the project with the Alt+Home key combination (or drag the button in the horizontal scrollbar all the way to the left).

 4. Use the Go To Next Overallocation tool (with the bottom pane activated) to find the next time period when the selected resource is overallocated.

5. Decide which task will be reassigned to another resource and select that task in the lower pane.

 6. Click the Resource Assignment tool to display the Resource Assignment dialog box (see Figure 13.7).

7. Select the resource you want to replace (the assigned resources are checked), and click the Replace button to display the Replace Resource dialog box (see Figure 13.8).

8. Select the name of the resource that you want to assign as a substitute.

9. Change the Units assigned for the new resource, if desired.

▲ 10. Click OK to complete the substitution.

In this example, I reassigned the task Design Access Permission to Mary, which reduces Pat's assignments for the day of February 19 to just 8 hours (see Figure 13.7).

FIGURE 13.7

Use the Resource Allocation dialog box to change the resource assignments.

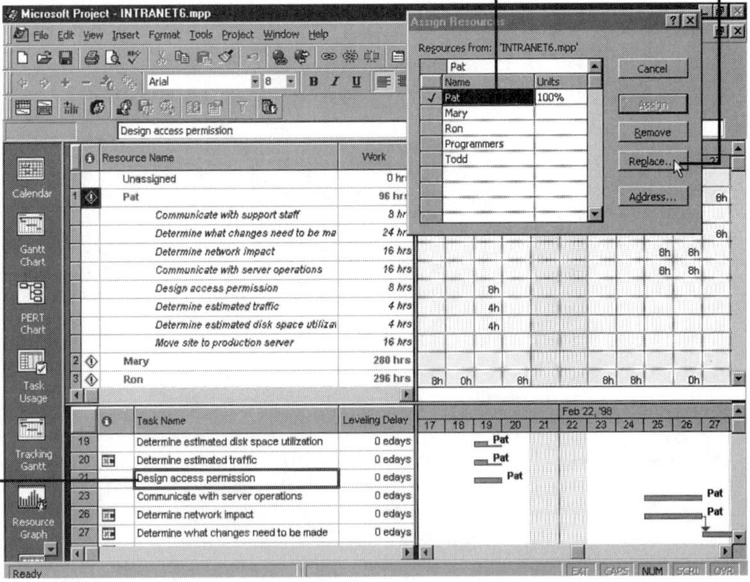

Assign Resources dialog box
with assigned resource selected

Replace button

Task to be reassigned

Figure 13.8

Select the replacement resource in the Replace Resource dialog box.

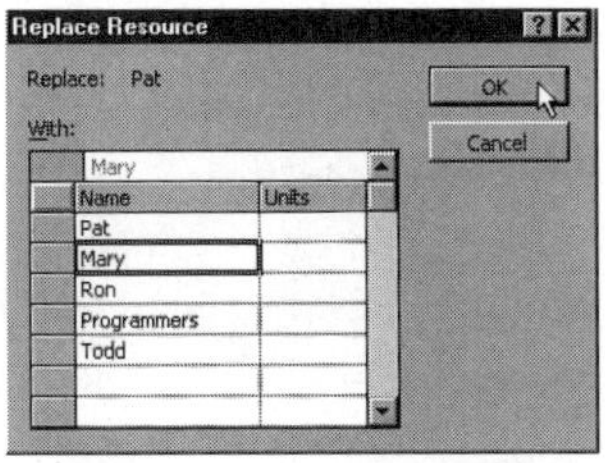

After changing the assignment, the task disappears from Pat's list of assignments and can be seen in Mary's list (see Figure 13.9). Pat's assigned work for the day is now within his availability of 8 hours.

Figure 13.9

The reassigned task now appears in Mary's list of things to do.

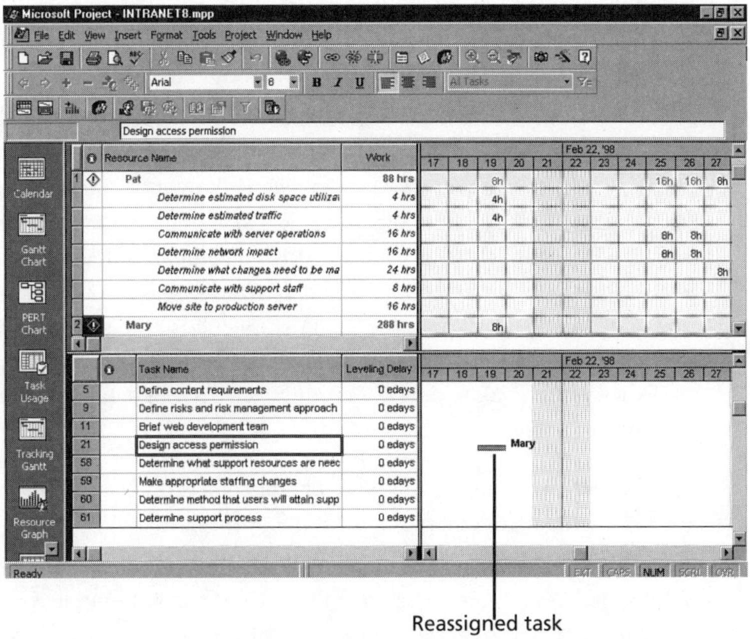

Reassigned task

13

Substituting resource assignments is often the most effective approach to resolving resource overallocations. The drawback is the time it takes to analyze the situation and reach a decision.

Using Delays to Level Out the Workload

If you can't resolve an overallocation by increasing resource availability or removing assignments, then you need to spread the assigned work out over a longer period so that the overallocated resource can finish its assigned tasks. Spreading the work out requires that some of the bunched-up assignments be shifted to later or earlier dates.In a project that's scheduled from a fixed start date, all tasks are scheduled as close to the start date as possible. When you attempt to level out the workload in these projects, you can shift assignments only by delaying them to later time periods. A special task field, called the Leveling Delay field, is used to record the amount of the delay for a task. As you will remember from the previous Hour, there's also an Assignment Delay field you can use to delay the scheduled work of just one resource without delaying the other resources assigned to the task. You learned how to use that field on the Task Form in Hour 12.

New Term **Delay**   A *delay* is an amount of idle time inserted in the schedule to shift the work to later or earlier time periods. In a fixed start date project, the idle time is inserted at the beginning of a task or assignment and has the effect of causing the assignment to start and finish later than originally scheduled. In a fixed finish date project, the idle time is inserted at the end of a task or assignment and has the effect of causing the assignment to start and finish earlier than originally scheduled.

Delaying some assignments to later dates could mean that successor tasks are also delayed—indeed, it might mean you can't finish the project when originally planned. The amount of time you can delay a task without affecting the project finish date is called *total slack* time (or sometimes just *slack* time). The amount of time you can delay a task without affecting any other task's schedule is called *free slack*. If there is free slack, then there has to be total slack. If you want to resolve an overallocation by delaying assignments, you cause the least disturbance to the schedules of other tasks (and to the finish date of the project) if you delay tasks that have free slack. If you can't find tasks with free slack to delay, you can at least avoid delaying the project's finish if you choose tasks that have total slack.

New Term **Slack**   The amount of *slack* time measures how long a task can be delayed without affecting the rest of the schedule.

Total slack is the amount of delay that will leave the scheduled completion of the project unchanged. *Free slack* is the amount of delay that not only leaves the project's finish unchanged, but also leaves the schedules for other tasks undisturbed.

The Resource Allocation view includes the Leveling Delay field as a column on the left of the Leveling Gantt chart in the bottom pane (see Figure 13.10). The bars in the timeline area are customized to show the amount of free slack as a thin line extending to the right of the task bar and the amount of the leveling delay as a thin line on the left of the task bar (from the original start date for the task to the delayed start date).

The Leveling Delay field uses time amounts the way people use them in everyday conversation: A day is 24 hours and a week is 7 days. This measurement is called *elapsed time* in Microsoft Project. Elapsed time is continuous time; unlike the term *duration*, it makes no distinction between working and nonworking time, nor is it governed by your definition of "day" and "week" in the **T**ools, **O**ptions dialog box.

FIGURE 13.10

The Leveling Gantt is designed to help manage task delays when leveling assignments.

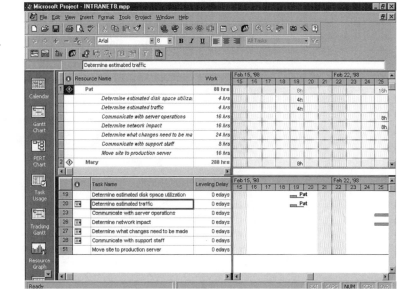

NEW TERM   **Elapsed Time**   *Elapsed time* is Project's name for the standard measures of time used by people in normal conversation: One day is 24 hours and one week is 7 days. Elapsed time is entered with an *e* before the time unit. For example, "2 edays" is two elapsed days.

In Figure 13.10, Pat has two tasks scheduled at the same time on February 19 that produce an overallocation (on an hour-by-hour basis). If one is delayed by 4 hours, then the overallocation will be resolved. The delay is shown in Figure 13.11, where the second task is delayed by 4 elapsed hours (4 ehrs). The task bar is shifted to the right by 4 hours, as shown by the delay bar that replaces the original task bar. The free slack is now gone for this task.

You can use Undo (Ctrl+Z) immediately after entering a delay amount to restore the previous value to the delay field, and you can remove a delay by entering a zero in the delay field. Note that you can't delete a delay value and then leave the entry blank.

13

FIGURE 13.11

Delaying the Determine Estimated Traffic task removes the overallocation for Pat on February 19.

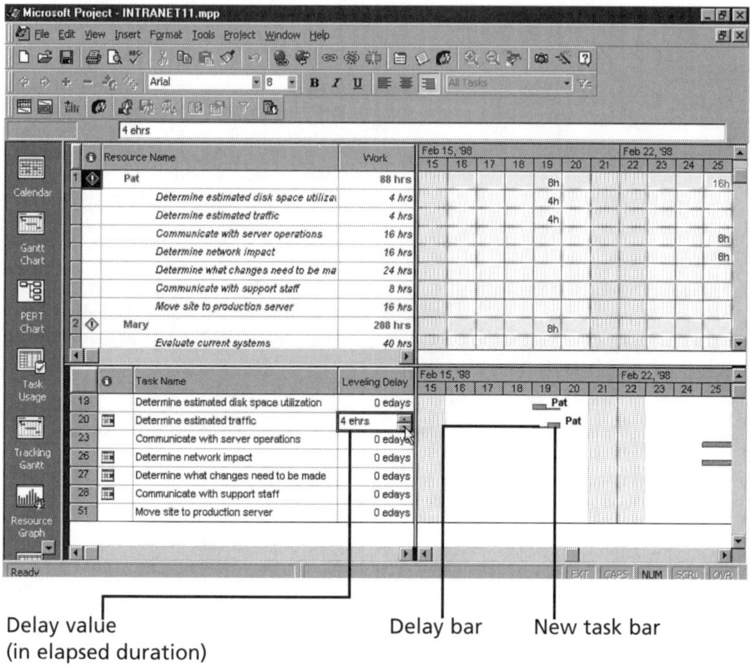

Delay value
(in elapsed duration)

Delay bar   New task bar

Other Delaying Techniques

Recall from Hour 4, "Turning the Task List into a Schedule," that you can split a task into disconnected time periods, which is sometimes a helpful technique for resolving overallocations. You could split a long task around a shorter task that has a date constraint or a higher priority for being completed as scheduled. If some of the work has already been finished on a task that's competing for an overallocated resource, you can split the task to reschedule the remaining work at a later time.

When tasks have multiple resources assigned to them, and only one of the resources is overallocated, it might be better to resolve the overallocation by delaying the assignment for just that resource, leaving the other resources unchanged. You learned how to delay and split assignments in Hour 12. Use those same techniques to resolve overallocations at the assignment level rather than the task level.

Letting Project Level Overallocated Assignments

Instead of manually leveling overallocations as described in the previous sections, you can take the easy route and let Project do the work for you. However, Project can resolve overallocations only by calculating delays; it can't increase resource availability on its own, or adjust the work content of tasks, or substitute one resource for another. It can simply do a mathematical trick and calculate delays as a substitute for the more intelligent methods. You will almost always produce a better schedule if you level assignments manually. If you want to try the automated leveling feature you must use the Tools, Resource Leveling menu command to display the Resource Leveling dialog box and choose the Level Now button. A full discussion of the leveling options is beyond the scope of this book. For complete coverage of the topic, refer to my more comprehensive book, *Special Edition Using Project 98*, published by Que Corporation.

13

PART V

Finalizing and Publishing Your Plan

Hour

HOUR 14

Optimizing the Project Plan

After you have defined and entered your tasks and resources into a project plan, you might start to feel overwhelmed by all the details displayed in Project's different views. Project is certainly a tool for dealing with minutiae. Project also, however, gives you the ability to step back from the project and view the information so that you can see the big picture and evaluate the plan's effectiveness.

In this Hour, you learn to display a summary of the important statistics of a project, such as the start and finish dates. You also learn to use filters that allow you to view a selected subset of the project's tasks or resources. You learn how to identify the critical path for your project and work with strategies that help you reduce the project's duration. Finally, you learn how to review the cost schedule and find ways to reduce the project costs.

Looking at the Big Picture

As you have worked through the previous Hours in this book, you probably realize that one of Project's greatest strengths is its capability to provide every detail of your project plan. The different views of Project, such as the Gantt Chart and the Calendar, allow you to focus on the project's details in different formats.

Sometimes, however, after you've defined your tasks, determined durations and constraints, created dependency relationships, and assigned your resources, you might want to broaden your view of the plan to see how all the parts fit together. Several tools are available that can help you take a look at the plan's big picture; these tools include compressing the timescale, collapsing the task list, filtering, and reviewing the cost schedule. You will work with each of these tools this hour.

NEW TERM   **Duration**   *Duration* is the time period required to complete a particular task.

Dependency Relationship   Tasks are linked by dependencies. For instance, one task must be completed for the next task to begin. The second task is dependent on the first.

Constraints   A *constraint* is a restriction on the start or finish date of a task. You can specific that a task start on a particular date or finish no later than a certain date. The task is said to be *constrained*.

You can view an overall statistical summary of the Project by opening the Project Statistics dialog box. The information in this dialog box is calculated from the values found in your Project. This summary will only be as up-to-date as the information found in your plan.

To Do: Opening the Project Statistics dialog box

To open the Project Statistics dialog box, follow these steps:

1. Right-click on any of the currently displayed toolbars. On the toolbar menu, select the Tracking toolbar.

2. On the Tracking toolbar, click the Project Statistics button.

3. The Project Statistics dialog box opens and gives you a statistical summary of the current project, as shown in Figure 14.1.

The Project Statistics dialog box provides several different summary details. The following list describes the information given in this dialog box.

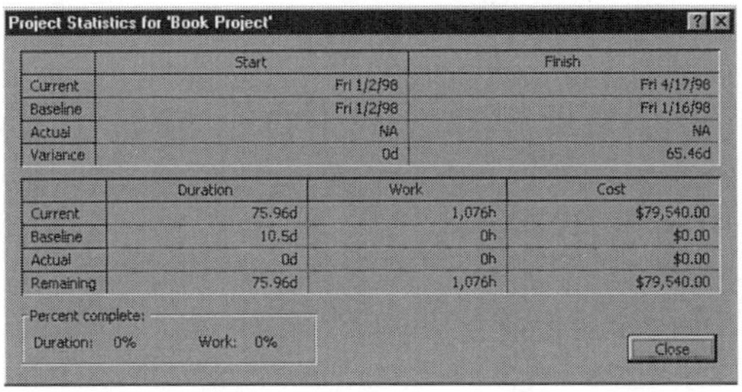

FIGURE 14.1

The Project Statistics dialog box gives you a summary of your project's start and finish dates and information on the current costs and hours of work performed.

NEW TERM **Baseline Dates** The *baseline* for a project represents your expectations for the project and the completion of its tasks. *Baseline dates* include projected start and finish dates for tasks and the project itself. See Hours 3, 4, and 5 for information on how to set up a new project and determine a baseline for the various aspects of the project.

- The top of the dialog box shows the current start and finish dates. A row is also provided for baseline dates if a baseline was set when the project plan was first designed. The Actual row gives you a start and finish date if the project has started and has been completed (this would be calculated from tracking information you enter). A Variance row is also provided for the start and finish dates to display the variance between the baseline dates and the actual dates.

- A second area in the dialog box lists summary information on the duration of the project, the work (in hours) completed on the project, and the cost of the project. A row is devoted to the Current data (duration, work, cost), Baseline data, Actual data, and Remaining data.

- A third area in the dialog box is reserved for information about the percentage of the project that has been completed. The Percent Complete section displays both the percentage of the duration and the work that has been completed.

Obviously, the statistics in the Project Statistics dialog box are dynamic in nature, meaning that the information given (except for the baseline information) changes each time you update the data in the Project file. You will find that it makes sense to periodically view the project summary statistics in this dialog box to get an overall feel for how your project is progressing.

Compressing the Timescale

Another strategy for broadening your view of the project details is to compress the timescale on the Gantt Chart, which gives you a good overview of the project's workflow. The default Major timescale for the Gantt Chart is weeks and the Minor timescale

14

is days. By compressing the timescales, you can effectively zoom out from the project details. For instance, you might want to change the Major scale to months and the Minor scale to weeks to get a much broader view of the bars and other information in the Gantt Chart. The simplest way to change the timescales is to use the Zoom Out and Zoom In buttons on the Standard toolbar.

To Do: Compressing the timescale for the Gantt Chart

To compress the timescale for the Gantt Chart, follow these steps:

1. In the Gantt Chart view, click the Zoom Out button on the Standard toolbar.

 2. Each click of the Zoom Out button selects a larger set of time units for both the Major and Minor scales (see Figure 14.2).

3. To decrease the time units on the scales, click the Zoom In button on the Standard toolbar.

Using the Zoom Out and Zoom In buttons can vary the detail (and scope) of your view of the task bars in the Gantt Chart. Project also gives you a way to zoom out and view the entire project. Choose **V**iew, **Z**oom to open the Zoom dialog box.

The Zoom dialog box has a number of standard timescale zooms and a custom zoom drop-down box. To zoom out to see the entire project, select the Zoom Entire Project radio button, and then click OK. You can then see your entire project in the Gantt Chart.

After you have finished viewing your project at a particular zoom setting, you can reset the view (return to the default timescale settings), by reopening the Zoom dialog box with the **V**iew, **Z**oom menu choice. In the Zoom dialog box, click Reset and then OK to return to the Gantt Chart.

> You can also make additional changes to the timescale by choosing **F**ormat, **T**imescale. The Timescale dialog box is discussed in Hour 7, "Formatting Views."

Collapsing the Task List Outline

Another way to step back from the project details and get an overview of the items in your project is to collapse the Task List outline. This can be done in any view that displays your tasks in a list table, and it's an excellent way to hide the subtasks in a project and just view the first-level summary tasks in the outline.

Zoom Out button

FIGURE 14.2

The Zoom Out button on the Standard toolbar offers a quick way to compress the timescale on the Gantt Chart.

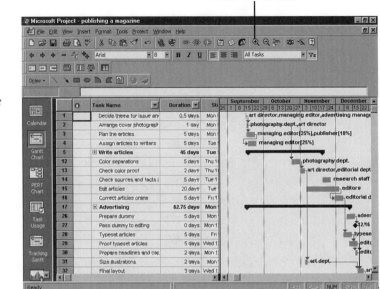

To Do: Collapsing the Task List Outline

To collapse the Task List outline, follow these steps:

▼To Do

1. In a view containing a task list (such as the Gantt Chart view), click the Task Name heading to select the tasks in the list.

2. To hide the subtasks in the list, click the Hide Subtasks button on the Formatting toolbar. The list collapses and only the summary tasks are shown (see Figure 14.3). A plus symbol appears to the left of your first-level tasks (in Figure 14.3, summary tasks are the first level).

3. To open the different levels of subtasks in the outline, click the Show Subtasks button on the Formatting toolbar. Each subsequent click of the Show Subtasks button opens a successive level in the outline.

▲

When you collapse the task list, you will also notice that the bars associated with the subtasks roll up and are not shown on the Gantt Chart. You can also collapse or expand the portion of the Task List outline related to a particular first-level task, such as a summary task. Each first-level task has a small plus (+) symbol to the left of the task name when the list is collapsed. To expand the subtasks for a particular first-level task, click the plus symbol. The subtasks related to the first-level task will appear, and all other subtasks (related to the other summary tasks) will remain hidden.

14

Hide Subtasks button

FIGURE 14.3

The Hide Subtasks button on the Formatting toolbar allows you to collapse the tasks shown in the task list.

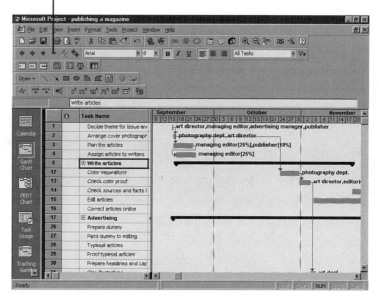

When you expand the subtasks for a particular first-level task, a minus (–) sign appears next to the task name. Clicking the minus (–) sign hides the subtasks for this primary-level task.

When you want to show all the subtasks on the task list, click the Show All subtasks button on the Formatting toolbar. All the tasks will reappear (as will their Gantt bars when you are in the Gantt Chart view). You can also expand or collapse a summary task by double-clicking on it.

An obvious overall strategy for getting an overview of information in your project is to move from very specific information (such as zooming out on the Gantt Chart or collapsing the Task List) to a more general view. Another approach, however, to reduce the clutter on your screen, is to look at specific portions of the information displayed by the different views of your project. The next section deals with filtering tasks and resources, which gives you a subset of the information in a particular view.

Collapsing the Task List outline and zooming out on the Gantt Chart timescale provides you with two informational overviews—text and chart— of the same information.

Filtering Tasks or Resources

Another strategy for viewing your information is to filter the information so that you can view a subset of the tasks or resources in a list.

NEW TERM **Filters** *Filtering* simply means that you set certain conditions so that only those tasks or resources meeting those conditions are displayed. For example, to reduce the tasks shown in a list, you could create a filter that shows only the milestone tasks.

You can also create filters that highlight the items meeting the conditions in the filter, but still display the entire list of tasks or resources. You have two options for using filters: You can use Project's predefined filters or create your own custom filters. The fastest way to filter information is through Project's AutoFilters.

Using AutoFilters

AutoFilters are the quickest way to view subsets of your tasks or resources. You can apply an AutoFilter to any Microsoft Project view, except the PERT Chart, Task PERT, or form views (filters are designed to act on the list pane of the current view).

To Do: Filtering a List Using an AutoFilter

To filter a list using an AutoFilter, follow these steps:

1. Choose **P**roject, **F**iltered, **A**utoFilter. A drop-down arrow will appear for each of the headings in the current list (for instance, the Task Name heading will have a drop-down arrow in the heading box).

2. Determine which headings you want to filter the list by. For instance, you might want to filter the tasks by their start date. Each drop-down list provides conditions for the filter that relates to the column of information under a particular heading. Click the drop-down arrow for a heading and select the filter condition as shown in Figure 14.4. As soon as you select the filter condition, the table is filtered, showing you only a subset of the information in the list. The column heading from which you selected the filter condition will turn blue.

 You can also invoke the AutoFilter command by clicking the AutoFilter button on the Formatting toolbar.

14

▼
FIGURE 14.4

AutoFilter allows you to quickly choose a condition or set of conditions to filter your list by.

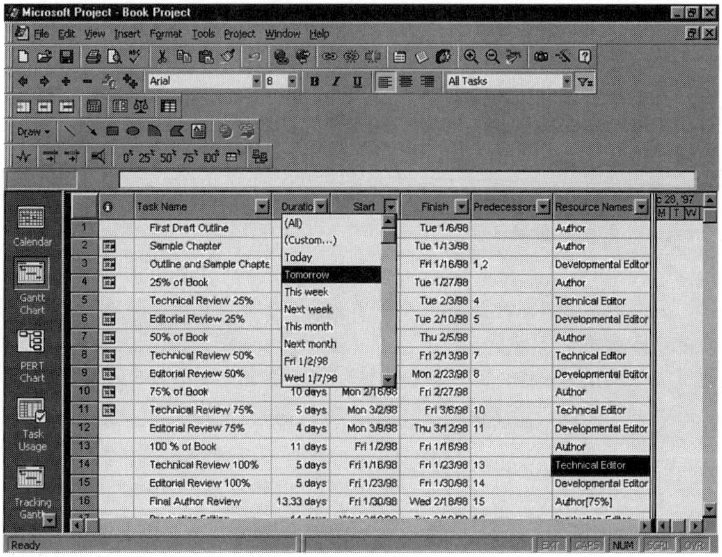

3. You can filter by more than one condition. To include additional conditions in the filter, use the drop-down lists for other column headings. For example, you might want to filter the list by start date (tasks that start tomorrow) and Resource Names (tasks related to one resource on the list).

▲

After you have completed the filtering process by using AutoFilter, you should return the list to its full complement of information. To remove the AutoFilter, choose **P**roject, **F**iltered, **A**utoFilter. This choice toggles the filter off.

AutoFiltering gives you a fast and fairly flexible method for filtering list data. Another possibility for filtering the information in your list is to use the predefined, standard filters that Project provides.

Using the Standard Filters

Project has several standard filters you can use to filter your lists. You can, for example, filter by critical tasks, milestone tasks, summary tasks, incomplete tasks, and tasks that use a particular resource.

You can also use the More Filters dialog box, which offers many predefined filters for filtering by tasks and resources.

To Do: Using a Standard Filter

To use a standard filter, follow these steps:

1. Choose **P**roject, **F**iltered for. On the cascading menu, select the standard filter you want to use (Completed Tasks, Critical, Incomplete Tasks, and so on, for a task list). The filter will be immediately applied to your list.

2. If the cascading filter menu does not have the particular standard filter you want to use, select **M**ore Filters to open the More Filters dialog box (see Figure 14.5).

 You can open a drop-down list of standard filters by clicking on the Filter button on the Formatting toolbar.

FIGURE 14.5

The More Filters dialog box offers several standard filters for filtering your lists.

You will find that a different list of standard filters appears on the filter cascading menu, depending on whether you are currently viewing a task list or a resource list.

3. Two radio buttons appear at the top of the More Filters dialog box: one for Tasks and the other for Resources. If you are filtering a task list, the Tasks button will be selected. Select the Filter you want to use from the Filter scroll box, and click the Apply button to activate the filter. The results of the filter will appear in your task or resource list.

You can also create your own filters by clicking the New button in the More Filters dialog box to open the Filter Definition dialog box. You can use it to set the conditional statements for a new filter by using a series of drop-down lists, as shown in Figure 14.6.

You might want to exhaust all the possibilities for filters using the standard filters before you attempt to create your own. Creating filters requires a good understanding of conditional statements and how they operate. Using the standard filters guarantees that the filter is performing correctly.

14

FIGURE 14.6

You can create your own filters in the Filter Definition dialog box.

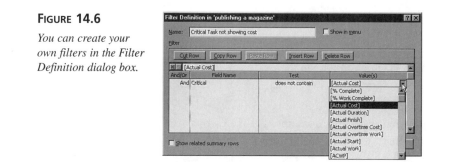

If you do create a new filter, its name will appear in the More Filters dialog box. Select it as you would any other filter and click Apply to filter the list.

To remove a filter that you have applied to your list, choose **P**roject, **F**iltered for. On the cascading menu, select All Tasks (for a resource list, select All Resources). The list will appear in its original form, showing all tasks or resources.

Sorting the Task and Resource Lists

Another way to manipulate your view of task and resource lists is to use the sort feature. This allows you to view the task or resource rows in an order that you define. You can sort tasks or resources by criteria such as task name, deadline, or start date. Sorting these items does not alter the ID numbers for the items or change the project schedule.

For instance, you might want to sort a list of tasks by their start date. After you have finished viewing your list in the new order dictated by the sort, you can easily return the items to their original order.

> Sorting order from your last sort is maintained when you switch views and is saved when you close a project file.

To Do: Sorting a List

To sort your list, follow these steps:

1. Choose **P**roject, **S**ort; several standard sorts appear for the type of list you are currently viewing. For the task list, standard sorts are available for Start Date, Finish Date, Priority, Cost, and ID. For the resource list, standard sorts are available for Cost, Name, and ID.

▼   2. Select a standard sort from the list. For instance, to sort a task list by task start date, select Start Date. The list will be ordered by the selected sort.

3. To return the list to its original order, sort by ID (this works for tasks and resources).

4. If you want to sort by more than one field, choose **P**roject, **S**ort, Sort By to open the Sort dialog box.

5. The Sort dialog box allows you to sort by three fields. For instance, you could sort tasks by type of task, then start date, and then cost. The field you want to sort by is selected from a drop-down scroll list. Use the radio buttons for Ascending and Descending to determine the direction of the sort for each field you want to sort by (see Figure 14.7). In the Sort By box, select the field you want to sort by first, and then place additional fields in the Then By boxes provided. Make sure to select Ascending or Descending for each field you select.

6. After you have selected the fields you want to sort by, click the Sort button. The
▲   list will be sorted by the fields that you chose (and in the direction you selected).

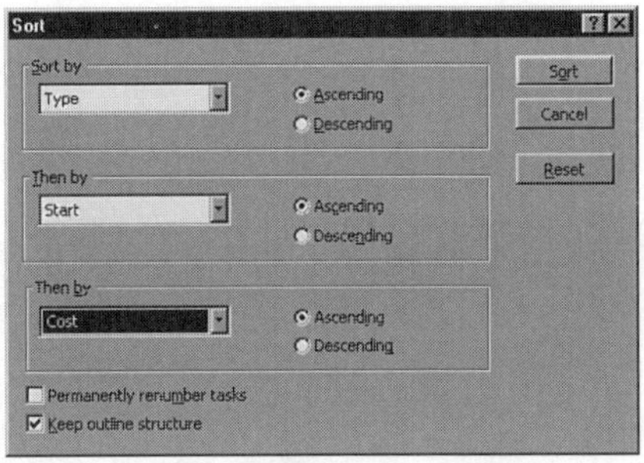

FIGURE 14.7

The Sort dialog box allows you to sort a list by more than one field.

You can also use the Sort dialog box to permanently renumber the tasks or resources in your list. Two check boxes are available in the Sort dialog box: Permanently Renumber Tasks and Keep Outline Structure.

The default selection is Keep Outline Structure, meaning the tasks will be sorted, but subtasks will remain tied to their summary tasks. If you select the Permanently Renumber Tasks check box, the tasks or resources will be renumbered according to the new sort order. To use the renumbering check box, the Keep Outline Structure check box must also be selected.

If you renumber your items according to the new sort, but then decide you want to restore the original ID sequence, choose **E**dit, **U**ndo Sort. A fast way to return your list to its original ID sequence after a sort is to open the Sort dialog box and then click the Reset button.

14

Viewing the Costs

The strategies discussed so far for helping you get a good overview of how your plan is laid out have focused on time issues for tasks and resources. Another view that you might find helpful as you optimize your plan is the Summary table. In the case of a task list, the Summary table lists information that focuses on the costs of the major events in your project and the duration of these important phases. For a resource list, the Summary table gives you information on the cost of the resource and the hours that the resource will be employed.

To Do: Viewing the Summary Table for a List

To view the Summary table for a particular list, follow these steps:

1. Choose **V**iew, **Ta**ble, **Su**mmary. A new set of columns will appear for the list, as shown in Figure 14.8. In the case of tasks, the summary columns are Duration, Start, Finish, % Complete, and Cost.

2. Use the Summary Table view of your tasks and resources along with filters and sorts to order the summary information to suit your particular needs (for instance, you might want to see only the summary information for critical or summary tasks, so you can use the filter feature to make this happen).

▲   3. To return to the original list view, choose **V**iew, **Ta**ble, **E**ntry.

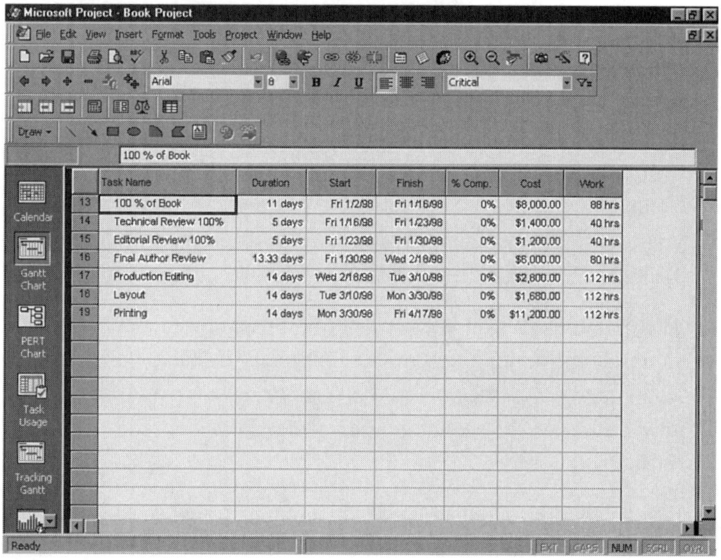

FIGURE 14.8

The Summary Table view for a list gives you a quick look at cost and duration information.

	Task Name	Duration	Start	Finish	% Comp.	Cost	Work
13	100 % of Book	11 days	Fri 1/2/98	Fri 1/16/98	0%	$8,000.00	88 hrs
14	Technical Review 100%	5 days	Fri 1/16/98	Fri 1/23/98	0%	$1,400.00	40 hrs
15	Editorial Review 100%	5 days	Fri 1/23/98	Fri 1/30/98	0%	$1,200.00	40 hrs
16	Final Author Review	13.33 days	Fri 1/30/98	Wed 2/18/98	0%	$6,000.00	80 hrs
17	Production Editing	14 days	Wed 2/18/98	Tue 3/10/98	0%	$2,800.00	112 hrs
18	Layout	14 days	Tue 3/10/98	Mon 3/30/98	0%	$1,680.00	112 hrs
19	Printing	14 days	Mon 3/30/98	Fri 4/17/98	0%	$11,200.00	112 hrs

When you use the Summary Table view on the Gantt Chart view, you may have to move the size of the Gantt Chart so that you can see all the columns in the Summary Table list. Place the mouse pointer on the left border of the Gantt Chart and use the sizing tool to drag the Gantt Chart border to the right.

The Summary Table view is another very good way to get a handle on the broader aspects of your project, particularly your costs for a certain major task or resource.

Shortening the Critical Path

Using the strategies for reviewing the various aspects of your project that have been covered so far in this Hour, might make you decide that you need to make some adjustments in your plan. In most cases, these changes revolve around time and money; there is seldom enough of both. For instance, you might need to reduce the time frame for your project. One way to do this is to add more resources to get the job done; however, adding resources greatly affects the project's final cost.

The most straightforward method of reducing the time it takes to complete the project is to determine which tasks are truly critical to completing the project—that is, which tasks in the project must be completed before the project can move on to the next set of tasks. (See Hour 5 for more information on scheduling and critical tasks). After you identify the critical tasks, you may be able to shorten their duration and compress the time frame for the project; this is called "shortening the critical path."

Identifying the Critical Path

You can use any of the task views to identify the critical tasks in your project. One of the best ways to view the critical tasks is to use the filter feature and filter the task list for critical tasks when you are in the Gantt Chart view. Choose **Project**, **Filtered**, **Critical** from the menu.

As you rework your project and the tasks it involves, you will find that non-critical tasks can become critical and critical tasks can become noncritical. Make sure you rerun the critical task filter after you make changes to your schedule so that you are looking at the critical path's most recent version. Press Ctrl+F3 to quickly rerun the filter.

14

If you want to show all the tasks on the list and highlight the critical tasks, hold down the Shift key and repeat the steps above to apply the filter. Figure 14.9 shows a task list where the critical tasks are highlighted.

FIGURE **14.9**

Hold down the Shift key when you run the critical task filter to highlight the critical tasks in the task list.

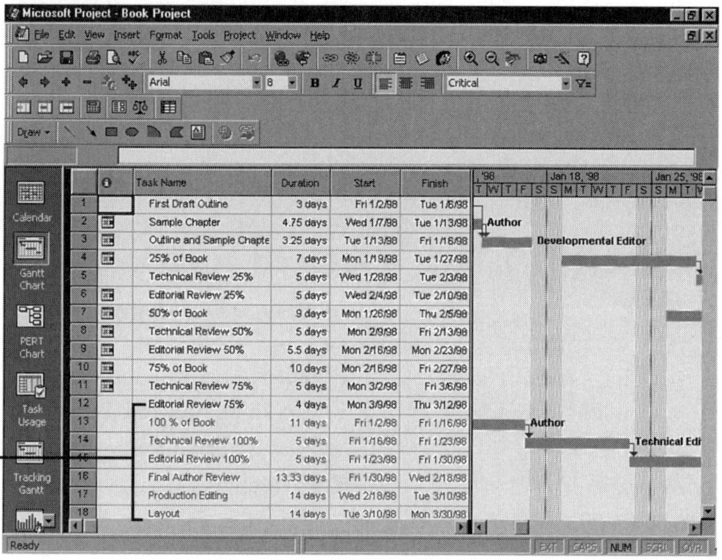

Critical tasks—

After you have the critical tasks displayed on the Gantt task list, it makes sense to split the Gantt Chart view with the task form. This allows you to select a critical task in the Gantt task list and view all its vital statistics in the task form. This viewing strategy also allows you to edit a task quickly while keeping your eye on the big-picture aspects of the project that the Gantt Chart provides.

To split the Gantt Chart view, right-click on the Gantt Chart, and select Split from the shortcut menu that appears. The window will be split between the Gantt Chart view (on the top) and the Task Form on the bottom (see Figure 14.10).

Strategies for Crashing the Schedule

After you have identified the critical tasks, you can move from critical task to critical task on the task list, looking for possible ways to reduce the duration of each task.

NEW TERM   **Crashing the Schedule**   *Crashing the schedule* is a strategy for reducing the critical path for your project.

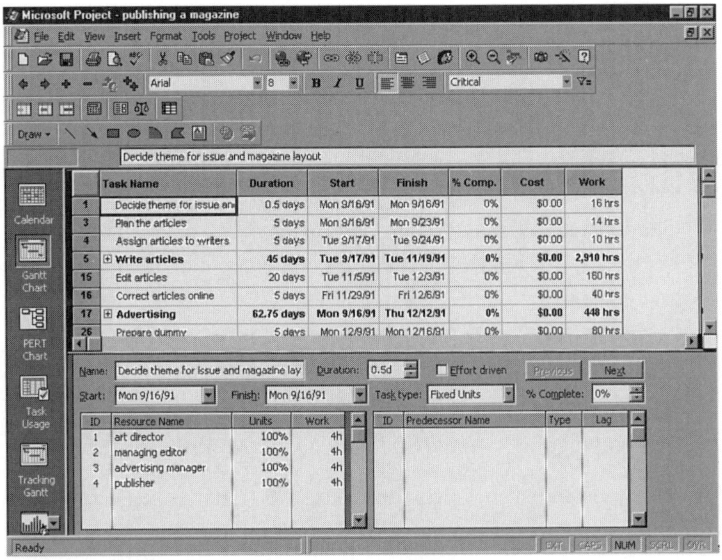

FIGURE **14.10**

You can split the Gantt Chart view so that the task list and the Task Form appear in the same window.

If you identify a task that can be compressed, you can quickly edit it in the Task Form. Keep in mind the strategies in the following list as you attempt to crash your schedule:

- The name of the game is to reduce the duration of critical tasks; assign more resources, if available, to a task to shorten the time frame for it.

- Examine the predecessor and successor of each task and see if tasks can be made to overlap. In some cases, tasks involved in a finish-to-start relationship can be realigned so that the second task (in the relationship) can be started before the first one is completed.

- You can always schedule overtime (budget permitting) to reduce the regular work hours for a particular task.

- Break large tasks into smaller tasks. Although it might require more resources, this approach may allow you to take a critical task and break it down into subtasks that can be completed simultaneously.

- Use your existing resources efficiently. You don't want to have resources sitting around on their hands. Make sure you are getting the appropriate amount of output from each resource. If you find you have resources with downtime, you might be able to use them on a critical task to shorten that segment of the schedule.

- Identify and correct errors in the project. If you have inadvertently scheduled a resource for more than one task at a time or placed a task at the wrong point in the schedule, correct these errors before trying to crash the schedule.

14

The most obvious suggestion for successfully optimizing a plan is to gain as much project management experience as you can. Managing small projects with Microsoft Project will give you the background you need to tackle those large, complex project plans.

Reducing Costs

The most significant portion of your project budget is related to the cost of your resources. It is very important that you keep tabs on the project's tasks and their current and projected costs. Having tasks exceed the budget because of neglect will never do.

Reviewing the Cost Schedule

An excellent way to keep tabs on your costs is to periodically review the Cost schedule by applying the Summary Table view to the Task Sheet.

When viewing your costs for tasks, it also makes sense to view the Task Form, which gives you information on the resources allocated to the particular task.

To Do: Viewing the Task Sheet and Opening the Task Form

To view the Task Sheet in the Gantt Chart view and to open the Task Form, follow these steps:

1. In the Gantt Chart view, choose **V**iew, Ta**b**le, **Su**mmary. This places the task list in the Summary view and shows you the cost of each task.

2. To show the Task Form, right-click the Gantt Chart and select Split from the shortcut menu. The Window will split between the Gantt Chart view and the Task Form. Use the mouse to drag the Gantt Chart border to the right so that you can see all the columns in the Task Sheet.

3. Select a particular task in the Task Sheet to view its budget information. The Task Form will give you information on the resources involved in the selected task.

> If you want to view your costs in a view that removes the Gantt Chart from the window, choose **V**iew, **M**ore views, and then select Task Sheet in the More Views dialog box. Use the **V**iew menu to assign the Summary Table view to the Task Sheet.

Strategies for Reducing Costs

To reduce costs, you must find ways to lower the price tag for the resources you use on your various tasks. One way to reduce costs is to use less-expensive resources. However, you should keep in mind the old adage "you get what you pay for" as you seek to reduce the cost of the resources you use.

Another significant way to reduce your overall costs is to keep a close eye on tasks that are threatening to go over budget. If the task is becoming too costly because of overtime pay (let's say you decided to use overtime to reduce the time frame for the task), you may want to reallocate resources to the project so that the particular task is still completed on time but only during regular working hours. With overtime pay rates out of the picture, you might be able to bring the task in on budget.

It also makes sense to take a hard look at the tasks in the project and see if any of them can be completely deleted. If other tasks do not depend on a particular task, you may find that it was an unnecessary step in the project. Having four quality control checks for a particular product might be a little redundant, especially if the first two quality control–related tasks are catching all the faulty product. Delete tasks that do not add to the plan's overall productivity. Reducing functionality or the quality of a task or set of tasks can help bring in a project on schedule and at a lower cost. However, this could also lower the "quality" of the final outcome, which is certainly important to your client.

14

HOUR 15

Printing Views and Reports with Resources

This hour shows you how to format and print views and reports that contain resource information. Project 98 can list your resources with detailed information about their task schedules, their assigned work, and their cost to a task or to the project. A number of predefined reports are available, and they can be customized to suit your style and needs. Also, the enhanced Usage views in Project 98 can display and print several lines of detailed resource information.

The highlights of this hour include the following:

- How to display detailed information in the usage views
- Which built-in reports focus on resource costing
- How to print resource assignments, schedules, and workloads
- How to customize standard resource reports to fit your needs

Formatting and Printing the Usage Views

Both the Task Usage and Resource Usage views let you see who is assigned to which tasks throughout the project. The assignment information is broken down by task. The Task Usage view groups the resource assignments with the task names; the Resource Usage view groups the assignments with each resource name. With either view, the right side of the screen presents a time-phased breakdown of detailed resource information.

When you create a new project file, the usage views display assigned work for each resource and each task on the right side of the screen (see Figure 15.1). However, you're not limited to seeing only the assigned work information. The following "Choosing the Details" section teaches you how to change the information displayed on the right side of a usage view. Also, you might want to adjust the timescale for the grid columns with Zoom In and Zoom Out on the toolbar.

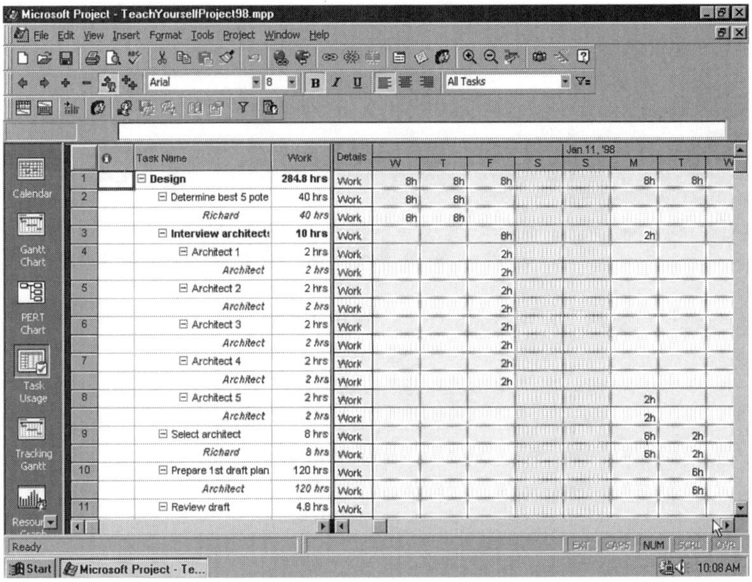

FIGURE 15.1

The standard Task Usage view shows detailed resource information for each task.

The Resource Usage view is similar to the Task Usage view, but is organized by resource instead of by task. The following notes and steps apply to both usage views.

Choosing the Details

A *detail* in Project 98 is a row associated with each resource in a usage view. The work detail row is shown by default. There are five other commonly used detail rows that can be displayed easily. Digging a little deeper reveals that any resource-related numeric field can be displayed as a detail row.

To Do: Displaying Detail Rows in Task Usage View

To display detail rows in Task Usage view, follow these steps:

1. Choose View, Task Usage or choose Task Usage from the View Bar.

2. Choose Format, Details and select the detail row you would like to display. Items with check marks will be displayed; items without check marks will be hidden from view (see Figure 15.2).

3. Return to Format, Details as many times as necessary to display or hide the common resource detail rows to fit your needs.

FIGURE 15.2

The most common usage detail fields are available from a cascading menu.

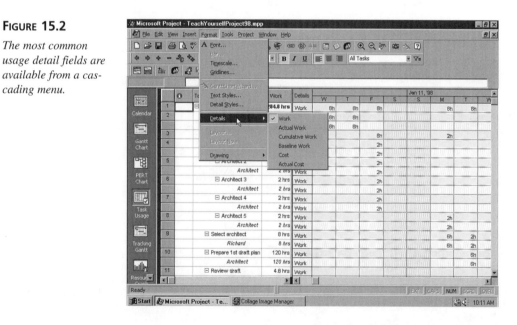

For faster access to the common detail options, right-click the right-side grid on a usage view.

You might want to display a detail row that's not among the common details list. For example, the amount of overtime allowed per person on a task could be of interest.

To Do: Displaying Additional Resource Rows in Task Usage View

To display additional resource rows in Task Usage view, follow these steps:

1. Choose **V**iew, Tas**k** Usage or choose Task Usage from the View Bar.

2. Choose F**o**rmat, **D**etail Styles, Usage Details tab. All available detail row fields are listed on the left side of the dialog box; all fields currently marked to be shown are listed on the right side (see Figure 15.3). Customize the usage view by showing or hiding fields and by ordering the rows with the Move buttons.

▲

> You can customize the pop-up details list by selecting the Show in **M**enu check box for each field at the bottom of the Usage Details tab.

FIGURE 15.3

Many Project fields are available for displaying on a usage view.

Formatting the Detail Styles

You can change the emphasis of each displayed detail row by changing the formatting. A different color or background pattern for more important rows can make the grid easier to interpret.

To Do: Choosing Colors and Patterns for Detail Rows

To choose colors and patterns for detail rows, follow these steps:

1. Choose F**o**rmat, **D**etail Styles.

▼

2. Highlight the field to be formatted from the Sh**o**w These Fields: list.

▼ 3. Make changes to the font, point size, and text color, as well as cell background color and pattern, for each detail field as needed.

4. Click OK when finished. Note that the special formatting is not applied to *each* detail row, but only to the first row of the *group*. That is, the formatting changes show on the Task Name lines in the Task Usage view, but not on each individual ▲ resource's line.

> The assignment rows in the Task Name or Resource Name column can be formatted to stand out, too. Choose Format, Text Styles, Assignment Row to make the change.

> Undo is not available for removing the formatting changes in Detail Styles or Text Styles.

Working with Cost Reports

In addition to the Task and Resource Usage views, there are several predefined reports in Project 98 that print resource-related information. One group of reports focuses on cost and the budget breakdowns for the project (see Figure 15.4). Tracking project costs over time, and budgeting accordingly, is usually a key management concern. Also, Project 98 computes and prints cost totals in the cost reports. The Cash Flow report, for example, shows total costs allocated in a time period, as well as the total cost of each task over the entire project.

> All reports supplied with Project 98 contain certain default settings. To make changes to the default settings for a report, see the section "Customizing the Standard Reports" later on in this Hour.

Cash Flow Reports

For a printout of expected cash flow over time throughout the project, choose the Cash Flow report. Expenses are displayed in time increments. The default time increment is weekly. The dollar amounts in each time period are calculated by Project based on assigned resources and their pay rates, fixed costs, and the accrual methods chosen for each. By default, resource costs are payable when the resource does the work, and fixed costs are payable at the end of a task. Per-use costs for resources are always payable at the beginning of the task. In the Cash Flow report, totals are computed and displayed at the bottom of the report for each time period and at the far right side of the report for each task.

FIGURE 15.4

Reports that focus on project costing are in the Cost report category

To Do: Previewing the Cash Flow Reports

To preview the Cash Flow reports, follow these steps:

1. Choose **V**iew, **R**eports.

2. Double-click on the Costs category, or choose the Costs category and click **S**elect.

3. Double-click on the **C**ash Flow report option, or choose the report option and then click Select.

Budget Reports

The Budget report prints a list of tasks with their associated fixed and total costs, remaining funds available for each task, and the current cost variance from the original baseline cost values. This is the same information available by applying and printing the Cost table on the Gantt Chart, with one important difference—the Budget report also computes and prints totals for each column of numbers.

> To see project totals for fixed costs, resource costs, and variances from the original project budget, print the supplied Budget report.

To Do: Previewing the Budget Report

To preview the Budget report, follow these steps:

1. Choose **V**iew, **R**eports.

2. Double-click on the Costs category, or choose the Costs category and click on Select.

3. Double-click the **B**udget report option, or choose the report option and then click ▲ Select.

15

Working with the Assignment Reports

The four standard reports in the Assignment reports group print resource assignment lists for your review and for distribution to project team members. The focus of each report is slightly different (see Figure 15.5). The key to managing a project team efficiently is knowing what the resources are responsible for over the life of the project. Important questions to review include who is supposed to be doing what work, when the work is due, and whether any resources are assigned more work than they can complete, based on their working calendars. The Assignment Reports are designed to answer these questions and more.

FIGURE 15.5

The supplied reports in the Assignment group help track resources and their workloads.

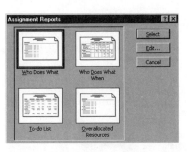

Who Does What Report

The **W**ho Does What report is good for getting a detailed view of your team and its efforts. This report lists every resource from the resource list, whether or not any work has been assigned to him or her. For each resource, the total amount of work on the project is given, along with a breakdown by task of the units per task (in % effort), work per task, and start and finish dates per task.

Who Does What When Report

As the name implies, the Who **D**oes What When report lists who is on the project resource list, which tasks each resource is assigned to, and when those work assignments occur. Totals for work per time period and work per resource are calculated and printed at the bottom and the right edge of the report. The time period for the report is a daily list by default.

> The Who **D**oes What When report could produce long multi-page printouts because of its daily timescale setting. You might want to change the timescale (see the section "Customizing Crosstab Type Reports") or print only a portion of the report (type in dates for the Timescale setting in the Print dialog box.)

To-Do List Report

The **T**o-Do List is a filtered report designed to focus on one resource at a time. Each time you preview the report, you must choose a resource name from the drop-down list of names that appear on the screen. The report lists all task assignments for the resource, including task details such as duration and start and finish dates. The assignments are listed in task ID order within calendar groups; by default, the grouping is weekly.

Overallocated Resources Report

The **O**verallocated Resources report is the result of taking the Who Does What report and filtering it to show only those resources that are overallocated sometime, and in one or more time periods, in the life of the project. For these resources only, the same task assignment details as in the **W**ho Does What report are listed.

Using the Workload Reports

The two supplied Workload reports are named Task Usage and Resource Usage. Don't let the names fool you, however; they are not simply printouts of the Task or Resource Usage views. Presented in a table format, known as a *crosstab*, the Workload reports list only one detail line of tasks and resource assignment information by time period, as shown in Figure 15.6. The default time period for each report is weekly. The option to add detail rows, as with the usage views, is not available in the usage reports. You can, however, define and print multiple usage reports with different detail information in each report. Also, Project calculates and prints totals by task, or by resource, and by time period in the usage reports, but not in the usage views.

FIGURE 15.6

Workload reports focus on resources and their assigned work by time periods.

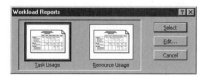

Task Usage Report

The supplied **T**ask Usage report lists all tasks in the project with the accompanying resource assignments. For each resource, the assigned hours within the time period are given. For each task, the total of the assigned resource hours is also given.

Resource Usage Report

In an orientation different from the **T**ask Usage report, the supplied **R**esource Usage report provides a resource list and their task assignments. Assigned hours per task per time period and total hours for the resource in each time period are given. Project calculates and displays the total work hours per time period for all resources and total work per resource over the life of the project. The default time period for this report is weekly.

Customizing the Standard Reports

As comprehensive as the supplied reports are, they might not meet your needs exactly. You might want to change some text formatting or the sort order in a report, for example. Because reports are a combination of table information, filters, and detail settings, this section shows you how to change these features in the supplied reports. If you prefer to keep the original report and create one that's similar to it, see the section "Creating a New Report Based on an Existing Report" in Hour 22, "Creating Custom Views and Reports."

If you follow these procedures and customize the supplied reports, the original settings are lost. To return to the original report, you must either re-edit the settings or use the Organizer feature to copy the report definition from the global.mpt.

Common adjustments made to the supplied reports include setting and removing page breaks, modifying the header and footer information, adding emphasis with text formatting, rearranging the report information by sorting a different way, and adding or removing detailed information on a report for enhanced readability.

Controlling Page Breaks in a Report

There's no method for setting or controlling page breaks within a report. However, manual page breaks can be set on views, which will affect some reports. Any report that's simply a list—that is, it has no time period data—will not be affected by manual page breaks; there's no way to directly control the page breaks in these reports. The resource reports explored in this Hour that can be controlled by manual page breaks set on views are the following:

- Cash Flow
- Who Does What When
- Task Usage
- Resource Usage

To Do: Setting a Manual Page Break for a View

To set a manual page break for a view, follow these steps:

1. Display a view by choosing one from the View Bar.
2. Select a cell on the row that will be at top of a new page, as shown in Figure 15.7.
3. Choose Insert, Page Break. The page break is inserted above the row with the selected cell.

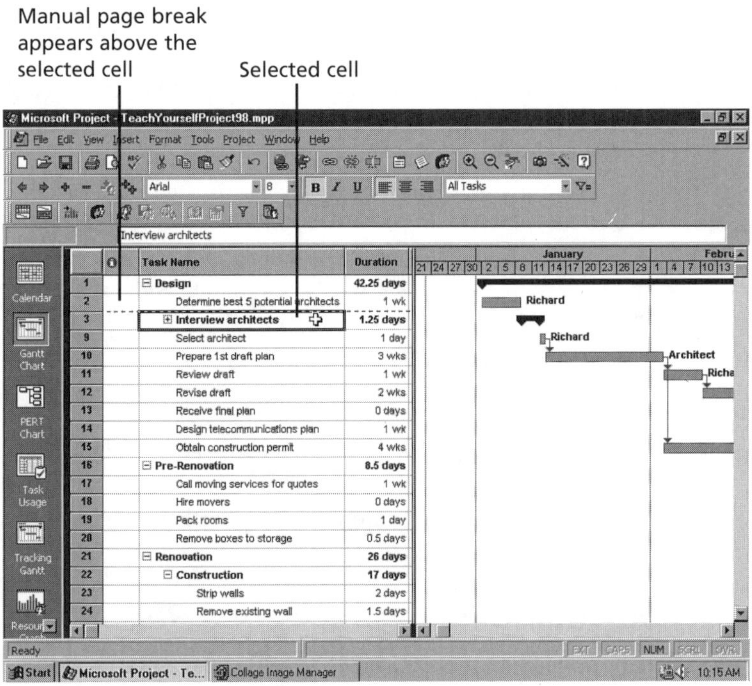

Manual page break
appears above the
selected cell   Selected cell

FIGURE 15.7

Selecting a cell to set or remove a manual page break.

To Do: Removing Manual Page Breaks

To remove manual page breaks, follow these steps:

1. Display a view by choosing one from the View Bar.

2. Select a cell on the row below an existing manual page break.

3. Choose Insert, Remove Page Break.

To remove all manual page breaks from a view, click the Select All area above the ID numbers and to the left of the column names as shown in Figure 15.8. The Insert menu will then show an option to Remove All Page Breaks.

FIGURE 15.8

Select all project tasks and fields with the Select All area above the task ID numbers.

Select All ————

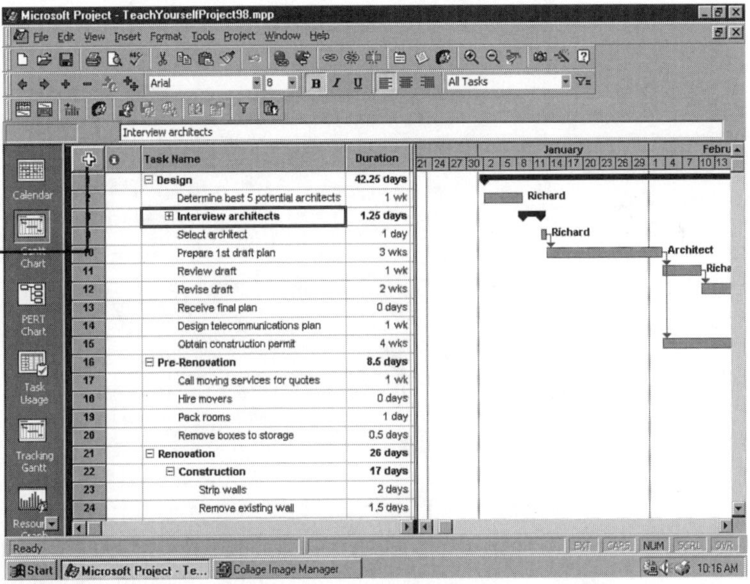

Choosing the Page Setup Options for a Report

After a report is previewed on the screen, the Page Setup options for the report become available. These options include the print orientation (portrait or landscape), printed page margins, and header and footer settings.

To Do: Accessing Page Setup Options for a Report

To access page setup options for a report, follow these steps:

1. Choose **View, Reports**.

2. Double-click a report category, or click the category and choose **Select**.

3. Double-click the report option, or click the report option and then choose **Select**.

4. At the top of the Preview screen, click the Page Setup button. The Page Setup dialog box appears, as shown in Figure 15.9.

5. Make your selections on the Page, Margins, Header, and Footer tabs. Initially, the default settings for the specific report will be chosen, but after they're changed, the new settings stay with the report. You don't need to change the Page Setup options every time you run a report.

6. Click Print Preview to display and review the new settings.

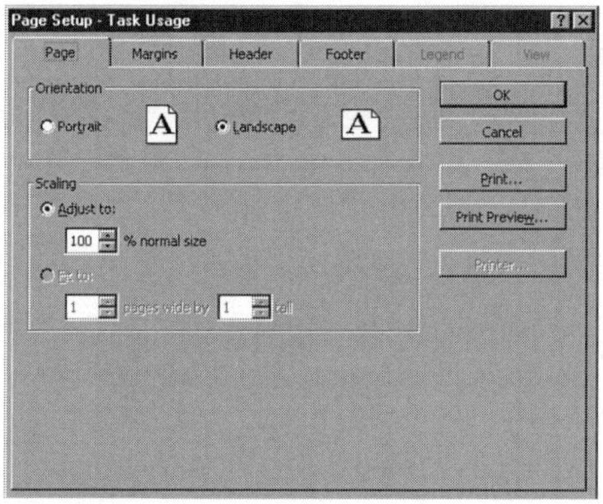

FIGURE 15.9

Change print settings in the Page Setup dialog box.

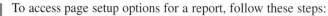

> Two new features in Project 98 give you more flexibility with headers and footers. Text formatting can be applied to any text in a header or footer section; no longer do you have to format an entire section. Also, you can now add graphics to headers and footers—great for inserting the company logo directly onto the Project printout. Use the shortcut buttons on the Header and Footer tabs in Page Setup to apply these new features.

Formatting Text in a Report

15

Unlike setting manual page breaks, text formatting for reports is changed in the report definition itself. Manual or text style formatting applied to a view is not carried over to reports. Within a report, text formatting is done by type of item. Tasks or resources can't be formatted individually in reports; text formatting must be applied by item types only.

Task items that can be formatted could include summary tasks, critical tasks, or milestones, for example. In resource reports, items might be all overallocated resources, all allocated resources, or resource cost or work totals. Several different items can be formatted in distinctly different ways within the same report, and each report can have its own combination of text formatting applied to items.

To Do: Changing the Text Formatting in a Supplied Report

▼ To Do

To change the text formatting in a supplied report, follow these steps:

1. Choose **V**iew, **R**eports.

2. Double-click a report category, or click once on a category and choose Select.

3. Click once on the report you want to modify.

4. Click the **E**dit button to open the report definition dialog box.

5. Make certain the options on the Definition tab are displayed. Click the Te**x**t button, and the Text Styles dialog box appears, as shown in Figure 15.10.

6. Use the **I**tem to Change drop-down list to select the items of interest, making your changes to one item type at a time.

7. When all items have been formatted, click OK on the formatting dialog box, and click OK again on the report definition dialog box.

8. Now preview the revised report by double-clicking its name or by clicking once and choosing **S**elect.

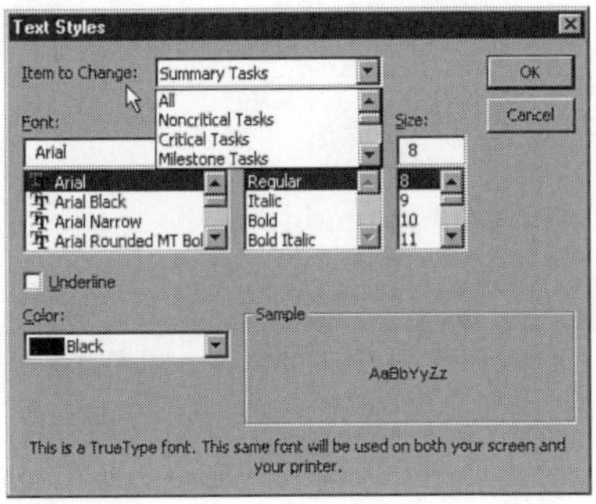

▲

FIGURE 15.10

Formatting in reports is applied to item types.

Changing the Sort Order for a Report

The order in which tasks and resources are printed is predefined in each report. You can change the report sort and print orders by using Project's three-level sort capabilities.

To Do: Changing the Sort Order of a Report

To change the sort order of a report, follow these steps:

1. Choose **V**iew, **R**eports.
2. Double-click a report category, or click once on a category and choose **S**elect.
3. Click once on the report you want to modify.
4. Click the **E**dit button to open the report definition dialog box.
5. Select the Sort tab in the dialog box.
6. Use the drop-down lists to choose the field to **S**ort By and select **A**scending or **D**escending order for the list. Make choices for the second and third sort levels, if you like. For task reports, these lists will include only task fields; for resource reports, they will be resource field lists.
7. Click OK on the Sort dialog box.
8. Now preview the revised report by double-clicking its name or by clicking once and choosing **S**elect.

Displaying or Hiding Task Detail in a Report

Some supplied reports might give you more data than you need, resulting in information overload. Unfortunately, some reports might not give you all the detailed information you want. The type and amount of supporting information supplied in each report can be changed by displaying or hiding detail options in the report definition.

To Do: Displaying or Hiding Report Details

To display or hide report details, do the following:

1. Choose **V**iew, **R**eports.
2. Double-click on a report category, or click once on a category and choose **S**elect.
3. Click once on the report you want to modify.
4. Click the **E**dit button. The report definition dialog box appears.
5. Select the Details tab in the dialog box, as shown in Figure 15.11.
6. A square check box next to a detail option indicates that the option can be set to be displayed (a check mark in the box) or to be hidden (no check mark in the box), independently of any other options. Turn on the details you would like to see; leave the other check boxes blank.

▼   7. The available details vary by report type. Timescaled reports let you choose the
        date formatting for that report only, for instance. Other options include whether to
        include summary tasks in the report, which could duplicate some information on
        the report, or whether to show numeric totals on the report.

     8. Click OK on the Details dialog box.

     9. Now preview the revised report by double-clicking its name or by clicking once
▲   and choosing Select.

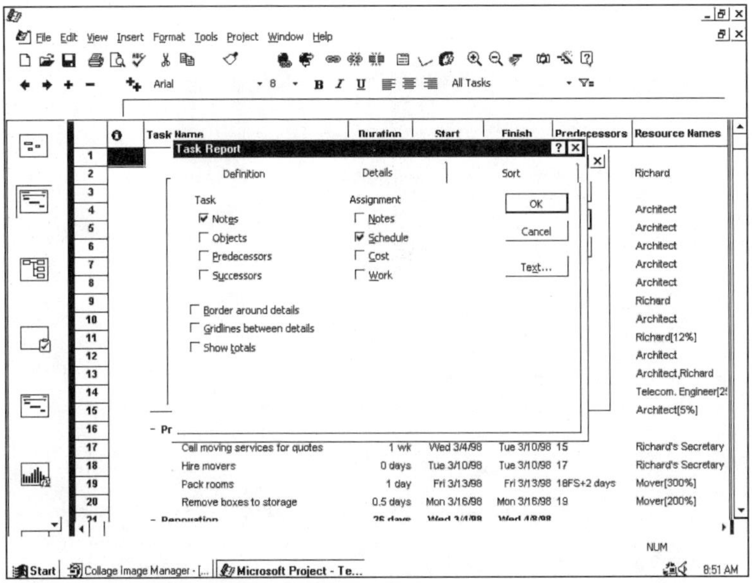

FIGURE 15.11

*The Details tab allows
you to show or not
show several types of
supporting information
per task or resource.*

Customizing Specific Report Types

Despite the quantity of supplied reports in Project 98, most reports are based on one of
three report types:

- Task reports
- Resource reports
- Crosstab reports

Task and Resource reports are simply lists of project data focused on either task or
resource information. The Crosstab report adds a time period dimension to reports and
can be focused on either task or resource information.

The remaining report types (not listed previously) are the Project Summary report and a
few calendar-based reports.

Because there are many more options for customizing the Task, Resource, and Crosstab reports than for the other report types, only these reports are covered here.

Customizing the Project Summary Report

The Project Summary report prints the "big picture" of the project. It provides information similar to the project Statistics display. The contents of this report, found in the Overview report category, can't be changed, and there are only four items on the Summary Report that can even be reformatted:

- Project Name
- Company Name
- Manager Name
- Details

Project uses the Project Name, Company Name, and Manager Name you entered on the File, Properties, Summary tab. If you did not supply this information, Project simply leaves the spaces for them on the Summary Report blank. The fourth item, Details, is all the other project information summarized on the report.

Formatting the Details information on the Summary Report with a larger point size could cause the numbers in certain fields to be too large to print in the allotted space. In that case, all you will see are pound signs (###) where numbers should be. Experiment and preview before printing the report.

To Do: Editing the Formatting for the Project Summary Report

To edit the formatting for the Project Summary report, follow these steps:

1. Choose **View**, **Reports**.
2. Double-click the **O**verview report category, or choose the category and click **S**elect.
3. Select the **P**roject Summary report option.
4. Click the **E**dit button.

▼

5. Use the **I**tem to Change drop-down list to modify the formatting for the four possible items discussed previously.

6. Click OK on the formatting dialog box.

▲

7. Now preview the revised report by double-clicking its name or by clicking once and choosing **S**elect.

> To get the "big picture" of your project at any time, display the project statistics. Choose Project, Project Information and select the Statistics tab. To print this information, use the Project Summary report.

Customizing the Calendar Type Reports

As with the Project Summary report, the editing options for the Calendar reports are limited to formatting changes—and not very many of those. Only two items can be modified: the calendar name itself and the calendar details taken as a whole group.

Customizing Task Reports

All Task reports list task name or IDs first on a report line, and include columns of project data from task tables in the project file. A Task type report discussed in this Hour is the Budget report. Task reports can include information on all tasks or only a group of tasks, if a filter is specified in the report definition. In addition to the text formatting and sort order changes discussed previously, the report definition dialog box, shown in Figure 15.12, allows you to do the following:

- Change the report name, although this is not recommended for the supplied reports.

- Break up the report into groups of calendar time, such as printing by quarters. This is not the same as creating a crosstab report type; it merely breaks the report into calendar segments.

- Apply and print data from a different task table. Any custom tables you create will be among your table choices.

- Apply any filter to the list, including custom filters you might have created. Filters can also be applied as highlighting filters; that is, instead of temporarily hiding the tasks that do not match the filter, all tasks appear, but the tasks that *do match* the filter are highlighted, or displayed differently.

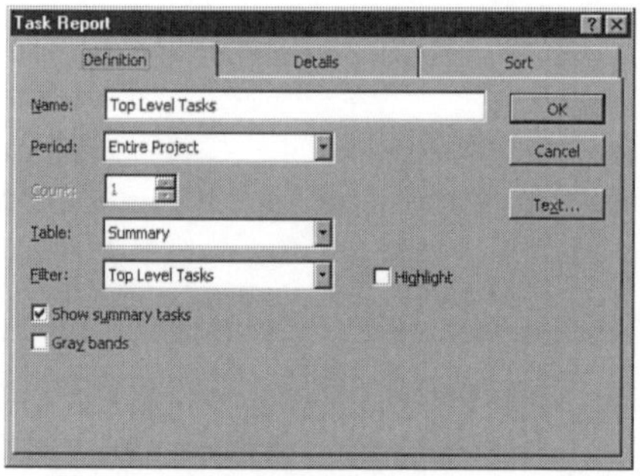

FIGURE 15.12

*The definition tab in
the Task Report dialog
box allows you to cus-
tomize some parts of
the Task report.*

To Do: Customizing a Task Type Report

To customize a Task type report, follow these steps:

1. Choose **View, Reports.**

2. Double-click a report category, or click once on a category and choose **Select.**

3. Click once on the report you want to modify.

4. Click the **Edit** button to open the report definition dialog box.

5. Select the Definition tab in the dialog box.

6. Make changes to the **Name, Period** (and **Count), Table,** and **Filter** fields.

   The Period and Count fields work together. Count sets the increment for the period. That is, with a Period of weeks and a Count of 1, a weekly report will be produced. With a Period of weeks and a Count of 2, a *biweekly* report will be produced.

7. Click OK on the report definition dialog box.

8. Now preview the revised report by double-clicking its name or by clicking once and choosing **Select.**

Customizing Resource Reports

Resource reports are very similar to task reports. The emphasis has just been shifted to resource information. In fact, the customization choices are the same for the two report types: Name, Period (and Count), Table, and Filter. Follow the procedures given for customizing task type reports to customize resource reports instead.

Resource type reports discussed in this Hour are the **W**ho Does What, **T**o-Do List, and **O**verallocated Resources. Now the differences between these reports should become clear:

- The **W**ho Does What report, filtered for resources who are overcommitted in some timeframe in the project, becomes the **O**verallocated Resources report.

15

- The **T**o-Do List is simply the **W**ho Does What report, filtered for a single resource with information grouped by a period of weeks, count 1. Changing the count to 2 on this report would produce a biweekly listing instead.

Customizing Crosstab Type Reports

The third report type that's most commonly used is the Crosstab report, which breaks project information into time periods and prints it out in a grid instead of a list format. As with Task and Resource report types, a Crosstab report can be sorted by up to three levels, and the amount of detail displayed in the report can be controlled. The Sort and Detail tabs in the report definition dialog box control those options. However, a Crosstab report can be either task or resource oriented. This focus and the time period settings are controlled on the Definition tab of the Crosstab Report dialog box.

The **C**ash Flow report, the Who **D**oes What When report, and the **T**ask Usage and **R**esource Usage reports are all Crosstab type reports.

To Do: Customizing a Crosstab Report

To customize a Crosstab report, follow these steps:

1. Choose **V**iew, **R**eports.
2. Double-click on a report category, or click once on a category and choose **S**elect.
3. Click once on the report you want to modify.
4. Click the **E**dit button. The Crosstab Report dialog box appears, as shown in Figure 15.13.
5. Select the Definition tab in the dialog box to make changes to the Crosstab fields.

FIGURE 15.13

Choose a row, a column, and a detail setting for a Crosstab report.

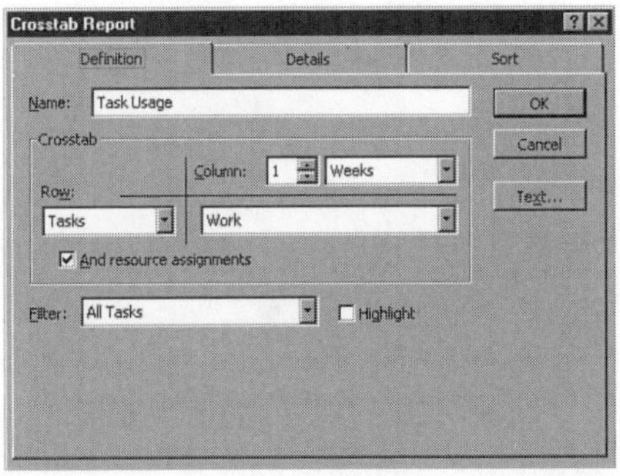

Crosstab Report

| Definition | Details | Sort |

Name: Task Usage

Crosstab

Column: 1 Weeks

Row: Tasks Work

☑ And resource assignments

Filter: All Tasks ☐ Highlight

OK
Cancel
Text...

- The Row setting will be either Task or Resource—the focus of the report.
- The Column settings define the time periods in the report columns.

▼

- The intersection of a row and a column can be any of the fields in the drop-down list on the Definition tab. The choice of fields vary, depending on whether Row is set to Task or to Resource.

- Do you also want to print assignments for the tasks or the resources? Turn on the And Resource Assignments box.

6. Select the Details tab to display or hide row and column totals and to choose a date format for this report only.

7. Select the Sort tab to alter the printed order of the report.

8. When finished, click OK on any tab in the report definition dialog box.

9. Now preview the revised report by double-clicking its name or by clicking once and choosing Select.

▲

Hour **16**

Publishing Projects on the Web or an Intranet

In this Hour, you see how you can save your project file as an HTML document that can be published to the Internet or your corporate intranet. This chapter introduces you to all of Microsoft Project 98's Web features and shows you how to create HTML documents to communicate important information about your project.

Overview of Project 98's Internet Features

Microsoft Project 98 has many new and exciting features that take advantage of the Internet's power. As with all the other Microsoft Office applications, Project 98 gives you the ability to save your project as an HTML document that can be viewed with a Web browser, such as Microsoft Internet Explorer or Netscape Navigator (see Figure 16.1).

FIGURE 16.1

Your project can be saved as an HTML document that can be viewed through a Web browser, such as Microsoft Internet Explorer.

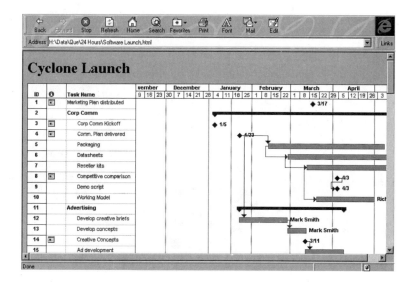

Some other Microsoft Project 98 Web-related features include the following:

- The ability to navigate to a Web site on the Internet or a document on your network from a hyperlink field on a task or resource.

- The ability to track your project's progress by collecting actual work and remaining work estimates from project team members on your corporate intranet (see Hour 20, "Using Microsoft Project in Workgroups").

- The ability to create an Import/Export map that allows you to select the specific task, resource, and resource assignment information you want to publish in your HTML document.

- The ability to easily include a picture of your project's Gantt Chart in your Web document.

- The ability to customize your HTML document to include a header row (resource assignment rows indented below their associated task) or to be based on a customized HTML template that includes your company logo or other graphics.

Exporting Project Data to Web Pages

In this section, you will step through the process of saving your project file as an HTML document. Each of the following examples uses the Software Launch.mpt project template that comes with Project 98. This file is typically located in the Microsoft Office\Templates\Microsoft Project directory. Or, you can work through the following examples using one of your actual projects.

Saving Your Project as an HTML Document

One of the key benefits of being able to save your project as an HTML documnent is that it offers the ability to publish the information *you* want to communicate about your project *without* giving people in your organization access to the project file itself.

> It's a good idea to save your project as a standard .MPP file before saving it as an HTML document.

16

To Do: Saving Your Project File as an HTML Document

1. Open your project file, and from the menu, choose **F**ile, Save As **H**TML. The File Save dialog box will be displayed (see Figure 16.2).

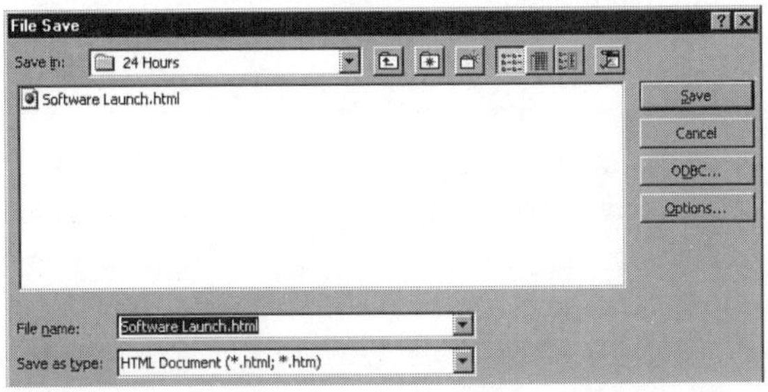

FIGURE 16.2

The File Save dialog box allows you to save your project as an HTML document.

2. Click Save, and Project displays the Export Format dialog box (see Figure 16.3), where you can select the "map" on which to base your HTML document. Project comes with 12 predefined map files you can use to create your HTML document, or you can create your own map files.

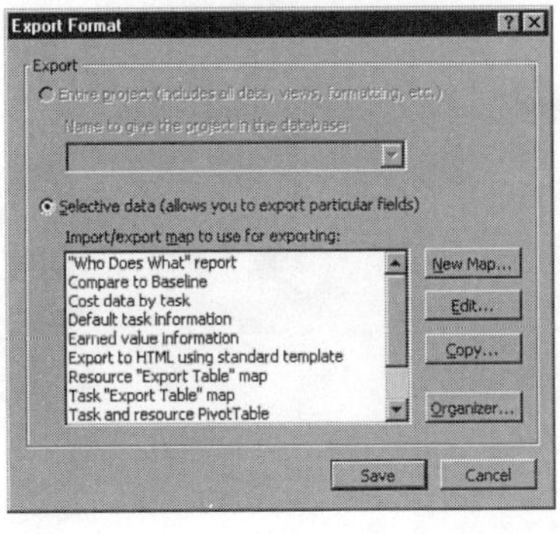

FIGURE 16.3

The Export Format dialog box allows you to select the map file used to determine which data to export to your HTML document.

▼ **NEW TERM** **Map** A *map* is essentially a set of instructions that tells Project the type of data you want to save in your Web document. For example, you might choose to export all tasks in danger of finishing late or all resources currently over budget.

> By default, Microsoft Project 98 saves your HTML file to the same directory and assigns it the same name as your project file (but with the extension html). You can override these defaults in the File Save dialog box by selecting the directory and filename as you would in any other Windows application.

3. From the **S**elective Data option on the Export Format dialog box, select the Task List With Embedded Assignment Rows map, and click Save. Your project is now
▲ saved as an HTML document.

Viewing Your Project as an HTML Document

Now comes the reallyproject file, fun part: You get to view your project file through your Web browser to see how it will look when it's actually published on your intranet or on the Internet. In this section, you view the HTML file created in the previous section ("Saving Your Project as an HTML Document") using Microsoft Internet Explorer 3.0*x*, but most browsers have a similar feature you can use to follow the example.

To Do: Viewing Your Project File with a Web Browser

To Do

1. Start Microsoft Internet Explorer, and from the menu, choose **F**ile, **O**pen. The Open dialog box will be displayed (see Figure 16.4).

2. Click the Browse button to navigate to the HTML file you want to view, and from the Browse dialog box, click **O**pen. From the Open dialog box, click OK, and your
▲ HTML document will be displayed in the browser (see Figure 16.5).

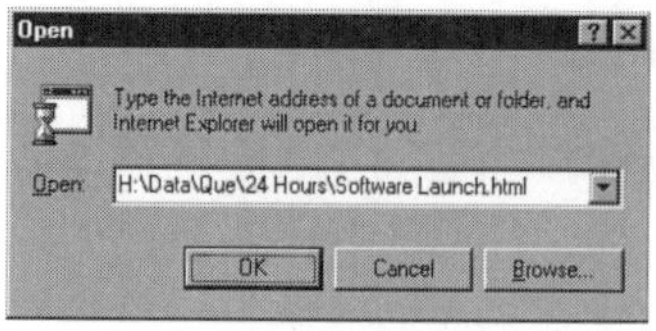

FIGURE 16.4

The Open dialog box in Microsoft Internet Explorer allows you to select the HTML file you want to view in the browser.

Open	? X
Type the Internet address of a document or folder, and Internet Explorer will open it for you.	
Open: H:\Data\Que\24 Hours\Software Launch.html	
OK Cancel Browse...	

FIGURE 16.5

Microsoft Internet Explorer allows you to view the HTML document based on the Task List With Embedded Assignment Rows map.

Microsoft Project Exported Information - Microsoft Internet Explorer

File Edit View Go Favorites Help

Back Forward Stop Refresh Home Search Favorites Print Font Mail Edit

Address H:\Data\Que\24 Hours\Software Launch.html   Links

Cyclone Launch

Project Start Date: Fri 1/2/98
Project Finish Date: Thu 6/4/98

Tasks with Assignments

ID	Task Name	Work	Duration	Start	Finish	% Work Complete
1	Marketing Plan distributed	0 hrs	0 days	Tue 3/17/98	Tue 3/17/98	0%
2	Corp Comm	1,680 hrs	104 days	Mon 1/5/98	Thu 5/28/98	0%
3	Corp Comm Kickoff	0 hrs	0 days	Mon 1/5/98	Mon 1/5/98	0%
4	Comm. Plan delivered	0 hrs	0 days	Fri 1/23/98	Fri 1/23/98	0%
5	Packaging	480 hrs	12 wks	Fri 2/13/98	Thu 5/7/98	0%
1	*Joe Franklin*	480 hrs		Fri 2/13/98	Thu 5/7/98	0%
6	Datasheets	520 hrs	13 wks	Fri 2/27/98	Thu 5/28/98	0%
1	*Joe Franklin*	520 hrs		Fri 2/27/98	Thu 5/28/98	0%
7	Reseller kits	440 hrs	11 wks	Fri 3/13/98	Thu 5/28/98	0%

Done

16

For more information about saving your Project files to the Web, including using Project to create your own import/export maps, see *Special Edition Using Project 98*, published by Que.

Working with Hyperlinks in Tasks and Resources

In addition to being able to save your project as an HTML document, Microsoft Project 98 includes several hyperlink fields that allow you to navigate to another document or Web site from a task or resource in your project. For example, suppose you have developed a task checklist in Microsoft Word that includes all the detailed processes for a task in your project. You can add a hyperlink to the task, so that when you click on it, you go directly to the task checklist.

Adding a Hyperlink

It's fairly easy to add a hyperlink to a task, resource, or assignment from any view. However, it's easiest to use the hyperlink if you display a view that has an indicator column so you can simply click on the hyperlink indicator icon to jump to the hyperlink target. In this example, I will be adding a hyperlink to a task using the Gantt Chart view.

To Do: Adding a Hyperlink

1. Open a project in any view.

2. Select the task, resource, or assignment to which you want to add a hyperlink, and from the menu, choose Insert, Hyperlink. The Insert Hyperlink dialog box will be displayed (see Figure 16.6).

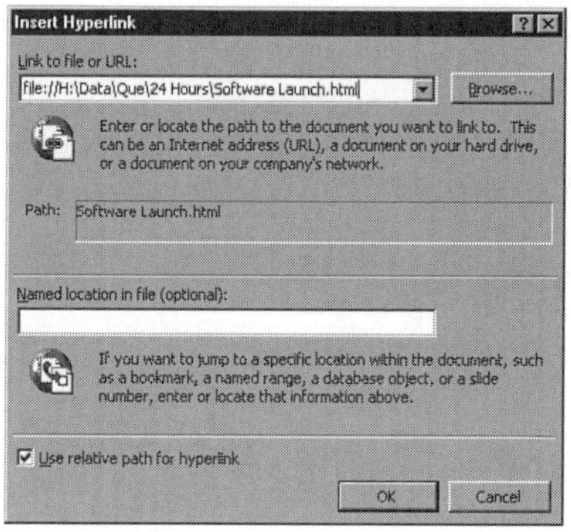

FIGURE 16.6

The Insert Hyperlink dialog box allows you to add, delete, or modify a hyperlink in your project.

3. In the Link to File or URL field, enter a Web site URL or a filename.

4. In the Named Location in File field, you can optionally point to a specific section of a document to navigate to. For example, you could navigate to a bookmarked section of a Word document or to a cell or named-range in an Excel file.

▲   5. Click OK, and the hyperlink will be created for the selected task.

You can delete a hyperlink by selecting the task, resource, or assignment and choosing Edit, Clear, Hyperlinks. To jump to the hyperlink reference, simply display the project in a view that has the indicator column displayed and click on the hyperlink icon on the row for the task, resource, or assignment.

Publishing Your Web Documents

After you have created your HTML documents, you need to publish them on the Internet or your corporate intranet.

If the Web documents will be viewed from your intranet, you need to copy all your HTML files (and related graphics files, if you included an image of your Gantt Chart, for example) to a location on your network server (as specified by your intranet administrator).

If you will be publishing your Web documents to the Internet, a convenient way to do this is with the Web Publishing Wizard included on the Microsoft Office 97 CD-ROM. The Web Publishing Wizard can walk you through the process of publishing your Web pages in an easy-to-follow, step-by-step fashion.

To see if you have the Web Publishing Wizard installed on your computer, from the Windows 95 task bar, click the Start button, and choose Programs, Accessories, Internet Tools. The Web Publishing Wizard should be listed in the Internet Tools folder. If you don't have it installed on your computer, you can download it for free from Microsoft's Web site at **http://www.microsoft.com/windows/software/webpost/**.

16

For more information about using the Microsoft Office Web Publishing Wizard, see *Teach Yourself Office 97 in 24 Hours, Second Edition*, also published by Sams Publishing.

So now you are all ready to become a Web publishing mogul! Let's just review the basic steps for publishing your project as an HTML document:

- Make sure your plan has been updated to reflect the latest information about your project. You want to make sure the information you're publishing is current.

- Choose the Save as HTML option from the File menu, and select the Import/Export map you want to use. Remember, the Import/Export map determines the specific project task, resource, and assignment information you will be publishing. It also contains information about the Web template that gives your HTML document its own "look."

- Use the Web Publishing Wizard to publish your HTML documents to the Internet or your corporate intranet.

PART VI

Managing and Tracking the Project

Hour

HOUR 17

Tracking Work on the Project

If you have been applying the lessons in this book to your own project, then you should have a finalized schedule or plan for completing the project on time and within budget—like an architect's plan for a building that meets all the builder's requirements. After work on the project gets underway, you will find that your plan, like the blueprints, will be consulted constantly, and it will be revised as you discover new information about the tasks and the resources you assigned to them. Sometimes actual events even threaten to make the plan unravel, but having your schedule already entered in Microsoft Project makes it much easier to figure out how to get things back on track, as in the following examples:

- If it appears that a task is going to take longer than you planned, and therefore delay other tasks and maybe even the finish of the project itself, then you can enter the new estimated duration in Microsoft Project and see the calculated effects on other tasks and resource assignments. You can use Microsoft Project to try "what if" scenarios to find the best way to minimize the impact on the project's finish date and cost.

- If a resource becomes unavailable or costs more than anticipated, you can quickly evaluate alternatives, including ways to substitute less expensive resources.
- If you have to add a task to the schedule, you can add it, find ways to minimize the impact on the timeline and costs, and alert all those who are affected by the change.

In this hour, we look at how you make the transition from using the Microsoft Project document as a preproduction planning device to a working blueprint that helps you manage the project and meet the project goals on time and within the budget.

- You will make a copy of the current schedule just before you start work on the project. This copy will serve as a *baseline* to use for comparing with later, revised schedules, especially the final schedule that shows what actually happened. Project calculates *variances* that show the difference between the baseline and scheduled entries.
- Then you will start using the current schedule to tell resources when to start work on specific tasks.
- When work actually starts and finishes on tasks, you will put those *actual* dates back into the Project file to replace the scheduled dates. If the actual dates differ from the scheduled dates, Project recalculates the schedule for the remainder of the project so you can better predict what is likely to happen. By entering actual data in the document, you improve the accuracy of the current schedule and are in a better position to assess how well the project is going.
- If you want to manage costs carefully, you should also record how much work was actually done on the tasks and what the costs actually were. You can then compare that data with the baseline costs to see if you're staying within budget.

NEW TERM   **Current**   The *current schedule* is the one you have been working with so far— it's made up of the fields you use to enter estimates for tasks and assignments. Microsoft Project uses this schedule to do calculations and changes as you enter new information into the project.

NEW TERM   **Baseline**   The *baseline schedule* is a set of fields that Project uses to preserve a copy of the current schedule at a specific point, usually the moment just before work actually starts. Baseline fields are not changed by your revisions to the schedule; they are changed only by explicit commands to set aside baseline copies of the current schedule.

NEW TERM   **Variance**   The *variances* are calculated by subtracting the baseline field from the corresponding current schedule field. Variances tell you how much the schedule value has changed since the baseline was created.

NEW TERM **Actual Fields** The *actual fields* are where you enter actual dates, work, and costs to show what actually happens. Project automatically copies these actual values into the corresponding fields of the current schedule to update it.

This process of monitoring progress, updating the schedule, and comparing the new schedule with the baseline schedule helps you assess whether you're likely to meet your goals in a timely fashion. This information can let you know that you need to make changes before it's too late. When the project is finished, your efforts should leave you in the position to gloat over how you finished early and for less cost than originally planned. Even if the project takes longer or costs more than planned, however, the tracking data you have recorded can help you explain where time was lost or why costs went over budget. You have also gathered information that will be useful in planning future projects.

In this hour, we will focus on the mechanics of updating the schedule. The variances and other analysis techniques are covered in the next Hour.

17

Understanding the Tracking Fields

The date, duration, work, and cost fields we have been working with in Microsoft Project are fields in the *current schedule*. These are the fields you use to plan and calculate a schedule. They tell you what your latest and best thinking is about how to complete the project.

Table 17.1 lists the current schedule fields that have tracking counterparts: baseline, variance, and actual fields. There are baseline and actual fields both for tasks and for resource assignments. Therefore, the baseline schedule shows not only when a task was scheduled to start and how much work was supposed to be done, but can also show when each resource assignment for the task was scheduled to start and how much work each resource was scheduled to perform.

TABLE 17.1. THE FIELDS USED IN TRACKING

Task Fields			
Current Schedule	*Baseline*	*Variance*	*Actual*
Start	Baseline Start	Start Variance	Actual Start
Finish	Baseline Finish	Finish Variance	Actual Finish
Duration	Baseline Duration	Duration Variance	Actual Duration (and Remaining Duration)

continues

TABLE 17.1. CONTINUED

Task Fields

Current Schedule	Baseline	Variance	Actual
*Work	*Baseline Work	Work Variance	*Actual Work (and Remaining Work)
*Overtime Work			*Actual Overtime Work (and Remaining Overtime Work)
*Cost	*Baseline Cost	Cost Variance	*Actual Cost (and Remaining Cost)
Overtime Cost			Actual Overtime Cost (and Remaining Overtime Cost)

Resource Assignment Fields

Current Schedule	Baseline	Variance	Actual
Start	Baseline Start	Start Variance	Actual Start
Finish	Baseline Finish	Finish Variance	Actual Finish
*Work	Baseline Work	Work Variance	*Actual Work (and Remaining Work)
*Overtime Work			*Actual Overtime Work (and Remaining Overtime Work)
*Cost	Baseline Cost	Cost Variance	*Actual Cost (and Remaining Cost)
Overtime Cost			Actual Overtime Cost (and Remaining Overtime Cost)

Fields in Table 17.1 marked with an asterisk also have timephased components—the data can be displayed and tracked for specific time periods (hourly, daily, and so on) in the Task Usage or Resource Usage view.

Notice that you can track actual overtime work and overtime costs, but there's no baseline record of how much overtime work or cost was in the schedule when the baseline was captured. Also note that *duration* is a task-level phenomenon—there's no duration measurement at the assignment level.

Project's *variance* fields show the difference between the current value and the baseline value for each task. The formula is *current scheduled value* minus *baseline value*. Positive variances mean the current schedule calls for more than the baseline plan called for: You'll be running late or doing more work or spending more on costs than you had planned.

For example, if a currently scheduled date is 5/10/99 and the baseline date is 5/12/99, the variance would be 5/10/99 minus 5/12/99 or -2 days. A negative variance of 2 days means you'll finish 2 days earlier than planned; a positive variance means you'll be finishing later than planned.Therefore, positive variances are bad (it took longer or cost more), and negative variances are good (it took less time or cost less).

The actual date fields have NA values in them until you indicate that work has started or finished on a task (see the Actual Finish column in Figure 17.1). The actual duration, work, and cost fields have Remaining… counterparts. That is, if 20 hours of work are scheduled for a task and 15 hours have been completed, you can enter either 15 hours in the Actual Work field or 5 hours in the Remaining Work field to update a task's progress. Project then calculates a value for the field you leave blank. (More on the Remaining… fields is covered later in this hour.)

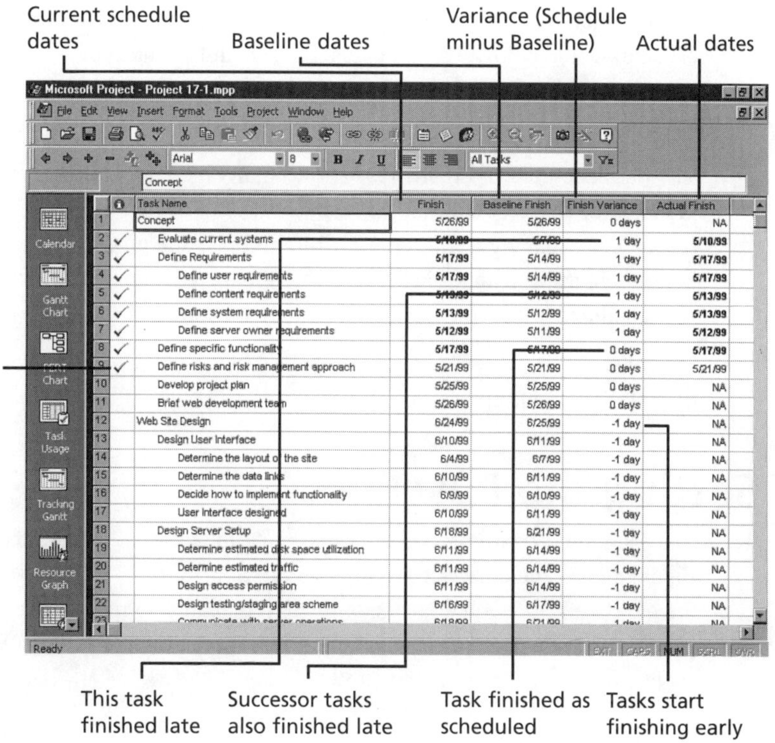

17

FIGURE 17.1

Actual values replace scheduled values and make the scheduled values fixed, as far as Project's calculator is concerned.

Check mark indicator for completed tasks

Current schedule dates

Baseline dates

Variance (Schedule minus Baseline)

Actual dates

This task finished late

Successor tasks also finished late

Task finished as scheduled

Tasks start finishing early

When you enter a value in an actual field for a task, Microsoft Project does three essential things (there are even more calculations covered later in this chapter):

- The value is entered in the actual field you are editing.

- The actual value is also copied into the current schedule field, replacing the estimated value with the actual value. This replacement could cause Project to recalculate current schedule values for successor tasks.

- Project tags the current schedule field as "fixed" now that an actual value is known and will not recalculate it again. For example, after you enter an actual start date for a task, Project won't recalculate that start date even if a predecessor task changes. Only you can change the field now by entering a new value in it or its actual counterpart.

As you track actual performance, the current schedule changes from its original speculative values to the known actual values. By the end of the project, the current schedule is identical to the actual schedule.

In Figure 17.1, you can compare the tracking fields for finish dates. The Finish column is the currently scheduled finish date for each task. I've bolded the actual dates that have been entered and the corresponding scheduled dates that are now fixed to those same values. Below the bolded (fixed) dates, the scheduled dates are free to be recalculated as circumstances change, but as new actual dates are entered for those tasks, their scheduled dates will become fixed, too.

The Variance field in Figure 17.1 shows that Task 2 took 1 day longer than originally planned. Because of that, the next several tasks finished late also. Task 8 finished on time (probably by having a shorter duration) and gets the project back on track (the variance is zero). Starting with Task 12, some time is saved somewhere, and all the project tasks are scheduled to finish a day early (variance is minus 1 day).

Now that we've surveyed the fields to be used in tracking, let's get on to the mechanics of putting data into those fields.

Setting the Baseline

The Planning Wizard prompts you to create the baseline when you first save a file (see Figure 17.2). Thereafter, it prompts you to update the baseline whenever it detects that the baseline is out of date or incomplete. You can also manually update the baseline from the menu at any time or save up to 10 interim versions of the baseline to show how the project plan has changed over time.

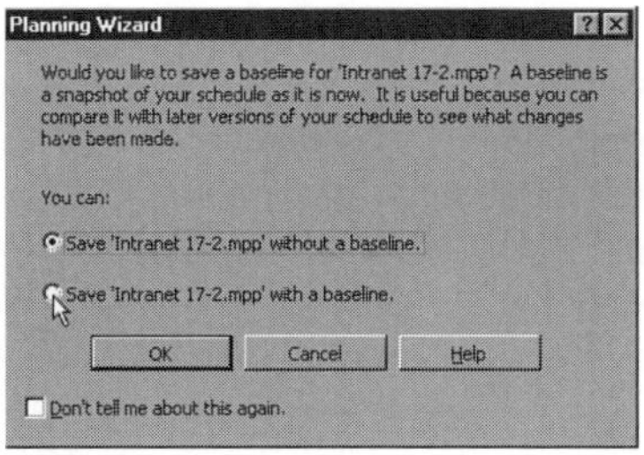

FIGURE 17.2

*The Planning Wizard
stands ready to save
baseline information
when you first save a
project file.*

Capturing the Baseline

The first time you save a file, after you have supplied the filename, the Planning Wizard
asks if you want to save a baseline as part of the saved file (see Figure 17.2). In a depar-
ture from standard Microsoft practices, clicking OK on the default selection does *not*
save the baseline: It saves the file without creating the baseline. You have to select the
second option and then click OK to make Project save the baseline. If you don't want to
be bothered with this dialog box, you can fill the check box labeled **D**on't Tell Me About
This Again. Doing so makes the Planning Wizard stop checking for the baseline when
you close a file. Just remember—it's up to you to remember to capture the baseline
before you start recording actual events. If you save the baseline and then subsequently
make changes that should be in the baseline, you are prompted to update the baseline
when you attempt to close the file after those additions (see Figure 17.3). This time, the
default selection does what the prompt advertises: It updates tasks and resources that
don't have baseline information saved. You can also choose to update baseline values for
all tasks at this point, to leave the baseline unchanged, and to discontinue being warned
about baseline changes.

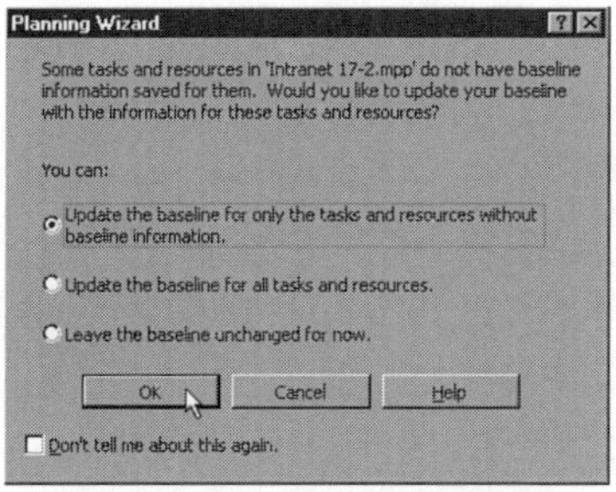

FIGURE 17.3

*You are also prompted
to include new tasks in
the baseline.*

17

The prompts to save the baseline were added to Project just to remind users about the importance of saving the baseline. You can safely ignore them, and even discontinue displaying them, as long as you can remember to save the baseline before you start entering actual values. On the other hand, it does no harm to continually update the baseline during the planning process.

You can use the Save Baseline command on the menu at any time to update the baseline. You should use this command just before you get ready to start tracking actual dates and costs to be certain that the baseline is updated to reflect the final plan. You can also use this command to update the baseline just for selected tasks. For example, if you add a task after the project has started, you could select that task and then use this command to record baseline values for that one task without disturbing the baseline values for any other tasks.

To Do: Saving the Baseline Manually

▼ To Do

1. Choose Tools, Tracking, Save Baseline from the menu to display the Save Baseline dialog box (see Figure 17.4).

2. Select Save Baseline to copy the task and assignment field values from the current schedule to the baseline fields.

3. At the bottom of this dialog box, you can choose whether to update all tasks and assignments or just the tasks that were selected when you started the command. (If you started from a resource view, this choice is not available.) Select Entire Project to save baseline values for all tasks, or Selected Tasks to save values for just the task you selected beforehand.

▲ 4. Click OK to start the save process and close the dialog box.

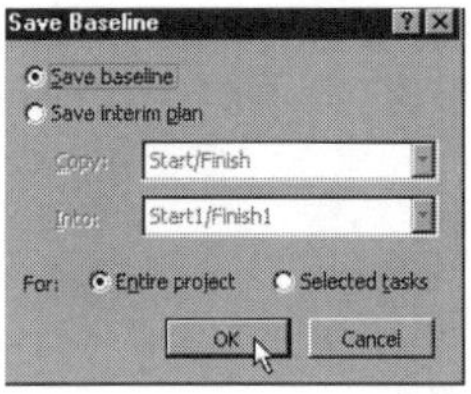

FIGURE 17.4

The Save Baseline dialog box allows you to save the baseline at any time, for all tasks or just for selected tasks.

Tracking Actual Performance

There's a wide range in the level of detail you can choose to record when tracking actual work on your project. Tracking can be simple or sophisticated, depending on your reporting needs and the time you have to do it. The time it takes to keep a project file updated can be a considerable drain on the project manager's schedule, so you must choose the level of detail based on the tradeoff between the time it takes you to keep the project updated and the value of the information that results. Here are some guidelines to keep in mind when tracking actual work:

- At the very least, you should record when tasks actually start and finish. If tasks finish late, the rest of the project might be in jeopardy of finishing late. If tasks finish early, resources could be freed that can help out with other tasks.

- For longer tasks that have started but not yet finished, you can record not only when the task started, but also how far along the task is—what percent of the scheduled task duration has been completed. You probably wouldn't want to take the time to do this for shorter tasks.

- Instead of tracking the percent of the task duration completed, and letting Project calculate how much work that involves, you can record the actual work itself for the task. Or, for even greater accuracy, you can record the work completed by each resource assigned to the task.

- By default, actual costs are always calculated by Microsoft Project, and you can't overwrite its calculations until the task is 100% complete. You have the option to supplement the cost calculations by entering actual costs for each resource assignment yourself. This option takes more time (unless you use the automated workgroup messaging described in Hour 20, "Using Microsoft Project in Workgroups"), but it can be the most accurate of all tracking methods.

In the following sections, we'll look at how you use Project's tracking facilities for each of the tracking approaches just outlined. Most of this discussion assumes that you will update the task fields and that you want Project to calculate appropriate actual values for the task assignments. The choice between this and the alternative, for you to enter actual work for each resource directly, is governed by a choice on the Calculation tab of the Options dialog box.

Collecting the Tracking Information

Before we get started, just a word about gathering the information you need to track progress. You should decide in advance how you will collect the progress data and then give the human resources a way to supply it to you. You might want to print forms to be

17

completed and sent to you on a regular basis or schedule meetings when the resources can report their progress. If all your resources have access to a computer and share email, you can use Microsoft Project's workgroup feature to automatically send notices of task assignments and changes in assignments and to automatically request progress reports after tasks are scheduled to be in production. Then, after reviewing the progress reports sent by the resources, you can upload them automatically into Project to update the schedule. However you do it, you need to establish the mechanism in advance.

Tracking Start and Finish Dates

You can enter the actual start and finish dates for a task in a variety of ways, but I'll show you only the most commonly used methods. One of the most useful views for tracking task dates is to display the Tracking Gantt Chart and apply the Tracking table to that view (see Figure 17.5). The Actual Start and Actual Finish columns are easily accessible next to the Task Name. The Tracking Gantt Chart shows a baseline task bar (in gray) beneath the current task bar (in color). Completed work is shown in a darker color on the current task bar.

FIGURE 17.5

Check marks in the task list indicate the completed tasks.

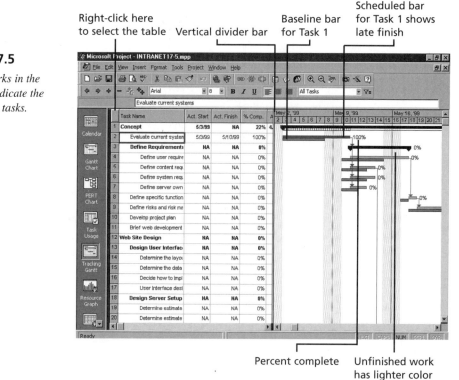

To Do: Tracking Start and Finish Dates

▼ To Do

1. Choose **V**iew, Tracking Ga**n**tt from the menu or use the Tracking Gantt icon on the View Bar to display the Tracking Gantt view.

2. Right-click in the header row above the task ID numbers to display the shortcut menu for Tables and choose **T**racking to display the Tracking table. If necessary, drag the vertical divider bar to the right to see the tracking columns.

3. Enter actual start dates in the Act. Start column and actual finish dates in the Act. Finish column.

The actual date fields display "NA" until you take a step that sets an actual date. You can remove the actual date by typing NA in an actual date field.

17

If you enter an actual finish date without having entered an actual start date, Microsoft Project assumes the task started on schedule and puts the scheduled start date in the actual start date field.

When you enter a date in the Actual Finish date field, Project performs several calculations, described in the following list, to supply values for all the task's actual fields:

- As described earlier, Project changes the scheduled finish date to match the new actual finish date and tags the Finish field as fixed and not to be rescheduled by changes in other tasks.

- If the actual start date has not been manually entered, Project sets it to equal the scheduled start date.

- Project calculates the Actual Duration field, based on the actual start and finish dates, and also enters that duration value into the scheduled Duration field.

- Project sets the Percent Complete (which is the percentage of duration completed) to 100%. See the following section for more on the Percent Complete field.

- If resources are assigned to the task, Project sets the actual start and finish dates of all assignments, calculates the actual work for each assignment, and then calculates the actual cost for each assignment.

- With the assignment work and cost calculated, Project then sums those amounts and puts the result in the task's Actual Work and Actual Cost fields.

- Finally, if the task was a "critical" task, Project changes it to noncritical. Recall from Hour 14, "Optimizing the Project Plan," that the purpose of the critical flag is to point out the tasks you could shorten or reschedule if you want to shorten the overall project. Because the task is now finished, it's no longer a candidate for helping you shorten the project, and the critical status is removed.

When the task is finished, Project will have calculated values for all the actual fields you didn't place an entry in.

> Project doesn't show a summary task as finished until the last of its subtasks is finished.

If you want to enter actual work and cost information that differs from the work and cost that Project calculates, see the sections that follow.

Tracking Progress for Unfinished Tasks

After a longer task has started, you might want to keep track of how the work is going while it's still far from being finished. Project has several ways to show partial completion of a task. If a task is partially completed, then some of the scheduled duration (calendar periods when work takes place) must have already occurred. You can enter the progress on the task in three ways:

- You can enter Actual Duration as an amount (like 2 days or 40 hours).
- You can enter the Percent Complete, which is the Actual Duration divided by the scheduled Duration. When nothing has been done on a task, the Percent Complete is zero; when the task is finished, it's 100%.
- You can enter the Remaining Duration, which is the scheduled Duration minus the Actual Duration.

 Actual Duration *Actual Duration* is the amount of calendar time that one or more resources have actually been working on the task.

 Remaining Duration *Remaining Duration* is the difference between the scheduled Duration field and the Actual Duration field.

 Percent Complete *Percent Complete* is calculated by dividing Actual Duration by the scheduled Duration field. It's the percent of scheduled Duration that has been completed.

If you enter any one of these three actual amounts, Project calculates the other two for you, using the value you entered and the scheduled Duration. However, if you enter values in both Actual Duration and Remaining Duration, Project assumes you're trying to tell it something like this: "We've spent this much time on the task, and we estimate that we need this much time to finish." By entering both the Actual Duration and the Remaining Duration, you're telling Project to change the Duration in the current schedule; therefore, it adds Actual Duration and Remaining Duration and puts that value in the scheduled Duration field.

Similarly, if you enter an Actual Duration greater than the scheduled Duration, Project assumes that the task is finished and took longer than scheduled. Project changes the current scheduled duration to match the new, longer actual duration, and then the Percent Complete and Remaining Duration fields are set to 100% and 0 (zero), respectively, to indicate that the task is complete.

You can enter all these values in the same view used earlier, the Tracking Gantt with the Tracking table applied. You just need to drag the vertical divider bar to the right or scroll to the right to bring the columns labeled % Comp, Act. Dur, and Rem. Dur. into view.

You can also use the tools on the Tracking toolbar to update tasks if you don't want to change the view you're using at the moment.

To Do: Using the Tracking Toolbar to Update a Task

1. Display the Tracking toolbar, shown in Figure 17.6.

2. Select the task you want to update.

3. Click one of the Percent Complete buttons if it fits the percentage you want to register.

4. Otherwise, click the Update Task tool to display the Update Tasks dialog box (see Figure 17.6).

5. Record the Actual Start date if different from the scheduled start date.

6. Record the progress on the task in the % Complete field, the Actual Dur field, and/or the Remaining Dur field.

7. If the task is complete, enter the Actual Finish date.

8. Click OK to close the dialog box.

Recording Actual Work

By default, when you enter values in the actual duration fields (Actual Duration, Remaining Duration, Percent Complete) for a task that has resource assignments, Project uses those entries to calculate actual work for each of the assignments, uses the actual work to calculate actual cost, and then sums the assignment work and costs in the task fields.

You can also enter actual work for the assignments manually instead of accepting the values Project creates. This method can add more precision to your records for resource work and costs, especially when some of the resources work more than others on a task. If you enter amounts directly into the assignment's Actual Work field, Project updates the task's Actual Duration and Percent Complete fields to incorporate your entries.

FIGURE 17.6

Record tracking information for one task at a time in the Update Tasks dialog box.

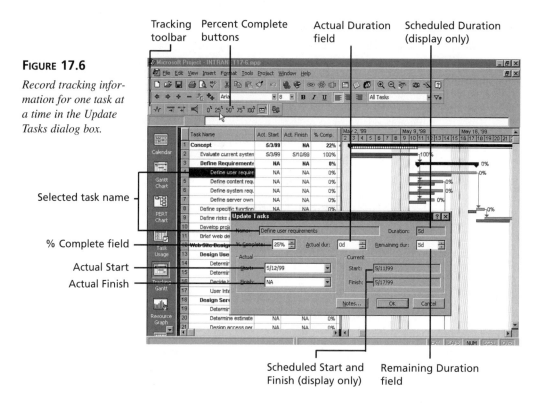

For Fixed Work tasks, you should avoid changing either the Scheduled or Actual Duration fields; change the task's Work or Resource fields instead. Project can then redistribute the fixed work over a longer or shorter time instead of calculating how much work has been completed. I advise you to change the task from Fixed Work to Fixed Units when you get to the tracking stage. The Fixed Work status was there only to help you calculate a realistic schedule.

As was the case with entering an actual finish date and no actual start date, if you enter Actual Duration, Remaining Duration, or Percent Complete without having entered an actual start date, Project uses the scheduled Start field value to fill in the actual start date.

Similarly, if you haven't entered an actual finish date when you enter values that imply the task is finished (by entering 100% in the Percent Complete field, zero in the Remaining Duration field, or an actual duration that's equal to the scheduled duration), Project supplies an actual finish date, based on the actual start date and the actual duration.

If you make entries into the task's Actual Duration field (by changing it directly or by changing either the Percent Complete or the Remaining Duration fields), Project recalculates the actual work for assignments and you will lose any actual work amounts you might have entered for the assignments. To avoid this problem, you must remember not to manually update the task's Actual Duration or Percent Complete fields after you have manually entered actual work for an assignment. Or, you can break the computational link between a task's actual duration and an assignment's actual work, as described in the following numbered list of steps.

17

If you want to keep Project from recalculating the assignment work fields when you change the task duration, you must break the computational link between the task's actual duration and the assignment's actual work.

To Do: Preserving Manual Updates to an Assignment's Actual Work

▼ To Do

1. Choose **T**ools, **O**ptions to display the Options dialog box and select the Calculation tab (see Figure 17.7).

2. To keep changes in the task's actual duration from changing the resource assignment's actual work, clear the check box labeled U**p**dating Task Status Updates Resource Status.

   Fill the check box to have changes in the task's actual duration calculate changes in the actual work for assignments. Note that this change affects only the current project unless you click the Set as **D**efault button; then it affects only new projects created after this point.

▲

3. Click OK to close the dialog box.

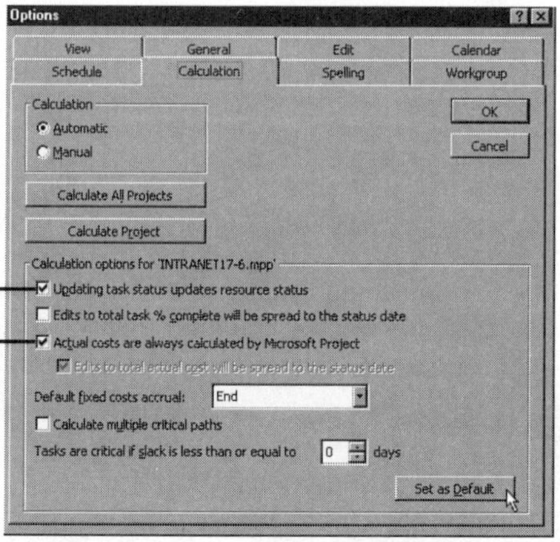

FIGURE 17.7

Choose how Project links the task's duration and an assignment's work in the Options dialog box.

Links the task's duration and an assignment's work

Protects actual cost calculations

If you break this computational link between the task's actual duration and an assignment's actual work, Project will no longer change a resource assignment's actual work values when you update the task's actual duration, but neither will it update the task's Actual Duration or Percent Complete fields when you record actual work for the resource assignments. If you break the link, you have to enter the task's Percent Complete values yourself in the Task Usage View. You just can't have it both ways.

Entering Actual Costs

By default, the Actual Cost fields for tasks and assignments are calculated by Project based on actual work and can't be changed by the user as long as there are unfinished resource assignments. In Figure 17.8, I've added the actual cost details to the grid. The amounts were calculated by Project based on the actual work.

If you want to enter task costs yourself (or if you want to import them) even though you have resources assigned, you can allow the Actual Cost fields to be edited.

To Do: Allowing Actual Cost Fields to Be Edited

1. Choose **T**ools, **O**ptions to display the Options dialog box and select the Calculation tab (refer to Figure 17.7).

2. To allow direct entries into Actual Cost fields, clear the check box for Actual Costs Are Always Calculated By Microsoft Project. To have Project calculate these values, fill the check box.

FIGURE 17.8

By default, actual costs are calculated by Project until work is completed.

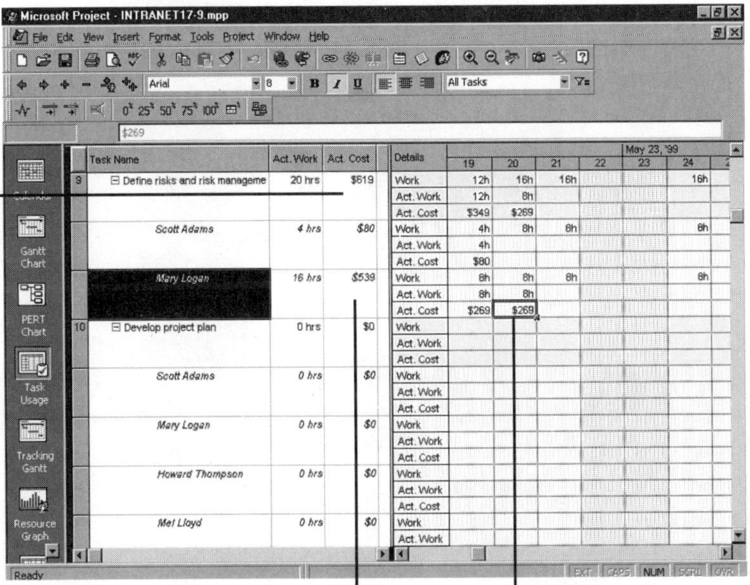

Change task costs only after all work is complete

Change assignment costs only after work is complete

Normally, you can't change timephased amounts at all

If you have been allowing direct entries into Actual Cost fields and decide to revert to having Project calculate the fields, you will lose all the manual entries you have made for actual costs.

17

HOUR 18

Analyzing Progress and Revising the Schedule

Project management is sometimes compared to risk management. The purpose of tracking, updating, and revising a schedule is to not only meet the stated goals, but also to correct problems quickly along the way. One common analogy is that you, as the project manager and captain of the ship, need to see that small black dot on the horizon long before it gets close enough to be recognized as a 200-ton tanker about to crash into your ship.

What warnings will you have? An overall project report can give you a reading on the pulse as a whole. Also in Project 98, variances point toward tasks and work drifting off schedule. For detailed assessment of work versus cost, an Earned Value Analysis is included, and there are visual clues to progress available on custom Gantt Charts.

The highlights of this hour include the following items:

- Understanding variance definitions and calculations
- Techniques for investigating task slippage

- Reporting on resource costs
- Steps to creating Earned Value reports
- Methods for rescheduling interrupted tasks
- Techniques for revising a project plan

Analyzing Variances and Revising the Schedule

Despite your best efforts, projects usually do not track exactly as planned. Investigating the difference between the current schedule and the baseline plan is an important part of the project manager's job. The sooner you know how the project is diverging from the original plan, and by how much, the sooner you can take corrective action.

NEW TERM   **Variance**   The calculated difference between a baseline value and the most current data value. See Table 18.1 for several common calculations used to determine the variance.

The differences between the baseline information and the most current data are known as *variances*. What can vary?

- Tasks might not start as planned, creating a start variance.
- Tasks might start on time but might not be completed as planned, creating a finish variance.
- Certainly costs can exceed estimates, creating cost variances for tasks, for individual resources, and for total resource assignments on a task.

Not all variances are harmful to the overall project. Some tasks might start and finish ahead of schedule, or they might not have required as much time as the original duration estimate. These variances, which will show as negative variance values, won't hurt the project as long as they don't create unproductive gaps in the schedule.

Notice that the calculations shown in Table 18.1 can result in negative values. If your current value is less than the baseline, you're ahead (generally speaking)!

TABLE 18.1. COMMON VARIANCE CALCULATIONS

Value/Field	Calculation
Task Start Variance	Currently scheduled start (the Start field) - Baseline start
Task Finish Variance	Currently scheduled finish (Finish field) - Baseline finish
Task Work Variance	Current total resource work assigned to the task (Work) - Baseline work for the task
Resource Cost Variance	Current cost of the resource over the project - Baseline cost of the resource

Project includes variance fields in several predefined tables. With a task view displayed, such as a Gantt Chart, apply the Variance table to view task start and finish variances, or apply the Work table to view work variances by task. For resource variances, display a resource view, such as the Resource Sheet, and apply the Cost or Work table.

To Do: Applying Tables to Views

To apply tables to views, follow these steps:

1. Display a task view (Gantt Chart, Task Usage) or a resource view (Resource Sheet, Resource Usage).

2. Choose View, Table.

3. Select from the cascading table name list, or select More Tables to display the complete list.

Analyzing Progress

How do you measure progress on a project? The first consideration is whether the project will finish on time. Of equal importance for most projects is whether they are staying within budget. You can get this information, and a general feel of the project progress, by examining the overall project summary.

If progress is lacking, however, specific causes need to be investigated. Tasks that are behind schedule, resources that are not completing work in a timely fashion, and general delays caused by competing company projects are all likely causes for a project not meeting its goals. The following sections cover methods for examining these project characteristics.

Reviewing Summary Progress Information

Overall project summary information can give you an indication of the project's general "health." If it's not progressing satisfactorily, you need to investigate further by examining detailed task or resource information.

To Do: Getting a Snapshot of the Project's Status

1. Choose **P**roject, **P**roject Information.
2. Click the Statistics button. The Project Statistics dialog box is displayed, as shown in Figure 18.1.

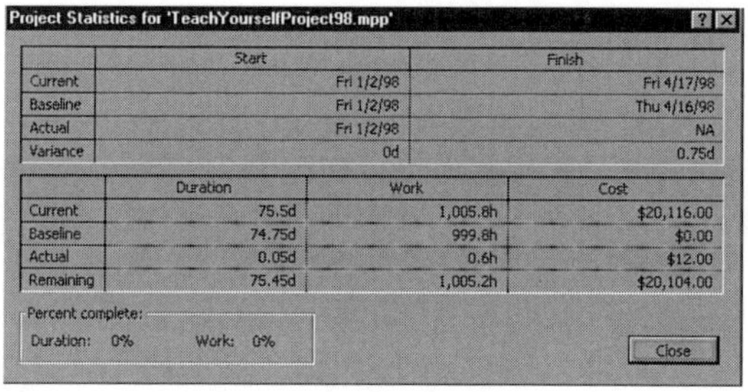

FIGURE 18.1

The Project Statistics dialog box gives you a snapshot of your project.

Project Statistics for 'TeachYourselfProject98.mpp'			? X
	Start		Finish
Current		Fri 1/2/98	Fri 4/17/98
Baseline		Fri 1/2/98	Thu 4/16/98
Actual		Fri 1/2/98	NA
Variance		0d	0.75d

	Duration	Work	Cost
Current	75.5d	1,005.8h	$20,116.00
Baseline	74.75d	999.8h	$0.00
Actual	0.05d	0.6h	$12.00
Remaining	75.45d	1,005.2h	$20,104.00

Percent complete:
Duration: 0% Work: 0%

[Close]

You can also open the statistics dialog box by clicking the Statistics button on the Tracking toolbar. As with other buttons, this one can also be added to another toolbar for convenience. See Hour 24, "Customizing Toolbars and Menus," for the steps needed to add buttons to toolbars.

The Project Statistics dialog box can't be printed directly. Instead, print out a Project Summary report.

To Do: Printing the Project Status Summary

1. Choose **V**iew, **R**eports.
2. Double-click the **O**verview category.
3. Double-click the **P**roject Summary report to preview it.
4. Click **P**rint to print out the report.

Reviewing Progress Information at the Task Level

The task Variance, Cost, and Work tables discussed previously are helpful for viewing progress and variance information at the task level. The entire group of Current Activity reports can also be helpful.

Another way to see whether tasks are progressing on schedule is to display a task *progress line*. Setting a progress date and displaying a progress line causes Project to draw a vertical line on a Gantt Chart on the progress date. The line connects tasks that begin before the progress date or cross the date, and aren't completed yet. If the line bulges or peaks to the left of the vertical line, that task is behind schedule. However, if the line peaks to the right, a task is ahead of schedule.

To Do: Displaying a Progress Line

▼ To Do

1. First set a progress "as of" date: Choose **P**roject, **P**roject Information and select a **S**tatus Date. If you skip this step, Project notifies you that it will use the current date when you create a progress line.

2. Choose **T**ools, Trac**k**ing, Progress **L**ines. The Progress Lines dialog box will appear, as shown in Figure 18.2.

3. On the Dates and Intervals tab, select the dates or intervals for progress lines:

   • Turn on Always Display Current Progress Line for the line to always be visible on the Gantt Chart, either on the current date or the status date you entered in step 1.

   • Enable Display Progress Lines At Recurring Intervals, if you would like more than one progress line displayed at regular intervals on the Gantt Chart. Also, define the interval (daily, weekly, monthly; displayed from the project start date or lines not appearing until later in the project).

   • Turn on Display Selected Progress Lines to show lines at any arbitrary dates you enter in the Progress Line Dates list.

4. Use the Line Styles tab to adjust progress line formatting.

5. Click OK when finished. Progress lines are then displayed on the Gantt Chart, as shown in Figure 18.3.

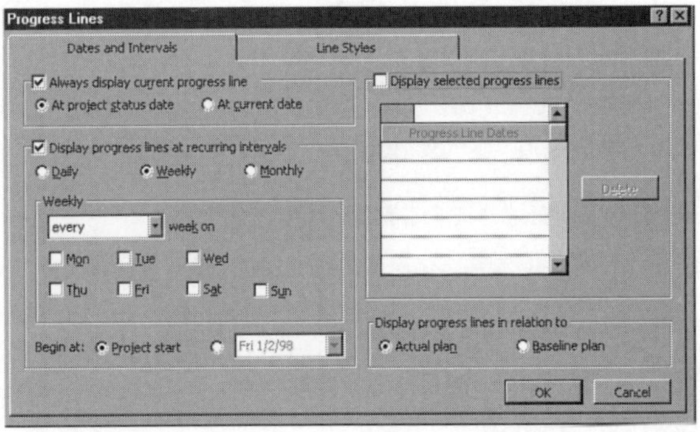

▲

18

FIGURE 18.2

Project progress lines can be displayed for fixed dates or at regular intervals.

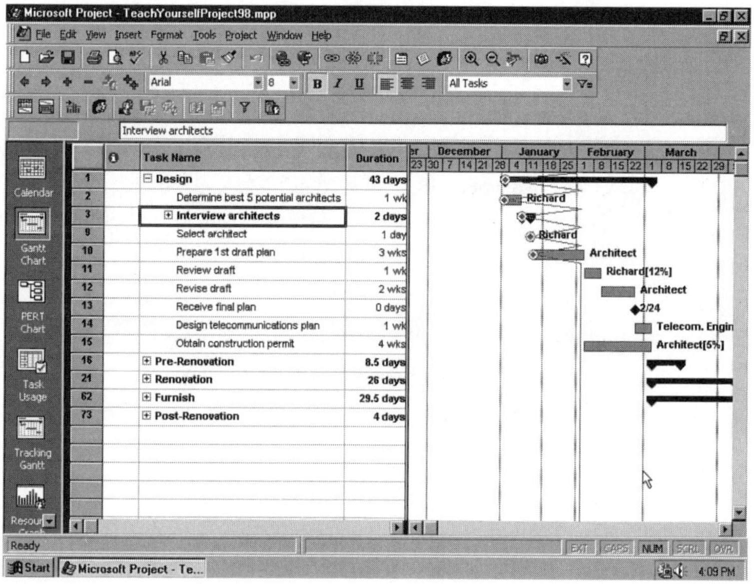

FIGURE 18.3

Left peaks indicate tasks that are behind schedule.

There is also a quick and easy way to display progress lines on a Gantt Chart.

To Do: Displaying Progress Lines on a Gantt Chart

1. Choose **V**iew, **T**oolbars and select Tracking.

2. Click the Add Progress Line toolbar button. The mouse pointer changes shape.

3. Move the mouse to the right side of the Gantt Chart. A pop-up dialog box shows which date you are pointing to. Click to display a progress line on that date.

4. Repeat for additional progress lines.

5. To turn these manual progress lines off, choose **T**ools, **T**racking, Progress **L**ines and turn off **D**isplay Selected Progress Lines.

The Slipping Tasks Report

Project defines a task as "slipping" if it's currently scheduled to finish after its original, baseline finish date. This assumes that a baseline was set for the project or the task.

To Do: Viewing the Slipping Tasks Report

1. Choose **V**iew, **R**eports.

2. Double-click the **C**urrent Activity category to display icons for reports in that category, as shown in Figure 18.4.

▼   3. Double-click the Slipping Tasks report to preview it.

   4. Use the start and finish information provided by the Variance table, and the Successors lists, to analyze the slippages.

▲   5. Click Close to return to the Reports dialog box.

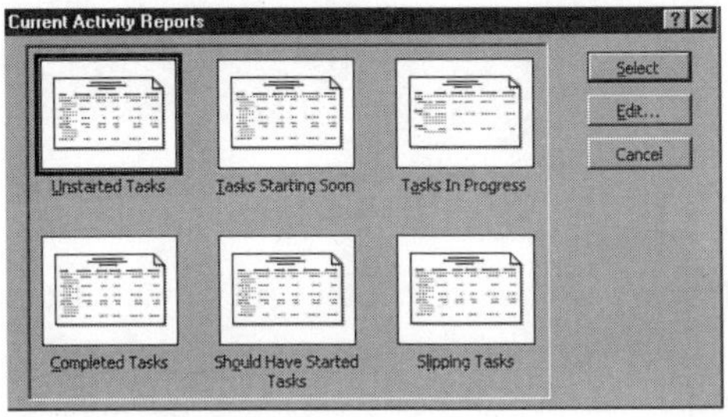

FIGURE 18.4

Print a list of slipping tasks from the Current Activity Reports dialog box.

The Overbudget Tasks Report

A task is considered "overbudget" if the current scheduled cost is greater than the baseline cost set for the task. Tasks can become overbudget for a number of reasons:

* More resources have been assigned to the task than anticipated
* More expensive resources have been substituted
* Fixed costs for the task have been modified

To Do: Viewing the Overbudget Tasks Report

1. Choose View, Reports.

2. Double-click the Costs category to display icons for reports in that category, as shown in Figure 18.5.

3. Double-click the Overbudget Tasks report to preview it.

4. Review the Cost table information to identify tasks that might need adjustments in the project plan.

▲   5. Click Close to return to the Reports dialog box.

Reviewing Progress Information at the Resource Level

How is a resource's progress measured? Two ways, typically—actual versus scheduled work, and cost versus scheduled cost. The task Work table, discussed previously, shows work variances by task, and the task Cost table shows cost variances by task. The supplied Overbudget Resources report might also help pinpoint resource cost variances.

18

FIGURE 18.5

Print a list of tasks currently running over budget from the Cost Reports dialog box.

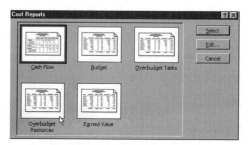

The Overbudget Resources Report

Typically, resources show as overbudget if they are now assigned to do more work than originally planned. More work means higher costs. It's also possible that a resource got an increase in pay rates in some project period.

To Do: Viewing the Overbudget Resources Report

To Do

1. Choose **V**iew, **R**eports.

2. Double-click the Costs category.

3. Double-click the Overbudget Resources report to preview it.

4. Review the resource cost information to identify resources who are working more hours than originally planned.

5. Click **C**lose to return to the Reports dialog box.

Updating the Schedule

The essentials of project tracking were discussed in Hour 17, but sometimes there's a major interruption to a project. Perhaps another company project has become more critical and all resources have been reassigned to it temporarily. Your project plan is still correct, but all or many of its tasks must be postponed. Project has methods for rescheduling uncompleted work on tasks in progress and for postponing tasks that have not yet started. Without these tools, each task would have to be modified manually.

Rescheduling Remaining Work

Tasks that have started but are not yet complete might need to have the unfinished work postponed. You could simply divide the existing task into two separate tasks and track them individually, but another way to represent the interruption is to split the single task into two sections:

- The completed portion
- The portion yet to be done

To Do: Rescheduling Work on a Single Task

Follow these steps to reschedule work on a single task:

1. Choose **View, G**antt Chart.

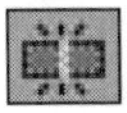

 2. Click the Split Task button on the Standard toolbar.

3. Position the mouse over the bar of the task to be split into finished and remaining work portions.

4. Click the task bar and drag the unfinished portion to the right. Let the Start and Finish dates in the pop-up dialog box, shown in Figure 18.6, be your guide.

5. Let go of the mouse button when finished.

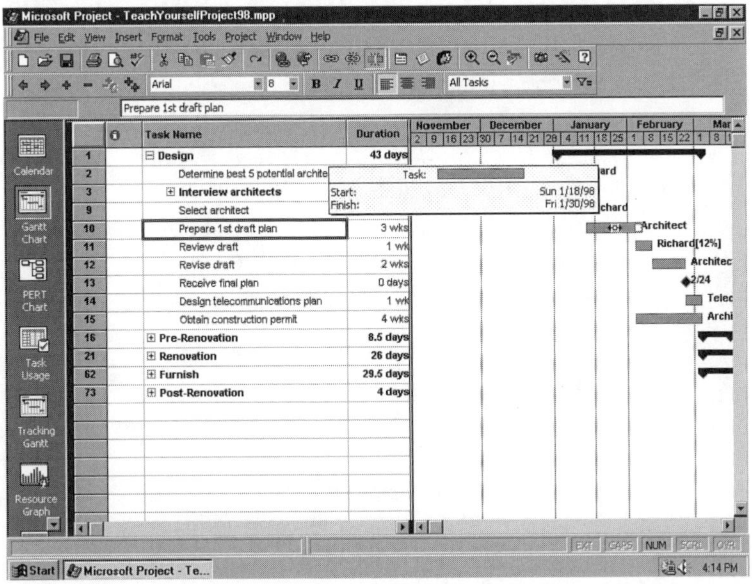

FIGURE 18.6

A pop-up box shows the task split dates while the mouse button is still pressed.

18

The preceding steps for task splitting must be followed for each task being rescheduled. If there are several tasks that will be rescheduled to resume at the same time, a dialog box can adjust all selected tasks at once.

To Do: Splitting and Rescheduling More Than One Task

1. Select all tasks that will resume work at the same point in time.

2. Choose **T**ools, Trac**k**ing, Update **P**roject. The Update Project dialog box will appear, as shown in Figure 18.7.

3. Select the option to **R**eschedule Uncompleted Work To Start and choose a date.

▼ 4. Select an option to reschedule the Entire Project to this date or only Selected
      Tasks.

▲ 5. Click OK when finished.

FIGURE 18.7

*Reschedule remaining
task work for several
tasks at one time.*

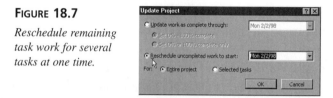

Rescheduling Tasks that Haven't Started

You can also postpone tasks that have not yet started. The technique is similar to
rescheduling remaining work for more than one task.

To Do: Rescheduling Unstarted Tasks

1. Select all tasks that need to be rescheduled.

2. Choose Tools, Tracking, Update Project. The Update Project dialog box will
   appear, as shown previously in Figure 18.7.

3. Select the option to Reschedule Uncompleted Work To Start and choose a date.

4. Select the option to reschedule the Entire Project to this date.

5. Click OK when finished.

> For a visual presentation of how far each task had to be postponed, display
> the Detail Gantt (choose View, More views, Detail Gantt). The narrow line
> before each task is the task slippage—the current start compared to the
> baseline start.

PART VII

Beyond One Project, One Application

Hour

HOUR 19

Working with Multiple Projects

In the simplest project management environment, there is a single ongoing project—but life is usually not so simple. A single project might grow so large that it should be broken into discrete phases or task groups, or each department in a company could have a single project to manage, or many departments might have several projects each to track. Projects within and across departments might depend on each other for information, such as completion dates. Instead of creating one huge project across the company, Project allows you to manage smaller files individually and then combine and link them as necessary. These smaller files can be opened one at a time or in a group, and each file can be placed in its own window. A critically important aspect of using multiple project files is balancing workloads for employees or equipment that are assigned between several projects.

In this hour, I'll show you techniques for consolidating many projects into one and how to share resources between several projects using a resource pool.

Consolidating Projects

The best method for creating a consolidated project file requires you to open a new or existing file and then insert other project files into it. The individual files don't need to be open; you can browse the folders to find the projects to include. This method gives you more control over the order of the individual projects in the combined file, the ability to set the linking relationship between the individual and combined files, and a choice of whether to display all project subtasks or only a project summary task row for each file.

In general, projects inserted into a consolidated file behave like "normal" project files. Tasks can be cut, copied, and pasted within the consolidated file. Projects and individual tasks can be linked in any of the four types of linking relationships. With few exceptions, tasks and groups of tasks can also be indented and outdented to alter the outline structure and, therefore, the summary information in the consolidated file.

Working with Inserted Projects

If the projects you would like to see in a consolidated view are not already open, the insertion method for combining projects is your fastest option.

To Do: Creating a Consolidated Project File with the Insertion Method

▼ **To Do**

1. Create a new project file or open an existing file to insert projects into.

2. Display a task view, such as the Gantt Chart.

3. Click on the task where the inserted project should begin.

4. Choose **I**nsert, **P**roject. The Insert Project dialog box will be displayed, as shown in Figure 19.1.

5. If necessary, navigate through file folders to display project filenames.

6. Decide how the inserted files will be associated with their original files:

   • **L**ink to Project allows changes in the individual file and the consolidated file to affect each other.

   • **R**ead Only inserts the most recently saved version of the file when the consolidated file is opened, but changes at the consolidated level are not sent back to the individual file.

   • **H**ide Subtasks causes individual files to be displayed *initially* as a single summary row for each project.

▼ 7. Click on the name of each file to be inserted into the consolidated file.

FIGURE 19.1

Use the Insert Project dialog box to select settings and which projects to insert.

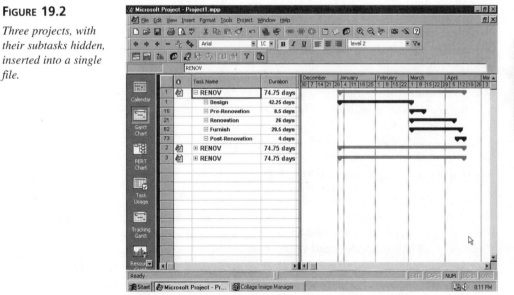

• Use the Ctrl key while clicking to add filenames to the selection.

• The order in which the filenames are selected determines their order in the consolidated file.

8. When finished, click Insert. The restructured file is then created and displayed, as shown in Figure 19.2.

9. Choose File, Save to name and save the consolidated file for future use; otherwise, you must re-create the consolidated file next time you need it.

FIGURE 19.2

Three projects, with their subtasks hidden, inserted into a single file.

19

Identifying Tasks that Are Inserted Projects

An icon in the Indicators column identifies a project summary task of an inserted project file. Also, the Task Information dialog box for these inserted project summary tasks is slightly different. Figure 19.3 shows an example of the new dialog box; its name is changed to Inserted Project Information. The Advanced tab allows you to unlink the inserted file and keep only the most recent information in the consolidated file. By clicking Project Info in the Inserted Project Information dialog box, you can view the vital statistics for the individual project file. This feature is particularly convenient for observing the results of "what if" experiments in the consolidated file.

FIGURE 19.3

The information dialog box for inserted projects is slightly different from the standard Project Information dialog box.

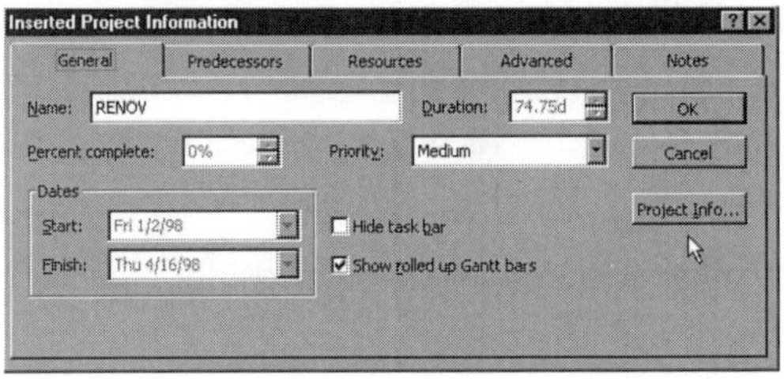

Templates for similar projects will emerge over time if you are following good project management practices. When similar projects, from similar templates, are consolidated, there will be a repetition of task names. For example, a task named "Prepare 1st draft" might appear in more than one project. There's no default method for seeing onscreen which "Prepare 1st draft" originated from which underlying project file.

There are several remedies for this confusion. You might already be using a custom field in individual files to assign project names or numbers. If so, display that field by inserting a column for it in the consolidated file. If not, you can use the standard field called "Project" for this purpose. As shown in Figure 19.4, the inserted Project column displays the source filename on each line of the consolidated file.

Working with Inserted Projects

Inserted projects in a consolidated file can be manipulated in a number of ways. Individual tasks or groups of tasks can be copied or moved from one project file area into another project, or deleted altogether. Changes such as these affect the individual project files if they are linked into the consolidated file.

Keep in mind that copying, cutting, or deleting summary tasks also copies, cuts, or deletes the subtasks underneath them.

FIGURE 19.4

The inserted Project field column identifies the source file for each task line.

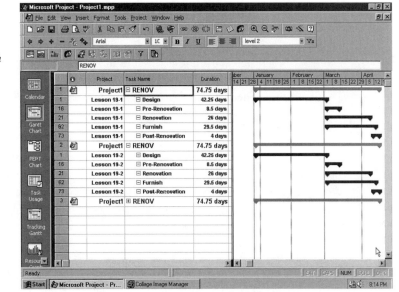

Tasks can be indented or outdented in the consolidated file outline structure to more accurately represent the relationships between projects. For example, the original file might contain a simple list of major phases of a company's project, such as Design, Finance, Production, and so on. The project manager for the design group can insert his entire project under the Design phase heading in the outline structure of the combined file. He should make sure his entire project was inserted as a subtask under the Design heading; that is, the inserted design project would need to be indented one level farther to the right of the Design phase task.

19

> Recall from Hour 3, "Starting a New Project File and Working with Tasks," that indenting a task one level to the right makes it a subtask and creates a summary task out of the task immediately above it. Outdenting a task moves it one outline level to the left and causes the task above it to no longer be a summary task.

The outline level at which projects are inserted are determined by the following rules:

- Projects are inserted at the outline level of the task immediately above the inserted row if that row is not a summary task.

- Projects inserted below summary tasks are inserted at one outline level to the right, one more indentation.

- Projects inserted at the bottom of a file, where there are only blank rows below them, are inserted at the outline level of the last visible row. If the last row in the consolidated file happens to be a collapsed summary task, the inserted project will assume the outline level of that summary task, not of its hidden subtasks.

One useful feature of consolidation is that a single project can be inserted into more than one consolidated file. This can focus a consolidation on a particular department or manager, for example. Finance and Production projects might be of interest to the financial officer, and the information systems department might need to see Finance and Networking projects combined. A little planning should be done in regards to who has read/write privileges to prevent having "too many cooks in the broth."

Consolidated files can also be inserted into other consolidated files, which effectively creates a hierarchy of projects. The absolute limit is 1,000 consolidated files; realistically, you will be limited by your computer's capabilities.

Individual tasks and entire projects can be linked within a consolidated file to create true cross-project dependencies.

Linking Consolidated Projects

After projects have been consolidated into a single, larger file, they can easily be linked in any of Project's four dependency relationships. It doesn't matter if the consolidation resulted from the New Window method or from inserting projects into another file.

Recall that the four basic dependency relationships in Project are Finish-to-Start, Start-to-Start, Finish-to-Finish, and Start-to-Finish (rarely used).

See Hour 5, " Turning the Task List into a Schedule—The Rest of the Story," for detailed information on task dependencies.

To Do: Creating Links Between Consolidated Projects

1. Create a consolidated file by choosing **Window**, **New** Window for open files or by choosing **Insert**, **Project** to select from lists of files.

▼   2. Link *tasks* in a default Finish-to-Start relationship by the usual linking techniques. One method is to select the first task name, press and hold the Ctrl key, select the second task name from another project, and click the Link Tasks button on the Standard toolbar.

Link *entire projects* by linking the project summary tasks.

3. To change the type of linking relationship, open the Task or Project Information dialog box for the *successor* task or summary task, move to the Predecessors tab in the dialog box, click in the Type cell, and select a different relationship from the drop-down list.

▲

> Click the Project Info button in an Inserted Project Information dialog box to see the effects of linking on the successor project's start and finish dates.

Deleting Inserted Projects

What happens if you inserted a project in the wrong spot in the combined file? If it was your last step, you can simply use the Undo command, or you could cut and paste the entire project elsewhere in the outline. If you don't catch your mistake, or simply change your mind later on, delete the inserted project from the combined file.

To Do: Deleting a Project from a Consolidated File

To delete an inserted project from a consolidated file, follow these steps:

1. Select the project summary task for the inserted project.

2. Press Delete. The project is removed from this consolidation but the underlying file remains stored on disk.

To Do

19

> Make sure you select the summary task for the entire inserted project before pressing Delete. By selecting either individual tasks or other summary tasks, you will remove those tasks from the original individual file if it's linked to the consolidated file.

Breaking a Large Project Apart Using Inserted Projects

Projects tend to take on a life of their own as tasks are added or steps to completion modified. It's not uncommon for a simple project to become large and somewhat unwieldy. Even at this point, however, there are usually logical groups of tasks, which should be managed together. This type of project is a good candidate for being broken into individual, more manageable files. These smaller files can then be inserted back into a consolidated file for projectwide analysis.

To Do: Breaking a Large Project into Several Inserted Projects

▼ To Do

1. Open the large project file.
2. Select a group of tasks that logically could be tracked in a single separate file.
3. Cut the selected tasks from the large project.
4. Create a new file.
5. Paste in the tasks cut from the large project.
6. Save and name the new, smaller file.
7. Repeat for other segments of the original large file.
8. When the large project has been broken into smaller files, use the Insert Project procedure given previously to create a consolidated file from the new smaller files.

▲ 9. Save and name the consolidated file.

Two notes of caution when using this technique:

The start date of the new, smaller files might need to be adjusted (use Project, Project Information). Also, links between tasks in the original file are *not* carried over into the individual files. They need to be re-established as external links to the other small files.

Sharing Resources Among Projects with a Resource Pool

A small company or single department might have only one ongoing project that commands all available resources. The Engineering staff could be dedicated to a new product development with the Marketing department focused on selling the new product when it becomes available. It's more likely, however, that even within a single department, there will be several projects in progress or under consideration. Engineering could be developing more than one new product, or different phases of a single product development might be managed by separate project leaders. In this case, several projects in Engineering might require work by the same engineering personnel. This requirement creates a need to manage a list, or pool, of resources.

Project allows you to create a resource pool of all available employees, equipment, or contractors, and maintain the pool separately from individual project files. An individual project file then points to this pool as its source of resources, instead of creating a list of resources within each individual file. With all shared files pointing to the pool, project managers can look across the ongoing projects to make resource assignments and correct allocation problems.

Creating the Resource Pool

Any Project .MPP file containing resource names and other resource information, such as resource calendars, can serve as the resource pool. However, often the resource pool file is simply a Project file that contains resource information and nothing else; that is, there are no tasks in the resource pool file itself. The tasks to which resources are assigned are actually in other individual files.

To Do: Creating a Resource Pool

To create a resource pool in a separate file, follow these steps:

1. Create a project file by choosing File, New.

2. Choose View, Resource Sheet.

3. Enter resource information, such as name, maximum units, pay rates, and base calendar, for each resource.

4. Choose File, Save and type a name for this resource file.

The list of resources you want to use might already exist in a project file. If so, there are three additional methods for creating a resource pool:

- Leave the existing file as is but let Project know it will also serve as the resource pool by attaching other files to it. This could create file lock-out problems with other users sharing the pool.

- Open the existing file, delete all tasks, and save the file under a new name by using File, Save As. This new file will become the resource pool.

- Open the existing file, copy all resource information, open or switch to a different file, and paste the resource information into the second file. Be sure when copying resource information to either click and drag through the resource ID numbers or select all resources by clicking in the unlabeled Select All cell at the upper-left of the resource sheet. Copying the resource names is not enough!

Sharing the Resource Pool

After the resource pool file has been created and saved, each individual file that will share resource information needs to be attached to the pool. Project describes this as sharing the resource pool. It simply means "don't look for a resource list in this file; look for it in a different file." To set up the sharing, both the pool file and the file with tasks *must* be open. After making the connection, the pool file can be closed to save system overhead.

To Do: Sharing a Resource Pool with an Individual Project

▼ To Do

1. Choose **File, O**pen to open the file that's serving as the resource pool (resource file).

2. Choose **File, O**pen again to open the individual project file (task file).

3. Make sure the task file is active.

4. Choose **T**ools, **R**esources, **S**hare Resources. The Share Resources dialog box will be displayed, as shown in Figure 19.5.

5. In the Share Resources dialog box, select the **U**se Resources option.

6. Also select the name of the pool file in the **F**rom drop-down list.

▲ 7. Click OK when finished.

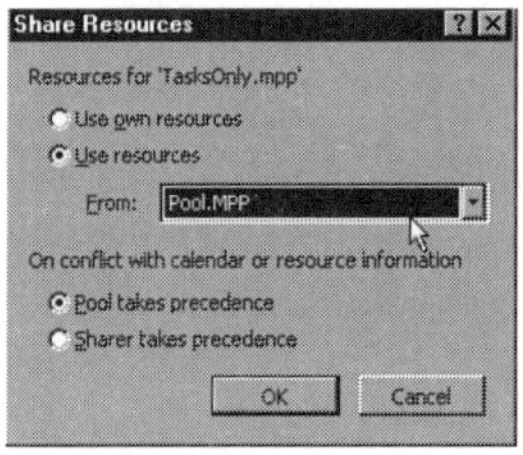

FIGURE 19.5

Connect to a resource pool with the Share Resources dialog box.

When sharing has been established, the complete list of resources from the pool are available for task assignments in the attached file. Any assignment or calendar changes made to the task file are automatically updated in the pool file, if the pool is still open. Any other sharing files are also updated.

Project keeps track of which file is serving as a resource pool and which other project files are sharing from the pool. When you later open a file being used as a resource pool, you are given the option of opening the pool as read-only, so others can update the pool while you are working. You can also choose to open the pool file read-write, which prevents others from updating the pool while you work. Figure 19.6 shows the options available when opening a resource pool file.

Similarly, when you open a file that's attached to the pool, you have options as to how that sharing file and the pool will be opened. Figure 19.7 shows the options available when opening a file that shares resources with the pool. You can choose to open the pool file to see the most recent pool information, or you can choose to open the pool file and all other sharing files if you need to look at other users' projects. The last option is to leave the pool and other sharing files closed. Your computer will work faster that way, but you will need to send out pool update messages periodically.

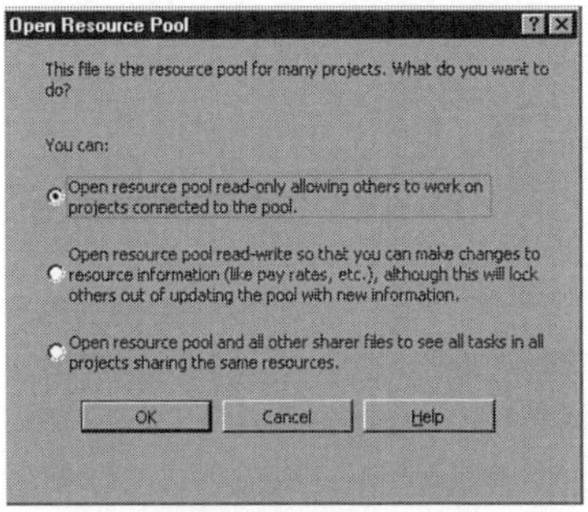

FIGURE 19.6

Options when opening a resource pool file.

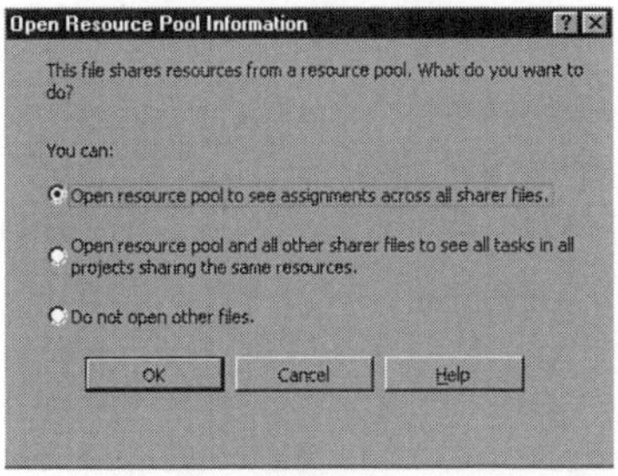

FIGURE 19.7

Options when opening a connected file if the pool is currently closed.

If the pool file was closed while changes were being made to resources in individual files, and then the pool is opened read-only, you must tell Project to update the pool so that its information stays current for other sharing files and users. The command to Update the Resource Pool will be available if Project has recorded that this step needs to be taken.

To Do: Updating the Resource Pool

Follow these steps to manually update the resource pool:

1. Make the resource pool file active on the screen.

2. Choose **T**ools, **R**esources, **S**hare Resources.

3. On the cascading menu, select **U**pdate Resource Pool. If a task file was active on the screen instead of the pool file, select **R**efresh Resource Pool instead of Update.

Identifying Resource Pool Links

It's certainly possible that you could lose track of which task files have been set up to share a resource pool, but with Project, you can see a list of all attached files in the Share Resources dialog box of the pool file. The dialog box will be slightly changed from its original appearance when sharing was being established.

To Do: Viewing a List of Files

To view a list of all files linked to the resource pool, follow these steps:

1. Open the resource pool file and make it the active file on the screen.

2. Choose **T**ools, **R**esources, **S**hare Resources. The Share Resources dialog box will open, as shown in Figure 19.8.

3. The Share Resources dialog box for an active pool file looks different from the box for a file that's not serving as a pool. Now, a list of all task files sharing the pool are displayed in the Sharing **L**inks area.

4. To open an attached file, click once on its name and click **O**pen. To open all attached files, click Open **A**ll.

   You can also indicate that attached files be opened read-only so that they won't be accidentally altered. Turn on the Open Files **R**ead Only check box before clicking Open or Open All.

5. The Share Resources dialog box closes automatically after you click Open or Open All.

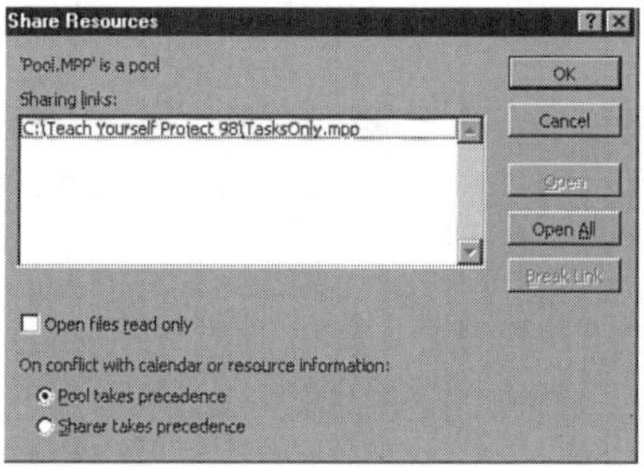

▼ To Do

FIGURE 19.8

The Share Resources dialog box in a pool file has a slightly different appearance.

Discontinuing Resource Sharing

A project file does not have to be attached to a resource pool forever. For example, you might be using the resource pool as a simple repository of resource information, not as the record keeper for resource allocations across many projects. In that case, you can attach a task file to the pool to automatically copy down resource information, instead of having to type it into the file, and then detach from the pool so Project doesn't have to maintain file links.

To Do: Discontinuing Resource Sharing

To discontinue resource sharing, follow these steps:

1. Open the resource pool file and make it the active file on the screen.

2. Choose **T**ools, **R**esources, **S**hare Resources.

3. The Share Resources dialog box will open.

4. In the Sharing **L**inks area, click once on the name of the task file that will discontinue sharing.

5. Click **B**reak Link. The resource sharing link will be broken and the dialog box will close.

19

HOUR **20**

Using Microsoft Project in Workgroups

Projects are rarely single-person undertakings. Typically, the project manager, project team members, and company managers all have interests in the progress of the project. Communication is the key to accurate project planning, tracking, and managing. Other hours in this book discuss creating and printing reports as well as exporting Project information to other software applications. This hour focuses on electronically communicating specific Project information such as resource assignments, completed work, and updated task status. It also looks at methods for circulating the actual Project file electronically.

Here is a list of the highlights of this hour:

- System considerations for electronic communication
- Methods for communicating with email
- Communicating with a Web site
- Steps to communicating with team members electronically
- Setting Project task reminders in Microsoft Outlook

Exploring Project's Workgroup Features

A project is only as good as its last update. Out-of-date information can easily lead to poor management decisions, unachievable end dates, and unmanageable resource allocations. Printed reports and information exchanged at team meetings may lose timeliness between reporting periods. Electronic communication of a project's status within a *workgroup* is the ideal way to keep the project on track.

NEW TERM **Workgroup** In the context of this book, a workgroup is the group of people directly involved with a project. The workgroup includes the project manager, who typically "owns" the Project file; project resources doing work on the project; affected managers; and possibly external contacts such as customers or contractors.

You decide who is in your workgroup and include in the Project file a method of communicating with each person in that group. After the group has been determined, the project manager can send out resource work assignments and receive updated actual work reports. The manager and resources can also exchange project updates. Another approach is to transmit a complete file to other users who are running Project and ask them to directly modify the project. Microsoft Project can take advantage of email systems, a local intranet, or the World Wide Web on the Internet.

For more information on publishing your Project information to the Web—either on the Internet or your corporate intranet—see Hour 16, "Publishing Projects on the Web or an Intranet."

Setting Up Project Messaging

After deciding on a messaging method and verifying software and hardware configurations for the workgroup manager and members, you must configure settings within the Project file. Every resource to be assigned in the project must appear on the resource sheet in the project and be uniquely identified. Normally, each resource is given a unique name anyway. If the resource name matches the email name for the resource, Project uses that resource name for communications. However, that is *not* normally the case; you will have to enter unique resource email addresses. Display the Email Address field on a resource sheet table and carefully enter all the email addresses for the people in the workgroup.

Project also must be set for the communication method you chose. If you are going to use an intranet or Internet system, you must verify the server addresses and enter them into the Project file.

Email addresses can be copied from an existing electronic address book and pasted into the Project email field. It's best to do this in a template or resource pool file so that you have to do it only once.

See Hour 19, "Working with Multiple Projects," for information on setting up resource pools.

To Do: Setting Up Workgroup Communications in Project

To set up workgroup communications in Microsoft Project, follow these steps:

1. Select **T**ools, **O**ptions from the menu to display the Options dialog box.

2. Select the Workgroup tab to see the dialog box shown in Figure 20.1.

3. Choose an option from the Default Workgroup **M**essaging for Resources drop-down list box. If resources can use either email or Web servers for communications, choose the Email and Web option.

4. In the Web Server URL (for Resource) field, type the address identification for the Web server and server folder for this workgroup (it will probably start with http://).

5. In the Web Server Root (for Manager) field, type the address path to the Web server software (this address may start with C:\ if a personal Web server is in use).

6. If you want, adjust the settings for notification and hyperlink colors.

7. Click OK when finished.

FIGURE 20.1

Set up workgroup communications in Project by selecting Tools, Options, Workgroup.

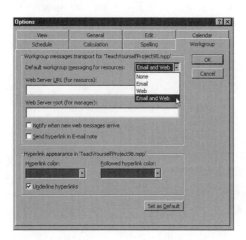

20

> Keep your manager on his or her toes. Ask your manager to turn on the Notify When New Web Messages Arrive feature so that he or she will automatically be notified of your messages. If this feature is not turned on, a Web system does not notify recipients of the arrival of messages, and the manager has to diligently check his or her WebInbox for team member correspondence.

Team members and mangers who use email only will communicate using the standard email Inbox and Reply features. On a Web system, two new messaging features are created: one for team members and one for the team manager. Members use an added feature called the TeamInbox to read, reply to, and track team messages. You view the TeamInbox in a Web browser. An opening screen in the browser prompts the member to log in to the Inbox. A member password is optional when accessing the TeamInbox.

On the other end of the Web communication arrangement, the project manager uses the added WebInbox feature. The manager opens the WebInbox from within Project. The manager uses the WebInbox to view team member responses and to accept the feedback into the project file.

Sending Task Requests with TeamAssign

When resources have been assigned to tasks in a project, the team members must be notified of those assignments. First, the workgroup or project manager sends a TeamAssign form to each resource with his or her assignment. The team member then responds to the manager, either accepting or rejecting the assignment. Finally, the manager opens the response and decides whether to update the project with the resource's answer.

To Do: Sending a TeamAssign Request

To send a TeamAssign request to a resource, follow these steps:

1. Display a task view, such as the Gantt Chart view.
2. Select **T**ools, **W**orkgroup, TeamAssign or click the TeamAssign button on the Workgroup toolbar.
3. Choose an option to send resource assignments for all tasks or only selected tasks.
4. Click OK. The TeamAssign dialog box appears as shown is Figure 20.2.
5. For the Subject field, accept the default TeamAssign option or type a subject for the message.

▼ 6. Accept or modify the text in the message area. It is good practice to give a desired response deadline in the message area.

7. In the list of tasks at the bottom of the dialog box, the To field is the only field you can edit. It is not recommended that you change these fields.

8. Click Send when finished. An icon indicating that a TeamAssign request has been made, but not yet responded to, appears in the Indicators column for the selected

▲   task.

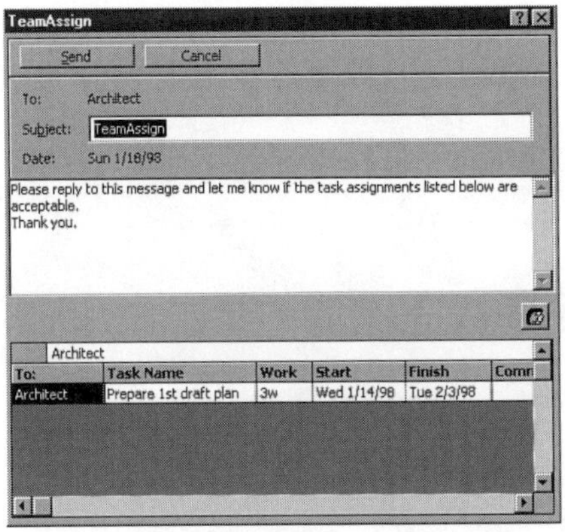

FIGURE 20.2

Use the TeamAssign feature to notify resources of their task assignments.

Composing the TeamAssign Form

A standard TeamAssign form is included with Project. It sends and requests information about predefined Project fields. The workgroup manager can add and reorder additional Project fields on the form.

To Do: Adding or Reordering Project Fields

To add or reorder Project fields on a TeamAssign form, follow these steps:

1. Select Tools, Customize, Workgroup. The Customize Workgroup dialog box appears as shown in Figure 20.3.

2. Click Add to include additional fields in the electronic form. Note the description for each field; this text can help you determine the usefulness of each field you might include in the form.

3. Use the Move Up and Move Down buttons to reorder the selected field on the form.

▼ 4. Select a reporting period from the Ask for Completed Work drop-down list box.

20

▼   5. If you want resources to record overtime work using these forms, select the Track
            Overtime Work check box.

        6. If you are giving resources the option of refusing assignments sent to them using
            the TeamAssign form, select the Team Members Can Decline Tasks check box.

        7. To cancel the changes you have made and close the dialog box, click the Return to
            Default Settings button.

▲   8. Click OK when finished.

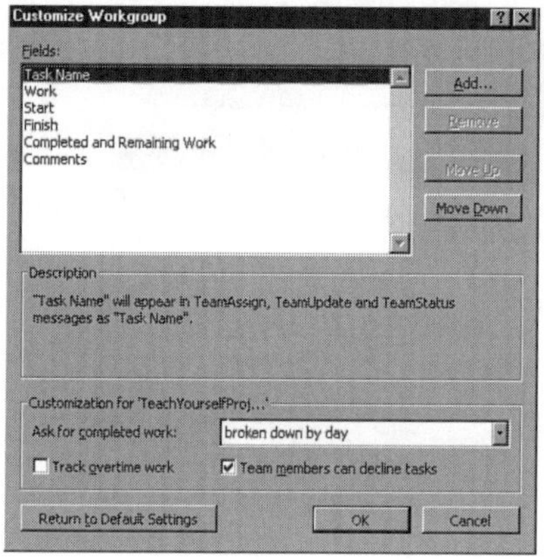

FIGURE 20.3

*The Fields list in work-
group messages can be
modified.*

Responding to TeamAssign Requests
==================================

Responding to TeamAssign Requests

If you are a member of a workgroup, it's likely that you'll need to respond to
TeamAssign messages from your manager.

To Do: Responding to a TeamAssign Message

To respond to a TeamAssign message your manager has sent to you, follow these steps:

        1. From your email Inbox, select the TeamAssign message to which you want to
            respond and click Reply.

            Alternatively, Web users can run their Web browsers to display the Workgroup
            Login box as shown in Figure 20.4. After logging in, messages addressed to the
            resource who logged in are displayed in the TeamInbox, as shown in Figure 20.5.
            Click the envelope icon next to a TeamAssign message to open that message.

        2. If you want, you can type a reply in the message area.

        3. Email users can accept or decline the assignment by typing Yes or No in the
▼   Accept? field.

▼   TeamInbox users can select or deselect the Accept? check box to accept or decline
         the assignment.

▲   4. Click Send when finished.

FIGURE 20.4

*Display the Workgroup
Login screen with your
Web browser.*

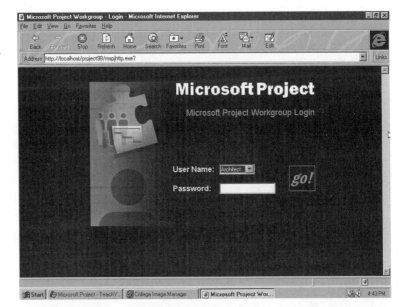

FIGURE 20.5

*Web team members
respond to task assign-
ments using a browser
and the TeamInbox.*

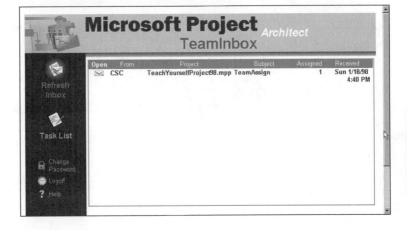

20

Workgroup Manager Feedback to Resources

After resources have responded to TeamAssign messages, the manager must incorporate these responses into the Project file. Accepting resource feedback is simple:

- Email managers can open the email Inbox and double-click the response.

  Email managers can send further communication to the team member: Click Reply, enter a message, and click Send. (The team member's accept or decline choice is not entered into the Project file at this point.)

- Web managers can select **T**ools, **W**orkgroup, WebInbox or click the WebInbox icon on the Workgroup toolbar. The WebInbox dialog box appears as shown in Figure 20.6.

  The manager should review each resource message for accuracy and completeness before accepting it into the Project file. Choosing **U**pdate Project automatically confirms the member's assignments in the Project file. Web managers can choose Update **A**ll to incorporate all TeamAssign messages into the Project file at once. Alternatively, you can choose Cancel to close the message without acting on it.

After the Project file is updated with a resource's response, the icon indicating that the manager is waiting for a TeamAssign response disappears from the Indicators column in the Gantt Chart view.

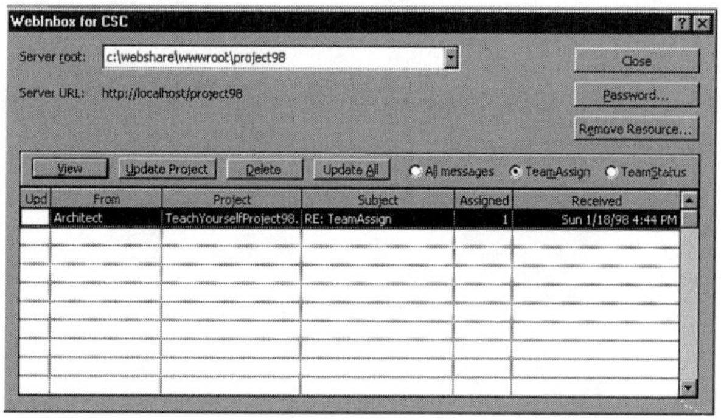

FIGURE 20.6

The manager updates the project with resource responses in the WebInbox in Project.

WebInbox for CSC					? ×
Server root:	c:\webshare\wwwroot\project98	▼			Close
Server URL:	http://localhost/project98				Password...
					Remove Resource...
View	Update Project	Delete	Update All	○ All messages ● TeamAssign ○ TeamStatus	
Upd	From	Project	Subject	Assigned	Received
	Architect	TeachYourselfProject98.	RE: TeamAssign	1	Sun 1/18/98 4:44 PM

Requesting and Submitting Status Reports with TeamStatus

TeamStatus messages are the key to communicating hard project data such as hours worked and hours remaining. In many ways, the submission and incorporation of task and resource progress keeps the project plan up to date. The workgroup manager may not have direct access to progress information and must rely on the team members to keep him or her posted. A team member can send a status update on any task assigned to him or her, whether or not a TeamStatus report has been requested by the manager.

To Do: Sending a TeamStatus Request

To send a request for a TeamStatus report, follow these steps:

1. In the Project file, select the tasks that you want to update.
2. Select **T**ools, **W**orkgroup, Team**S**tatus.
3. Send a request to the members on the selected tasks or on all tasks.
4. If you want, you can make changes to the Subject field and message area.
5. Click Send when finished. An icon indicating that a TeamStatus request has been sent, but not responded to, appears in the Indicators column for the selected task.

Team members have to respond to TeamStatus requests from their managers. They can also generate status messages without waiting for the manager's request.

To Do: Responding to a Status Message

For a team member to respond to a status message, follow these steps:

1. Open a TeamStatus message in your email Inbox or the TeamInbox. Figure 20.7 shows a message opened in the TeamInbox.
2. Enter actual data for the task, such as actual hours worked and so on.
3. If you want, modify the message area.

20

4. Click Send when finished.

 If assigned Project tasks are being tracked by members in Microsoft Outlook, task status reports can also be generated there: Use the Tasks, New TeamStatus Report feature in Outlook.

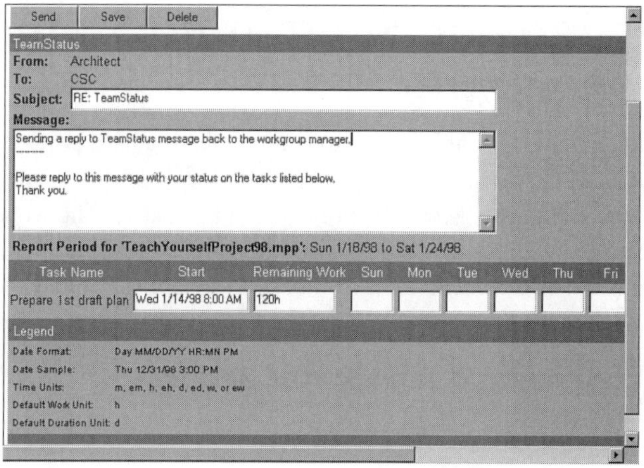

FIGURE 20.7

Members use the TeamInbox to respond to a TeamStatus request.

Hour **21**

Exchanging Project Data with Other Applications

In a number of situations, you will find it helpful to be able to export project data to other software applications or import data from other applications into Microsoft Project. For example, if you want to prepare a report or presentation about your project for a Web page or for a Microsoft PowerPoint presentation, you will have to export the data if you don't want to retype it. You also may want to export a picture of a Project view such as the Gantt Chart or the PERT Chart to be used in another application.

Similarly, you may want to use data already entered in another application as part of your Project document. For example, you could start a new task list by importing a list of tasks and dates created in a Microsoft Access database. You may already have a typed list of resources with their cost rates and email addresses in Microsoft Excel that you want to include in your resource pool. Importing the data directly into Project prevents typing errors and certainly saves you time. For small amounts of data, you can use the copy and paste facilities of the Windows Clipboard. Remember that pasting data from another application offers you the opportunity to paste dynamic links to the original source so that when the data source changes, the pasted copy of the data changes also. With that technique, you can link resource cost rates in Project, for example, to a pay-scale file in Excel or Access.

This Hour introduces you to Project's options for exchanging information with other file formats and software applications. The subject is too broad and too detailed to cover in depth in this book. This Hour shows you how to use a few of the features I think most readers of this book are likely to use. For complete coverage of the topic, refer to my more comprehensive book, *Special Edition Using Microsoft Project 98*, published by Que Corporation.

File Formats Supported by Microsoft Project 98

You can import and export entire projects or selected sets of project data with the **File, Open** and File, Save **As** menu commands. These commands allow you to read and write the project data in formats other than Project's native MPP format. Some of the formats Project supports are beyond the scope of this book or are less used these days. File formats supported by Project are listed here; their file extensions are given in parentheses:

- **Project Database (`*.mpd`)**
  This format uses the Microsoft Access 97 (version 8.0) data file format, although it has a proprietary extension (MPD). This format is replacing the MPX 4.0 format as the standard data exchange format for Microsoft Project.

- **MPX 4.0 (`*.mpx`)**
  You must save a Microsoft Project 98 document in this format if you want it to be opened in Microsoft Project version 4 or 4.1.

- **Microsoft Access 8.0 Database (`*.mdb`)**
  You can save all or part of the project data in the Access 8.0 format. Any application that recognizes this format can open and edit the file or query it for reports.

- **Microsoft Excel Workbook (`*.xls`)**
  Use this format to exchange task, resource, or assignment information with Microsoft Excel. Microsoft Project can import from the Excel 8.0 format, but it only exports to the Excel 5.0/7.0 format. You can also link field entries in Project with cell values in Excel.

- **Microsoft Excel PivotTable (`*.xls`)**
  This special format is used in Excel 5.0/7.0 for its PivotTable. Although you can export individual fields of Project data to a PivotTable, you cannot import an Excel PivotTable into Microsoft Project.

- **Hypertext Markup Language (*.htm)**

  This is the HTML format used by Web browser programs. You can export Project field data to the HTML format, but you cannot import HTML files into Microsoft Project.

> The file extensions used in the preceding list and in the following text are visible to you only if Windows 95 is displaying file extensions. To display file extensions, open Windows Explorer and choose **V**iew, **O**ptions from the menu. On the View tab, clear the check box for Hide MS-DOS File Extensions for File Types That Are Registered. Click the **A**pply button and then click OK.

As you can see in Figure 21.1, the File Open dialog box in Microsoft Project lists by default all files that match the pattern *.mp*. Consequently, the list of files you can open directly includes not only the standard Project documents (*.mpp) and templates (*.mpt), but also the MPX 4.0 documents (*.mpx) and the Project database documents (*.mpd). To save a Project file in these other formats, however, you must explicitly select the file type when you save it (see Figure 21.2).

FIGURE 21.1

All files in native Project formats are listed by default in the File Open dialog box.

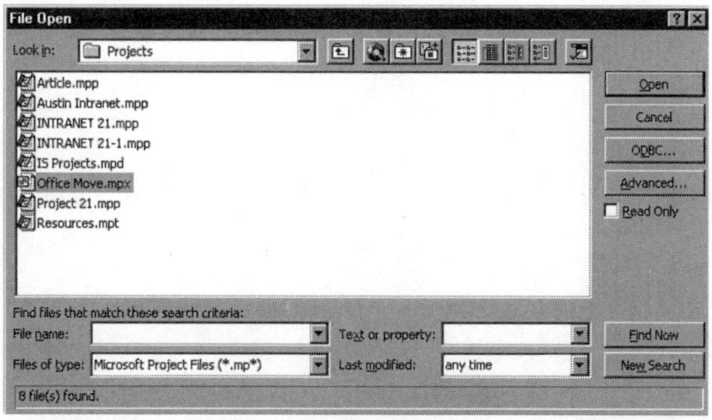

FIGURE 21.2

You can save a Project file in other formats with the Save As command.

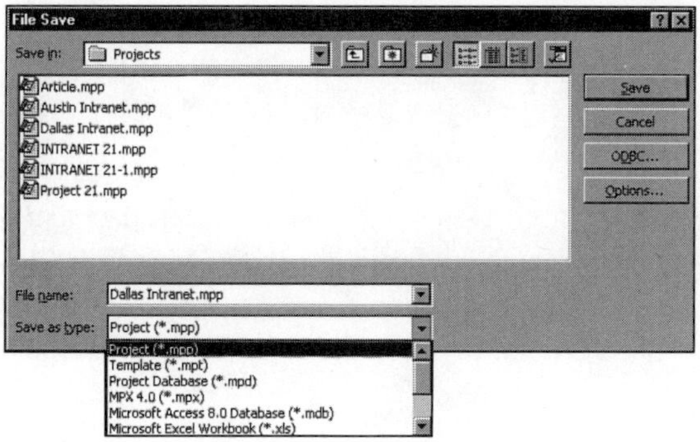

21

Exporting Project 98 Data to Older Releases of Microsoft Project

If you want your Project 98 document to be accessible to someone using version 4.0 or 4.1 of Microsoft Project, you have to save your project in the MPX 4.0 format. The earlier version of Project is no longer supported directly.

To Do: Saving Microsoft Project 98 Documents in the MPX Format

To save a Project 98 document in the MPX 4.0 format, follow these steps:

1. Open the document to be saved.
2. Choose **F**ile, Save **A**s from the menu to open the Save As dialog box.
3. Select MPX 4.0 from the Save As **T**ype drop-down list box.
4. Change the name and or directory as required and click OK.

Although you can open Project 4.0 and 4.1 documents directly in Microsoft Project 98, occasionally some file corruption will occur. If you open the file in version 4.0 or 4.1, save it into the MPX format from that version, and then open it in Project 98, you will usually get a clean copy of the project data.

You can open an MPX file in Microsoft Project 98 just as you can any other Project document.

Copying Selected Data Between Applications

In addition to exporting (or importing) data using the **F**ile, **O**pen or File, Save As command, you can also use the **E**dit, **C**opy and Edit, **P**aste commands to copy selected data from one document to another—and the receiving document can be in the same application or in a different application. For example, you can copy a wage rate from Excel into a Project Resource sheet or copy a picture of a Project Gantt Chart into a PowerPoint slide show.

You can also use the **I**nsert **O**bject command to insert data that is presented by another application—as long as both applications support Microsoft's OLE protocol (Object Linking and Embedding). For example, you can insert an Excel workbook into the task's Notes field or Objects field. If you insert a new Excel workbook file (that is, if you create the document from within Project), the data it contains resides within Project and the Excel "object" is said to be *embedded* in Project. If you insert an existing Excel file as an object into Project, the object is said to be *linked* because the data resides outside Project and can be edited independently of Project. When you open the Project document, the linked copy of the workbook can be automatically updated to reflect any new values that were created while Project was not open.

NEW TERM   **OLE**   OLE (Object Linking and Embedding) is a standard that allows you to share information that originates in one document with other documents—even documents in other applications. However, both applications must support the OLE standard if sharing is to take place.

Copying Data from Other Applications into Microsoft Project

You can use standard Office hot keys and menu commands to paste information into Project from other Office applications. For example, you can select a cell in an Excel workbook using the Ctrl+C hot key and then paste the value into a cell in a Microsoft Project table. If you use the **E**dit, Paste **S**pecial command, you can choose the Paste **L**ink option to create a link between the copy you paste in the Project document and the external cell in Excel. With a link, if the value in the Excel workbook changes, Project can automatically update the value in the Project document.

To Do: Pasting Linked External Data into a Project Table

To copy and paste data as a link from an external file into a Project table, follow these steps:

1. Select the data in the external application.
2. Use the **E**dit, **C**opy command in that application to put a copy of the data in the Windows Clipboard.
3. Select the location in Project to which the data is to be pasted.
4. Choose **E**dit, Paste **S**pecial to display the Paste Special dialog box.
5. Click the Paste **L**ink button; from the **A**s list of data types, select Text Data.
6. Click OK to paste the link.

A small gray triangle appears in the lower-right corner of any cell in Project that contains a linked value. When you open the Project file that contains linked data, an alert dialog box appears to warn you that the file contains linked data (see Figure 21.3) and offers you the opportunity to update the display by opening the source of the link and retrieving the current value stored there. Choose **Y**es to update the linked data now; choose **N**o to avoid waiting for the link to be refreshed at this time.

21

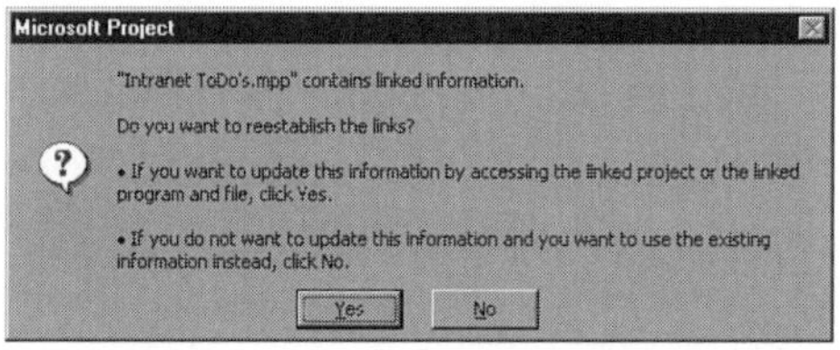

FIGURE 21.3

You are automatically alerted when a project you open has linked data that may be out of date.

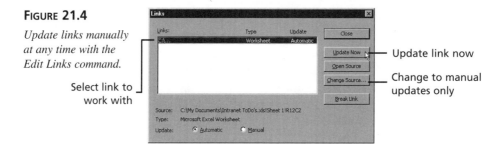

You can update linked data at any time while working with a document. To do so, select the **E**dit, Links command to display the Links dialog box (see Figure 21.4). Select the link you want to work with from the **L**inks list. Click the link you want to update and then click the **U**pdate Now button. You can also disconnect the link from the external source by clicking the **B**reak Link button.

FIGURE 21.4

Update links manually at any time with the Edit Links command.

Select link to work with

Update link now

Change to manual updates only

Copying Microsoft Project Data into Other Applications

You can copy Project data into another Office application by using standard Office techniques for copying with the Windows Clipboard. For example, you can paste a link to the total cost of a project into an Excel workbook that you can use to track the cost of all current projects.

To Do: Pasting a Link to the Total Cost of a Project

To paste a link from Microsoft Project into another Office application, follow these steps:

1. Open the project file and display a task view such as the Gantt Chart view.

2. Display the project summary task by choosing **T**ools, **O**ptions. The Options dialog box appears. Select the Pro**j**ect Summary Task option on the View tab.

3. Display the Cost table by choosing **V**iew, Ta**b**le, **C**ost. The Total Cost column shows the total cost of the project in the row for the project summary task.

▲ To Do ▼

▼

▼ 4. Press Ctrl+C or select the **E**dit, **C**opy command to copy the total cost value to the Clipboard.

5. Open the Excel workbook and choose **E**dit, Paste **S**pecial to display Excel's Paste Special dialog box.

6. Choose Paste **L**ink and select the Text type from the **A**s list box.

▲ 7. Click OK to complete the action.

As work on the project progresses, and actual costs update the Total Cost field in Microsoft Project, the Excel file also continues to show the most current cost of the project.

Copying Project's Views to Other Applications

One special method of copying Project data to other applications allows you to paste a picture of a Project view in another application. For example, you can save a picture of Project's Gantt Chart and paste it into a PowerPoint presentation.

To Do: Saving a Project as a Static Picture

To paste a picture of a Project view into another application, follow these steps:

1. In Microsoft Project, display the view you want to copy and format it to look the way you want the final picture to look.

2. If you want to include only selected tasks in the picture, select those tasks now. You can select tasks that are not adjacent (press the Ctrl key and click the desired tasks), and those tasks appear next to each other in the picture.

3. Click the Copy Picture tool on the Standard toolbar to display the Copy Picture dialog box. If the picture will be viewed only on screen, choose For **S**creen. Choose For **P**rinter if you have already selected the printer to be used and want to optimize the way the picture will look when printed on that printer. The option To **G**IF Image File is mainly for publishing on Web pages.

To include in the picture all rows currently visible on your screen, choose Ro**w**s On Screen. If you have selected the rows you want to include, choose Selected **R**ows.

To include the time periods visible on your screen, choose As Sho**w**n On Screen. To have the picture cover a specific span of time, enter **F**rom and **T**o dates.

4. Click OK to copy the picture to the Clipboard.

5. Open the document into which you want to copy the picture.

▲ 6. Choose **E**dit, **P**aste or press Ctrl+V to paste the picture into the new document.

21

Figure 21.5 shows the Project Gantt Chart view inserted into a new PowerPoint slide presentation.

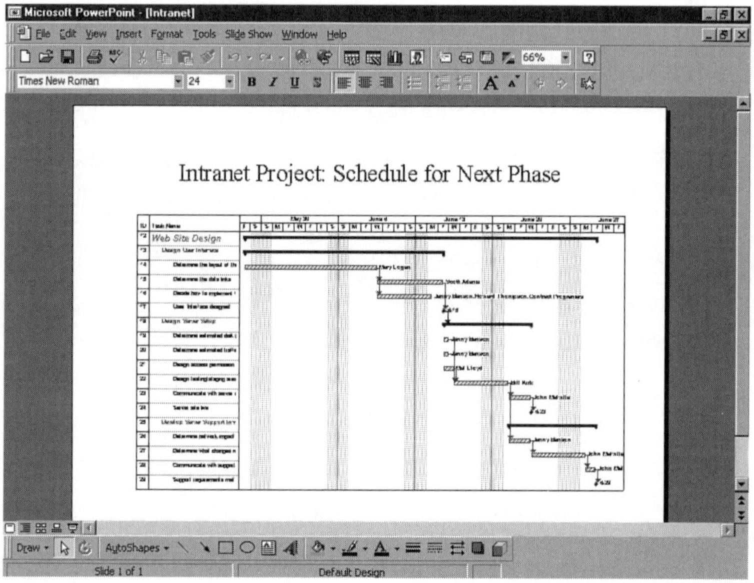

FIGURE **21.5**

The Gantt Chart from a Project document is displayed in a PowerPoint presentation.

Linking Selected Data Between Applications

If you select the Link check box when pasting an object into a project, the object is linked to its original application and will change if the original object is modified. To copy an object as a linked object rather than an embedded object, follow the instructions for inserting an embedded object but remember to select the Link check box. Alternatively, you can select the object to copy in another application; use **F**ile, **C**opy to copy it to the Clipboard, select **E**dit, Paste **S**pecial, and select the Link check box to insert the object into Project as a linked object.

PART VIII

Customizing Microsoft Project

Hour

HOUR 22

Creating Custom Views

The good news is that Microsoft Project 98 is a highly customizable product. The bad news is that Microsoft Project 98 is a highly customizable product. There are so many features you can modify to meet your needs within Project that it is not uncommon for inexperienced users to feel overwhelmed by the possibilities. There should be a logical order to your experimentation. Most users begin by customizing tables and reports. Many then create custom filters. Some go further and combine custom tables and filters into custom views. Although there are nine main components of Project that can be customized, this hour focuses on the two most commonly used: tables and views.

In this hour, you learn:

- How to create new tables
- How to create custom tables to display columns of interest
- How to modify an existing table onscreen
- How to choose view elements
- How to create a custom view

Creating Custom Tables

Project supplies 19 task-related and 8 resource-related tables. Each of these tables was designed with a theme in mind. For example, the Cost tables group task-related and resource-related cost fields in one location. The Work tables group task-related and resource-related work fields together, such as scheduled work, baseline work, actual work, and work variances. The Entry tables are the default tables for the Gantt Chart and the Resource Sheet views and were envisioned as your primary data entry tables.

But the supplied tables may not meet your display or printing needs exactly. Tables are the elements most commonly customized by Project users. There are essentially three methods for creating custom tables in Project:

- Create a new table from scratch
- Copy and modify an existing table
- Modify a supplied table, either using the Table Definition dialog box or directly onscreen

With the exception of onscreen editing, tables are customized by specifying choices in the Table Definition dialog box.

To Do: Creating Additional Tables

To create a new table from scratch, to modify an existing table, or to use an existing table as the starting point for a custom table, you start with these steps:

1. Select **V**iew, **T**able, **M**ore Tables. The More Tables dialog box appears as shown in Figure 22.1.

2. In the More Tables dialog box, display the list of interest by choosing a type of **T**able: Ta**s**k or **R**esource.

3. To create a new table from scratch, click the **N**ew button at the bottom of the dialog box. To modify an existing table and keep the same table name, click **E**dit. To use an existing table as the starting point for a custom table, click **C**opy.

4. The Table Definition dialog box opens. Make changes as desired, using the instructions in the following sections. Click OK when finished.

5. To see your new or custom table onscreen, click Apply from the More Tables dialog box.

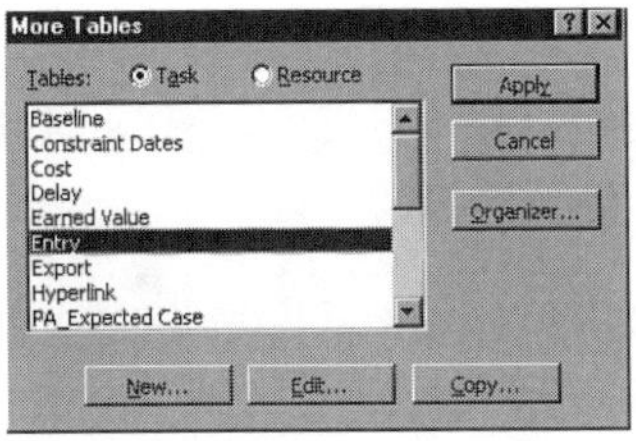

FIGURE 22.1

Get started customizing tables with the More Tables dialog box.

FIGURE 22.2 (dialog image area)

Entering a Table Name

After choosing New, Edit, or Copy from the More Tables dialog box, the Table Definition dialog box appears as shown in Figure 22.2. You use this dialog box to make explicit choices to define the custom table. The first step is to type a new **N**ame for the table, to distinguish it from any existing tables. Project gives a new table the default name of `Table` and a number; copies of existing tables are named `Copy of original table name`. Simply replace these Project defaults with names you choose.

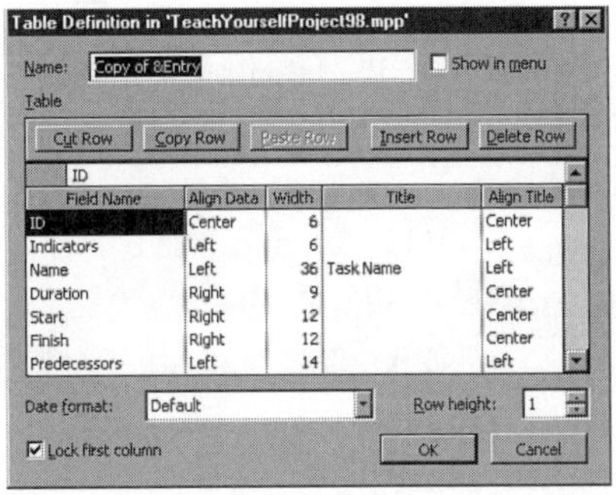

FIGURE 22.2

Use the Table Definition dialog box to choose project fields for a custom table.

Add custom tables to the **V**iew, **T**able cascading menu list by selecting the Show in **M**enu check box next to the table name in the Table Definition dialog box.

Adding and Changing the Columns in the Table

After typing a name for the table, the next step is to define the table by working in the **T**able area of the dialog box. The layout in this area is the reverse of the way the table is displayed on the screen: *Each row in the table definition defines a column for onscreen display.* For each box-row/screen-column, you must specify a field from the list of available Project fields. Other areas in the table definition are given default values by Project.

To Do: Completing the Table Definition Area

To define the table you began creating in the preceding exercise, follow these steps:

1. Click in the Field Name column.

2. Select a Project Field Name from the in-cell drop-down list. You can type the field name instead, but your typing must match a Project field name *exactly*; you cannot move the cursor away from the cell until it does.

3. Data in table columns is displayed right-justified by default. Move to the Align Data cell and use the in-cell drop-down list to choose left or center justification instead.

4. Table columns have a width of 10 characters by default. Move to the Width cell and use the in-cell spinner arrows to choose any width between 0 (the column is hidden) and 128 maximum.

5. The title that appears at the top of the table columns is the field name itself. If you want to label the column something else, move to the Title cell and type the desired label.

6. Titles are displayed center-justified by default. Move to the Align Title cell and use the in-cell drop-down list to choose left or right justification instead.

7. Use the row-editing features to rearrange the field rows. You can Cut, Copy, Paste, Insert, and Delete rows as you build the table. You can always return to the table definition later to make more row adjustments.

8. Repeat steps 1 through 7 to finish building and modifying the table.

> Undo is not available in the Table Definition dialog box. Work purposefully, or be prepared to redo some steps.

Completing the Definition of the Table

Before you finish with the Table Definition dialog box, there are three additional choices you can make from the bottom of the dialog box:

- Date Format. Choose how dates will be displayed in this table only.

> Use the Date Format option to create a special table to display the time of day for task start and finish dates, without changing the default display for all dates.

- **R**ow Height. How deep the rows of this table will appear, not how many bars will appear on the Gantt chart. Typically, leave this number at the default value of 1.

- **L**ock First Column. Turn this setting on to prevent the first column and only the first column of the table—usually the ID or Name field—from scrolling off the screen to the left as you move around in the table onscreen. Notice that Project differs from what you may be used to in Microsoft Excel: In Project, you can prevent only the first column from scrolling off the screen; you cannot freeze more than the first column. This limitation may influence the field you choose to display first in the table.

When you have finished making selections from the Table Definition dialog box, click OK.

To see your custom table onscreen, click Apply in the More Tables dialog box.

> The column headings are always displayed as you scroll down in the project task list. There is no setting to turn this feature on or off, or to modify it in any way.

Changing Table Features from the View Screen

You have an alternative to making changes to a table using the Table Definition dialog box: onscreen editing. You can change the settings for columns that already appear, as well as add and remove columns.

> Be aware that onscreen changes made to a table—adding or removing columns or changing column settings—actually edit the underlying table definition and affect all views that use that table. If you want to keep the original settings for a supplied table, you should create a copy of the table and work with the copy onscreen instead of the original.

To Do: Editing Columns in a Table

To change the columns in an existing table using onscreen editing, follow these steps:

1. Move the vertical divider bar if necessary so that the column you want to modify is visible.

2. Position the mouse pointer over the column title and double-click. The Column Definition dialog box appears as shown in Figure 22.3.

22

To Do
▼

▼ 3. The Column Definition dialog box lets you set the same five column characteristics that you can set for rows in the Table Definition dialog box; namely, Field **N**ame, **T**itle, **A**lign Title, Align **D**ata, and **W**idth.

4. When finished making changes to the columns, click OK to return to the screen
▲   and view the new table settings.

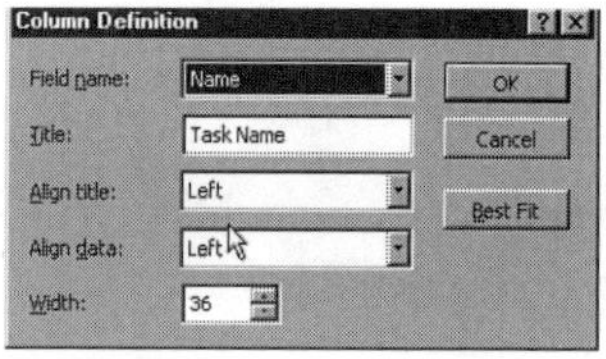

FIGURE 22.3

Column settings can be adjusted onscreen.

Column Definition		?	X	
Field name:	Name	OK
Title:	Task Name	Cancel
Align title:	Left	Best Fit
Align data:	Left	
Width:	36	

> From the Column Definition dialog box, choose **B**est Fit if you aren't sure how wide to make the column. But choose **B**est Fit after making other desired changes; clicking the **B**est Fit option closes the dialog box and applies all the column settings.

In addition to changing column settings, you can add and remove columns while viewing the table.

To Do: Adding a Column to a Table

To add a column to a table, follow these steps:

1. Select any cell in a column to the left of which you want the added column to appear. Existing columns to the right of the selected column are moved farther to the right; the new column is inserted to the left of the selected column.

2. Choose **I**nsert, **C**olumn. The Column Definition dialog box appears.

3. For the information to be displayed in this column, select a Project field name from the drop-down list box.

4. For the other fields, you can accept the default settings or make changes as desired.

▲ 5. When finished, click OK.

To Do: Removing a Column from a Table

To remove a column from a table, follow these steps:

1. Position the mouse pointer over the title for the column you want to remove.

2. Click the column title so that the entire column is selected.

▼ 3. Select **E**dit, **Hi**de Column. The selected column is removed and remaining
▲   columns to the right of the selected column move back to the left.

The phrasing for removing columns can be misleading. The **Edit, Hide** Column command implies to most users that the column width is set to zero, and can be displayed again (as is true in Microsoft Excel). In Microsoft Project, the column is actually removed from the underlying table definition. You must follow the procedures for inserting a column to redisplay the "hidden" column.

22

Creating Custom Views

Although a number of predefined views are supplied with Project, they may not meet your needs exactly. Perhaps you would prefer that the Summary table be displayed with the standard Gantt Chart instead of the Entry table. Or perhaps your boss wants all summary tasks on the Gantt Chart to be printed in 14-point bold text. You can create custom views from scratch, edit existing views by changing the default settings for the view, or create a custom view by copying an existing view that is close to what you need but not quite right. All three options are available from the **View, More** Views command. Project views are comprised of several components:

- The view *name*, such as Gantt Chart or Resource Usage
- The basic *screen type* for the view, such as Task Usage or Resource Sheet
- The *table* of Project fields displayed, either a supplied table or one you have customized
- The *filter* in effect, either no filter (to show all tasks or resources), a supplied filter, or a filter you have already customized

All these view components are selected or specified in a single dialog box. The choices you make are stored with the view definition. The next time you apply your custom view, the correct table and filter are applied to the basic screen type you chose for this view.

To Do: Creating a Custom View

To Do ▼

To begin the process of creating a custom view (whether you want to create a custom view from scratch, edit an existing view, or copy an existing view that is close to what you need), you start with these steps:

1. Select **View, More** Views. The More Views dialog box appears as shown in Figure 22.4.

2. To create a new view from scratch, click the **New** button at the bottom of the dialog box.

   To modify an existing view and keep the same view name, select a view from the list and click **Edit**.

▼

FIGURE 22.4

Edit or copy an existing view or create a new view in the More Views dialog box.

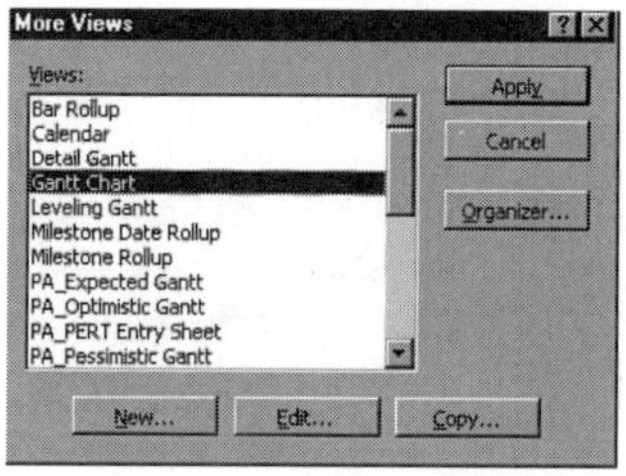

To use an existing view as the starting point for a custom view, select a view from the list and click Copy.

3. The View Definition dialog box opens, as shown in Figure 22.5. Make changes as desired, using the instructions in the following sections. Click OK when finished.

FIGURE 22.5

Define components of a custom view in the View Definition dialog box.

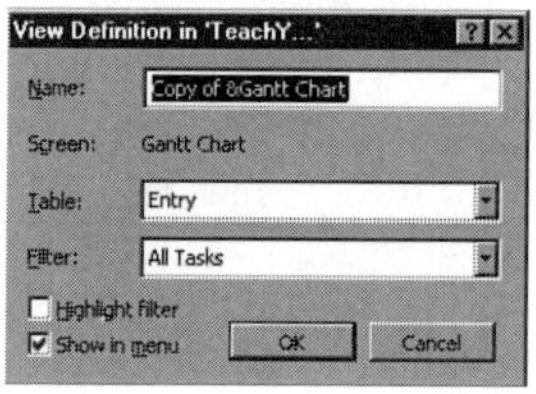

4. To see your new or custom view on the screen, click the Apply button in the More Views dialog box.

Entering the Name of the View

The first step in defining a custom view is to give the view a name. Microsoft Project gives the new or copied view a default name such as View 1. Replace the default name by typing any name that makes logical sense to you, up to a maximum of 50 characters (shorter is better). To create a keyboard shortcut key (the underlined character you see on other menu choices), type an ampersand (&) before the letter you want to use as the shortcut key.

Selecting the View Components

After providing a view name, you have to select a table and filter for the view. If you created a completely new view instead of copying or editing an existing view, you must also do the following:

- Identify the new view as a full-screen single view or a split-screen combination view; most views are full screen.

- Select a screen type for the view. In the View Definition dialog box shown in Figure 22.6, choose the basic layout from the drop-down list of possible Screen types.

FIGURE 22.6

Define a custom view as being either a full-screen or a split-screen type.

Selecting the Table for the View

Which columns of Project fields should be displayed in your custom view? Choose the appropriate fields from the **T**able drop-down list in the View Definition dialog box. Any custom tables you have created also appear in this list.

> You are not limited to displaying only the table named in the view defini-tion. After any view is displayed, select View, Table to show a different table on the screen. This action does not change the definition of the view; the next time it is displayed, the table in the view definition will be back.

Selecting the Filter for the View

Should you display all task (or resource) rows in this view or only some of them? Choose the appropriate rows from the **F**ilter drop-down list box in the View Definition dialog box. Any custom filters you have created also appear in this list. If you choose All Tasks or All Resources, you have effectively selected no filter. A filter does not have to hide rows. If you would rather see all rows in the view but have the rows that match the filter appear on the screen in blue, select the **H**ighlight Filter check box in the View Definition dialog box.

Saving the View Definition

Custom views, like custom tables and filters, are automatically saved with the Project file in which they were created. There is no additional "save to file" step to perform. Just be sure to save the file.

Hour **23**

Using Macros with Microsoft Project

Microsoft Project includes eleven built-in macros that are an extension of
the core program. Most of the macros are already assigned to toolbar buttons
to provide additional functionality in managing your project. You can also
create your own macros for tasks you perform repeatedly, which is the main
topic of this hour.

New Term   **Macro**   A *macro* is an automated list of instructions you use to
accomplish a specific task.

When you run a macro, it executes all the steps in its list, one after the other.
The macro saves you from having to execute each of the commands manually and from having to remember the correct sequence of commands
required. You can execute a macro from the Macro dialog box, from a toolbar button, or with a keystroke.

This hour discusses the basic steps in creating simple macros you can use in
Microsoft Project. If you are interested in learning more about creating and
editing macros, I strongly encourage you to refer to *Special Edition Using*

Project 98, published by Que. This *Special Edition* book provides detailed information on using the Visual Basic Editor and Visual Basic for Applications to work with your macros.

Introducing the Built-In Macros

To access the macros included in Microsoft Project, choose **T**ools, **M**acro, **M**acros. A list of available macros appears in the Macros dialog box, as shown in Figure 23.1.

FIGURE 23.1

Macros built in to Microsoft Project.

Macro names

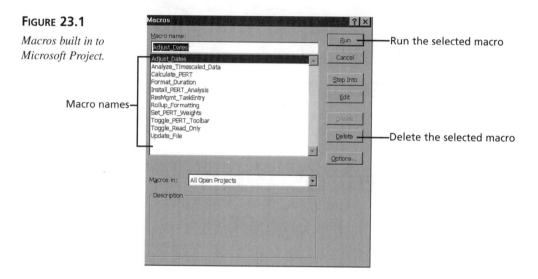

Run the selected macro

Delete the selected macro

Some of the built-in macros have been referred to in previous hours of this book. The following list briefly describes these macros:

- *Adjust Dates*. Changes the project start date and adjusts task constraints by the same change (see Hour 5). This button is available on the Analysis toolbar.

- *Analyze Timescaled Data*. Sends timescaled work and cost figures to an Excel PivotTable for further analysis (see Hour 18). This button is available on the Analysis toolbar.

- *Format Duration*. Changes all duration labels to the same unit (see Hour 7).

- *ResMgmt TaskEntry*. Displays the Task Entry view for managing resource assignments (see Hour 11). This button is available on the Resource Management toolbar.

- *Rollup Formatting*. Formats summary task bars (see Hour 7) to display markers for subtask dates. This button can be added to a toolbar.

- *Toggle Read-Only*. Releases or acquires write privileges when working with a file on a shared directory (see Hour 20). This button can be added to a toolbar.

- *Update File*. Updates a read-only file to the current version on the shared directory (see Hour 20). This button can be added to a toolbar.

- *Toggle PERT Toolbar*. Displays or hides the PERT Analysis toolbar. This and the remaining macros in this list are used for PERT analysis to provide statistical estimates for task duration, a topic not covered in this book but referenced in Hour 4.

- *Install PERT Analysis*. Installs the Microsoft Project PERT Analysis options and displays the PERT Analysis toolbar.

- *Calculate PERT*. For each task, this macro calculates a single PERT duration by taking a weighted average of its optimistic, expected, and pessimistic duration estimates.

- *Set PERT Weights*. Displays the Set PERT Weights custom form, enabling you to adjust the weights used to compute the PERT estimation of task duration.

You can run any of these macros from the Macros dialog box by clicking the **R**un button. For example, if you want to display all task duration entries in the same unit, Days, you can run the Format Duration macro. After clicking the **R**un button, the macro prompts you to select the unit to be used for all duration field entries and then goes through the entire task list and converts all duration values to day units.

To Do: Running a Macro

To run an existing macro from the Macros dialog box, follow these steps:

1. Select **T**ools, **M**acro, **M**acros to display the Macros dialog box (see Figure 23.1).

2. Select the macro you want to run from the **M**acro Name list.

3. Click the **R**un button to start the macro. You must respond to any prompts the macro presents you.

The Macros dialog box shown in Figure 23.1 contains a button used to delete macros. When you no longer need a macro, it is a good idea to delete it. But be careful! This button allows you to delete *any* macro—including the built-in macros that come with Project.

In Hour 24, you learn how to run a built-in macro from the **Tools** menu; you also learn how to add a button to a toolbar and then assign a macro to the toolbar button.

Planning Your Own Macro

In previous hours of this book, you have been introduced to many tools that can help manage your project. As you work on a project, pay attention to those actions you perform every day or more than once a day. These actions are good candidates for automating tasks by recording a macro.

Once an action or process is identified, you have to isolate the individual steps taken to achieve the desired results.

Creating a Macro

After you have determined the steps you want to include in your macro, you are ready to create the macro. With Project 98, there are two ways to create a macro:

- Write the macro in Visual Basic for Applications code
- Record (or capture) the steps desired for the macro

The simplest way to create a macro is to record the steps. Once created, the macro can be edited with the Visual Basic Editor. Refer to *Special Edition Using Project 98,* published by Que, for specific information on using the Visual Basic Editor.

> It is a good idea to save the project before you capture a macro. After the macro is recorded, you can close the project and reopen it to test the macro (assuming that you save the macro in the global template).

The first step in recording a macro is to set up the environment. This step can be difficult because you have to determine what steps should be done before you record the macro and what steps should be included in the macro. For example, the macros we've discussed and planned for in the first part of this hour all use the Gantt Chart view. To make sure that the Gantt Chart is the selected view for the macro, you can manually select it from the View Bar before you run the macro, or you can plan to select the Gantt Chart view as one of the steps in the macro. Think about what you are trying to do with the macro and what makes the best sense for the situation. If you want to be able to run the macro from one of the other views, then you should include a step in the macro that selects the Gantt Chart view. If you plan to activate the Gantt Chart view before you run the macro, it is not necessary to add a step for selecting the view.

To Do: Creating a New Macro

When you want to create a new macro, complete the following steps:

1. Complete any manual steps necessary to set up the environment for the process you want to automate (for example, select the appropriate view).

2. Choose **Tools, Macro, Record** New Macro to display the Record Macro dialog box (see Figure 23.2).

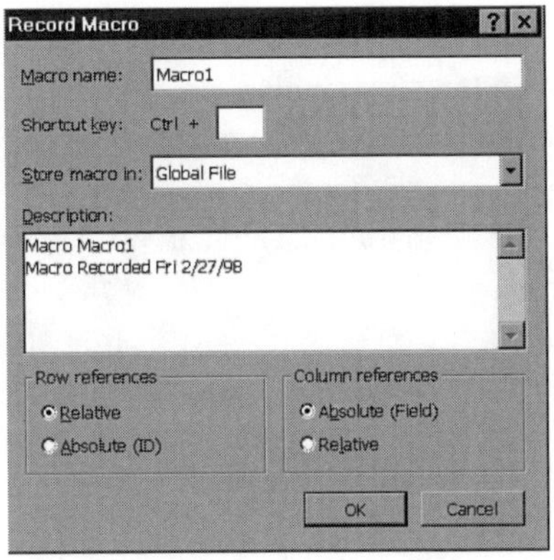

FIGURE 23.2

The Record Macro dialog box allows you to name and begin recording the macro.

3. Enter a name for the macro. The default name for a macro is the word Macro followed by a number (for example, Macro1). To make the macro easier to identify later, you should enter a custom name. When naming macros, use the following naming conventions:

   • The name must begin with a letter.

   • The name can have any letter, number, or special character *except* a space, period, or the following characters:
     , ! @ & $ #

   • The name cannot exceed 255 characters in length.

   • The name cannot be a Visual Basic for Applications reserved word.

   If the name you type doesn't adhere to these conventions, Microsoft Project displays an error message indicating the problem. Although Visual Basic doesn't distinguish between uppercase and lowercase letters, you may want to consider using a mixed-case name to make the macro name more readable.

4. Specify a Shortcut **K**ey if desired.

   The assignment of a shortcut key combination is very valuable for macros you use frequently, but it is not necessary if you intend to create a toolbar button for the macro.

▼   The shortcut key combination starts with the Ctrl key and a letter of the alphabet. Although you may think you have up to 26 combinations, many key combinations are already in use by Microsoft Project (for example, Ctrl+X is already used to execute the **E**dit, **Cu**t command). After you eliminate all the reserved combinations, you are left with only eight combinations: You can assign Ctrl plus A, E, J, L, M, Q, T, or Y. If you do not assign a shortcut key combination, you have to assign the macro to a button on the toolbar or use the **T**ools, **M**acro, **M**acros command to run the macro.

5. Indicate where you want to store your macro.

   You can store the macro within an individual project or place it in the global project file. The Global File is `global.mpt`. If a macro is placed in the global project, you can access it from all projects. For the macros we will be creating, the best place to store them is in the Global File. The macros aren't specific to a particular project, just a particular view.

6. Add a description for the macro. This step is optional. You do not have to enter a description, but doing so makes it easier to understand the purpose of the macro at a later date.

7. Indicate how you want to reference your rows and columns.

   When you are planning your macro, you have to determine whether a particular row or column reference in the Gantt Chart table is required by the macro. For a macro, the positioning can be Absolute (which means that if you are in row 1, the macro always runs starting at row 1) or Relative (which means that the macro begins in the row that is selected at the time you run the macro).

   The same referencing applies with columns. The default setting for rows is Relative positioning. Columns use Absolute positioning as the default.

8. Click OK.

9. Perform the actions you want to automate.

▲   10. Select **T**ools, **M**acros, Stop **R**ecorder.

Running a Macro

After the macro has been recorded, that isn't the end of the development process. You want to make sure that the macro works.

To Do: Running (Testing) a Macro

To test a macro, follow these steps:

1. Close the project.

▼   2. Select No when prompted to save the project.

▼ 3. Open the project again.

4. Select the PERT Chart view from the View Bar.

5. Select **T**ools, **M**acro, **M**acros. The Macros dialog box appears (see Figure 23.3).

6. Select the macro from the **M**acro Name list.

▲ 7. Click the **R**un button.

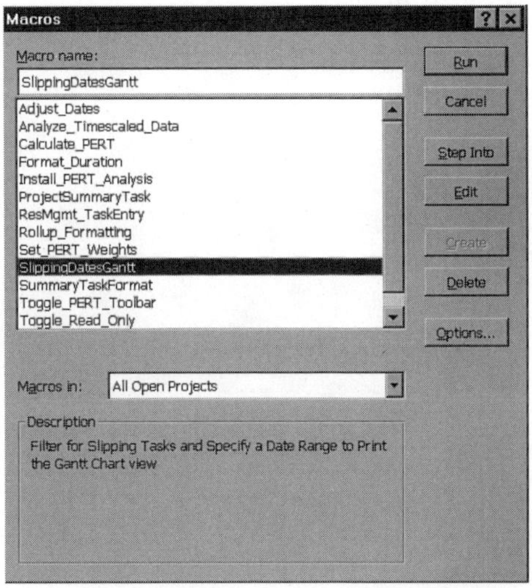

FIGURE 23.3

The Macros dialog box allows you to run, view, and edit your macros.

Macros	? ✕
Macro name:	
SlippingDatesGantt	**R**un
Adjust_Dates	Cancel
Analyze_Timescaled_Data	
Calculate_PERT	
Format_Duration	**S**tep Into
Install_PERT_Analysis	
ProjectSummaryTask	**E**dit
ResMgmt_TaskEntry	
Rollup_Formatting	
Set_PERT_Weights	Create
SlippingDatesGantt	
SummaryTaskFormat	**D**elete
Toggle_PERT_Toolbar	
Toggle_Read_Only	
	Options...

Ma**c**ros in: All Open Projects

Description

Filter for Slipping Tasks and Specify a Date Range to Print the Gantt Chart view

After you click the **R**un button, you may see the mouse pointer change to an hourglass. The view should shift to the Gantt Chart view automatically and execute the remaining steps of the macro you selected. There are two other ways to run a macro: If the macro has been assigned to a shortcut key combination, you can press the shortcut keys instead of running the macro from the dialog box. If the macro has been assigned to a toolbar button, you can simply click the toolbar button to run the macro.

If you intend to use the macro frequently, assign it to a toolbar button as discussed in Hour 24.

23

Hour **24**

Customizing Toolbars and Menus

As you have discovered, commands on both the toolbars and menus offer an efficient way for you to interact with the projects you design. Although most of the toolbars and menus give you the commands you need, other commands might be unavailable or buried so deeply on a menu that they aren't convenient to use. Project provides several different features that let you customize the toolbars and menus to make your work easier and more efficient.

If you have modified toolbars and menus in other programs, such as Word or Excel, you will discover that customizing these items in Project is very similar.

Creating and Customizing Toolbars

As you continue to work with Microsoft Project, you will find that some of the buttons on the toolbars are vital to the way you work, and others are rarely used. This use of buttons is often determined by the type of work you do. In addition, you might find that some tasks you perform frequently have no toolbar buttons available. You can customize toolbars to remove the buttons you rarely use and replace them with buttons to help perform those tasks you use more frequently.

Each button on a toolbar runs a *macro*—a series of steps designed to perform a task. When you click the Open button, a macro runs that contains the same steps you would take to perform that task using the menus, in this case, **F**ile, **O**pen. When you create macros to perform tasks you use most often, you can assign the macros to toolbar buttons.

> Customizing toolbars is different from other types of customization. Toolbars are part of the *application* file, rather than a *project* file. As a result, when changes are made to a toolbar, those changes appear whenever you access any project file. The toolbar settings are stored as part of the global.mpt file automatically.

Displaying Toolbars

You can show and hide toolbars in two ways: right-click on any toolbar to display the toolbar shortcut menu (see Figure 24.1) or choose **V**iew, **T**oolbars.

Some toolbars are set to dock themselves at the top of the screen; others appear to float in the project window (such as the Tracking toolbar in Figure 24.1). To reposition a docked toolbar, click and drag the vertical separator bars on the left edge of the toolbar. As you drag, the outline of the toolbar changes. When you have the toolbar placed where you want it, release the mouse button. To reposition a floating toolbar, click and drag the toolbar's title. You can also double-click the title of a floating toolbar; the toolbar will be docked at the place it was previously docked.

Reviewing the Built-In Toolbars

Microsoft Project 98 includes 12 built-in toolbars. The Standard and Formatting toolbars appear by default when you start Microsoft Project. You can display any of the remaining 10 toolbars as you need them.

- *Standard toolbar*. Provides access to the main Microsoft Project features.
- *Formatting toolbar*. Buttons on this toolbar give you access to outlining, filters, and text formatting features.
- *Custom Forms toolbar*. The buttons on this toolbar display forms that have already been designed.

FIGURE 24.1

The toolbar shortcut menu indicates active toolbars with a check mark.

Vertical separators

Docked toolbar

Displays the Customize dialog box

Floating toolbar

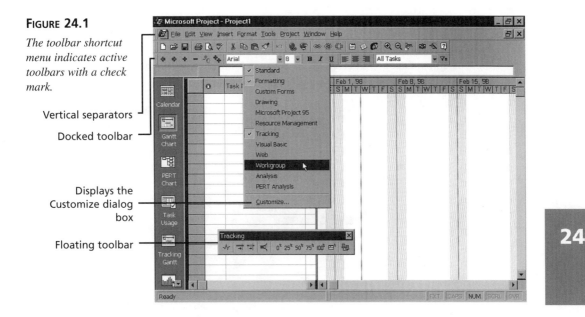

24

- *Drawing toolbar.* Gives you access to graphic drawing tools for drawing figures and text boxes in the Gantt Chart timescale.

- *Microsoft Project 95 toolbar.* Displays the Standard toolbar from Microsoft Project 95.

- *Resource Management toolbar.* Provides access to tools for resolving resource overallocations, managing pooled resources used in several projects, and managing resource communications.

- *Tracking toolbar.* Provides access to the commands necessary to track progress and reschedule work on uncompleted tasks.

- *Visual Basic toolbar.* Displays buttons for recording, running, and editing macros.

- *Web toolbar.* Displays buttons that activate your World Wide Web browser (such as Microsoft Internet Explorer or Netscape Navigator), keeps a list of your favorite Web sites, and helps you move through Web pages.

- *WorkGroup toolbar.* Contains tools you can use to automatically communicate scheduling changes, request progress updates, and share project files with others in your workgroup.

- *Analysis toolbar.* Contains tools for adjusting and evaluating your project.

- *PERT Analysis toolbar.* Displays analysis tools used with the PERT Chart view for indicating best-case, expected, and worst-case scenarios for task durations, start dates, and finish dates.

Using the Customize Dialog Box

Before you can create a new toolbar or customize an existing toolbar, you must display the Customize dialog box. It's used to create new toolbars, add buttons or remove buttons from any active toolbar, and rearrange the order of the buttons on a toolbar.

To display the Customize dialog box, right-click on any toolbar and select Customize, or choose View, Toolbars, and select Customize. Figure 24.2 shows the Customize dialog box.

FIGURE 24.2

Drag the Customize dialog box away from the toolbars if it blocks the toolbars you want to customize.

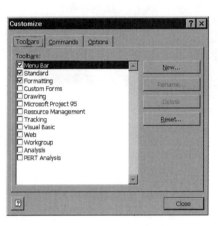

The Customize dialog box displays the custom choices on three tabs:

- *Toolbars*. Display or hide a toolbar by marking or unmarking the toolbar name. New toolbars can be created, renamed, or deleted, and toolbars you have customized can be reset back to display their original buttons.
- *Commands*. Using the button categories, you can add a tool to a toolbar.
- *Options*. You can enlarge the tool button size, control what is displayed in the toolbar button ScreenTip, or control how the menus are animated.

To Do: Customizing Toolbars

To customize a toolbar, follow these steps:

1. If the toolbar you want to customize is not active, right-click on any toolbar and select the desired toolbar from the shortcut menu.
2. Right-click on any toolbar and choose Customize to display the Customize dialog box, or choose View, Toolbars, and select Customize.
3. In the Customize dialog box, select the Commands tab (see Figure 24.3).

List of categories

FIGURE 24.3

*Use the **Commands** tab in the Customize dialog box to add or remove buttons from a toolbar.*

Commands in the selected category

24

4. Select a category from the list on the left side of the dialog box. The commands in that category appear on the right side of the dialog box.

5. To see the ScreenTip for the selected command, click the Description button. The ScreenTip appears when you rest the mouse pointer over a button on a toolbar. In Figure 24.4, the [Task/Resource Notes] command from the Project category has been selected.

FIGURE 24.4

You can find out more about a command by displaying its description.

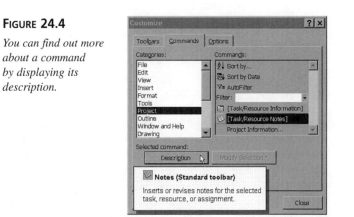

6. To add a command to a toolbar, click the command and drag it into any position on the toolbar. When dragging a command to a toolbar, your mouse pointer changes to the shape of a white arrow with a gray box on the tip of the arrow and an × on the stem of the arrow. When you move the mouse pointer into the toolbars, it becomes a thick capital *I*. Commands you add to the toolbars may or may not have icon buttons; those that don't are displayed as text buttons.

▼   To remove buttons from a toolbar, select the button on the toolbar; a heavy black
     border indicates which button is selected. Drag the button off the toolbar, being
     careful to release it away from other existing toolbars. When dragging a command
     off a toolbar, your mouse pointer changes to the shape of a white arrow with a gray
     box on the tip of the arrow and an × on the stem of the arrow.

▲   7. After you have finished customizing a toolbar, close the Customize dialog box.

In Figure 24.5, the Close and Properties commands from the File category have been
added to the Standard toolbar. A third tool is being added.

FIGURE 24.5

*Commands can be
added to any active
toolbar. Some appear
as icons, and others as
text.*

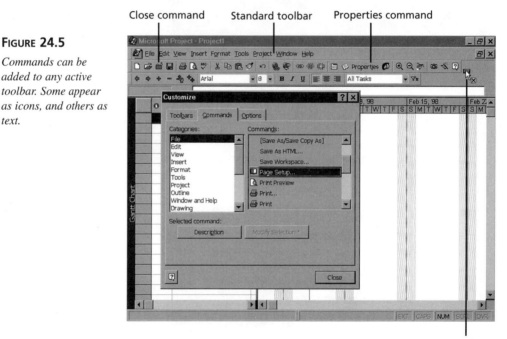

Close command   Standard toolbar   Properties command

Mouse pointer

Creating New Toolbars

Sometimes the buttons you use most frequently are on several different toolbars. Instead
of having four or five toolbars displayed, you might want to have one or two toolbars that
contain most (if not all) the command buttons you use. At other times, you might want to
create a customized version of an existing toolbar without affecting the original toolbar.

To Do: Building a New Toolbar

To build a new toolbar, follow these steps:

1. Right-click on any toolbar and choose **C**ustomize to display the Customize dialog box, or choose **V**iew, **T**oolbars, and select **C**ustomize.

2. In the Tool**b**ars tab, click **N**ew to open the New Toolbar dialog box. Project assigns a generic number sequentially to each new toolbar and identifies the toolbar name as "Custom *number*," such as "Custom 1."

3. Type the new toolbar name. Toolbar names must be unique and are limited to any combination of 50 characters and spaces.

4. Click OK.

5. An empty floating toolbar window appears onscreen (see Figure 24.6). If necessary, move the toolbar window by dragging its title bar.

6. Select the **C**ommands tab and drag command buttons onto the toolbar. The custom toolbar will enlarge as you add command buttons. You can dock the toolbar or leave it floating.

    You can also drag copies of buttons on existing toolbars to the new toolbar by holding down the Ctrl key as you drag the button.

Restoring the Built-In Toolbars

Changes you make to toolbars could become out of date or may not fit every project you create. As a result, you might want to restore the default buttons to a toolbar.

To Do: Restoring the Default Buttons

To restore the default buttons to a toolbar, follow these steps:

1. Right-click on any toolbar and choose **C**ustomize to display the Customize dialog box, or choose **V**iew, **T**oolbars, and select **C**ustomize.

2. In the Tool**b**ars tab, select the toolbar you want to restore to its default settings.

3. Click **R**eset.

4. A confirmation window appears. Click OK.

5. Close the Customize dialog box.

24

FIGURE 24.6

*Drag buttons you want
to include on the new
custom toolbar.*

Title bar ——————

New custom toolbar ——————

Adding a command ——————

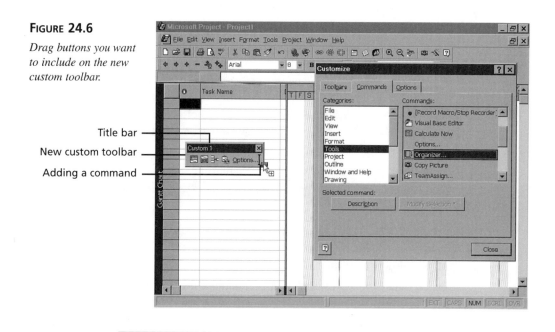

Resetting a toolbar removes all customized changes you have made to that
toolbar—not just the most recent changes. If you have placed custom buttons on a toolbar that you plan to reset, you lose the custom buttons. Drag
the custom buttons to another toolbar if you want to preserve them.

Customizing Command Buttons

Some of the commands available in the Customize dialog box have a blank button image
associated with them. When the command is added to a toolbar, only the name of the
command is displayed. Additionally, when you create a macro, there's no command button image for the macro; when the macro command is added to a toolbar, only the name
of the macro is displayed. You can change the blank button image to one of the available
images or design your own image for the command button by using the Modify
Selection options in the Customize dialog box.

Using the Modify Selection Options

With the Modify Selection options, you can customize a button image in three ways:

- Copy an image from one button to another
- Choose a button image from the button library
- Design an image from scratch

To use the Modify Selection options, the toolbar containing the button you want to modify must first be displayed, and a button must be selected on the toolbar. Right-click on any toolbar and choose **C**ustomize to display the Customize dialog box, or choose **V**iew, **T**oolbars, and select **C**ustomize. Select the **C**ommands tab in the Customize dialog box.

Copying a Button Image

One way to edit a button is to copy an existing button design; this method is especially useful when another button resembles the one you want to use on the new button. Copying the design does not copy the function of the original button to the new button. After you paste the design on the blank button, you can then modify the design to customize it for the new button.

To Do: Copying an Existing Button Design

24

To copy the design of an existing toolbar button to another button, follow these steps:

▼ To Do

1. Right-click the button on the toolbar containing the design you want to copy and the Modify Selection options will appear (see Figure 24.7).

2. Choose **C**opy Button Image.

3. Right-click on the button to which you want to apply the copied design.

▲ 4. From the Modify Selection options, choose **P**aste Button Image.

FIGURE 24.7

You can also use the Modify Selection button in the Customize dialog box to display the options.

Modify Selection options

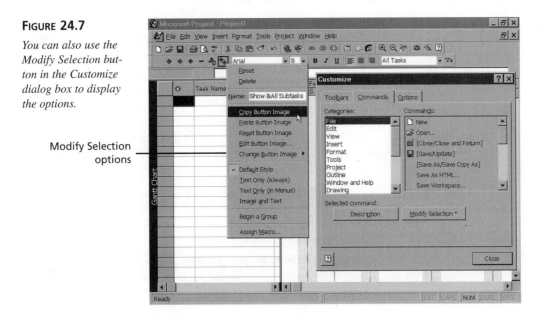

Using an Image from the Button Image Library

If an existing button image doesn't resemble what you want the image to look like, perhaps one of the images in the Button Image Library will be what you're looking for.

To Do: Using the Button Image Library

To use one of the images from the Button Image Library, follow these steps:

1. Right-click the button on the toolbar whose image you want to change and the Modify Selection options will appear (refer back to Figure 24.7).

2. From the Modify Selection options, choose Change **B**utton Image.

3. Choose the image you want from the Button Image Library.

Editing the Button Image

When a command has a blank button image, or the image you copied or used from the Button Image Library needs to be modified, you can design your own button image with the Button Editor.

To Do: Using the Button Editor

To display the Button Editor, follow these steps:

1. Right-click the button on the toolbar whose image you want to change and the Modify Selection options will appear.

2. From the Modify Selection options, choose **E**dit Button Image. The Button Editor dialog box appears (see Figure 24.8).

3. The button design is enlarged so that individual pixels can be identified in the Picture box. You can then change the location of each pixel in the picture using the mouse to get the design you want.

The Colors box is your palette for selecting colored pixels for your design. The Move arrows help you position the image in the button design area by moving it one row or column at a time. The Preview area shows you what the current image looks like.

To change the image, use any of the following techniques:

- To change the color of any pixel, click a color in the Colors box and then click the pixel or drag the color across all pixels you want to color.

- To erase or clear pixels, click the Erase box and then click all pixels you want to clear, drag the pointer across pixels you want to clear, or click a pixel a second time to clear the existing color.

- To reposition the picture on the button, clear an area along the edge toward which you want to move the design, and then click the desired move button.

FIGURE 24.8

Alter an existing button image or create a new one from scratch.

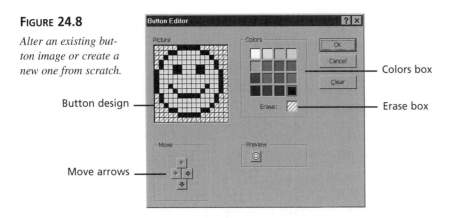

Button design

Move arrows

Colors box

Erase box

- To clear the image canvas completely, click Clear.
- To cancel changes to start over, click Cancel or press Esc.

When the design looks the way you want it to, click OK. The new design now appears on the new button.

> Create a new toolbar to hold "library" copies of the button faces you have created. If you accidentally delete a custom button, the graphic on the button face will be lost forever.

Managing Toolbars with the Organizer

Toolbars are global objects in Microsoft Project that are attached to the *application* rather than to a specific project. As a result, toolbars are stored as part of the global.mpt template and are available for all projects you create. Changes you make to the toolbars are also stored in the global.mpt template. When you want to share a custom toolbar with other users, it must be copied to the global.mpt file on the computer system they are using. It's as simple as copying the custom toolbar to a project file, and then copying the custom toolbar from the project file to the Global template file (global.mpt) on the other person's machine. The specific steps are outlined in the following list.

When you need to include a special toolbar with a particular project file, you can use the Organizer to copy the toolbar. You've used the Organizer before—in Hour 4, "Turning the Task List into a Schedule," you used it to copy calendars to global.mpt and in Hour 7, "Formatting Views," you used the Organizer to copy views between project files.

To Do: Sharing a Custom Toolbar

Follow these steps to share a custom toolbar:

1. Open the project to which you want to copy the toolbar.

2. Choose Tools, Organizer. The Organizer dialog box is displayed.

3. Select the Toolbars tab.

4. On the left side of the dialog box, pick the toolbar in the global.mpt file that you want to copy. You can select multiple toolbars by pressing the Ctrl key as you click additional toolbars.

5. Click Copy to copy the selected toolbars to the project file on the right side of the dialog box. Figure 24.9 shows that a copy of the toolbar Custom Resource Management has been placed in the New Product project file.

6. Click the Close button or press Esc to close the Organizer dialog box.

7. Use File, Save As to save the project file on a floppy disk or a network drive that the other user has access to.

8. Open the project file on the other user's machine.

9. Activate the Organizer and copy the file from the project file to the Global template on the other user's machine.

The custom toolbar will now be available to the other user. Choose View, Toolbars to display the toolbar.

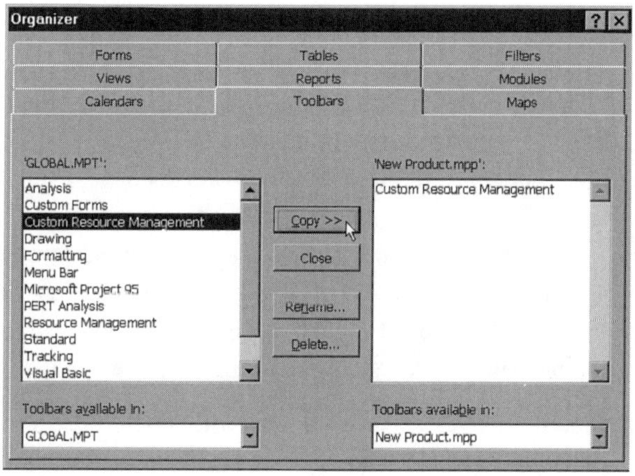

FIGURE 24.9

Toolbars copied into a project file can't be displayed, but they can be copied into global.mpt templates on other computers.

If you accidentally hold down the Ctrl key and click on a button, the Customize Tool dialog box appears. This shortcut enables you to quickly change an existing button to another command—but be careful! It also changes the button face as well. To reset the toolbar, display the Customize dialog box (**V**iew, **T**oolbars, **C**ustomize). On the Toolbars tab, select the toolbar and click **R**eset.

Customizing the Menu Bar

Like toolbars, the Menu Bar can be customized to store commands you use frequently. When you make a change to the Menu Bar, the change becomes a permanent part of the application and is not a specific change to the active project file. Changes to the Menu Bar are stored as part of the global.mpt file.

In Project 98, the Menu Bar acts much like the toolbars. By default, it's docked at the top of the screen, but like toolbars, it can be moved and docked at the side or bottom of the screen or left floating in the middle of the screen. Additionally, the ways you can customize the Menu Bar are very similar to how you customize toolbars, described earlier in this Hour.

In Microsoft Project, any command that has a pointing triangle is considered a menu. In Figure 24.10, the **E**dit menu is active. Within the **E**dit menu are three other built-in menus: Fi**ll**, Cle**a**r, and **O**bject.

FIGURE 24.10

The Menu Bar is customized in the same way toolbars are customized.

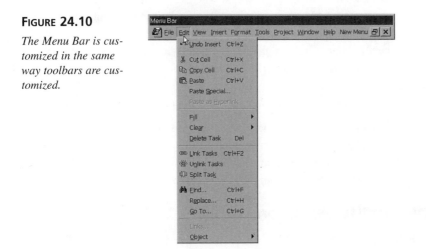

Customizing menus offers a wide range of possibilities. You might simply want to attach commands to existing menus. Items such as frequently used views, tables, filters, and macros can be attached to existing menus quite easily.

When you want to change the name of a Menu Bar item or create a new one, you are, in effect, creating a custom menu bar.

Adding a New Command to the Menu Bar

To Do: Adding a New Command

To add a new command to the Menu Bar, follow these steps:

1. Right-click on the Menu Bar (or any toolbar) and choose Customize to display the Customize dialog box, or choose View, Toolbars, and select Customize.

2. In the Customize dialog box, select the Commands tab.

3. Select the New Menu category at the bottom of the Categories list. The New Menu command will then appear in the Commands list.

4. To add a new menu to the Menu Bar, drag the New Menu command from the Commands list to the Menu Bar. The mouse pointer becomes a thick capital *I*. Position the I-pointer where you want the new menu to appear, release the mouse button, and the new menu drops into place. In Figure 24.11, a new menu is being added to the Menu Bar.

   To add a new menu (a submenu) to an existing menu, drag the New Menu command to the menu on the Menu Bar. For example, to create a submenu under the Tools menu, drag the New Menu command to the Tools menu. The menu on the Menu Bar will become active, showing you the commands currently available on the menu. When the mouse pointer changes into the I-pointer (turned sideways), position it where you want the new menu to appear and release the mouse button to drop the new menu into place.

5. After you have added the new menu, you can then add items to it.

6. Proceed with adding commands to the new menu. Adding items to a new menu is identical to adding buttons to a toolbar. Simply select the category and item you want to add and drag it onto the Menu Bar. By positioning the command between two existing commands, the new item drops into place.

Using the Modify Selection Options

The Modify Selection options are used to edit the new menu or the commands on an existing menu. To display the Modify Selection options, right-click on the Menu Bar and choose Customize to display the Customize dialog box. You can also choose View,

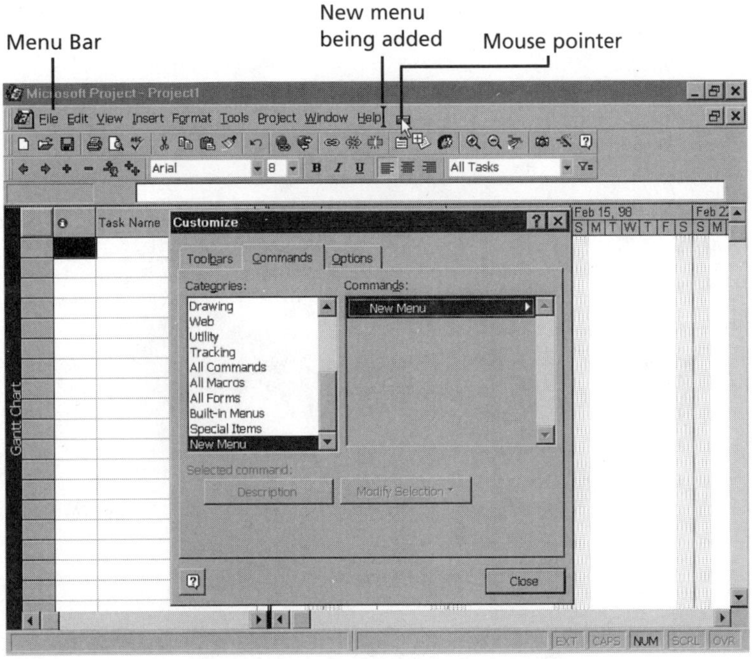

FIGURE 24.11

Adding a new menu command is easy with the New Menu Category on the Commands tab of the Customize dialog box.

Menu Bar

New menu being added

Mouse pointer

Toolbars, and select **C**ustomize. After the Customize dialog box is displayed, select the Commands tab.

To display the Modify Selection options, right-click on the menu you want to change, or select the menu and click the **M**odify Selection button in the Customize dialog box. Figure 24.12 shows the Modify Selection options, with all the choices available. Depending on the menu or command you have selected, some of the choices will be grayed out. When you create a new menu, you should assign it a name that reflects the special feature attached to the menu.

To Do: Changing the Name of a Menu

You can name a menu you are creating or change the name of an existing menu through the Modify Selection options. Follow these steps:

1. From the Modify Selection options, choose **N**ame.

▲ 2. Type the new menu name in the **N**ame text box and press Enter.

If you want to restore the original settings on the Menu Bar, select the **T**oolbars tab in the Customize dialog box. Select Menu Bar from the list of toolbars and click the **R**eset button. A warning message appears to confirm resetting the Menu Bar; click OK.

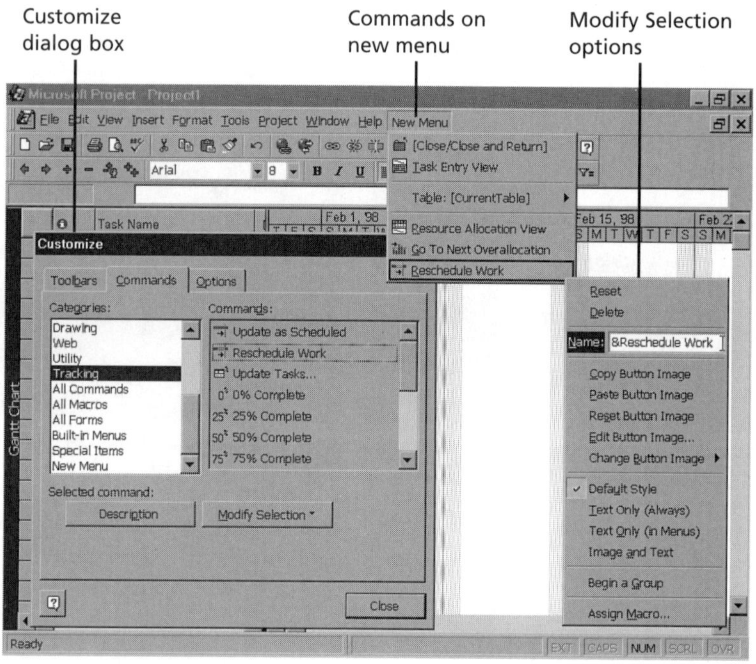

Customize
dialog box

Commands on
new menu

Modify Selection
options

FIGURE 24.12

*Use the Modify
Selection options to
name a menu and to
group menu
commands.*

INDEX

S